Strategic Management for Travel and Tourism

To my wife Michelle and daughters – Lydia, Megan and Laura

N.E.

Strategic Management for Travel and Tourism

Nigel Evans
David Campbell
and George Stonehouse

AMSTERDAM BOSTON HEIDELBERG LONDON NEW YORK OXFORD
PARIS SAN DIEGO SAN FRANCISCO SINGAPORE SYDNEY TOKYO

Butterworth-Heinemann
An imprint of Elsevier
Linacre House, Jordan Hill, Oxford OX2 8DP
200 Wheeler Road, Burlington MA 01803

First published 2003
Reprinted 2003

British Library Cataloguing in Publication Data
A catalogue record for this book is available from the British Library

Library of Congress Cataloguing in Publication Data
A catalogue record for this book is available from the Library of Congress

ISBN 0 7506 4854 6

For information on all Butterworth-Heinemann publications visit
our website at www.bh.com

Composition by Genesis Typesetting Limited, Rochester, Kent
Printed and bound in Great Britain

Contents

Preface

There are of course a number of existing strategic management titles, including *Exploring Corporate Strategy* by Johnson and Scholes (Financial Times/Prentice Hall, 2002), *Corporate Strategy* by Lynch (Financial Times/Prentice Hall, 2001) and *Business Strategy: an Introduction* by Campbell, Stonehouse and Houston (Butterworth-Heinemann, 2002). There are, however, few textbooks that apply strategic management concepts to a 'services' context and particularly to the travel and tourism industry and the hospitality sector. The important human phenomenon of tourism and the industry which has grown up in order to support it – the travel industry – have grown to represent one of the world's most important industrial sectors. Furthermore, travel and tourism is an industry which exhibits a number of distinctive characteristics and has a growing academic literature associated with its study. Consequently, it is appropriate that a dedicated text should consider the strategic implications of managing in this important and rapidly developing industry in particular.

This textbook aims to be the textbook of choice for students studying strategy units on courses related to travel, tourism and hospitality. The book represents a 'contextualization' of generic strategic material content. This is achieved through:

- the application of concepts and principles;
- the emphasis of key points affecting this industry in particular; and
- the use of short illustrative examples and longer case studies.

The purpose of the textbook will therefore be to provide an in-depth review of the subject area but applied to the travel and tourism industry and its component sectors. Each chapter contains specific references to travel and tourism, but it should be stressed that this book is concerned with strategic management *for* travel and tourism, thereby implying that the theory is generic but it is adapted and applied to the needs of this particular industry. The book explicitly recognizes that the industry's sectors are service rather than manufacturing based. Consequently certain aspects of strategic management are particularly emphasized and the language used modified accordingly. For example, 'operations' will be used in place of 'production' and the intangibility, perishability, cash flow implications, and difficulty of maintaining quality standards etc. of service based products are emphasized.

It can be argued that 'hospitality' represents a separate sector with its own literature and constructs. It can further be argued that the term has rather different meaning in North America than elsewhere. Whilst in North America it broadly tends to encompass travel and tourism, elsewhere hospitality has come to represent that part of the travel and tourism product that deals with accommodation and catering. The approach here will be to include hospitality as a part of the broad travel industry since many of the companies involved are integrated and to exclude accommodation from consideration would be to exclude a major part of the tourist product offering. Furthermore hospitality (at the strategic level) shares many of the same characteristics as other areas of the travel industry. For example, the focus on customer service, the perishability of the product, price discrimination, yield management techniques, distribution etc. are common to hospitality and other parts of the travel industry.

The use of the word 'tourism' sometimes causes problems. Whilst the 'travel industry' can be identified broadly as a certain sub-set of mostly larger companies (such as airlines, hotel groups and tour operators) providing services to tourists, 'tourism' also encompasses a diverse, highly fragmented network of small to medium sized companies and other organizations. Much of the strategic management literature relates primarily to larger businesses. However, many of the principles embodied in the literature are applicable to smaller businesses and 'not for profit organizations', but they need to be applied in a rather different way. The approach adopted here is to focus primarily on larger scale businesses but the principles can usually be adapted and applied to smaller and not for profit organizations.

The book features:

- Short illustrative cases throughout, while longer cases for analysis appear at the end of the text.
- Each chapter includes a brief introduction and overview.
- Each chapter includes a number of learning objectives, clearly stated at the start of the chapter.
- Definitions and key concepts are clearly labelled throughout the text.
- Each chapter includes references and a guide to further reading.
- A glossary of terms is included for reference.

The authors would be grateful for any and all feedback or criticism, good or not so good, on this volume. It is likely that the second edition will contain a larger suite of cases and the authors are grateful to Amanda Miller for donating her case on Leicester Promotions. Comments on the book would be most welcome. In the first instance, please contact the publishers.

Nigel Evans
David Campbell
George Stonehouse

Part One

An introduction to the strategic process

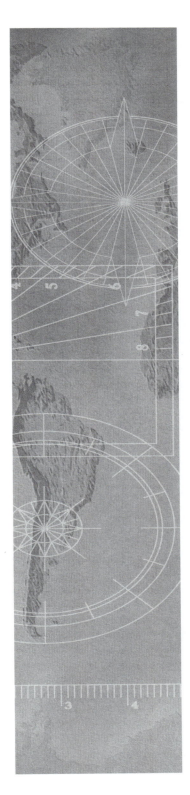

Introduction

Why do we refer to strategy as a *process*? The answer is that it is never a once for all event – it goes on and on. There is a need to continually review strategic objectives because the environment is always changing. The purpose of strategy is to make an organization to fit into its environment. By achieving this, the probabilities that it will survive and prosper are enhanced. The first section of this book is concerned with introducing the subject matter of strategy in a specific context, namely that of travel and tourism. Thus in Part One concepts, definitions and the nature of objectives are discussed in Chapter 1 whilst Chapter 2 highlights the particular characteristics of travel and tourism which are relevant to understanding the way in which organizations within the industry are managed in a strategic way.

The subsequent parts of this book are concerned with examining the distinct 'stages' in the strategic process. It can be argued that strategy is a process because it contains distinct 'stages' and that there are three stages in all, as shown by Figure 1.

Strategic analysis

The purpose of strategic analysis is to gather information. None of us would be wise to make an important decision about anything in life without adequate and relevant information, and neither would a travel and tourism organization.

There are two main stages in strategic analysis. First, strategic analysis involves an examination of an organization's internal environment (*internal analysis*). This takes the form of a thorough analysis of the internal processes and structures of a business in much the same way as a doctor might carry out a thorough

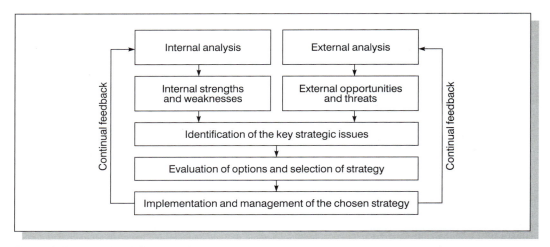

Figure 1 A schematic of the strategic process

medical examination on a person. The purpose of internal analysis is to establish what the organization is good at (its strengths) and what it is not so good at (its weaknesses). We discuss the internal environment in Part Two of this book.

The second stage in strategic analysis is an examination of the organization's external environment (an *external analysis*). This takes the form of a thorough analysis of two 'layers' of external environment – the micro- or 'near' environment, and the macro- or 'far' environment. We will encounter the external environment in Part Three of the book.

The macroenvironment contains a range of influences that affect not only an organization in an industry, but also the whole industry itself. It follows that a single organization is usually unable to affect the factors in the macroenvironment – successful strategy usually involves learning to cope and adapt to changes. This book explains the macroenvironment in terms of five main areas of influence – socio-demographic, political, economic, environmental and technological influences. We discuss this in Chapter 7.

The microenvironment comprises the industry in which the organization competes. The organization is usually affected by the factors in this environment and it may be able to have an influence upon it. However, unlike the internal environment the organization does not have control over its microenvironment. We sometimes refer to the micro-environment as the competitive environment because it is within this sphere that an organization competes, both for resource inputs and to sell its product outputs. We discuss this in Chapter 8.

From the information gathered from the external analysis, we seek to establish which influences represent opportunities, and which are, or might develop into, threats.

Once we have established the organization's internal strengths and weaknesses, and its external opportunities and threats, the challenge becomes to select a strategy that will address the weaknesses and threats whilst, at the same time, will build upon its strengths and exploit its opportunities. It is important to understand that a detailed internal and external analysis is a necessary prerequisite for the SWOT information – it emerges from the internal and external analyses.

The process sometimes involves an additional stage of condensing the strengths, weaknesses, opportunities and threats (SWOT) into a survey of the 'key issues.' These are the most pressing or most important elements of the SWOT statement – those which require the most urgent action or which the strategy should be particularly designed to address. The SWOT is discussed in Chapter 9.

Strategic choice

The second stage in the strategic process involves taking the important information gathered from the strategic analysis and using it to make an intelligent and informed choice or selection of the most appropriate courses of action for the future. These strategic choices are covered in Part Four of the book. Choices are required about how the travel and tourism organization (or its constituent parts) will compete, the strategic direction it will take and the methods which will be utilized. These aspects of strategic choice are discussed in Chapters 10 and 11.

It is at this stage that we come to appreciate the importance of the strategic analysis. If we have gained insufficient or flawed information from the analysis, then we cannot be sure that the strategy selection we make will be the right one.

Strategic choice therefore begins with an examination of the strategic analysis. Once we are acquainted with it, we normally generate a list of the options open to the organization, paying particular attention to how each option will address the key issues. After this, we evaluate each option using a number of criteria. Finally, the most appropriate strategic option is selected. We discuss this matter in Chapter 12.

Strategic implementation and management of change

The third stage in the strategic process involves taking the selected strategic option and actually putting it into practice. We discuss this stage in Part Five of the book.

This is a complex part of the process as it concerns putting detailed aspects of the strategy into practice. It involves *doing* the strategy and this brings into focus a number of other managerial issues. There are a number of areas of which we need to be aware in order to effectively implement a strategy for a travel and tourism organization.

Implementation typically involves taking into account the following:

- the adequacy of the organization's resource base (Chapter 13);
- the readiness of the organization's culture and structure to undertake the proposed strategy (Chapter 13);
- the management of any changes that are needed to implement the strategy (Chapter 13);
- the extent to which the organization positions itself in respect to its geographic coverage and international presence (Chapter 14).

In implementing the strategic process it is necessary to be aware not only of changes occurring to the internal and external environment, but also of changes to the subject matter itself. Thus Chapter 15 considers the present and future trends occurring in the study of strategic management.

The 'feedback' link

Finally, the progress of strategy is monitored continually through feedback from the implementation stage back to the analysis stage. As a strategy proceeds, it may affect the organization's internal environment and it may have an effect on the external environment. In addition, independent influences may have brought internal or external changes about since the strategic analysis was first carried out.

In order to ensure that the selected strategy is still appropriate, therefore, a review of the strategic analysis is necessary. If nothing has changed, then the company may decide that no amendment to the strategy is necessary. If the environment (internal or external) has changed, however, some modification to the strategy may become necessary.

CHAPTER 1

Strategy and strategic objectives for travel and tourism organizations

Introduction and Chapter Overview

Strategic thinking and strategic management are the most important activities undertaken by any business or public sector organization. How skilfully these activities are carried out will determine the eventual long-term success or failure of the organization. In this chapter, we introduce the most basic concepts in the study of these activities. The various definitions of the word *strategy* are discussed and then we explore the levels of decision-making in successful strategic management (at the strategic, tactical and operational levels). These are defined and the links between the levels are discussed. Finally, we discuss the nature of strategic objectives – who is responsible for setting them and what they are essentially about.

Learning Objectives

After studying this chapter, students should be able to:

- define the word *strategy* using Mintzberg's five Ps framework;

- distinguish between deliberate (prescriptive) and emergent strategy;

- explain what strategy contains in practice;

- describe what is meant by *strategic, tactical* and *operational* decisions;

- explain what is meant by *hierarchical congruence* and why it is important;

- employ the stakeholder model to explain how strategic decisions are arrived at;

- define mission and describe the purpose and typical contents of a mission statement;

- explain the most typical types of objectives that are sought through strategic management.

What is strategy?

Definition

At the beginning of a book on strategy, the question 'What is strategy?' seems to be the most obvious starting point. The answer to the question is rather more complicated than it might at first appear. The growth of the subject of study has led to the use of the term strategy (and strategic management) in various ways.

Many organizations are hindered by short termism, concentrating on the most pressing immediate tasks at hand rather than looking ahead and taking a longer-term view. This is understandable given the pressures on modern business, but is not the most sensible way to manage. It is difficult to plan ahead (in the same way as it is difficult to forecast the weather) because there are so many sources of uncertainty and change, but concepts, frameworks, tools and techniques have been developed to facilitate the process. The overall aim of strategic management is thus to develop a framework for thinking ahead – for thinking strategically.

Historically, the term strategy has military roots, with commanders employing strategy in dealing with their opponents (see for example Keegan, 1988). Indeed, dictionaries often continue the military theme, defining strategy as 'the art of war'. Viewing strategy in such a way, the fundamental underlying premise of strategy becomes the notion that an adversary can be defeated (even a larger, more powerful one) if it can be out-manoeuvred using strategic skill.

Since the beginning of commercial transactions, businesses have had strategies determining their future courses of action. It is only since the 1960s, however, that the subject area has been widely considered as a topic of academic interest and hence widely taught in business schools and on business based courses. The subject is also widely taught as part of some tourism related courses and has received some attention in the tourism literature (see for example: Go and Pine, 1995; Hall, 2000; Holloway, 1998; Olsen *et al.*, 1998; Phillips and Moutinho, 1998; Moutinho, 2000; Poon, 1993; Teare and Boer, 1991; Tribe, 1997).

As in the military arena so in business: organizations attempt to out-manoeuvre their rivals. In so doing, strategies have to be developed that rely on various disciplines such as marketing, finance and human resource management.

It is evident, then, that people use the word *strategy* in different ways. You may have heard people talk about a strategy for a business, a strategy for a football match, a strategy for a military campaign or a strategy for revising for a set of exams. It was this multiplicity of uses of the term that led Henry Mintzberg at the McGill University in Montreal (Mintzberg, 1987) to propose his 'five Ps' of strategy.

Mintzberg's 'five Ps'

Mintzberg suggested that nobody can claim to own the word 'strategy' and that the term can legitimately be used in several ways. A strategy, he suggested, can be:

- a plan;
- a ploy;
- a pattern of behaviour;
- a position in respect to others;
- a perspective.

It is important not to see each of these Ps in isolation from each other. One of the problems of dividing ideas into frameworks like the five Ps is that they are necessarily simplified. The five Ps are not mutually exclusive, i.e. it is possible for an organization to show evidence of more than one interpretation of strategy.

Plan strategies • • •

A plan is probably the way in which most people use the word strategy. It tends to imply something that is intentionally put in train and its progress is monitored from the start to a predetermined finish. Some business strategies follow this model. 'Planners' tend to produce internal documents that detail what the company will do for a period of time in the future (say five years). It might include a statement on the overall direction that the organization will take in seeking new business opportunities as well as a schedule for new product launches, acquisitions, financing (i.e. raising investment capital), human resource changes, etc.

A large tour operator, for instance, might decide that it plans to implement a strategy concerned with expanding its share of the market and that this will be achieved by setting prices at lower levels than competitors and by acquiring smaller firms. It might write its plans down in some detail and circulate them to all of its key managers so that, at any given point in time, the entire organization can be shown to be acting in accordance with the predetermined plan.

Ploy strategies • • •

A ploy is generally taken to mean a short-term strategy, and is concerned with the detailed tactical actions that will be taken. It tends to have very limited objectives and it may be subject to change at very short notice. Mintzberg describes a ploy as, 'a manoeuvre intended to outwit an opponent or competitor' (Mintzberg *et al.*, 1998: 14) He pointed out that some companies may use ploy strategies as threats. They may threaten to, say, decrease the price of their products simply to destabilize competitors.

One example of a ploy strategy is that employed in a soccer match. If the opposing team has a particularly skilful player, then the team manager may use the ploy of assigning two players to mark him for the duration of the game. However, this tactic will only last for the one game – the next game will have a completely different strategy. Furthermore, the strategy will only operate only as long as the dangerous player is on the pitch. If he is substituted or gets injured, the strategy will change mid-game

Thus the tour operator (introduced above) may have an overall planned strategy which includes offering lower price levels than competitors, but as a short term ploy, it might suddenly discount its prices within six weeks of departure in order to destabilize its competitors and to sell excess capacity.

Pattern strategies • • •

A 'pattern of behaviour' strategy is one in which progress is made by adopting a consistent form of behaviour. Unlike plans and ploys, patterns 'just happen' as a result of the consistent behaviour.

On a simple level, a small specialist tour operator offering summer villa and apartment holidays to a particular Greek island to a small but loyal group of customers might be viewed as following a pattern strategy. The company is unlikely to produce elaborate plans – simply renewing contracts with property owners and transport providers annually. If offered a new villa on favourable terms, then the operator would probably contract the property and feature it in its brochure without thinking much about it. It is an opportunity that is taken, as it appears too good to miss. However, the operator would probably not feature a hotel in Majorca although it may be available to the company because that would be outside their pattern of business behaviour.

Such patterns of behaviour are sometimes unconscious, meaning that they do not even realize that they are actually following a consistent pattern. Nevertheless, if it proves successful, it is said that the consistent behaviour has *emerged* into a success. This is in direct contrast to planning behaviour.

Key concepts: Deliberate and emergent strategy

There is a key difference between two of Mintzberg's Ps of strategy – plan and pattern. The difference is to do with the *source* of the strategy. He drew attention to the fact that some strategies are deliberate whilst others are emergent.

Deliberate strategy (sometimes called *planned* or *prescriptive* strategy) is meant to happen. It is preconceived, premeditated and usually monitored and controlled from start to finish. It has a specific objective.

Emergent strategy has no specific objective. It does not have a preconceived route to success BUT it may be just as effective as a deliberate strategy. By following a consistent pattern of behaviour, an organization may arrive at the same position as if it had planned everything in detail.

Position strategies • • •

A position strategy is appropriate when the most important thing to an organization is how it relates, or is positioned with respect to, its competitors or its markets (i.e. its customers). In other words, the organization wishes to achieve or defend a certain position.

In business, companies tend to seek such things as market share, profitability, superior research, reputation, etc. It is plainly obvious that not all companies are equal when one considers such criteria. Some airlines, for instance, have enviable reputations for reliability and quality whilst others are not so fortunate. The competitors with a reputation to defend will use a position strategy to ensure that the reputation they enjoy is maintained and strengthened. This may even include marketing messages that point out the weaknesses in competitors' products whilst pointing out the features of their own.

Perspective strategies • • •

Perspective strategies are about changing the culture (the beliefs and the 'feel', the way of looking at the world) of a certain group of people – usually the members of the organization itself. Some companies want to make their employees think in a certain way, believing this to be an important way of achieving success. They may, for example, try to get all employees to think and act courteously, professionally or helpfully.

The elements of strategy

Chandler's definition

Given the foregoing definitions by Mintzberg, we might think that writers in business strategy are unable to agree on a single definition of the word strategy. This is partly true, but some have tried to sum it up succinctly to make it easier for students to understand. One such definition, still widely quoted, was offered by Professor Chandler of Harvard Business School in 1962. Given that Chandler predated Mintzberg, it is perhaps not surprising that it is rather more simplistic than Mintzberg might have accepted.

> Strategy is the *determination of the basic long-term goals* and objectives of an enterprise, and the adoption of *courses of action* and the *allocation of resources* necessary for carrying out these goals. (Chandler, 1962 – emphasis added)

Three components of strategy

This is a useful definition because it shows the scope of what 'good' strategy is. The italics in this quote show the three important contents of strategy.

The *determination of the basic long-term goals* concerns the conceptualization of coherent and attainable strategic objectives. Without objectives, nothing else can happen. If you do not know where you want to go, how can you act in such a way as to get there?

The *adoption of courses of action* refers to the actions taken to arrive at the objectives that have been previously set. If, for example, your objective is arrive in London when travelling from Edinburgh there are various courses of action available to you. You might travel by train, by car, by coach or by plane. You might travel on certain days or at certain times of day. You might take advantage of certain concessionary fares, and you might make a booking through an intermediary such as a travel agent or book directly with the principal company (the airline or train company). Thus as a result of wanting to travel to London, a whole range of options need to be considered and detailed decisions have to be taken as to which options to select.

The *allocation of resources* refers to the fact that there is likely to be a cost associated with the actions required in order to achieve the objectives. If the course of action is not supported with adequate levels of resource, then the objective will not be accomplished.

Hence, strategy contains three things. In the example of travelling from Edinburgh to London:

1 Your *objective* is clearly stated as arriving in London at a certain date and time.
2 In order to achieve this objective certain *actions* are necessary. It is decided that flying is the best option. Thus a specified flight is booked through a travel agent, leave is taken from work and a plane is boarded at the airport.

3 However, the actions would not be possible if they could not be resourced. You need the *resources* of a plane with a suitably qualified pilot, an airport, money to pay for your flight and other such 'inputs.' If any one of these is missing, you will be unable to meet your objective.

Key concept: Resources

Resource inputs (sometimes called *factors of production*) are those essential inputs that are essential to the normal functioning of the organizational process. These are the inputs, without which an organization simply could not continue to exist or meet its objectives. We can readily appreciate that human beings rely upon certain vital inputs such as air, water, nutrition, warmth, shelter, etc., but organizations have similar needs. An organization's resource inputs fall into four key categories:

1 *financial resources* – money for capital investment and working capital. Sources include shareholders, banks, bondholders, etc.
2 *human resources* – appropriately skilled employees to add value in operations and to support those that add value (e.g. supporting employees in marketing, accounting, personnel, etc.). Sources include the labour markets for the appropriate skill levels required by the organization.
3 *physical (tangible) and operational resources* – land, buildings (offices, warehouses, etc.), plant, equipment, stock for production, etc. Sources include estate agents, builders, trade suppliers, etc.
4 *intellectual (intangible) resources* – inputs that cannot be seen or felt but which are essential for continuing business success. e.g. 'know-how', legally defensible patents and licences, brand names, registered designs, logos, 'secret' formulations and recipes, business contact networks, databases, etc.

Levels of strategic decisions

Different 'levels'

It is useful at this stage to understand what characterizes strategic decisions. Management decisions within any organization can be classified in three broad (and sometimes overlapping) categories: strategic, tactical and operational. These can be illustrated as a hierarchy in which higher level decisions tend to shape those at subordinate levels.

Strategic, tactical and operational decisions within an organization differ from each other in terms of:

- focus;
- the level in the organization at which they are made;
- scope;
- time horizon;
- degree of certainty or uncertainty;
- complexity.

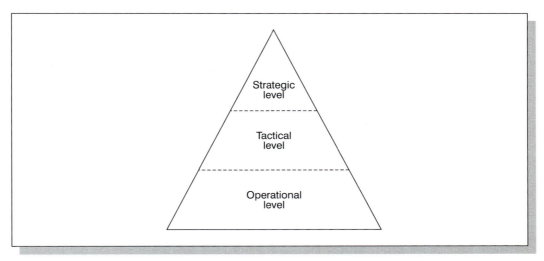

Figure 1.1 Levels of strategic decision-making

The strategic level

Strategic decisions are concerned with the acquisition of sustainable competitive advantage which involves the setting of long-term corporate objectives and the formulation, evaluation, selection and monitoring of strategies designed to achieve those objectives. Strategic decisions are made by senior managers (usually directors), they affect the whole organization, are long-term in nature, are complex and are based upon uncertain information. Managers at the strategic level require multiconceptual skills – the ability to consider the effects of multiple internal and external influences on the business and the possible ways in which strategy can be adjusted to account for such influences.

The decision early on in the company's history for easyJet to operate as a low cost, no frills airline is an example of a strategic decision. It was taken at the most senior level, it affected the whole competitive position of the business, it was long-term in nature and it affected all members of the business.

The tactical level

Tactical decisions are concerned with how corporate objectives are to be met and how strategies are implemented. They are dependent upon overall strategy and involve its fine-tuning and adjustment. They are made at head of business unit, department or functional area level and affect only parts of the organization. They are medium-term in timescale, semi-complex and usually involve some uncertainty but not as much as at the strategic level.

The operational level

Operational decisions are concerned with the shorter-term objectives of the business and with its day to day management. They are dependent upon strategy and tactics. These decisions are made at junior managerial or supervisory level, are based on a high degree of certainty, and are not complex. The procedures in a sales office are typical operational activities – processing orders that have a tactical purpose in pursuit of the overall strategy.

	Strategic	Tactical	Operational
Focus of decision	Achieving sustainable competitive advantage	Implementation of strategy	Day-to-day operations
Level of decision-making	Senior management, board of directors	Head of business unit or functional area	Supervisory
Scope	Whole organization	Business unit or functional area (e.g. Marketing)	Department
Time horizon	Long-term (years)	Medium-term (months to years)	Short-term (days, weeks, month)
Certainty/ uncertainty	High uncertainty	Some uncertainty	High certainty
Complexity	Highly complex	Moderately complex	Comparatively simple
Examples	Decision to launch new product, enter new market, investment decision etc.	Decision to advertise, alter price etc.	Decision to re-order stock, scheduling of jobs

Table 1.1 Comparing strategic, tactical and operational decisions

Congruency and 'fit'

The success of strategy rests upon a very important, but rather obvious principle. Once the strategic level objectives have been set, the operational objectives must be set in such a way so that they contribute to the achievement of the tactical and strategic objectives. In other words, the operational decisions must 'fit' the higher levels of decision-making. This introduces the concept of *congruence*.

The decision-making framework can be visualized as a pyramid (Figure 1.1). The top, where the strategic decisions are made, is thin whilst the bottom (operational decisions) is fatter. This representation is meant to show that strategic decisions are taken infrequently whilst operational decisions are taken often. Strategic decisions are few and far between whilst operational decisions are taken weekly, daily or even hourly. For every one strategic decision, there may be hundreds of individual operational decisions. Tactical decisions are between the two.

Time and planning horizons

One of the key differences between the three levels of decision-making in organizations is the timescale with which they are concerned. It is usually considered that the higher up the organization, the longer the timescale with which management is concerned. Certainly this is true in most manufacturing companies, but in service companies where service delivery is of prime importance relatively senior staff can often be involved in operational decision making.

On an airline flight, for example, the flight crew, including the captain, are typically concerned with ensuring that the daily schedule runs safely and to time, whilst the chief executive may be worrying about potential threats that are some years away. Meanwhile, middle managers, say those in charge of graduate recruitment or the preparation of financial statements, will be planning a few months in advance – possibly as far as one year ahead.

Strategic management involves taking account of a large number of environmental variables. The longer ahead that a manager seeks to plan for, then the more uncertainty is introduced into the analysis.

Mission and mission statements

An organization's *mission* can be described as its overarching *raison d'être*. It is the objective that subsumes all others beneath it. For some organizations, the mission is very easy to articulate but for large commercial businesses, it tends to be more complex.

The purposes of a mission statement

Some organizations attempt to frame their mission in a formal statement, which is often to be seen adorning office walls, printed on employee identity cards and published in annual reports. Mission statements are commonly found both in the commercial sector and in the non-commercial (*not for profit*) sector. Such a statement has a number of possible purposes. It can be used to clearly communicate the objectives and values of the organization to the various stakeholder groups and it can be argued that it assists in promoting hierarchical congruence. It may also have an effect in influencing the behaviour and attitudes of employees, although this is somewhat debatable as anecdotal evidence suggests that many employees have not in fact read their organization's mission statement.

A mission statement can be seen as the starting point for an organization's entire planning process since it requires senior management to sit down and seriously consider where the firm is and where it should be in the future. This point was emphasized by two leading management writers, when they stated that, 'in business like in art, what distinguishes leaders from laggards, and greatness from mediocrity, is the ability to uniquely imagine what could be' (Hamel and Prahalad, 1994: 25).

However, establishing an organization's mission is not easy or without controversy, and as a result styles and content vary enormously. Drucker (1974: 94) pointed out that:

> defining the purpose and mission of the business is difficult, painful and risky. But it alone enables a business to set objectives, to develop strategies, to concentrate its resources and to go to work. It alone enables a business to be managed for performance.

Campbell and Yeung (1998) emphasized that whilst the mission statement itself is clearly important, it is also important for managers to instil a 'sense of mission' in employees. The success of the mission requires the behaviour of employees to match the values of the company, but such harmony is difficult to achieve and requires the mission as it is implemented to become embedded as part of the organizational culture.

Effective mission statements

- **Clearly articulated**. The mission statement should be simple to comprehend so that employees and other stakeholders can clearly understand the principles and values that will guide them in their dealings with the organization. The statement must be specific enough to have an impact upon the behaviour of individuals.
- **Relevant**. The mission statement should be appropriate to the organization in terms of its history, culture and shared values. The mission should not be too broad or too narrow. Too broad may result in lack of focus. Too narrow may mean factors that are potentially important to the organization will be overlooked
- **Current.** An unchanged mission statement may no longer be able to act as a driving force guiding the organization into the future.
- **Positive tone**. The mission statement should be written in such a way that encourages commitment and energizes or inspires employees.
- **Individuality**. The mission statement should set it apart from other organizations establishing its individuality if not its uniqueness through an emphasis on the advantages of the organization based on an objective assessment of organizational strengths and weaknesses.
- **Enduring**. The mission statement cannot be continually altered, as this would be confusing, so they are likely to remain in place for a number of years. Consequently they must be written to allow for some flexibility.
- **Adapted**. Mission statements are written with various target audiences in mind, some for employees only, some for shareholders and other external groups, and others for all audiences. The information and style should reflect the relevant target audience.

Source: Adapted from Stone (1996)

What does a mission statement contain?

The style, content and terminology of mission statements vary enormously. Some are long and detailed whereas others are short and to the point. Some are focused on a particular audience (such as employees or customers) others are written with multiple target audiences in mind. There are probably no 'rights' or 'wrongs' of how it should be presented or what it should contain it all depends upon the organization and its culture. In assessing mission statements the reader will find many examples of the use of language that is ambiguous in its meaning or is questionable in its use of 'hype' to inflate the image of the organization. In practice, mission statements usually contain one or more of the following:

- Some *indication of the industry* or business the organization is mainly concerned with.
- An indication of the *realistic market share* or market position the organization should aim towards.
- A brief summary of the *values and beliefs* of the organization in relating to key stakeholder groups such as customers and employees.
- An indication of the *ownership* or control of the organization.
- A summary of the *geographical location* or scope of organizational activities.
- Specific and *highly context-dependent objectives* are sometimes expressed in the mission statement.

A selection of mission statements taken from a range of tourism organizations in various sectors of the industry is presented below.

British Airways

British Airways introduced a new mission statement after a consultation process involving employees in 1997. The mission statement replaced an existing statement, which had been drawn up in 1995 in the run-up to privatization, and many employees have received training in its meaning for their particular jobs. In introducing its new mission British Airways cited four vital challenges for change facing the company:

- What customers are asking for.
- What people want.
- The global economic climate.
- The challenge of competition.

> 'Whatever it is called, a vision, mission or strategic intent, its purpose is to provide a guiding light for the future. Companies without a mission are prone to opportunism, incrementalism, to constant changes of direction, to being driven by short-term budgetary pressures and to corporate confusion.
>
> A unifying mission is especially important in large companies where staff and managers are expected to take decisions themselves, without constant referral back to headquarters or to their seniors. If everyone understands where the company is aiming, then independent decisions are more likely to be aligned with each other and with the companies' ultimate objective.
>
> A mission also helps an organization set stretching goals and then drive its short-term plans and budgetary trade-offs to achieve the long-term aim.'

Source: British Airways News, 2 May, 1997

British Airways Mission Statement Post 1997	British Airways Mission Statement Pre 1997
OUR MISSION	**OUR MISSION**
'To be the undisputed leader in world travel' We are passionately committed to excellence and to the highest levels of customer service	'To be the best and most successful company in the airline business'
OUR GOALS	**OUR GOALS**
Customers' Choice – Airline of first choice in our key markets. Strong Profitability – Meeting investors' expectations and securing the future.	Safe and Secure – To be a safe and secure airline Financially strong – To deliver strong and consistent financial performance Global leader – To secure a leading share of air travel business world-wide with a significant presence in all major geographical markets

Truly Global – Global network, global outlook: recognized everywhere for superior value in world travel.
Inspired People – Inspired teams of people, building and benefiting from the company's success

OUR VALUES

Safe and Secure
Honest and Responsible
Innovative and Team-spirited
Global and Caring
A Good Neighbour

Service and Value – To provide overall superior service and good value for money in every market segment in which we compete
Customer driven – To excel in anticipating and quickly responding to customer needs and competitor activity
Good employer – To sustain a working environment that attracts, retains and develops committed employees who share in the success of the company
Good neighbour – To be a good neighbour, concerned for the community and the environment

FOUR KEY OBJECTIVES

To be genuinely the world's favourite airline
To be pre-eminent in customer service
To be truly global
To be the UK's best managed company by the year 2000

Source: British Airways Fact Book 1999

Source: British Airways Fact Book 1996

Southwest Airlines

The mission of Southwest Airlines is dedication to the highest quality of customer service delivered with a sense of warmth, friendliness, individual pride, and company spirit.

To Our Employees

We are committed to provide our Employees a stable work environment with equal opportunity for learning and personal growth. Creativity and innovation are encouraged for improving the effectiveness of Southwest Airlines. Above all, Employees will be provided the same concern, respect, and caring attitude within the organization that they are executed to share externally with every Southwest Customer.

Source: www.southwest.com

Maldives Tourism Promotion Board

VISION

- Be the most exclusive destination in South Asia
- Be the top tourism earner in south Asia
- Be an example of sustainable tourism development in small island nations

MISSION

The Maldives Tourism Promotion Board will promote quality and sustainable growth in the tourism industry of the Maldives to foster a well utilized and financially healthy private sector industry – in this way enabling the industry to deliver long-term economic, social and cultural benefits to the people of the Maldives, whilst at the same time contributing to enhancements to the Maldives' unspoiled marine environment to the benefit of the people and visitors of the Maldives.

OBJECTIVES

- To strengthen and enhance the exclusive image of the destination in the source markets
- To position the Maldives as the 'premium' destination world-wide
  To achieve growth targets set for the destination in the Marketing Plan for each year
- To diversify the source markets as well as the market segments to the destination
- To undertake market research to monitor the world economic conditions and travel trends in order to identify market opportunities
- To monitor and support the private sector in their operations to maintain viable bed occupancy levels and to iron out seasonal fluctuations in visitor arrivals.

Source: www.visitmaldives.com

Holidaybreak plc

Holidaybreak is the UK's leading operator of specialist holiday businesses. Group companies retain a distinctive identity whilst sharing expertise and exploiting opportunities in areas of common interest.

Our aim is to achieve continuing profitable growth by developing our existing businesses and market leading brands in the UK and European holiday markets and through acquisitions in the travel sector.

Certain core values will be common to all:

- High levels of customer service
- Excellent value for money for all customers
- An open and cooperative working environment where individual initiative and responsibility are encouraged
- A commitment to the welfare and development of all employees
- The maintenance of good supplier relations
- Continuous improvement in everything we do.

Source: www.holidaybreak.co.uk

How do businesses set objectives?

Earlier in this chapter, we introduced the idea that strategic objectives, since they represent the most important level of decision-making, are set by an organization's senior management, usually the board of directors. In setting objectives, however, senior managers are likely to be influenced by a range of different groups, which have an interest in the organization. *Who or what influences the senior management in their objective-setting?* This question cuts to the heart of an important debate that is taking place both in universities and in business circles. This debate revolves around two differing approaches towards objective-setting: the stockholder and stakeholder approaches.

The stockholder approach

The stockholder approach argues that businesses exist primarily for their owners (usually shareholders). Accordingly, any business behaviour that renders profit performance sub-optimal is not only theft from shareholders but will also, eventually, lead to a level of business performance that will harm all other groups such as employees, customers and suppliers.

In 1970, the Nobel Laureate Professor Milton Friedman contended that 'the moral obligation of business is to increase its profits.' Friedman argued that the one and only obligation of company directors (which are the legal agents of shareholders' financial interests) is to act in such a way as to maximize the financial rate of return on the owners' shares. The capitalist system upon which the Western economies rests in large part upon the presupposition that investments made in shares (e.g. in pension funds, unit trusts, etc.) will perform well. The profitable performance of shares lies in an increase in the share's value and in the rate of dividend per share – objectives that can only be served by financial profits.

The stakeholder approach

A stakeholder can be defined as:

> *Any group or individual who can affect or is affected by the achievement of an organization's objectives.* (Freeman, 1984: 46)

This definition draws in almost everybody that is, or may be potentially involved in the life of an organization. It consequently goes without saying that not all stakeholders are equal in their influence on an organization's objectives.

The stakeholder approach (as advocated by Freeman, 1984; Donaldson and Preston, 1995 and Campbell, 1997a), argues that organizations, like individual people, are characterized by their relationships with various groups and individuals such as employees and customers. A group or individual qualifies as a stakeholder if it/he/she has a legitimate interest in the organization's activities and thus has the power to affect the firm's performance and/or has a stake in the firm's performance.

The implications of this proposition are far-reaching. In essence, stakeholder theory argues that shareholders are neither the sole owners of a business nor the sole beneficiaries of its activities. Whilst shareholders are undeniably one stakeholder group, they are far from being the only group who expect to benefit from business activity and, accordingly, are just one of those groups who have a legitimate right to influence a company's strategic objectives. Some of these groups are internal to the organization

Internal stakeholders	External stakeholders
Board of directors	Shareholders
Employees collectively	Creditors (existing and potential)
Individual employees (e.g. founding entrepreneur)	Suppliers (existing and potential)
Employees' representatives (trade unions, trade associations etc)	Customers (existing and potential)
Functional business areas (marketing, finance etc)	Trade bodies (e.g. ABTA)
Geographical areas of the organization (e.g. Europe, Asia etc.)	Pressure groups (e.g. environmental)
	Competitors (current and future, national and international)
	Government (legal, fiscal, and regulatory impacts)
	Private individuals
	International regulatory bodies (e.g. IATA)
	The local community

Table 1.2 Examples of internal and external stakeholders

whilst others are external. Stakeholder groups, which might be able to exert an influence over the setting of objectives, are shown in Table 1.2.

Stakeholders and objectives

One widely used and useful model for understanding how stakeholders exert influence on an organization's objectives was proposed by Mendelow (1991). According to this model, stakeholders can be 'ranked' depending upon two variables: *interest* and *power*:

- stakeholder *power* refers to the *ability* to influence the organization;
- stakeholder *interest* refers to the *willingness* to influence the organization.

In other words, interest concerns the extent to which the stakeholder cares about what the organization does.

It then follows that:

Stakeholder influence = power × interest

The actual influence that a stakeholder has will depend upon where the stakeholder is positioned with respect to ability to influence and willingness to influence. A stakeholder with both high power and high interest will be more influential than one with low power

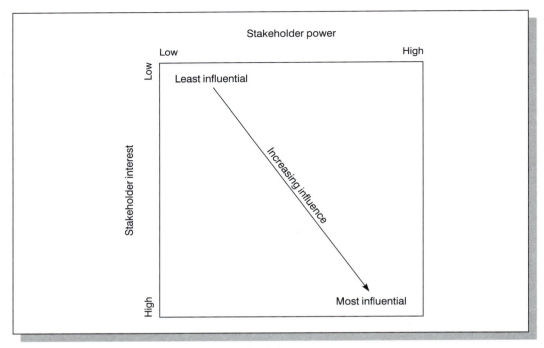

Figure 1.2 The stakeholder map (adapted from Mendelow, 1991)

and low interest. We can map stakeholders by showing the two variables on a grid comprising two intersecting continua (Figure 1.2).

Once constructed, we can use the map to assess two things:

1 which stakeholder is likely to exert the most influence upon the organization's objectives, and;
2 the stakeholders that are most likely to be in potential conflict over strategic objectives (where two or more stakeholders are in close proximity in the high power–high interest part of the map).

The managing director and the board of directors are examples of stakeholders with both high power and high interest. This is because they manage the business, depend upon it for their jobs and their positions within the organization give them power with which to implement their decisions. The local community (in most cases) will not concern itself with the setting of organizational objectives and have limited power to impose their views.

The content of corporate objectives

The importance of objectives

In strict terms, the most important of all objectives is simply to survive as a going concern. Other objectives depend upon the type of organization and the nature of its environment. Objectives are not necessarily mutually exclusive in that an organization can usually pursue more than one type of objective at the same time. Juach and Glueck (1988) defined an objective as 'the end the firm seeks and the criteria the firm uses to determine its effectiveness'. The objectives can be written in a *closed* manner in that they are stated in quantitative terms and are specific in relation to form and timescale, or an *open* manner in that they are stated in qualitative terms and are general in form and timescale.

Objectives are essential to the successful accomplishment of the managerial function in any formal organization in that they:

- provide a sense of direction;
- provide a standard of measurement and a means of controlling performance;
- project an image of the organization's style.

Corporate objectives

Corporate objectives translate the mission into specific long-term targets that can usually be quantified and measured. Corporate objectives are strategic level objectives that can be used as a starting point in the setting business (or tactical) and operational objectives which are more detailed objectives set lower down the organizational hierarchy (see the foregoing discussion). The business objectives will usually relate to important constituent parts of the overall organization – often termed strategic business units (SBUs), whilst the operational objectives will usually relate to smaller units or teams within each SBU.

Corporate objectives normally:

- relate to the whole organization;
- apply to the medium to long term;*
- are set by senior management;
- relate to a number of key areas of concern;
- can be pursued simultaneously.

Care must be taken in writing corporate objectives so that they are clear and easily understood. A common view is that objective writing is a 'CRIME' in that corporate objectives should be:

- *Communicable* – capable of being easily communicated down the line to the workforce and other internal and external stakeholder groups.
- *Realistic* – capable of being achieved within the timescale.
- *Internally consistent* – consistent with the overall organizational mission, the operational objectives and the strategy for achieving the objectives set.
- *Measurable* – capable of being quantified so that they can be measured and it is possible to assess whether the objectives have been achieved.

* Note time horizons vary considerably and will depend largely upon the nature of the business, especially the lead time taken to launch new products and services. In some industries such as pharmaceuticals and chemicals where heavy capital expenditure is required and where research and development are time-consuming, lead times may be long. In many sectors of travel and tourism lead times will be comparatively short, since launching a new destination or a new route for example can be achieved fairly quickly. However, where large capital investment is required, as with hotel construction or new aircraft purchases, lead times are likely to be quite long. As a working rule the long term is often considered to be 5+ years, the medium term 1–5 years and the short term less than 1 year.

- *Explicit* – written in clear unambiguous language, precise in relation to both targets set and to timescale.

Corporate objectives often relate to economic and social concerns, and to matters of growth and competitive advantage which will now be considered.

Economic objectives

Economic objectives are those that can be measured in financial ways. For commercial organizations, objectives will usually include measures such as *return*. Return is an accounting term to describe the proportion of either sales or investment capital that is left over as profit. In commercial organizations the economic objective is often referred to as the *primary objective*, with other objectives being *secondary* to the achievement of the financial objective.

Return on sales, sometimes referred to as profit margin, is an indication of how well the company has controlled its costs whilst *return on assets* (or *return on capital employed*) is an indication of how efficiently the company has used its investors' money. Both of these are important business objectives – to provide sufficient return to retain some profits for future investment and to provide investors with a dividend on their shareholding.

Not-for-profit organizations also have economic objectives, but they are measured in different ways. Organizations like destination marketing offices, charities and government departments tend to measure economic performance by using cost–benefit or value-for-money objectives. These organizations usually rely in large part on income over which they have little control – it may, for example, be fixed by central or local government. The objectives set will typically involve extracting the maximum benefit in terms of outputs from the income they have.

A destination marketing office for a country, a city or a resort for example, will have a certain income which it uses as carefully as possible to ensure it can deliver as many tourists of required type as possible to the destination within its allocated budget.

Social objectives

We should not assume that all organizational objectives are financial in nature. Many exist, either in part or totally, to deliver social benefits. Many publicly funded organizations such as museums, art galleries, heritage attractions and so on exist to deliver services to society in general. Charities exist primarily to provide social benefit to one or more allegedly worthwhile constituencies. For organizations of this type, economic objectives may be secondary to their desire to deliver socially desirable ends.

Commercial organizations are also gradually adopting social objectives in their strategic planning. Although they are usually subordinate to their economic objectives, commercial organizations may espouse social or environmental causes that they purport to believe in. They may, for example, recognize the social value of supporting local community projects or seconding (at their own expense) some of their people to serve with charities.

Growth or market share objectives

At some stages in the life of an organization, objectives concerning growth and expansion become among the most important. This is especially true of businesses who must grow and maintain market position in order to 'keep up with' or 'keep ahead of' competitors.

Size and market position offer a number of advantages and it is these that an organization seeks when growth is a key objective. Size gives an organization economy of scale advantages in both product and resource markets. It means that a larger organization attracts resource inputs at preferential unit cost compared to smaller concerns and its larger presence in its product markets increases its pricing power and its ability to subjugate competitors

Competitive advantage objectives

Finally, and importantly, many strategic objectives concern the company's position in respect to its competitors. Competitive advantage objectives concern how the company's position compares to others – especially to competitors. The objectives are limited to ensuring simply that 'we beat you', or 'we are better than you'. Superior performance is the only objective and if a company can achieve ascendancy over its nearest competitors, then the objective will have been accomplished.

Objectives in British Airways

An illustration of the cascading of objectives is provided by British Airways.

The mission sets the long-term direction, which is used to identify the strategic goals needed to achieve the mission. The mission and strategic goals provide a planning horizon of 10 years between 1997 and 2007. The combined mission and corporate goals provide the parameters and relevance for 3-year business plans for each of the key areas of business (the SBUs), which in turn are used to set each year's budget for each department. The business plan and budget determine the actions required by each department which in turn determine individuals' work programmes. Relevant key performance indicators (KPI) are set for each individual employee.

Source: Adapted from *British Airways News*, 2 May 1997

References and further reading

Argenti, J. (1997) Stakeholders: the Case Against. *Long Range Planning*, 30(3), 442–445.

Athiyaman, A. (1995) The Interface of Tourism and Strategy Research: an Analysis. *Tourism Management*, 16(6), 447–453.

Athiyaman, A. and Robertson, R.W. (1995) Strategic Planning in Large Tourism Firms: an Empirical Analysis. *Tourism Management*, 16(3), 199–205.

Baetz, M.C. and Bart, C.K. (1996) Developing Mission Statements Which Work. *Long Range Planning*, 29(4), 526–533.

Bart, C.K. (1997) Sex, Lies and Mission Statements. *Business Horizons*, November-December.

British Airways News (1987) To be the Undisputed Leader in World Travel. No. 1158, 2 May.

Campbell, A. (1997a) Stakeholders: the Case in Favour. *Long Range Planning*, 30(3), 446–449.

Campbell, A. (1997b) Mission Statements. *Long Range Planning*, 30(6), 931–932.

Campbell, A. and Yeung, S. (1998) Creating a Sense of Mission, in S. Segal-Horn (ed.), *The Strategy Reader*. Oxford: Blackwell, ch. 14, pp 284–295.

Chandler, A.D. (1962) *Strategy and Structure*. Boston, MA: MIT Press.

David, F.R. (1989) How Companies Define Their Mission. *Long Range Planning*, 22(1), 90–97.

Dev, C.S. (1989) Operating Environment and Strategy: the Profitable Connection. *Cornell Hotel and Restaurant Administration Quarterly*, 30(2), 9–14.

Donaldson, T. and Preston, L.E. (1995) The Stakeholder Theory of the Corporation: Concepts, Evidence, and Implications. *Academy of Management Review*, 20, 65–91.

Drucker, P.F. (1974) *Management: Tasks, Responsibilities, Practices*. New York: Harper and Row.

Freeman, R.E. (1984) *Strategic Management: A Stakeholder Approach*. Boston, MA: Pitman.

Go, F. and Pine, R. (1995) *Globalization Strategy in the Hotel Industry*. London: Routledge.

Hamel, G. and Prahalad, C.K. (1994) *Competing for the Future*. Boston, MA: Harvard Business School Press.

Hall, C.M. (2000) *Tourism Planning: Policies, Processes and Relationships*. Harlow: Pearson Education, pp 75–96.

Juach L.R. and Glueck, F. (1988) *Strategic Management and Business Policy*, 3rd edn. New York: McGraw-Hill.

Keegan, K., (1988) *The Mask of Command*. New York: Viking Penguin.

Holloway, S. (1998) *Changing Planes – A Strategic Management Perspective on an Industry in Transition*. Volume 1: *Situation Analysis*. Aldershot: Ashgate.

Holloway, S. (1998) *Changing Planes – A Strategic Management Perspective on an Industry in Transition*. Volume 2: *Strategic Choice, Implementation, and Outcome*. Aldershot: Ashgate.

McKiernan, P. (1997) Strategy Past; Strategy Futures. *Long Range Planning*. 30(5), 790–798.

Mendelow, A. (1991) Proceedings of 2nd international conference on information systems, Cambridge, MA. Described by

Johnson, G. and Scholes, K. (1997) *Exploring Corporate Strategy*, Hemel Hempstead: Prentice Hall.

Mintzberg, H. (1987) Five Ps for Strategy. *California Management Review*, Fall. Reprinted in Mintzberg *et al.* (1998), p. 13ff.

Mintzberg, H., Quinn, J.B. and Ghoshal, S. (1998) *The Strategy Process: Revised European Edition*. Hemel Hempstead: Prentice Hall.

Moutinho, L. (2000) Strategic Planning, in L. Moutinho (ed.), *Strategic Management in Tourism*. Wallingford: CABI, ch. 10, pp 259–282.

Olsen, M.D. (1991) Strategic Management in the Hospitality Industry: a Literature Review. *Progress in Tourism, Recreation and Hospitality Management*, 3, 215–231.

Olsen, M.D., West, J. and Tse, E.C. (1998) *Strategic Management in the Hospitality Industry*, 2nd edn. New York: John Wiley.

Phillips, P.A. (1996) Strategic Planning and Business Performance in the UK Hotel Sector; Results of an Exploratory Study. *International Journal of Contemporary Hospitality Management*, 15(4), 347–362.

Phillips, P.A. and Moutinho, L. (1998) *Strategic Planning Systems in Hospitality and Tourism*. Wallingford: CABI.

Poon, A. (1993) *Tourism Technology and Competitive Strategies*. Wallingford: CABI.

Sautter, E.T. and Leisen, B. (1999) Managing Stakeholders – a Tourism Planning Model. *Annals of Tourism Research*, 26(2), 312–328.

Schwaninger, M. (1986) Strategic Business Management in Tourism. *Tourism Management*, 7(2), 74–85.

Soteriou, E. C. and Toberts, C. (1998) The strategic planning process in national tourism organizations. *Journal of Travel Research*, 37 (August), 21–29.

Stone, R.A. (1996) Mission Statements Revisited. *SAM Advanced Management Journal*, Winter, 31–37.

Teare, R. and Boer, R. (1991) *Strategic Hospitality Management*. London: Cassell.

Tribe, J. (1997) *Corporate Strategy for Tourism*. London: International Thomson Business Press, ch. 2.

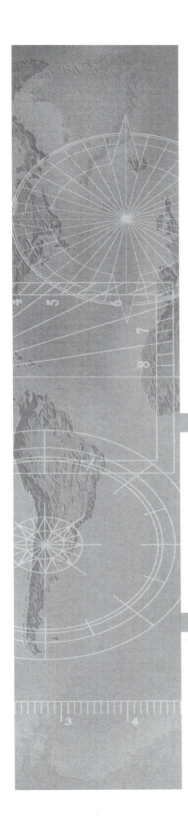

Introduction to strategy for travel and tourism

Introduction and Chapter Overview

Travel and tourism strategy represents a key challenge to managers because of the nature of the products being sold and of the complexities of the environment in which the industry exists. In particular, however, strategy is informed by the fact that most travel and tourism products are services rather than goods (i.e. they are intangible). In this chapter, we consider how the nature of a travel and tourism product informs strategy formulation, both in a general sense (because they are mainly intangible) and in a more specific discussion of the products themselves.

Learning Objectives

After studying this chapter, students should be able to:

- define goods and services;
- explain the product features of travel and tourism products;
- describe the key features of service products and how they relate to travel and tourism;
- describe six product factors that specifically apply to travel and tourism.

Travel and tourism as a service industry

Goods and services

In a book such as this on travel and tourism strategy, it is appropriate to define the products that comprise the central themes that we will be studying. If you have studied business or economics before, you will remember that there are two basic types of product – goods and services. Goods are tangible – things you can own, whilst services are intangible and are things done on your behalf or for your benefit. You do not 'own' service products but instead you have use of them. For example, as a customer you do not own an aircraft seat on a flight or a cruise ship you may be travelling on but you make use of the services offered.

Travel and tourism products have a number of characteristics which are of relevance to the way in which they are managed. These characteristics are discussed in the following section. Whilst some of these features are common to all service products, some other characteristics are unique to travel and tourism products.

Service product characteristics

Characteristics of service products

There are a number of factors which make services different from physical goods. These distinguishing factors are:

- intangibility;
- inseparability;
- perishability;
- heterogeneity;
- ownership.

We will consider each characteristic in turn.

Intangibility

Services cannot normally be seen, touched, smelt, tasted, tried on for size or stored on a shelf prior to purchase. Their intangibility makes them harder to buy but easier to distribute.

The fact that the tourism product is not a physical object but an amalgam of 'invisible' services does create certain problems for organizations operating in the sector. To overcome this intangibility, tour operators sometimes attempt to create some form of tangible offering that potential customers can relate to. With the growth in the home ownership of video-recorders and computers for example, tour operators and destinations are now able to record the features of their holidays on video or make them available on the Internet for home viewing by potential customers. This takes away some of the uncertainty the customer may have when buying a holiday. Similarly, travel brochures help to overcome the intangibility problem and this is why so much effort, expense and creativity are devoted to their design.

Key concept: Packages and tour operators

A 'package' can be defined as a pre-arranged combination, sold or offered for sale at an inclusive price, of not less than two of the following three elements:

- transport;
- accommodation;
- other tourist services not ancillary to transport or accommodation and accounting for a significant part of the package.

The growth of the package has been a major cause of the increase in the holiday market since the 1950s. The role of the package company goes beyond that of the wholesaler, in that they not only purchase or reserve the separate components in bulk but, in combining these components into an 'inclusive tour', they also become producers in the holiday market. The traditional appeal of the tour operators' product has been to offer a complete holiday package at the lowest price to a population often lacking the linguistic knowledge or the knowledge and confidence to organize independent travel. Consequently the tour operation has become the dominant feature of the holiday market in many tourist-generating countries.

Inseparability

The production and consumption of services are inseparable. To take advantage of an air flight or a bus service, for example, both you and the means of transport must make the journey at the same time. The implication of this inseparability is that the consumers have direct experience of the production of the service. They are, in effect, in the 'service factory' at the time of production. This has profound implications for the staff in service industries.

When a physical product is purchased, it comes packaged and the customer is likely to assess the product purely upon its product features (such as taste, size, specification, etc.). Managers have time to plan these aspects of product management to ensure that customer satisfaction is achieved. The circumstances under which the product is produced and how it is delivered are usually of little relevance to the customer.

In the case of a service product, however, customers are likely to be very concerned about the way in which the product is delivered, i.e. the level of customer service. At a hotel reception desk, for example, the customer is likely to notice if the receptionist is rude or unwelcoming. Similarly, the customer will also experience the production of the product if the receptionist is efficient, courteous and helpful.

The task of satisfying customers for the provider of a service is in many ways much more difficult than it is for the manufacturer of a product. In service industries everything has to be right first time, all the time and any mistake can prove very costly in terms of lost future custom. How service personnel conduct themselves in the customer's presence, what they say, what they don't say, how competent they are, how personable they are or how presentable they are, can determine whether the customer buys from the business again.

Perishability

Since production and consumption are simultaneous, services are instantly perishable if they have not been sold at the time of production. The empty train seat, the empty hotel bed or the unsold holiday all represent lost opportunities. They are lost sales that can never be recovered (empty hotel rooms cannot be 'stored' for when demand increases). Unlike manufacturers of goods, they cannot just keep on producing services and store them for future sales and striking the correct balance between capacity and sales (supply and demand) is extremely difficult.

Key concepts: Capacity, occupancy rate and load factors

In travel and tourism, capacity refers to the number of people that can be accommodated in a hotel, aircraft, bus, resort, etc. It may be, for example, that a hotel has a capacity of 300 and an aircraft might be able to accommodate 130.

The important figure, however, is how much of the capacity is actually used at any time. This is the occupancy rate for accommodation or the load factor for transportation. If a hotel, for example, is only full on a quarter of the nights in a year, then it is paying the fixed costs on the empty rooms without any income from them. This is particularly important when considering seasonality and also explains why hotel prices fall in the low season – to maintain as high an occupancy rate as possible to help to cover the hotel's total costs.

The problems of perishability can be made even more acute by fluctuating demand but fixed supply. Demand can vary during the day, during the week or from season to season of the year. Many resort hotels, for instance, are full for only a few months of the year. Capacity may therefore be insufficient to meet demand at peak times, but in excess of what is required at slack times.

Demand can fluctuate for all sorts of reasons, such as seasonal changes, changes due to the level of economic activity, and changes due to climatic conditions. Changes in demand can also occur very suddenly and can have a dramatic impact on service suppliers. For instance a single reported terrorist attack in a destination area could severely limit demand. Or more widespread instability such as the Gulf War of 1991 can also curtail demand. In the case of the Gulf War, the airline industry worldwide faced a major downturn in demand.

Supply, however is much more difficult to alter, at least in the short term. For example, a hotel has a fixed bedstock (number of beds) that it has to try to fill. A scheduled airline has an obligation to fly between advertised points regardless of the number of empty seats on the aircraft. A tour operator enters a contractual obligation, often months in advance of the date of travel, with the providers of accommodation to fill a certain specified number of rooms.

The management challenge, therefore, is to make sure that the company is operating at full capacity for as much of the time as possible. To be successful, the company will need carefully designed strategies to stimulate demand, lengthen seasons, or to offer appropriate pricing levels to manage and 'smooth out' occupancy levels.

Heterogeneity

Services, unlike mass-produced manufactured goods, are never identical. One hotel in a chain of hotels, or one person's holiday, will never be identical to another. The human element and other factors in delivering services, ensures that services will be heterogeneous, i.e. varied.

Tourism products are 'people oriented', and the human factor plays a key role. The enjoyment gained from a holiday cannot be separated from the personalities who go to make up that holiday – the personnel employed in the travel agency, the airline crew, the hotel staff, the tour operator's overseas representative, and of course, the holidaymaker. All of these have a role to play in ensuring that the holiday lives up to the customer's expectations.

Human behaviour, however, is highly variable and it is difficult for a company to ensure that its employees display good customer relation skills all of the time. Similarly, the company has no influence over the behaviour of the customer when on holiday. The customer's attitudes and behaviour will also contribute to the pleasure gained from the holiday. This means that there is an uncontrollable element inherent in the production of the travel or tourism product which can lead to the holidaymaker being satisfied or disappointed with the holiday.

To take account of this problem, it is important that as much information as possible is provided in advance to the potential customer, both by the tour operator and the travel agent. This will reduce the risk of the customer purchasing an unsuitable holiday at the outset. Special attention has also to be paid to the personnel who will deal with the client on a face-to-face basis to make certain that they have suitable personalities for dealing with the public.

In many cases in travel and tourism, the customer is actually attracted by the heterogeneity. Tourists would become bored if every tourist destination was identical, and hotel chains try hard to maintain a consistent brand image whilst at the same time trying to differentiate each hotel through varying design features. This heterogeneity is understandable, but it does make it very difficult for potential purchasers to evaluate services and for managers to deliver products of a consistent quality.

Managing 'heterogeneity' at Radisson Hotels International

Radisson Hotels is part of the privately owned Carlson group of companies based in Minneapolis. Other companies in the group include a leading US travel agency chain and the international Carlson Wagonlit business travel agencies. Radisson has grown rapidly in recent years, despite problems elsewhere in the hotel sector because it focused on management contracts and franchising in its hotels rather than in real estate investment, i.e. another party owns the physical structure of the hotels. The company has concentrated on its strengths in management, marketing and sales. The company has some 400 hotels with 97000 rooms, in 53 countries. Radisson owns very few of these hotels and manages about 50 while the rest are franchised, i.e. they are managed by franchisees operating in partnership with Radisson.

Radisson's goal is to be the fastest growing quality hotel chain, seeking to operate in the upmarket business travel and leisure destination markets. It relies on a variety of upmarket products, including deluxe Plaza hotels, all-suite hotels, inns and resorts. Plans for future development call for targeting Europe (especially eastern Europe), Asia Pacific, the Caribbean, South America and Canada.

The challenges for a company such as Radisson include ensuring that the same levels of quality are provided around the world, when:

- staff come from many cultural and linguistic backgrounds;
- locations vary greatly in their geographical characteristics;
- the company does not actually own the buildings.

The strength of a brand such as Radisson relies upon such standards being ensured, but in practice it is a very difficult management task, since even communicating effectively with worldwide locations in different time zones can be problematic.

Radisson relies heavily on alliances with local 'quality' hoteliers, places a great emphasis on training, standardizes procedures where possible, carefully words all its management and franchising agreements, and has sophisticated international communications including its 'Pierre' transcontinental toll-free reservations service.

Ownership

When a customer buys a manufactured product there will usually be a document, such as a receipt, which transfers ownership from seller to buyer. When a consumer buys a service he or she does not usually receive ownership of anything tangible. A car is hired, but ownership is not transferred, a hotel room is reserved for a period of time but nothing in it is ever owned by the customer. Even a credit card actually remains the property of the issuing company.

Service buyers are therefore buying only access to or use of something, which has important management implications. Since transfer of ownership is not involved the task of building a relationship with customers, of retaining their custom, and building brand loyalty become more difficult.

Travel and tourism-specific characteristics of service

Six travel and tourism-specific factors

The five special characteristics of services cited in the preceding section change the emphasis of a manager's task when compared to the sale of goods. However, these characteristics, whilst applicable to the travel and tourism industry, are not unique to it but could be applied to other service sectors.

Six further factors, however, might be added in the travel and tourism context:

1 High cost
2 Seasonality
3 Ease of entry/exit
4 Interdependence
5 Impact on society
6 The effect of external shocks

Whilst these factors are not unique to travel and tourism, they are certainly very important to any consideration of strategic management in a travel and tourism context.

The fifth of these factors, tourism's impact on society, is unique to the industry, in that no other service industry can claim to have such a visible impact which can be highly significant in the way in which organizations and destinations are managed. Finally, managing in the travel and tourism industry is carried out at the mercy of events.

High cost

Travel and tourism products usually represent a relatively high cost purchase for the consumer. Taking a holiday, buying an airline ticket or staying at a hotel are expensive. Indeed in some cases such purchases will represent the largest single item of expenditure for a consumer in a given year. Consequently, making such a purchase does not usually occur without a great deal of thought and a comparison of alternative offerings. It is not like buying a fast moving consumer good, which may be done on impulse. This feature of travel and tourism products is important when formulating strategy, especially with regard to marketing.

Seasonality

Bull (1995) argued that 'Tourism has one of the most highly seasonal patterns of demand for any product, having less variation than the demand for Christmas cards or air conditioners, but more than nearly all high value individual purchases.' This seasonality has implications for the price and quantity of tourism products supplied between seasons. One way in which management can respond to these problems of seasonality is to develop or acquire counter-seasonal businesses, i.e. to develop from their own resources or to purchase businesses that operate primarily at other times of the year.

Season	Period of application	Fare (UK £)	Index
Basic	16 Apr – 15 Jun	860	100
Off-peak	01 Feb – 15 Apr 16 Jun – 31 Jul	1045	122
Shoulder	01 Aug – 09 Dec 25 Dec – 31 Jan	1245	145
Peak	09 Dec – 24 Dec	1400	163

Source: Bull (1995), based on IATA 1994 Air Tariffs/Galileo CRS

Table 2.1 Example of seasonal market for air travel: economy class excursion fares London–Sydney 1994/95

Table 2.1 shows the four different seasonal markets for air travel between London, UK and Sydney, Australia which have developed over a number of years with prices varying by up to 63%.

Managing variations in seasonal demand at First Choice Holidays plc

First Choice Plc is the UK's fourth largest outbound tour operator, with about 13% of the total Air Inclusive Tour or 'package' (AIT) market. The UK AIT market is highly seasonal, being concentrated in the months of June, July and August and with almost 50% of customers choosing Spain as their holiday destination.

Such seasonality of demand causes some managerial problems:

- Profits are concentrated in the second half of the financial year, and losses usually incur for the first 6 months. First Choice lost £39.7 million in the six months to the end of April 2001, but recorded a profit of £79.6 million in the full financial year to October 2001. Such uneven performances can make the financial markets uneasy and this, in turn, can make it more difficult to raise new finance.
- Large fluctuations in cash flow occur. Typically cash flows in during the early part of the calendar year as bookings are made and paid for, but then cash is drained over the course of the summer months as the companies have to pay accommodation, airline and other expenses. Net cash levels are usually at their lowest levels during the autumn and early winter. Many companies have to rely on bank borrowing facilities to support them during this period and some companies have failed due to banks' refusal to support AIT companies through their cash deficit months.
- 'Integrated' travel companies such as MyTravel and First Choice own charter airlines. Whilst it is not difficult to keep the airlines flying with very high load factors over the summer season, capacity has to be carefully managed so that aircraft capacity is not underutilized during the winter.

Managerial responses:

- Owing to the severity of climatic conditions the Canadian outbound market has a very strong winter demand, particularly to the Caribbean. In 1994 First Choice purchased International Travel Holdings now known as 'Signature Vacations', a Canadian tour operator which carries about 700 000 passengers a year.
- Charter airlines owned by UK tour operators (including Air 2000 owned by First Choice) have developed long-haul routes. On these routes market demand is strongest during the European winter period.

Ease of entry/exit

In some areas of travel and tourism it is relatively easy to set up in business or to leave the business, i.e. entry and exit costs are relatively low (compared to some other industries which have higher capital set-up costs). For a tour operator for example, most of the travel services included in the holidays are leased, or are purchased as and when required. The greatest initial cost involved is often in producing the brochures and marketing the holidays to travel agents and the public. Similarly, travel agents do not purchase products from tour operators until the customer pays for them, and so do not incur the risk of unsold stock or stock-holding costs.

Therefore, entry to the industry might be considered to be relatively straightforward and this means that if one company is seen to be successful in a particular segment of the market then it is not difficult for a competitor to offer a similar product.

Interdependence

The travel and tourism industry can be viewed as being comprised of five component sectors:

- accommodation;
- attractions;
- transport;
- travel organizers;
- destination organizations.

Each of these sectors can be further broken down into several sub-divisions (as shown in Figure 2.1). Some of the sub-divisions, such as tour operators, are operated for profit while others such as museums and national parks are often operated on a non-commercial basis. The important point to note in this context, however, is that the sectors are all linked and depend upon one another, i.e. there is an interdependence between them. The accommodation sector, for example, relies upon the transport sector to transport guests to and from the accommodation. Similarly, the transport and accommodation sectors both rely upon the travel organizers sector to provide them with customers.

If one sector fails to deliver a service it has a 'knock on' effect on other sectors. For example, if a tour operator organizes a holiday including seats on an aircraft, the quality

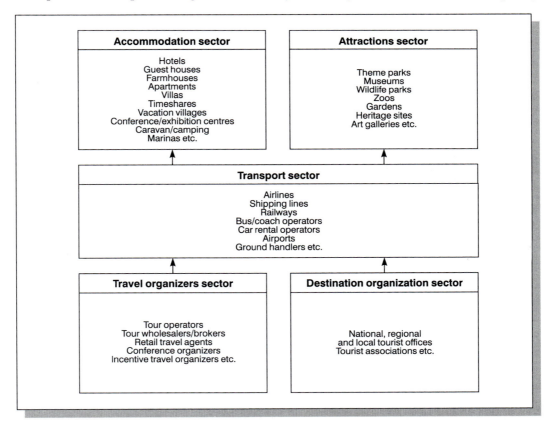

Figure 2.1 The sectors and sub-divisions of the travel and tourism industry (adapted from Middleton and Clarke, 2001)

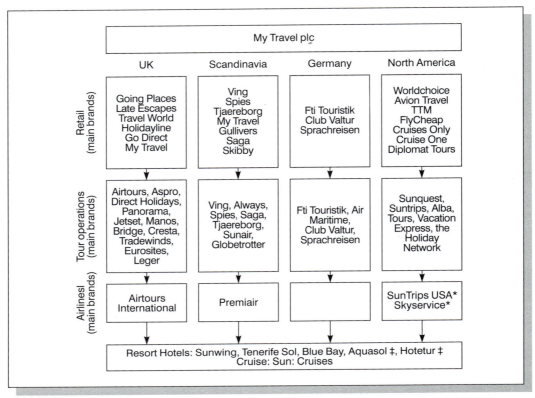

Figure 2.2 Vertically integrated structure of MyTravel plc. *Long-term contract. Associate. ‡Joint ventures (Airtours plc, 2001)

of the holiday will be judged partly upon the quality of the airline regardless of whether the tour operator has any direct control over that airline's activities.

Figure 2.1 shows how the various sectors in the industry 'fit' together. In reality, the world is not as simple as the diagram suggests. Individual companies will often straddle two or more sectors. Some hotel companies, for example, organize inclusive tour packages and thereby also operate in the travel organizers sector. In the late 1990s travel companies in the UK and elsewhere undertook strategies of 'vertical integration' whereby a single company may sell travel arrangements to customers (retail), provide travel arrangements (tour operations), transport customers (airline operations) and in some cases also own accommodation. As the industry stood in 2002, the 'big 4' outbound travel companies in the UK: Thomson, MyTravel (Airtours), First Choice and Thomas Cook, were all vertically integrated in this way.

This vertically integrated structure can be illustrated by looking at the structure of MyTravel Plc (prior to their acquisitions in Canada) in Figure 2.2.

Impact of tourism

Perhaps the one area where tourism is unique is in its impact on society. It is probably fair to say that no other industrial sector comes close since tourism by definition involves the transportation of people (often in large numbers) to a destination area away from home. But

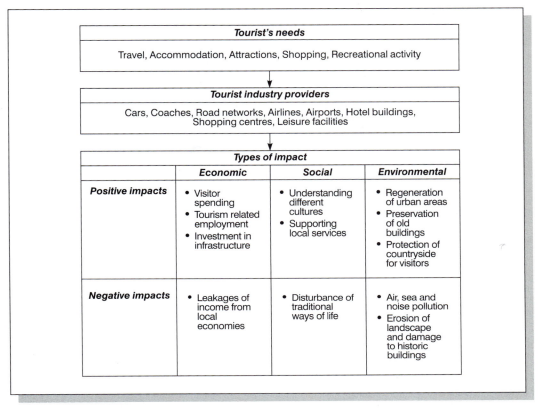

Tourist's needs		
Travel, Accommodation, Attractions, Shopping, Recreational activity		

Tourist industry providers		
Cars, Coaches, Road networks, Airlines, Airports, Hotel buildings, Shopping centres, Leisure facilities		

Types of impact		
	Economic	**Social**	**Environmental**
Positive impacts	• Visitor spending • Tourism related employment • Investment in infrastructure	• Understanding different cultures • Supporting local services	• Regeneration of urban areas • Preservation of old buildings • Protection of countryside for visitors
Negative impacts	• Leakages of income from local economies	• Disturbance of traditional ways of life	• Air, sea and noise pollution • Erosion of landscape and damage to historic buildings

Figure 2.3 The basic impacts of tourism on destination areas

the impacts that tourism has are both wide-ranging and controversial. The focus of attention is usually upon the impact tourism has upon host destinations, as shown in Figure 2.3, but tourism can also have an impact on tourist generating areas. The changed perceptions towards food and culture in northern Europe is evidence of this as tourists have gained an insight into other cultures as a result of the increase in travel since the early 1970s.

The holidaymakers

Krippendorf (1987), in his influential work *The Holidaymakers – Understanding the Impacts of Leisure and Travel*, discussed aspects of the impact tourists have on their destination.

'In the early 1960s a leading tourism researcher wrote:

Tourism brings [people] together, it is instrumental in their dialogue, it leads to personal contact in which people can understand attitudes and beliefs, which were incomprehensible to them, because they were distant. In this way it helps to bridge gaps and erases differences. Since its focal point is man and not the economy, tourism can be one of the most important means, especially in developing countries, of bringing nations closer together and of maintaining good international relations. Hunziker (1961)

'This was the theory twenty years ago. Today, when travelling has become a mass phenomenon, the tale of understanding among peoples is nothing more than wishful thinking. Friedrich Wagner (1970), a veteran German travel journalist, argues that the faith in the mission of tourism as promoting international understanding can be supported by a great deal of practical evidence.

'I do not share this faith nor do I know many positive experiences and examples. On the contrary, I believe that the chances for real human contact between holidaymakers and locals could hardly be less hopeful. The contact is usually only skin deep, the relationship a mere illusion. Where the main reason for travelling is to get away from things, where the tourist ignores the existence of other people; where assembly line techniques are the only way of dealing with huge numbers, where profit making rules supreme, where there are feelings of superiority and inferiority, no communication can develop.'

Source: Krippendorf (1987)

Any discussion on the impacts of tourism usually centres on the effects of so-called 'mass tourism'. Mass tourism has been defined as, 'a phenomenon of large-scale packaging of standardized leisure services at fixed prices for sale to a mass clientele' (Poon, 1993).

Poon went on to identify five key forces as being responsible for the spread of this mass, standardized and rigidly packaged tourism:

1 Consumers: sun-lust, and inexperienced mass consumers.
2 Technology: jet aircraft, automobile, computer reservations and accounting systems, credit cards.
3 Production: cheap oil, charter flights, packaged tours, hotel overbuilding, mass production.
4 Management: economies of scale, hotel and holiday branding, promotional airfares, mass marketing.
5 Frame conditions: post-war peace and prosperity, paid holidays, regulation of air transportation, incentives to attract hotel chains to establish operations.

In North America and Europe, different agents facilitated the development and spread of mass tourism. In the USA, multinational hotel chains, airlines and the growth in car usage were prevalent whereas in Europe by comparison, powerful tour operators, charter flights and packaged tours to Mediterranean 'sun' destinations, were the key agents in the rapid growth of mass tourism.

One of the key questions facing marketing in a travel and tourism context today is the extent to which mass tourism will continue. Poon (1993), in her book *Tourism, Technology and Competitive Strategies*, claimed that increasingly what she termed as a 'new tourism' is emerging. The signs of the emerging new tourism include:

- The growing demand for 'independent' non packaged holidays.
- The growing demand for choice and flexibility.
- Information technologies, such as Computer Reservations Systems (CRS) and the Internet are rapidly diffusing and allowing customers to deal directly with companies and organizations as a means to flexibly make travel arrangements as an alternative to package holidays.
- The rate of growth of the traditional sun package tour business is slowing.

- There is increasing environmental planning and control of tourism in host countries such as Belize and Bermuda.
- There is an increasing 'segmentation' of travel markets to cater for differing lifestyle characteristics.
- The travel behaviour and motivation of tourists are changing with more shorter breaks and activity oriented travel.

Port Douglas, Queensland, Australia

Tourist destinations and companies are increasingly coming to realize that limits have to be placed on growth if the impacts of tourist developments are not to destroy the attractions that tourists sought in the first place. In the tourism literature the terms 'tourist carrying capacity' and 'sustainable tourism' have been used to describe the maximum desirable level of tourism development that could be sustained over a medium- to long-term period.

Port Douglas is situated about 40 miles north of Cairns on a coast of beautiful beaches, reefs and rainforest. Port Douglas is sharing in the boom of 'Tropical Far North Queensland', the name by which the region markets itself. Once a port handling sugar cane, until 20 years ago it was a sleepy town. Today its permanent population is still only 4000. Port Douglas's resort centre covers only a few streets and traditional wooden buildings surrounded by dense vegetation give the town much of its character. The main 'Four Mile Beach' runs along a strip of land on which Port Douglas is situated. Numerous trips to 'The Great Barrier Reef', 'The Atherton Tablelands' and the 'Daintree Rainforest' world heritage site, also leave the resort.

In 1996 Port Douglas gained a major new hotel with the opening of the 300-room Treetops Resort. It is the latest venture of Port Douglas Reef Resorts and has been designed to the strictest environmental standards and largely leaves the rainforest canopy and tropical foliage intact. The developer also owns the Reef Terraces Resort while Radisson has developed the Radisson Royal Palms Resort close to Four-Mile Beach. Nearby is the Sheraton Mirage Resort while two smaller hotels are located in the centre of the town.

John Morris, Chief Executive of Port Douglas Reef Resorts, has had a big influence on the development of the resort: 'Port Douglas is one of the unique resorts in the world, not just because of its natural attractions but because it will not be changing in any major way. We have about 2000 beds and only a couple more hotels will be allowed. Visitors can rest assured that there will never be a glitzy resort here. It will never go over the top.'

The relevance of the preceding discussion on the impacts of tourism to managers is twofold:

1 Modern consumers are becoming sensitive to the impacts of what they consume, whether it is the effect that the detergents they use might have on the environment or the impacts that tourism has particularly on the host community. In successfully managing their tourism products, managers and marketers must be sensitive to this issue in a way in which they often were not in the past.

2 Whilst mass tourism may be here to stay, changes are nevertheless taking place in the marketplace. Consumers are becoming more knowledgeable, experienced and

sophisticated in their tastes and rather more complicated to understand. Managers have to research and attempt to understand these changes. Furthermore, in the highly competitive travel and tourism industry, they have to design their products to appeal to these changing tastes and then to promote, distribute and price the products appropriately.

The effect of external shocks

The travel and tourism industry is particularly prone to external shocks beyond the control of its managers. Wars, hurricanes, terrorist attacks, pollution, adverse publicity or accidents can have a dramatic and speedy affect upon levels of business. For example The 1990–91 Gulf War led to a severe downturn in travel and tourism in the early 1990s, whilst the terrorist attacks in New York and Washington on 11 September 2001 had a similar effect upon the industry. Managers, whilst not able to plan directly for such events, need to be able to assess the risks that the business is prone to and have contingency plans in place so that they are able to react quickly and effectively when necessary. One approach is to spread the risks so that one upset does not destroy the business entirely. Thus a tour operator specializing in tours to only one country would be vulnerable if a war or environmental catastrophe were to occur in that country. By operating to several countries, however, the risks are spread and the overall vulnerability is reduced.

The effects of September 11 on Accor

Accor is a Paris based multi-brand network of 3600 hotels in 90 countries which are fully integrated in terms of sales and technology. For several years this network has been coordinated under the well known banner of 'Accor Hotels'. Hotel development is based on well-known international brands (such as Sofitel, Novotel, Mercure, Ibis, Formule 1, as well as Motel 6 and Red Roof Inns in the United States), which cover the full range of hotel segments, from budget to luxury class. Accor properties are now well represented around the globe, particularly in America, Europe and Asia.

The travel industry, faced with a slowdown that was already perceptible in the spring of 2001, had to cope with one of the worst crises in its history with the events of September 11 of the same year. The tragic events had two consequences. The first was immediate and of an unprecedented magnitude – a psychological shock. The second was the aggravation of the global economic slowdown affecting America, Europe and Asia simultaneously. As a result of the events, some hotel investments were postponed but very few were cancelled and the group still planned 250 new hotel openings in the early to middle years of the decade. The group was protected to some extent from the worst effects of the downturn by the diversity of its hotel portfolio both geographically and in terms of quality. However, some effects on hotel bookings were inevitable. For example, the luxury hotel industry in Paris was severely affected, whereas the economy hotel segment in Europe held up well. Thus, Sofitel's bookings dropped by 33% in October and 18% in November 2001, while Formule 1 and Ibis budget brands in Europe recorded an increase of 3.5% in their October bookings and 4.6 in November. In the US, Sofitel's bookings declined by 25–30%, whereas Red Roof Inns and Motel 6 (budget brands) registered a limited drop of 8.2% in October and then 6% in November 2001.

References and further reading

Airtours plc (2001) *Annual Report and Accounts.*

Bull, A. (1995) *The Economics of Travel and Tourism*, 2nd edn. Melbourne: Longman.

Krippendorf, J. (1987) *The Holidaymakers – Understanding the Impacts of Leisure and Travel.* London: Heinemann.

Middleton, V.T.C. and Clarke, J. (2001) *Marketing in Travel and Tourism.* Oxford: Butterworth-Heinneman.

Moutinho, L. (2000) *Strategic Management in Tourism.* Wallingford: CABI.

Poon, A. (1993) *Tourism Technology and Competitive Strategies.* Wallingford: CABI.

Scott, N., Parfitt, N. and Laws, L. (2000) Destination Management: Co-operative Marketing, a Case Study of the Port Douglas Brand, in B. Faulkner, G. Moscardo and E. Laws (eds), *Tourism in the 21st Century: Lessons from Experience.* London: Continuum.

www.accor.com

www.firstchoiceplc.com

Part Two

Internal analysis

Introduction

Purposes of internal analysis

Internal analysis is concerned with providing the management of travel and tourism organizations with a detailed understanding of their organizations, how effective current strategies are and how effectively resources have been deployed in support of chosen strategies. In carrying out internal analysis managers may gain insights and understanding of how competitive advantage might be achieved and also an appreciation of where remedial action must be taken in order to ensure survival. This next section of the book introduces and evaluates the main techniques and frameworks which are employed to enable travel and tourism managers to produce a comprehensive internal analysis of their organization.

Travel and tourism organizations should carry out an internal analysis for a number of reasons, including the following:

- to identify resources, competences and core competences to be developed and exploited;
- to evaluate how effectively value added activities are organized;
- to identify areas of weaknesses to be addressed by the formulation of future strategies and their successful implementation;
- to evaluate the performance of products;
- to evaluate financial performance;

- to evaluate investment potential if finance is being sought from external sources;
- to assess the performance and future requirements for human resources;
- to provide the analytical underpinning for the 'strengths' and 'weaknesses' section of the SWOT.

The components of internal analysis

An internal analysis will usually cover some or all of the following aspects:

- Resource analysis.
- Competence identification and analysis.
- Analysis of internal activities using Porter's value chain analysis.
- Financial resources and financial performance.
- Products and their position in the market.

These aspects of internal analysis are covered in Chapters 3 to 6, which comprise Part Two of this book. A number of 'techniques' and frameworks are introduced to help travel and tourism managers in carrying out the analysis and in organizing the information.

CHAPTER 3

The travel and tourism organization – competences, resources and competitive advantage

Introduction and Chapter Overview

In Chapter 1 we encountered the concept of competitive advantage as one of the key objectives of business strategy. There has been considerable debate in the academic literature as to the causes of competitive advantage. Essentially, the debate asks the question, 'How do organizations achieve superior performance?' Two positions have emerged as the most prominent.

The *competitive positioning* school of thought, based primarily on the work of Professor Michael Porter of Harvard Business School (1980, 1985), stresses the importance of how the organization is positioned in respect to its competitive environment or industry (which we discuss in Chapter 8). The *resource* or *competence* school (Prahalad and Hamel, 1990;

Heene and Sanchez, 1997), on the other hand, argues that it is the competences (abilities) of the business and the distinctive way that it organizes its activities, which determines the ability to outperform competitors. As with most controversies, we suggest that both schools of thought have their merits – both are partial explanations of the source of competitive advantage.

This chapter concentrates on developing an understanding of the major factors governing the level of performance of the business, namely its resources, competences, particularly its core competences, and its 'value adding' activities.

Learning Objectives

After studying this chapter students should be able to:

- explain the concepts of *core competences*, *competences*, *resources* and the relationships between them;

- explain the concept of the *value chain* and the value chain framework;

- explain the relationships between core competences and core activities;

- explain how the value chain framework 'works';

- explain how the configuration of value adding activities can improve business performance;

- identify the potential benefits of collaboration with suppliers, distributors and customers.

Resources, competences, core competences and competitive advantage

In all industries, regardless of whether the average profitability for the sector is relatively high or low, some organizations are more successful than others. This is as true for the component sectors of travel and tourism as for any other industry. The superior performers conceivably possess something special that weaker competitors do not have and this enables them to outperform their rivals. The sources of *competitive advantage* lie in combining the superior application of competences (skills) and the deployment of superior resources (assets) in creating value for consumers. Strategy and tourism texts often use the term *sustainable* (or sustainability) in connection with the notion of advantage. Sustainability is achieved when the advantage resists erosion by competitive behaviour (Porter, 1985: 20). In other words, in order to achieve the goal of reaching a position of sustainable competitive advantage, a business's competitive advantage must be capable of resisting duplication or emulation by other companies (Barney, 2002).

Definitions

The terms *competence* and *capability*, *core competence* and *distinctive capability* are often used interchangeably in textbooks on strategy. Although some writers (Stalk *et al.*, 1992) argued that there are significant differences between the terms *competence* and *capability*, here the terms will be taken to mean broadly the same things based upon the following definitions.

Competences ● ● ●

A *competence* is an attribute or collection of attributes possessed by all or most of the organizations in a sector of industry. Without such attributes a business cannot enter or survive in the industry. Competences develop from resources and embody skills, technology or 'know how'. For example, in order to operate as an outbound tour operator involved in air inclusive tours a company must possess a range of competences in arranging:

- a means of distributing, marketing and selling the product;
- licences to operate the required capacity to the specified destinations;
- air transportation to and from the destination;
- suitable accommodation at the destination;
- ground handling activities to ensure customers are checked on to their flights and that they are transported to and from their accommodation.

Every successful survivor in the industry must possess these areas of competence.

Core competences ● ● ●

A *core competence* or *distinctive capability* is an attribute, or collection of attributes, specific to a particular organization, which enables it to produce performance above the average for the industry. It arises from the way in which the organization has employed its competences and resources more effectively than its competitors. The result of a distinctive capability is an output which customers value more highly than those of competitors. The basis upon which their core competences are achieved is considered later in the chapter.

Resources ● ● ●

A *resource* is an input employed in the activities of the business. Success rests in large part upon the efficiency by which the business converts its resources into outputs. Resources fall into five broad categories – human, financial, physical (buildings, equipment, stock, etc.), operational (aeroplanes, ships, coaches etc.) and intangible (e.g. 'know how', patents, legal rights, brand names, registered designs, etc.).

Key concept: Competitive advantage

Competitive advantage is often seen as the overall purpose of strategy. Some texts use the phrase *superior performance* to mean the same thing. Essentially, a business can be said to possess competitive advantage if it is able to return higher profits as a proportion of sales than its competitors. The higher profits mean that it will be able to commit more retained profit to reinvestment in its strategy, thus maintaining its lead over its competitors in an industry. When this superiority is maintained successfully over time, a *sustainable* competitive advantage has been achieved. Competitive advantage can be lost when management fail to reinvest the superior profits in such a way that the advantage is not maintained.

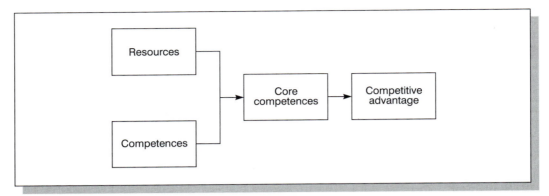

Figure 3.1 The links between resources, competences and competitive advantage

How core competences 'work'

Core competences tend to be both complex and intangible so that it is necessary to explore the nature of resources and competences which underpin them before exploring the concept further. The purpose of such analysis is to allow managers to identify which resources and competences act as the foundation of existing or potential core competences. It is important to note that not all the competitors in an industry will possess core competences or distinctive capabilities (Kay, 1993). It is only those organizations that are producing above average performance which can be considered as possessing core competences. Those with only average or below average performance possess competences and resources (without which they could not compete in the industry at all) but not core competences. See Prahalad and Hamel (1990), Kay (1993), Heene and Sanchez (1997) and Petts (1997) for further discussion of these concepts.

Made simple

Core competence (distinctive capability) = superior deployment of resources + superior application of 'general' competences
Core competence (distinctive capability) when applied in a market creates value for customers and this represents competitive advantage

---

These terms will now be considered in greater detail.

Resource analysis

Tangible and intangible resources

Resources can be either *tangible* or *intangible*. They are the inputs or assets which enable an organization to carry out its activities. Tangible assets include stocks, materials, machinery, buildings, human resources, finance and so on. Intangible assets include skills, knowledge, brand names and goodwill, patent rights, etc. (see Coyne, 1986; Hall 1992), but in a tourism context they also refer to what economists typically refer to as 'free resources'.

Tangible resources are obtained from outside organizations. Such resources are obtained in resource markets in competition with organizations from within and outside the industry. Intangible resources can often be developed within an organization, but as with tangible resources, they have a value attached to them which, although sometimes difficult to quantify, can often be bought and sold in markets. Relationships with the suppliers of resources can form an important part of the organization's core competence, as for example with its ability to attract the most appropriately skilled human resources in the job market.

Tourism is different from most other industries in that free resources are a vital part of the product. Free resources are those resources available in such abundance naturally, such as air, the sea, climate and culture, etc., that there is no need for an allocative mechanism (a market), in order to allocate them to users or consumers. Scarce resources on the other hand are the tangible and intangible resources, which are limited in their supply relative to the demand of consumers, and are therefore allocated in a market.

Bull (1995) argued that the basis for tourism lies in building upon free resources (or 'renewable resources' as they are sometimes termed), with a mixture of public sector and private sector resources. Free resources together with the scarce resources are combined to form what most tourists perceive as the tourist 'product'. It may be argued, as Bull (1995) pointed out, that in today's world there are few truly free resources since any human activity makes demands on the world's resources and, as a consequence, ultimately someone will have to pay a price. Indeed the concept of *sustainable tourism* largely rests upon the recognition of such a line of argument.

All resources have competing demands made upon them so that if they are used for one form of activity they cannot be used in other ways. For example, a large flat coastal area might be suitable for the development of a resort area for tourism or as a site for heavy industry. If tourism is chosen ahead of heavy industry an opportunity to develop heavy industry on this site has been lost. The cost of this choice is known as the *opportunity cost*, which represents the potential economic returns that are being given up in favour of the chosen option (in this example, developing tourism).

Features of tourism resources

A number of points are pertinent to a consideration of tourism's use of resources and to their management in the industry. Particular challenges presented to tourism managers in the use of resources include the following.

Resource immobility ● ● ●

Many resources that are used cannot be moved either in terms of place or time. For example, a particular beach or mountain, the Empire State Building or the culture of Spain are geographically fixed. The Alpine snows of February cannot be replicated in May and the 'midnight sun', a tourist attraction in far northern latitudes, can be observed only during midsummer.

Resource substitution ● ● ●

It is often difficult to substitute one resource category with those of another. For example, in a car factory efficiency gains may be possible, and indeed have been achieved, through replacing employees by machines, i.e. the substitution of human resources with operational resources. In the case of a luxury hotel, an airline or a cruise ship, for instance, the quality of service is often perceived as being closely linked with the quality and number of staff. Consequently it is difficult to replace human resources with operational resources such as computers, and as a result tourism is usually viewed as a labour intensive industry.

Resource conflict and competition • • •

Tourism frequently makes extensive demands on the use of certain resources, which can be in serious conflict or competition with other uses. Such resource conflict or competition may be partially resolved through pricing mechanisms by which the activity that is able to pay the most is able to use the resources. Similarly, regulatory restrictions such as the geographical zoning of areas to permit specified activities only within a particular zone may resolve some conflicts. Some degree of conflict frequently remains. Thus the competing demands of the British army in using gunnery ranges in the Isle of Purbeck, Dorset (an Area of Outstanding Natural Beauty) and in the Northumberland National Park at Otterburn, Northumberland, are in conflict with tourist demands for unspoilt environments. In a local government setting, tourism has to compete for funding with other activities such as education and social services.

Resource ownership and control • • •

Tourism frequently has to utilize resources that are neither owned nor controlled by the companies operating within the sector. This results in a high degree of interdependence between tourism based businesses.

Thus airlines depend upon the physical resources provided by airports and the operating resources provided by air traffic control services. Although the airlines may have some influence over the way in which these resources are managed, they are rarely directly owned and managed. Projects aimed at regenerating decaying urban environments often have tourism at their heart. Such projects are often developed as public–private partnerships in which the public sector (local and national government) manage and control the overall redevelopment and provide limited funding (often termed 'pump priming'). Private sector companies in such cases provide the major part of the financial resources. Examples of such public–private partnerships include the redevelopment of Cardiff Bay in the UK and of the Baltimore waterfront in the USA.

Seasonality • • •

Demand for most tourism resources and hence products, whether business or leisure based, is highly seasonal. This in turn is the result of factors such as climate, the distribution of holiday entitlements, the timing of events and festivals, and historic travel patterns. Consequently, the price that organizations have to pay for their resource inputs and the prices that consumers have to pay those organizations vary according to the season. For example long haul airline flights frequently have a low season, a high season and a 'shoulder' season with prices that reflect periods of relatively high, low and medium levels of demand respectively.

Low rewards • • •

Tourism is often viewed as a low margin area of business. Whilst this is not necessarily the case, it is certainly true to say that the rewards from tourism are often slow to materialize and are susceptible to wide swings in cash flow and profitability. As Bull (1995) pointed out, rewards in tourism may be low for several reasons. The industry is often perceived as being relatively clean and pleasant both to invest in and to work in. Consequently, employees may be prepared to work for lower wages as they would rather work in such an attractive industry than elsewhere. Destinations are often situated in areas with few alternative land uses and employment opportunities and therefore little competition is provided for the use of resources. This puts an effective upper limit on rewards in terms of prices paid for land and development, and wages paid to employees. For example the development of tourism in the Yucatán Peninsula on the Caribbean coast of Mexico, has taken place over recent years in an area that is economically poorly developed and which is remote from major markets for goods and services. Hence the development of tourism in this beautiful region does not face strong competition from other industries for the use of resources and the costs of rewarding resources (in terms of land costs and wages) are relatively low.

Capacity constraints • • •

The capacity of tourism resources is frequently constrained in some way. Thus in tourism the *carrying capacity* for a destination is often referred to. This refers to the ability of a site, resort, or a region to absorb tourism use without deteriorating. The notion of carrying capacity is central to the concept of sustainability. The rapid development of Spain's Costa del Sol for instance from the 1950s onwards demonstrates the need to constrain development. Extensive linear development along the coast to the west of Málaga led to overbuilding with poor planning controls. The relative popularity of the resort area subsequently diminished as consumers opted for more recent and better-planned resorts elsewhere. Thus the over use of resources led to the carrying capacity being exceeded and deterioration in the environment that had attracted tourists in the first place.

Similarly the capacity of physical and operational resources in tourism is often constrained, at least in the short to medium period. If a hotel (physical resource) is full or an airline flight (operational resource) is fully booked it is difficult to add capacity quickly whereas if additional demand is apparent for a manufactured product capacity can often be increased by overtime working, by putting on an extra shift of work or by running production lines at a faster rate. Thus in the tourism industry supply is often relatively fixed whereas demand fluctuates.

The managerial implication of this is that managers will often (in the short to medium term) try to influence demand rather than supply. Thus pricing measures and promotional activities will be altered in order to increase or reduce demand so that it matches the supply that is available. For example it has become common for UK tour operators to alter prices in a very active manner in the weeks immediately prior to the date of departure and hotels often make late alterations to their accommodation rates. This active management of prices (which can be moved upwards or downwards to inhibit or encourage demand respectively) is a way of managing the demand so that it matches the supply which has been previously fixed.

Time • • •

Unlike the purchase of household goods or many services, tourism consumers must also give up a scarce resource in addition to money, namely time. In a similar way to money, time has an 'opportunity cost' attached to it, i.e. other ways in which it might be spent to which a value can be attached. Whilst much time is spent on tourism willingly, other time spent travelling may be viewed by some consumers as a burden that if at all possible should be avoided or curtailed. The managerial implication of this is that consumers may choose different products or may be willing to pay a premium for certain services or alternatively take advantage of discounted travel in return for some extra inconvenience.

For example, flights to Australia from Europe have become increasingly popular for leisure travellers in recent years as newer aircraft types (primarily the Boeing 747 400 series) have needed only one refuelling stop, thereby reducing journey times to about 21 hours. The more efficient use of time also explains why overnight long haul flights and early morning trains are more expensive. The recent rapid growth in the popularity of 'no-frills' airlines is explained partly by the fact that passengers are willing to trade some degree of inconvenience for lower fares. The airlines usually utilize 'secondary airports' (such as London Luton airport in the UK or Dallas Love Field in the USA) which are further away from the main urban centres that they serve.

Analysing resources

When we analyse a company's resources as part of an internal analysis, several frameworks can be employed to provide a comprehensive review.

Analysis by category • • •

First, we might consider them by *category* – physical, operational, human, financial and intangible resources. These resources are then evaluated quantitatively (how much or how many) and qualitatively (how effectively they are being employed). Much of this analysis is covered in Chapters 3, 4 and 5.

- Physical resources (buildings, land, materials) and operational resources (computers, machines, aircraft, systems etc.) are typically be audited for capacity, utilization, age, condition, contribution to output and value.
- Financial resources (the amount and type of finance available to the organization) are considered in terms of the balance between different types of finance and the relative cost of each of these types.
- Human resources (employees, junior, middle and senior management, board directors) are considered in terms of numbers, education, skills, training, experience, age, motivation, wage costs and productivity in relation to the needs of the organization.
- Intangible resources (brand, reputation, goodwill, skills and 'free' resources) are assessed in terms of their overall value to the organization.

Resource analysis for Marriott International

Marriott International is a leading worldwide hospitality company which operates and franchises hotels under a number of recognized international brand names including Marriott, Renaissance and Ramada International.

Resource category	Analysis of Marriott resources
Physical resources	• Over 2200 operating units in the United States and 59 other countries • Properties range from luxurious (Ritz-Carlton) to budget (Courtyard and Fairfield Inn)
Operational resources	• Each brand has a detailed set of operating procedures which is constantly updated and refined • Worldwide reservations system with industry leading costs per reservation • Common reservations system for all brands allowing for cross selling opportunities • Large web sales volume • Marriott Rewards is the largest frequent guest programme in the hospitality sector and is linked to over 30 international airlines
Financial resources	• Most hotels are financed by third parties with only 1% of properties being company-owned • As a hotel manager and franchiser significant and more stable cash flows are generated than through real estate ownership • Strong balance sheet and profitability record
Human resources	• 153 000 employees • Extensive staff training and advancement opportunities • Largest employer in 'Fortune' list of 100 best companies to work for in United States
Intangible resources	• Strong range of brand names many of which are clear leaders within their market tiers • Customer and owner loyalty achieved through a strong rewards programme, • Distinct market positioning of each brand • Many hotels situated at scenic locations

Analysis by specificity • • •

Secondly, we can analyse resources according to their *specificity*. Resources can be specific or non-specific. For example, skilled workers tend to have specialized and industry-specific knowledge and skills. Some technology, for example computer software, is for general (non industry-specific) business use, like word-processing, database and spreadsheet software. Other computer software applications, like airline or hotel computer reservation systems, or yield management programmes, are written for highly specialized uses. Whereas non-specific resources tend to be more flexible and form the basis of competences, industry-specific resources are more likely to act as the foundations of core competences (for example the specialized knowledge of procurement managers responsible for contracting accommodation in the tour operating sector).

Analysis by performance • • •

Thirdly, resources can be evaluated on the basis of how they contribute to internal and external *measures of performance*. Internal measures include their contribution to:

- business objectives and targets – financial, performance and output measures;
- historical comparisons – measures of performance over time (e.g. against previous years);
- business unit or divisional comparisons.

External measures can include:

- comparisons with competitors, particularly those who are industry leaders and those who are the closest competitors and are in its strategic grouping;
- comparisons with companies in other service based industries.

By employing these techniques of analysis, an organization is able to internally and externally *benchmark* its performance as a stimulus to improving performance in the future. Performance, however, is based on more than resources, and competences must be similarly analysed and evaluated.

Competences

Competences are attributes like skills, knowledge, technology and relationships that are common among the competitors in an industry. For example, all companies in the airline industry possess similar competences (basic abilities) in operations, marketing and distribution. They are less tangible than resources and are consequently more difficult to evaluate. Competences are more often developed internally but may also be acquired externally or by collaboration with suppliers, distributors or customers.

Competences are distinguished from core competences by the fact that they do not produce superior performance and by the fact that they are not distinctive when compared to the competences possessed by other companies in the industry. On the other hand, competences are essential for survival in a particular line of business. Competences also have the potential to be developed into core competences.

Core competences

Distinguishing core competences from general competences

Core competences are distinguished from competences in several ways:

- they are only possessed by those companies whose performance is superior to the industry average;
- they are unique to the company;
- they are more complex;
- they are difficult to emulate (copy);
- they relate to fulfilling customer needs;
- they add greater value than 'general' competences;

- they are often based on distinctive relationships with customers, distributors and suppliers;
- they are based upon superior organizational skills and knowledge.

Core competence arises from the unique and distinctive way that the organization builds, develops, integrates and deploys its resources and competences. An existing core competence can be evaluated for:

- *Customer focus* – does it adequately focus on customer needs?
- *Uniqueness* – can it be imitated by competitors as if so, how easily?
- *Flexibility* – can it be easily adapted if market or industry conditions change?
- *Contribution to value* – to what extent does it add value to the product or service?
- *Sustainability* – how long can its superiority be sustained over time?

Competences, as opposed to core competences, can also be judged against these criteria in order to evaluate their potential to form the basis upon which new core competences can be built.

Core competences can never be regarded as being permanent. The pace of change of technology and society are such that core competences must be constantly adapted and new ones cultivated.

Sustaining core competences – Club Med

In 1950, with Europe at peace, Frenchman Gilbert Trigano together with Gérard Blitz, a Belgian, bought some American army surplus tents and camp beds, set them up in a pinewood on the Spanish island of Majorca and called the enterprise Club Méditerranée. The idea was a success from the start. Holiday camps were not new. In Britain Billy Butlin's camps had provided cheap refuges from rainy summers. But Club Med (as it became known) offered reliable sunshine and warm seas, along with what Gerard Blitz called 'an antidote to civilization'. He saw no need for Club Med to make money, as long as they covered their costs. What mattered was that people could be liberated from their working lives for a week or two and live as the noble savage, do some cooking if they wanted to and help with the rudimentary washing-up. It was Trigano who turned Club Med into a profitable business. Tents were soon replaced by thatched huts. During Mr Trigano's four decades with Club Med, bungalows and hotels were added with the soft comforts of home. Staff were hired to do the chores. There were Club Med establishments throughout the world from Tahiti to Bulgaria.

The romanticism that had made Club Med so appealing when Trigano and his early partner banged in the first tent pegs in Majorca was not discarded. Rather, Trigano made Club Med's hint of sensual pleasure a key part of its sales appeal. The partly Belgian idea, which had been launched in Spain with American equipment, became as French as Bardot. As a loyal Frenchman, Mr Trigano made Club Med a messenger of his country's superiority in food, wine, language and indeed culture. Then, suddenly, it seemed that paradise was lost.

After Club Med had showed losses for three successive years in the 1990s, Harvard Business School chillingly used the firm as a study to illustrate 'the death of a brand'. Club Med, which a survey revealed that 77% of Americans and 88% of Europeans had heard of, had become Club Red. The young people who were once its customers were now middle-aged and less thrilled by its offer of organized, communal living, however comfortable. The next generation saw Club Med as just another big hotel chain.

After a revolt by shareholders of Club Med in 1997 Mr Trigano and his son Serge, who had become chief executive, stood down from management. Philippe Bourgignon, who had revived Disney's sickly theme park near Paris, took over, with a promise to return Club Med back to health. Over the next three years the Group transformed its activities and staged a strong financial recovery. After being tested in the French market in 1998, the new group strategy was put into practice in 1999. Restoring the brand and distribution, regaining competitiveness and rationalizing management and organization all contributed to strengthening the Club's market position.

The Club now enjoys an improved image, better product–client fit, a fair price policy, rising volumes and profitable product delivery. A new leisure concept Club Med World (a city based product) was successfully launched, the Club Med product range was broadened to include active wear, body care and sun creams, sunglasses, watches, water sports, etc. and Club Med.com was developed as a new distribution channel. With its transformation plan, strong growth has been achieved utilizing its three strategic assets: its employees, its members and its brand (a 'club'). In so doing the company is repositioning itself from being a hotel company to a service company based on the concept of a 'club' and on the strong sense of belonging which its members (750 000 in France alone) enjoy, enabling it to embody a lifestyle.

Core competences and distinctive capabilities

Kay (1993) presented a slightly different explanation arguing that competitive advantage is based upon what he termed *distinctive capability*. According to Kay (1993), distinctive capability can develop from four sources:

- *Architecture* – A network of relationships within or around the organization. The relationships may be among employees (internal architecture), with suppliers and customers (external architecture) or among a group of organizations engaged in related activities (networks). For example, the strategic alliances that have been built up by the major international airlines in recent years are examples of using networks to strengthen the competitive position of individual airlines through shared activities and extending geographical scope.
- *Reputation* – In service markets reputation is an extremely important contributor to consumer choice of product, but given the intangibility of the product, reputation is usually built up slowly and at some cost as consumers gain experience. Given the high value and public profile of travel products, reputations can easily be damaged, for example through disaster. A coach or aeroplane crash, a ferry sinking or a hotel fire quickly erodes the reputation of the affected organization.
- *Strategic assets* – The strength of market position or dominance of a market is often based upon the possession of strategic assets. They can be of three types. First, an organization may benefit from a monopoly position in a market, secondly, an organization may have already incurred the costs of supplying a market which inhibits the ability of new entrants to compete effectively, and thirdly, some companies may benefit from the possession of licences or regulation that prevents competition. For example, the dominant position of major international airlines at their 'hub' airports (such as Lufthansa at Frankfurt, United at Chicago and American Airlines at Dallas/

Fort Worth) is often the result of costs expended over many years and local regulatory regimes that have allocated take-off and landing slots to these airlines over the years.

- *Innovation* – Through innovation companies are often capable of providing a distinctive product and/or reducing costs. However, innovations can often be copied (particularly in service industries) and the additional returns are often not forthcoming for the innovating company. For example, British Airways was the world's first airline to introduce flat beds for some of its business class passengers, but other airlines quickly followed its lead.

British Airways' core competences

In the airline sector all airlines have the competences and resources required to operate flights between certain destinations. A company like British Airways (Kay, 1993) possesses core competences relating to its:

- Dominance of take off and landing slots at London's Heathrow airport.
- Licences it holds to operate certain routes to which access is denied for other airlines.
- Brand attributes which act as the basis of its reputation for high quality service.

These core competences, although initially identified by the author in the early 1990s, are still valid in the contemporary market. However, it could be argued that the web of cooperative partnerships with other airlines through the 'One World' strategic alliance in allowing for greater destination choice and flexibility of arrangements provides a further area of core competence for the airline. Thus British Airways has distinctive capabilities in terms of strategic assets (Heathrow slots and licences), reputation (brand attributes) and architecture (strategic alliances).

The possession of these core competences enables the airline to charge premium prices for its products by targeting business travellers in particular and by altering aircraft seat configurations to accommodate a greater proportion of business and first class passengers. In this way, core competences are applied to the marketplace and in so doing form the basis of an organization's competitive advantage.

Outcomes of the analysis

Aims of the analysis

The aims of an analysis of resources, competences and core competences (distinctive capabilities) are, therefore, to:

- understand the nature and sources of particular core competences;
- identify the need for and methods of adaptation of existing core competences;
- identify the need for new core competence building;
- identify potential sources of core competence based on resources and competences;
- ensure that core competences remain focused on customer needs.

Resources, competences and core competences are obviously closely related to the ways that a business organizes and performs its value adding activities. It is therefore also necessary to analyse the way in which value adding activities are configured and co-ordinated.

Key concepts: Competence leveraging and building

Competence leveraging

Competence leveraging refers to the ability of a business to exploit its core competences in new markets, thus meeting new customer needs. It can also refer to the ability of the business to modify and improve existing core competences.

Competence building

Competence building takes place when the business builds new core competences, based upon its resources and competences. It is often necessary to build new competences alongside existing ones when entering new markets as it is unlikely that existing competences will fully meet new customer needs.

From distinctive capability to competitive advantage

According to Kay (1993), distinctive capability becomes a competitive advantage when it is applied in a relevant market. Each distinctive capability will have a market (or group of markets) in which the organization can achieve a competitive advantage. Competitive advantage is a relative rather than an absolute notion and can be viewed in several ways.

Organizations can enjoy a competitive advantage relative to:

- other suppliers in the same market;
- other firms in the same industry; or,
- other competitors in the same strategic grouping.

In establishing competitive advantage therefore, it is important that activities are correctly matched up to the organization's capabilities. It is also important that organizations are able to fully understand the inherent differences between: 'the market', 'the industry' and the 'strategic group'. The market refers to the needs of customers and potential customers, whereas the industry an organization is in refers to a group of products linked by common technology, supply or distribution channels. The strategic group refers to those organizations that are identified as primary competitors.

Markets, industries and strategic groups

The market
- Defined by demand conditions
- Based on consumer needs
- Characterized by 'the law of one price'.

The industry
- Determined by supply conditions
- Based on production or operations technology
- Defined by the markets chosen by organizations

The strategic group
- Defined by the strategic choices of firms
- Based on distinctive capabilities and market positioning
- Subjective in determination

During the 1980s Britain's largest brewer, Bass plc, viewed the market for beer as having unexciting growth prospects and redefined its core business as 'leisure'. Consequently the company bought Horizon Travel, a leading UK tour operator of the time. Bass was correct in its observation that pubs and holidays were alternative ways of spending leisure time and that they competed for the same share of consumer expenditure. However, the skills involved in brewing beer and managing an estate of public houses were quite different from those required to run a tour operator. As a result, the tour operator was subsequently disposed of through a sale to the market leader, Thomson. Bass, perhaps failed fully to appreciate that there is a leisure market but that there is not a leisure industry. They did not possess the necessary operating skills (in the industry) to service the market effectively.

Source: Adapted from Kay (1993)

Analysis of value adding activities

What is value adding?

Value chain analysis (Porter, 1985) seeks to provide an understanding of how much value an organization's activities add to its products and services compared to the costs of the resources used in their production. Although it has been applied widely in the manufacturing sector, several writers have applied the model successfully to a service setting. Poon (1993), for example, adapted the model to the travel and tourism industry. A given product can be produced by organizing activities in a number of different ways. Value chain analysis helps managers to understand how effectively and efficiently the activities of their organization are configured and coordinated. The acid test is how much value is added in the process of turning inputs into the outputs, which are products in the form of goods and services. Value is measured in terms of the price that customers are willing to pay for the product.

Value added can be increased in two ways. It can be increased by:

1 changing customer perceptions of the product so that they are willing to pay a higher price for a product than for similar products produced by other businesses; or by,
2 reducing unit costs of production below those of competitors.

Key concept: value added

In simple terms, the value added to a good or service is the difference in the financial value of the finished product compared to the financial value of the inputs. As a sheet of metal passes through the various stages in car production, value is added so that a tonne of metal worth a few hundred pounds becomes a motor car worth several thousand pounds. The rate at which value is added is dependent upon how well the operations process is managed. If the car manufacturer suffers a cost disadvantage by, say, holding a high level of stock or working with out-of-date machinery, then the value added over the process will be lower.

Similarly, a tour operator gathers together various inputs in terms of transportation, accommodation, on-site services and ground handling arrangements and 'packages' them together and in so doing adds value to the customer. Efficiencies in procurement, for instance, achieved through the use of buying in bulk can be passed on to the customer.

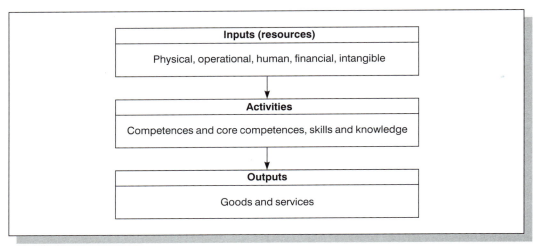

Figure 3.2 A simplified schematic of the value adding process

There are clear linkages between value adding activities, core competences, competences and resources. Resources form the inputs to the organization's value adding activities while competences and core competences provide the skills and knowledge required to carry them out. The more that core competences can be integrated into value adding activities, the greater will be the value added.

The value adding process

Businesses can be regarded as systems that transform inputs (resources, materials, etc.) into outputs (goods and services). This is illustrated in Figure 3.2.

The activities inside the organization *add value* to the inputs. The value of the products is equivalent to the price that a customer is willing to pay for them. The difference between the end value and the total costs is the *margin* (the quantity that accountants would refer to as the *profit margin* – before interest, taxation and extraordinary items). The rate at which value is added varies. If value is not being added as fast as it could be then *waste* is occurring and the organization is not operating as efficiently as it might. Poor quality, low utilization or occupancy and an under-skilled workforce are all examples of waste. Increased added value can be achieved through achieving a reduction in costs or increasing the price that the customer is willing to pay for the output.

The value chain

The activities of the organization can be broken down into a sequence of activities known as the *value chain* as described by Porter in 1985. Poon (1993) applied Porter's value chain to the travel and tourism industry (see Figure 3.3).

The activities within the chain may be classified into *primary* activities and *support* activities. Primary activities are those which directly add value to the final product. Support activities do not directly add value themselves but indirectly add value by supporting the effective execution of primary activities. Whilst the nature of the primary activities and the way in which they can add value vary greatly between differing types

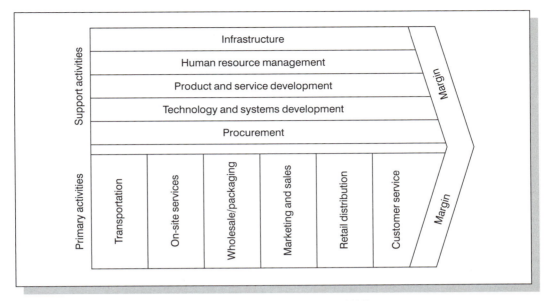

Figure 3.3 The value chain (after Poon, 1993, adapted from Porter 1985)

of tourism organization according to the organizational context, the secondary activities are common in most organizational contexts.

Tables 3.1 and 3.2 describe the primary and support relating to the travel and tourism industry and how they might add value.

Analysis of the value chain

An organization's value chain links into the value chains of other organizations, particularly those of suppliers and distributors. This 'chain' of value chains is sometimes called the *value system* or *total supply chain*. Linkages with suppliers are known as forward linkages while those with distributors and customers are backward linkages.

Different types of organization will have very different value chains. For example, the value chain of MyTravel plc, a vertically integrated UK based tour operator, includes transportation of clients and retail distribution. In a smaller tour operator such as the independent tour operator Sunvil, however, the position is somewhat different. In the case of this company (which operates air holidays primarily to Greece and Cyprus), retail distribution and transportation are undertaken by other companies on a commercially agreed basis. Consequently these aspects do not form a part of the company's value chain but are important elements of the value system described above.

Similarly, not all of an organization's activities are of equal importance in adding value to its products. Those, which are of greatest importance can be considered as *core activities* and are often closely associated with core competences. Thus in an upscale hotel, clients are willing to pay premium prices because the level, type and consistency of customer service are of a high standard. Thus, this aspect may be of greatest importance in adding value and the organization's core competences could be concentrated in this area.

A further point to stress is the importance of linkages between the component parts of the model. In some cases a key source of value added activity might lie in the way in

Activity	Description	Examples of how value might be added
Transportation services	Transportation to and from the destination and at the destination	Information provision Scheduling Gate operations Ticketing Baggage handling Passenger management In flight/on board services Reservations Route and yield management Equipment age and specification Timekeeping
Services on site	Services delivered to visitors at their destination	Repair and maintenance of accommodation Age and specification of accommodation Entertainment Added services provided, e.g. car hire, excursions Accommodation locations Quality of company representatives
Wholesaling and packaging	Assembling or 'packaging' the product or service	Commission negotiations Product development Pricing Assembling, integrating and coordinating aspects of the product
Retail distribution	Distributing the product to the market	Retail locations Choice of distribution channels Commission levels Cost of sales Client database management Customer retention levels
Marketing and sales	Making the product available to the market and persuading people to buy.	Brochure production and distribution Advertising Public relations Sales force management Frequent flyer programmes Brochure display Point of sale materials
Customer service	Installation and after sales support.	Customer complaint management Management and monitoring customer satisfaction Speed of responsiveness Client advice

Table 3.1 Primary activities (adapted from Poon, 1993)

Activity	Description	Examples of how value might be added
Procurement	Purchasing, leasing or renting of services and equipment	Lower prices Better contract terms
Technology and systems development	Developing and implementing technology and systems in support of primary activities	Computer reservation systems Internet applications 'Real-time' sales reports Yield management applications
Products and services development	Developing new products, services and market opportunities	New market segments New products New destinations Developing partnerships and alliances
Human resource management	Recruitment, selection, training, reward and motivation	Quality of employees and managers Employee empowerment Team working Level of training Outsourcing
Infrastructure	General management, financial control and accounting, planning, legal affairs, quality control	Speed and quality of decision making Costs of providing infrastructure Coherent and consistent standards

Table 3.2 Support activities (adapted from Poon, 1993)

which organizations link different parts of the value chain. For example for a tour operator it is important that demand and supply are closely coordinated so that excess capacity which cannot be sold is avoided and so that there is enough supply to meet customer demand. This involves close linkages between the transportation, wholesaling and packaging, retail distribution and marketing and sales components.

Analysis of value adding activities helps to identify where the most value is added and where there is potential to add greater value by changing the way in which activities are configured and by improving the way in which they are coordinated. It is important to note that an organization's value chain is not analysed in isolation but that it is considered in conjunction with its external linkages to suppliers, distributors and customers. Figure 3.3 provides a classification of various internal and external linkages encountered.

A value chain analysis would be expected to include:

- a breakdown of all the activities of the organization;
- identification of core activities and their relationships to core competences and current organizational strategies;
- identification of the effectiveness and efficiency of the individual activities;
- examination of *linkages* between activities for additional added value;
- identification of *blockages* which reduce the organization's competitive advantage.

Internal linkages		External linkages	
Type of activity	**Example**	**Type of activity**	**Example**
Primary–primary	Interdepartmental coordination	Links with suppliers – backward linkages (upstream)	Tour operator linking with a hotel group
Primary–support	Computer base sales management systems	Links with distributors – forward linkages (downstream)	Tour operator securing 'racking agreement' with a travel agency group for its brochures
Support–support	Training for new technologies	Links with other companies at same stage of operations	Airlines collaborating in some of their activities through the formation of strategic alliances

Table 3.3 Classification of internal and external linkages

A useful technique in value chain analysis involves comparison with the value chains of competitors to identify the benefits and drawbacks of alternative configurations.

The aim of value chain analysis is to identify ways in which the performance of the individual activities and the linkages between them can be improved. This may involve identification of improved configurations for activities or improved coordination of them. It is particularly important to consider the extent to which value chain activities support the current strategy of the organization. For example, if the current strategy is based upon high quality then the activities must be configured so as to ensure the creation of high quality products. On the other hand, if the organization competes largely on the basis of price then activities must be organized so as to minimize costs.

Core activities, non-core activities and outsourcing

An increasing trend in recent years has been for organizations to concentrate on core activities associated with core competences and to outsource activities which are not regarded as core to other organizations for whom those activities are core. This is why, for example, British Airways has outsourced some of its accounting and information technology functions to external suppliers. The combination of complementary core competences adds to the competitive advantage of all the collaborating companies. Value chain analysis should therefore also seek to identify where outsourcing might potentially add greater value than performing the activity in-house.

The service profit chain

During the 1990s an alternative framework was introduced by a team of researchers at Harvard University. The *service profit chain* (Heskett *et al.*, 1997) assesses the sources of profitability and growth in labour dominated service firms. Such companies are defined

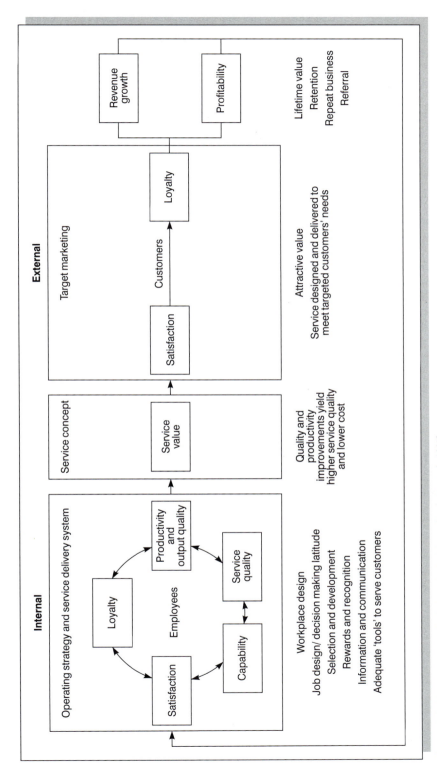

Figure 3.4 The service profit chain (adapted from Heskett *et al.*, 1997)

as those service companies where labour is both an important component of total cost and which are capable of differentiating the firm's service from that of competitors. The purpose of the service profit chain is to provide managers with a framework to help them manage such companies by enabling them to focus on (predominantly) quantifiable measures that lead to financial performance measures. In this regard it is similar in its approach to the 'balanced scorecard' approach to strategy developed by Kaplan and Norton (2001). The service profit chain is shown in Figure 3.4.

The Profit Impact of Market Strategy (PIMS) study initiated in the 1970s found, on examining thousands of companies in many industries, that one of the primary determinants of profitability was market share (Buzzell and Gale, 1992). However, other researchers (Reicheld and Sasser, 1990) questioned the findings in relation to service companies and concluded that customer loyalty is a more important determinant of profit in these companies. The service profit chain establishes links between profitability, customer loyalty and employee satisfaction, loyalty and productivity. The links in the chain (Heskett *et al.*, 1997) are as follows:

- Profit and growth are stimulated primarily by customer loyalty.
- Customer loyalty is a direct result of customer satisfaction.
- Customer satisfaction is largely influenced by the value of services provided to customers.
- Value is created by satisfied, loyal, and productive employees.
- Employee satisfaction results primarily from high quality support services and policies that enable employees to deliver results to customers.

References and further reading

Barney, J.B. (2002) *Gaining and Sustaining Competitive Advantage*, 2nd edn. Upper Saddle River, NJ: Prentice Hall.

Buzzell, R.D. and Gale, B.T. (1992) in J.I. Moore (ed.), *Writers on Strategy and Strategic Management*. London: Penguin.

Coyne, K.P. (1986) Sustainable Competitive Advantage – what it is, what it isn't. *Business Horizons*, Jan–Feb, 54–61.

Hall, R. (1992) The Strategic Analysis of Intangible Resources. *Strategic Management Journal*, 13, 135–144.

Hallowell, R. and Schlesinger, L.A. (2000) The Service Profit Chain, Intellectual Roots, Current Realities, and Future Prospects, in T.A. Swartz and D. Iacobucci (eds), *Handbook of Services Marketing and Management*. Thousand Oaks, CA: Sage.

Heene, A. and Sanchez, R. (1997) *Competence-based Strategic Management*. London: John Wiley.

Heskett, J.L., Jones, T.O., Loveman, G.W., Sasser, W.E. and Schlesinger, L.A. (1994) Putting the Service Profit Chain to Work. *Harvard Business Review*, March–April, 164–170.

Heskett, J.L., Jones, T.O., Loveman, G.W. Sasser, W.E. and Schlesinger, L.A. (1994) Service Profit Chain Audit. *Harvard Business Review*, March–April, 170–174.

Heskett, J.L., Sasser, W.E. and Schlesinger, L.A. (1997) *The Service Profit Chain*. New York: Simon and Schuster.

Kandampully, J. and Duddy, R. (2001) Service System: a Strategic Approach to Gain a Competitive Advantage in the Hospitality and Tourism Industry. *International Journal of Hospitality and Tourism Administration*, 2(1), 27–47.

Kaplan, R.S. and Norton, D.P. (2001) *The Strategy Focused Organization*. Boston, MA: Harvard Business School Press.

Kay, J. (1995) Learning to Define the Core Business. *Financial Times*, 1 December.

Kay, J. (1993) *Foundations of Corporate Success*. Oxford: Oxford University Press.

Petts, N. (1997) Building Growth on Core Competences – a Practical Approach. *Long Range Planning*, 30(4), August, 551–561.

Oliva, R. (2001) The Essence of Service Lies in Focus: Mastering Management. *Financial Times* Supplement, January 15.

Porter, M.E. (1980) *Competitive Strategy: Techniques for Analysing Industries and Competitors*. New York: Free Press.

Porter, M.E. (1985) *Competitive Advantage*. New York: Free Press.

Poon, A. (1993) *Tourism, Technology and Competitive Strategy*. Wallingford: CABI.

Prahalad, C.K. and Hamel, G. (1990) The Core Competence of the Organization. *Harvard Business Review*, 90, 79–91.

Reichheld, F.E. and Sasser, W.E. (1990) Zero Defections: Quality Comes to Services. *Harvard Business Review*, September/October, 105–111.

Stalk G., Evans P. and Shulmann L.E. (1992) Competing on Capabilities: the New Rules of Corporate Strategy. *Harvard Business Review*, March/April, 57–69.

The Economist (2001) Gilbert Trigano [Club Med founder] Obituary, 10 February, p. 129.

Zeithaml, V.A., Parrasuraman, A. and Berry, L.L. (1990) *Delivering Quality Service: Balancing Customer Perceptions and Expectations*. New York: The Free Press.

www.Clubmed.com

The travel and tourism organization – the human context

Human resources are one of the key resource inputs to any organizational process. A thorough analysis of this resource is an important part of strategic analysis and this chapter explains the resource audit – one of the most widely used tools for this purpose.

Closely linked to the human resource is the issue of an organization's personality or culture. We define culture and then go on to explain its importance to an organization. The cultural web is discussed – a model used to explain the way that the features of culture determine the organization's paradigm. Finally, we discuss two cultural typologies.

After studying this chapter, students should be able to:

- define and explain the importance of human resources to an organization;

- explain the employment and working conditions in tourism

- explain the purpose of a human resource audit;

- describe what a human resource gap is;

- explain what a human resource audit contains and what it can be used for;
- describe human resource benchmarking;
- explain what a critical success factor (CSF) is and how human resources can be CSFs;
- define culture, explain its determinants and why it is important;
- explain the components of the cultural web and the nature of paradigms;
- describe two typologies of cultural types.

Human resources

The importance of human resources

People are an important resource to most organizations, but in service based organizations in particular it is often the human resources (i.e. people) that represent the key factor in delivering successful performance. Lynch (2000) put it thus, 'There are some industries where people are not just important but they are the *key factor* for successful performance, as for example in leisure and tourism, where a company has a direct, intangible interface that relies on individual employees to give interest and enjoyment to customers'. Similarly, Baum (1997) considered the experience of the guest or consumer within the tourism industry to be both highly intense and intimate in a way rarely replicated in other service industries. Furthermore, their interactive experience is commonly with the industry's front-line staff who generally are those who have the lowest status, are the least highly trained and are the poorest paid employees. Several authors, including Baum (1995), Choy (1995) and Nickson (2000), have investigated these characteristics.

The importance of employee performance in tourism – Marriott Hotels

Notwithstanding the sales oriented language (designed to attract potential recruits), the following extract from Marriott Hotels clearly illustrates the importance the American based hotel chain attaches to selecting, recruiting and motivating its employees:

'Recognizing our associates [employees] for their hard work, providing for their health and the well-being of their family members, opening avenues of growth and career development, easing the balance between work and personal life – are all part of our associate-centred environment.

'At Marriott our success begins with our associates. The idea that highly satisfied associates provide better service to customers is the foundation of our philosophy. It's a great formula: when our associates delight our customers, those customers will return and add to our business. And a successful business means growth and greater opportunities for our associates.

'As a result you will find a culture that supports and inspires personal development both within the workplace and beyond. Mentoring, training, advancement paths, career mobility, and work-life programmes are just a few of the initiatives and programmes that bring to life our forward-thinking approach toward careers. Marriott's diverse environment readily recognizes the contributions of individuals and, at the same time, maximizes the synergy that close teamwork can bring. In addition, we are committed to promoting from within whenever possible.'

Source: *Adapted from Marriott.com*

Employment and working conditions in travel and tourism

Worldwide employment in tourism is estimated at 192.2 million jobs which is one in every 12.4 jobs. By 2010 this should grow to 251.6 million jobs (one in every 11 jobs) according to the World Travel and Tourism Council (WTTC, 2000). The industry employs a large proportion of young and female employees and has a large number of part-time and seasonal workers. The industry is also often characterized by:

- a large proportion of female employees;
- a large proportion of young employees;
- a large number of part-time and seasonal workers;
- high staff turnover rates;
- recruitment difficulties;
- poor levels of training;
- low pay.

A study in the United States (Woods *et al.*, 1998), for example, found that annual staff turnover in the hotel sector was running at 51.7% for 'front-line' employees (although the figures were somewhat lower for supervisory and managerial staff). As a counter-balance to some of the negative aspects of the industry, it must be said that the industry is often seen as an attractive industry in which to work. Staff often have access to concessionary travel and accommodation rates, opportunities are presented for meeting people and seeing something of the world and many employees are situated in attractive surroundings.

In such circumstances the challenge to managers is to recruit and retain well motivated employees. In order to do this employers may offer more training opportunities, provide higher levels of pay and bonuses and pay attention to the design of jobs and roles through:

- job enlargement – by which employees' jobs are made more worthwhile and interesting in that they are given a wider variety of tasks to carry out;
- job rotation – by which employees rotate jobs between them so that teamwork is encouraged, knowledge and skills are gained and everyone has to take a share of less popular tasks;
- job enrichment – by which employees are given a greater deal of discretion or empowerment to make decisions;
- job sharing – by which employees' jobs are shared between two or more employees thereby sharing burdens and responsibilities.

The management of the guest–employee encounter

The management of the guest (or customer)–employee encounter remains one of the most difficult but ultimately most important tasks for tourism managers (Baum, 1997). Thus, in fast moving markets, especially in service industries which are relatively 'labour intensive', the following factors are particularly important:

- the abilities and knowledge of individuals;
- the ability of individuals to learn;
- the ability of individuals to adapt to change (Pettigrew and Whipp, 1991).

Writers on service quality have suggested that, 'the proof of service [quality] is in its flawless performance' (Berry and Parasuraman, 1991) – a concept similar to the notion of 'zero defects' which is often discussed in a manufacturing context. From the customer's point of view, the most immediate evidence of service quality occurs in the service encounter or 'the moment of truth' when the customer interacts with the organization (Bitner *et al.*, 1994). The derivation of the term 'moment of truth' is often attributed to Jan Carlzon (1987), a past President of Scandinavian Airline Systems (SAS), when he used the terminology to describe every point of contact that a customer, or potential customer, has with the organization in question.

As Baum (1995) and Ryan (1996) have argued, the tourism industry presents particular challenges in the management of 'moments of truth' because of the fragmentation of the experience for many customers. For example, the purchase of a typical package holiday may involve contact with a wide range of intermediaries. The following list is indicative only (adapted from Baum, 1997). Each one is potentially involved in a 'moment of truth'.

- The retail travel agent
- Insurance companies
- Ground transport to and from the airport
- Airport handling agents (at outbound and inbound airports)
- Immigration and customs services
- Local ground transportation
- The hotel or other accommodation
- Tour services at the destination
- Companies selling goods and services at the destination
- Emergency services at the destination
- Service providers such as photography processing on return

The concept of the 'moment of truth' as a manifestation of the guest (or customer)–employee encounter clearly has applicability throughout the three parts (traveller generator region, transit route region and tourist destination region) of what Leiper (1990) called 'the tourism system'. Baum, building on Leiper's representation, produced a model of 'moments of truth' in relation to the wide range of organizations that go to make up the tourism system. The model presented as Figure 4.1 recognizes that 'moments of truth' need not carry equal weighting, i.e. some will be more important to customers than others, 'so that as far as the guest is concerned . . . a positive or negative experience in one area may elicit a very different response to a similar experience elsewhere in the guest cycle' (Baum, 1997). The model provides through its vertical axis a measure (albeit rather crude and subjective) of the intensity and therefore the importance of the interaction to customers. In so doing the model allows tourism managers who are responsible for the tourists' experience to attempt to predict those areas of greatest potential impact and consequently to recognize those areas on which resources might be focused.

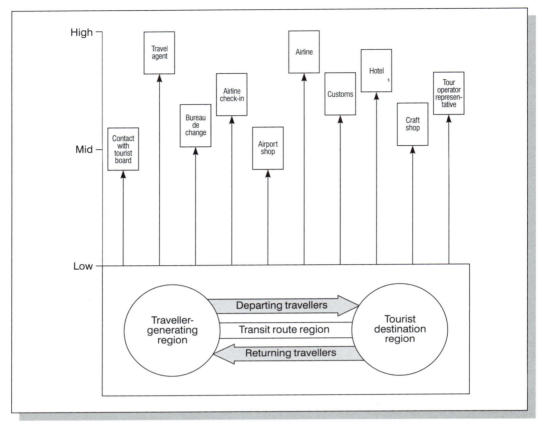

Figure 4.1 A model of the tourist experience and moments of truth (adapted from Baum, 1997)

Decisions about the future strategy of the organization are made by people and strategies are implemented by people. The success or failure of a current strategy will depend not only on decisions made in the past but also on how those decisions are being implemented now by people employed by the organization. It is therefore important to ask questions about who and how, and about why people are doing what they are doing and what they should do in strategic implementation. In short, human resources add value, manage the business and, conversely, can make spectacular errors that can be very costly to the organization.

An understanding of the capabilities of individuals and groups in terms of attitudes, abilities and skills, as well as an understanding of how individuals relate one to another, is an important part in the preparation and development of strategy. A key 'tool' in gaining an understanding of an organization's human resources is the human resource audit.

The human resource audit

The purpose of HR audit

The human resource audit is an investigation into the size, skills, structure and all other issues surrounding those currently employed by the organization. The audit reviews the ability of the human resources to implement a chosen strategy or a range of strategic options.

Most organizations employ accountants to maintain a constant review of financial resources, and each year limited companies subject themselves (by law) to a formal external financial audit. Human resources are another resource input and are equally important, and although they are not subject to legal verification, an organization would be foolish to pursue a strategy without a thorough review of its human resources, i.e. its people.

Once the audit has been completed, management should be able to answer the key question – are the human resources in the organization capable of implementing the proposed strategy? If any gaps are identified, then a human resource strategy may be put in place to close the gap.

Key concept: Human resource gaps

A 'gap' can occur in any area of human resource management. It rests upon a simple calculation:

Human resource characteristic necessary for the proposed strategy *minus* current state of the human resource characteristic *equals* the human resource gap

Gaps can occur in particular skills. In sectors like tourism, for example, skills gaps may be identified in particular areas such as those with knowledge and experience of computer reservation systems. It may be that the audit reveals a deficit of 30 people who can operate such systems – a negative gap. The task of the human resource department thus becomes to successfully appoint or retrain to gain the requisite number of skilled operators.

Positive gaps may also be identified – surpluses of a particular type of employee. The human resource strategy thus has to put measures in place to 'dispose' of the excess labour.

Gaps may be closed by using the 'five Rs' individually or in combination. The five Rs are:

- Retirement
- Retraining
- Redeployment
- Redundancy
- Recruitment

The contents of a human resource audit

The contents of a human resource audit may vary from organization to organization depending on its size, geographic coverage, and type of activity. However, a typical audit checklist is as follows.

- The number of employees by a number of counting methods: – the total number, by division, by location, by skill type, by grade or place in hierarchy, by age or length of service, by gender and by ethnic origin.
- Employee costs – usually measured by salary costs and 'add-ons' like national insurance, etc.

- The organizational structure and the position of employees within the structure.
- Recruitment and selection procedures and their effectiveness.
- The quality and effectiveness of training and development programmes used.
- The level of employee motivation and morale.
- The nature of employee or industrial relations between management and employees.
- The internal and external networks that employees in the organization have developed (and their effectiveness for various purposes).
- The monitoring of the effectiveness of existing human resource policies and control procedures.

Formal and informal human resource audits

The information provided by the audit can provide management with important information about the state of the organization's human resources. In most types of organization, regular audits are essential to success. However, for a professional soccer club or an orchestra, the state of the human resources is completely transparent and the audit occurs continually – although it may never be formally conducted. A football team that loses every match or an orchestra that sounds terrible will have obvious human resource skill deficits. A formal audit is hardly necessary in such a circumstance.

Formal audits may be carried out by personnel specialists on a regular basis (say annually), or whenever management needs the information for the purposes of a strategic analysis. Practitioners in this area make the point that the simple following of 'lists' like that outlined above, is only a starting point. As points of interest are raised, such as key skill deficiencies, then it is imperative that the reasons for the shortage (or surplus) are also examined as an integral part of the audit.

The outcomes of a human resource audit

The problem of measurement • • •

The various components of a human resource audit present differing problems of quantification. We can intuitively understand that entries like employee costs, numbers, skills shortages or surpluses can be measured in numerical terms. Industrial relations measures can usually be measured by such things as days lost through strikes, etc. Other parts of the audit present more difficulty in respect of measurement.

How, for example, might we measure staff morale or motivation? We might be able to say that staff morale is high or low, but any 'in-betweens' might be difficult to assign a value to in the same way as for, say, employee costs. The same problems arise with the levels of staff motivation and job satisfaction. It is also probably true to say that in most organizations, large disparities exist between employees in respect of these intangibles. Some employees will be highly motivated and will enjoy good morale whilst others will not. It is for these reasons that a 'checklist' approach to human resource audit is rarely possible – it usually contains some subjective assessments of some parts of the audit.

Human resource benchmarking • • •

The concept of benchmarking is one that we will encounter several times in this book. Essentially, benchmarking is a tool for comparing a feature of one organization with the same feature of another. It is particularly useful for comparison against the best in an industry for the feature in question. Followers of the best in the industry might then ask why the leader company has achieved the superior performance. Increasingly, however, companies in the service industries are also benchmarking themselves against companies in different sectors, so for example it may be that in the area of offering customer service, hotel companies are able to learn from practices in banking, airlines or car dealers for example.

The feature examined in a benchmarking analysis will depend upon what the organization needs to know. If, for example, a company identifies a negative gap in a key skill area which it has found difficult to close (say of good quality graduates), a benchmark study will enable the company to find out about its competitors. If Company A is known to be able to attract the best graduates, then an examination of its human resource policies will enable other companies (competitors) to benchmark their own practices against it. It may be that Company A is identified as offering the best career-progression planning, the highest salaries or the best development opportunities. If this is found to be the case, then competitors will want to examine their own provision in these areas to see where they can be improved.

Lead companies may also be analysed for the ways in which they not only manage their internal human resources, but also the ways in which they interact with external sources of labour. Many airlines, for example, close skills gaps by making extensive use of contract workers. They may also 'outsource' some of their work to outside suppliers or use consultants. The ability to attract these 'mobile' workers can be just as important as the ability to attract permanent employees.

Identifying human resources as critical success factors

As well as using a human resource audit to identify gaps, it can also be used to establish which, if any, employees or groups of employees are critical to strategic success. These are the people that the organization's success may have been built upon in the past and it is likely that the existing structures are centred on them.

In some organizations, critical success human resources may be found on the board of directors giving strategic direction to the company as a whole. In others, they might be found in research, developing the new products upon which future success will be built. Certain marketing personnel or operations people might also be critical in some businesses. For example, in some tour operators, the management of the operational aspects of tours may involve local knowledge and experience of destination areas and individual suppliers. This knowledge and experience may be held by key individuals, whose sudden loss to a company could cause operational problems. Well-managed companies try to reduce this risk through measures such as documented procedures, rotating staff to widen the experience base, and training procedures.

Key concept: Critical success factors

It is usually the case that there are one or more reasons why superior performers in an industry are in the positions that they are. These key reasons for success are called *critical success factors* (CSFs). Some companies have uniquely skilled employees, such as particularly skilled engineers or product development specialists. In this case, the CSF is a human resource. In other businesses, the CSF might be a unique location, a brand image, an enviable reputation, a legally protected patent or licence, a unique production process or technology. This is not to say that other parts of the organization are unimportant, but merely that the CSF is *the* key cause of the success.

In terms of competitive strategy, the approach to a CSF is to defend it – in some cases at whatever cost it might take. This usually takes to form of 'locking it in' to ensure that the advantage is maintained or that competitors are prevented from gaining the same advantage. If the CSF is in the form of a human resource this might involve contractual arrangements providing financial incentives, long periods of notice to leave the company or providing the right working environment to motivate employees.

The importance of the human resources in a business and the steps that may be taken to motivate and retain key staff is illustrated by the case of Bridge the World.

Motivation and employee retention in Bridge the World

Jerry Bridge, a veteran traveller and top-performing salesman at Trailfinders (a specialist London based travel agency and tour operator), founded the company Bridge the World in London during 1989. It quickly established a niche in the market when it took advantage of the war against Iraq and tumbling air passenger numbers to negotiate good deals with airlines. Since then it has branched out into tailor-made holidays, in which it offers anything from the trip of a lifetime for a retired couple with a pension lump sum to intercontinental adventures for students on a gap year. The company has grown at an annual rate of 23% for the past 10 years, achieving sales of £34 million. The company's employees are important ingredients in this success.

Bright ex-traveller sales staff are employed who are capable of organizing complex itineraries and communicating a passion for the product, and they are supported by imaginative marketing. Attracting good staff is not the only challenge. Retaining them is equally important. Despite the growth in sales, profit margins were being eroded because of a haemorrhage of sales staff, with 40% leaving within 15 months of starting. The unacceptably high rate was having a detrimental effect on profitability, not least because sales staff reached peak performance after a year in the job.

Managing Director Jerry Bridge tried to transform the situation by hiring a human resources director and consultants to investigate the problem. A new incentive scheme raised the threshold on sales bonuses and a Bridge the World sabbatical was introduced whereby sales staff who stayed with the company for 21 months qualified for a two-month sabbatical with access to discounted flights and hotels booked through the company. The sabbatical has proved immensely popular among travel-hungry staff, whose average age is 25.

Bridge the World has also sought 'Investors in People' accreditation (a UK government backed training initiative) and spent a lot of money and resources on training. The company now has its own trainer running courses on sales techniques and leadership skills, and has a share ownership scheme for directors and senior management, The company's annual sales staff turnover rate is now 32%, well below the sector's average and still dropping. A combination of measures – money, incentives and training – improved employee retention and performance.

Organizational culture

What is culture?

Culture is the organizational equivalent of a human's personality. As with human personality, organizational culture can be somewhat difficult to explain and define, and consequently many different definitions exist. Ralph Stacey (1996) provided one definition.

> The culture of any group of people is that set of beliefs, customs, practices and ways of thinking that they have come to share with each other through being and working together. It is a set of assumptions people simply accept without question as they interact with each other. At the visible level the culture of a group of people takes the form of ritual behaviour, symbols, myths, stories, sounds and artefacts.

According to Charles Handy, a leading writer on management, the difficulties encountered with defining culture mean that it cannot be precisely defined, for in essence it is 'something that is perceived, something felt' (Handy, 1996). Organizational culture can vary enormously from one organization to another, as Handy pointed out.

Organizations are as different and varied as the nations and societies of the world. They have differing cultures – sets of values and norms and beliefs – reflected in different structures and systems. And the cultures are affected by the events of the past and by the climate of the present, by the technology of the type of work, by their aims and the kind of people that work in them (Handy, 1996).

Culture can thus be explained in terms of the 'feel' of an organization or its 'character' or as it has sometimes been described as 'the way we do things round here'. Definitions can be a bit inaccessible, but the importance of an organization's culture lies in the fact that it can be 'felt' whenever it is encountered. From a strategic point of view the important point is that all organizations have culture and that it can have a significant effect upon organizational performance. Consequently, tourism managers must attempt to understand the culture of their organization and the effect it is having (positive or negative) upon organizational performance. Managers may subsequently find it necessary to take steps to implement a programme that attempts to change the prevailing culture in order to improve performance.

Organizations are as individual as people, and in many ways there are as many cultures as there are organizations – each one is unique. This is not to say, however, that we cannot identify common features between organizational cultures.

The determinants of culture

Why an organization has a particular type of culture is as complicated a question as asking why a human has a particular personality. It has many possible influences, the net effect of which forge culture over a period of time. Any list would be necessarily incomplete, but following are some of the most important.

- The philosophy of the organization's founders, especially if the organization is relatively young.
- The nature of the activities in the business and the character of the industry it competes in.

- The nature of the interpersonal relationships and the nature of industrial or employee relationships.
- The management style adopted and the types of control mechanism – for example, the extent to which management style is autocratic or participative.
- The national or regional character of the areas in which the organization's activities are located. This, in turn, can affect the power distance, which also influences culture.
- The structure of the organization, particularly its 'height' and 'width'.
- The dependency the organization has on technology and the type of technology employed (the growth of e-mail, for example, has had an influence of the culture of some organizations).

Key concept: Power distance

This is a term attributed to Hickson and Pugh (1995). They use the term to describe 'how removed subordinates feel from superiors in a social meaning of the word "distance". In a high power distance culture, inequality is accepted . . . in a low power distance culture, inequalities and overt status symbols are minimized and subordinates expect to be consulted and to share decisions with approachable managers.'

Why is culture important?

Culture is important because it can and does affect all aspects of an organization's activities. The metaphor of human personality may help us to understand this. Some people's personality means they are motivated, sharp, exciting to be with, etc. Others are dull, tedious and apathetic. These personality features will affect all aspects of their lives.

The same is true of an organization's 'personality'. Culture is important because of the following (not exhaustive) reasons. Culture can have an influence on:

- employee motivation;
- the attractiveness of the organization as an employer and hence the rate of staff turnover;
- employee morale and 'goodwill';
- productivity and efficiency;
- the quality of work;
- the nature of the employee and industrial relations;
- the attitude of employees in the workplace;
- innovation and creativity.

The point to make after such a list is simply that culture is *very* important. It is essential that management understand the culture of the organization both in analysing strategic position and then in the implementation of strategy.

The cultural web

One of the most commonly used ways of making sense of an organization's culture is to use the cultural web (Johnson, 1992). It is a schematic representation of the elements of an organization's culture in such a way that we can see how each element influences the paradigm.

Key concept: Paradigm

A paradigm is a worldview – a way of looking at the world. It is expressed in the assumptions that people make and in their deep-rooted beliefs. The paradigm of an organization or a national culture is important because it determines how it will behave in a given circumstance. Given a certain moral dilemma or similar choice, we might expect the paradigms of an orthodox Jew and an atheist Westerner to lead them to arrive at different conclusions. The things that cause one culture to adopt one paradigm and another culture to espouse a different one are set out in the cultural web.

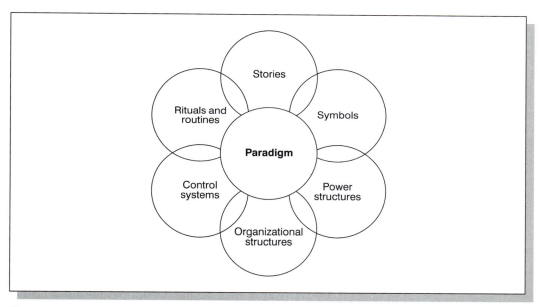

Figure 4.2 The cultural web (adapted from Johnson, 1992)

The main elements of the web are described below.

Stories

Stories are those narratives that people within the organization talk to each other about, what they tell new recruits and outsiders about the organization. The stories typically recount events and people from the past and present – stories of famous victories and defeats. They tend to highlight what is considered important to the members of the organization.

Routines and rituals

Routines are the procedures for doing things within the organization. They are repeated on a regular basis to the extent they are taken as 'the way things are done'. Rituals have a longer time frame and can be either formal or informal. Formal routines and rituals are a part of the organization's practice, such as the 'long service award' or the company Outward Bound course that work teams might go on from time to time. Informal routines and rituals might include the way that people behave at the annual Christmas party or the extent to which colleagues do (or do not) go for a drink together after work.

Symbols . . .

Symbolic aspects of organizational life concern those things that symbolize something to some people – a certain level of promotion, the company car they drive, the position of their office, their job title. In some companies, these symbols have no apparent importance at all. In others, they matter a great deal. The way that employees respond to these symbols can tell us a great deal about the culture.

Structure . . .

The structure of an organization can mean more than just those formal relationships that are shown on an organization diagram. Informal structures can also exist through interpersonal relationships that transcend the formal structures. Some organizations have highly developed informal structures whilst others do not.

Control systems . . .

The ways in which activities are controlled, whether 'tight' or 'loose', is closely aligned to culture. This has a strong link to power distance and the nature of the activities in which the organization is engaged. Control systems, by definition, concern activity in which performance is gauged against a predetermined standard and the methods of both standard-setting and monitoring performance vary significantly according to culture.

Power structures . . .

The core assumptions that contribute to the paradigm are likely to be made by the most powerful management groupings in the organization. In some companies, this power resides in the research department, in others it will be the production people or those from another department. In some organizations there may be arguments about what is important between one or more groupings.

Each component of the cultural web exerts its own influence upon the organization's paradigm. The paradigm describes the aggregate effects of all of the cultural influences on the way the members of the organization look at the world. This can apply to regions of the world just as it applies to organizations. People indigenous to the Middle East are often thought to have a different view of the world than citizens of countries in north-western Europe. This difference is because of the influence that each component of the cultural web exerts on the national or regional paradigm.

A cultural web for MyTravel plc

MyTravel plc (formerly Airtours plc) is one of the world's leading travel groups with involvement in tour operating, travel retailing, charter airlines, accommodation and cruising. Chaired by David Crossland, the business has a corporate headquarters in the Manchester suburbs and other offices elsewhere for its operating divisions. The business was founded in Lancashire some 30 years ago by Crossland, a former travel agency clerk, as a single travel agency (see the MyTravel case in the cases section at the end of this book for a more detailed discussion).

Stories
- £8000 start-up costs
- David Crossland went from coffee boy to Airtours Chairman
- Consolidation of UK position through takeover of First Choice not allowed
- Difficulties in German subsidiary

Symbols
- David Crossland hard-working family man
- Airtours logo
- Royal blue corporate colour

Power structure
- Head office in Manchester
- Crossland and family, senior management
- Strong management team
- Powerful influences over suppliers

Organizational structure
- Hierarchical
- Team working
- Empowerment of managers to make decisions
- Semi-autonomous divisional offices

Control system
- Economies of scale through central coordination and vertical and horizontal integration
- Partners in joint ventures
- Budgeting, target-setting and financial reporting

Rituals and routines
- Striving for quality
- Importance of advertising and promotion
- Attracting customer loyalty
- Producing 'the brochure'

Paradigm
- Value for money
- Family oriented
- The 'Airtours family'
- Entrepreneurial

Cultural typologies

A number of writers in organizational theory have attempted to group culture types together. The thinking behind such attempts at typology is that if organizations can describe their cultures by type, then this would help in strategic analysis. We will briefly consider two of these attempts.

Handy's culture types

Handy (1996) suggested that organizational cultures could be divided into four broad types: power cultures, role cultures, task cultures and person cultures.

Power cultures • • •

This type of organization is dominated by either a very powerful individual or a dominant small group. It is typified by an organization that has grown as a result of entrepreneurial flair. Strategic decisions and many operational ones are made by the centre and few decisions are devolved to other managers. As the organization is dependent on the abilities and personality of the powerful individual, the ability of the organization to change in response to changes in the environment are sometimes limited by the centre.

Power cultures are common in small entrepreneurial (owner-managed) companies and in some notable larger organizations with a charismatic leader.

Role cultures • • •

This type of culture is found in many long-established organizations that have traditionally operated in stable environments. They tend to be very hierarchical and rely on established procedures, systems and precedent. They often respond slowly to change as it takes time for change to be recognized through the reporting mechanisms. Delays are also encountered in the slow and considered decision-making process.

Role cultures are common in traditional bureaucracies such as the civil service. The task of management in a role culture is to manage procedure. There is usually a high degree of decentralization and the organization is run by rules and laid down procedures.

Task cultures • • •

Task cultures are found in organizations engaged in activities of a non-repetitive nature, often high value, one-off tasks. Activities are normally based around flexible multi-disciplinary teams containing expertise in the major disciplines required to complete the project. Teams tend to be small but flexible and find change easy to identify and adjust to. Strategic planning tends to concentrate on the task in-hand.

As their name suggests, task cultures can be found in organizations that are dedicated to a particular task. Consortia that work on large civil engineering projects may demonstrate task culture, as might missionary teams that work together on a medical project in the developing world.

Person cultures • • •

Person cultures are those that exist primarily for the benefit of the members of the organization itself and hence they tend to be rare in commercial businesses. They can have a very different 'feel' to the other cultures as all members of the organizations work for the benefit of themselves and the other members.

They can be found in learned professional societies, in trade unions, in cooperatives, in some charities and in some religious organizations.

In reality, few organizations fit perfectly into one just classification and they may demonstrate elements of two or more. Some diversified organizations may have divisions that fall into all the categories and the cultures may change over time. Many start as power cultures and then tend towards a role culture as size increases.

In assessing the appropriateness of the four cultural types Lynch (2000) suggested that three criteria might be used. Does the dominant culture identified:

- Fit with prescriptive or emergent forms of strategy formulation?
- Deliver competitive advantage for the organization?
- Have the ability to cope with strategic change?

Lynch's conclusions are shown in Table 4.1

	Prescriptive or emergent strategy	Delivery of competitive advantage	Ability to cope with strategic change
Power culture	Prescriptive	Enhanced but individuals may miss competitive moves	Depends on individual or group at centre
Role culture	Prescriptive	Solid, slow and substantive	Slow, will resist change
Task culture	Emergent	Good where flexibility is important	Accepted and welcomed
Person culture	Possibly emergent	Depends on individual	Depends on individual

Source: adapted from Lynch (2000: 319)

Table 4.1 An assessment of Handy's four cultural types

In assessing the four main cultural types however, three important qualifications should be made:

1 Organizations change over time.
2 Several types or variations of culture often exist in the same organization.
3 Different cultures may predominate depending on the headquarters and ownership of the company.

Miles and Snow's culture types

Miles and Snow (1978) categorized cultures into four types, based on how they tend to react in strategic terms.

Defenders • • •

These organizations tend to seek a competitive advantage in terms of targeting niche markets through cost reduction and specialization. They tend to operate in stable, mature markets and, as the name suggests, they favour defending their current market share by service improvements or further cost savings. Defenders therefore tend to be centralized, have rigid control systems and a hierarchical management structure that does not enjoy sudden change.

Prospectors • • •

These organizations enjoy the challenge of developing and introducing new product to the marketplace. They actively seek out new markets for their products. These favoured strategies require the organization to constantly monitor the environment and be willing and able to respond to quickly to changes that may occur. To that end, these organizations are decentralized and flexible.

Analysers • • •

These organizations are 'followers' and are conservative in nature. Steady growth through market penetration is the favoured option as this can be achieved without radical changes to structure. Moves into new markets and products only occur after extensive evaluation and market research. They learn from the mistakes of others and tend to balance power between the centre and divisions with complex control systems.

Reactors • • •

Reactors are a bit like analysers in that they tend to follow rather than innovate. They differ from analysers in that they are less conservative and sometimes behave impulsively, having failed fully to consider the implications of their actions. These organizations may lack proper control systems and typically have a weak but dominant leader.

Organizational culture at Southwest Airlines

The culture of Southwest Airlines, which emphasizes employees as the airline's 'first customers' and passengers as the second, has been integral to Southwest Airlines' success. Dallas-based Southwest grew significantly during the 1990s and continues to do so, drawing in thousands of employees new to the airline's ways and raising questions about whether it can keep its culture intact. In 1990, the airline had 8600 on its payroll, which rose to about 29 000 employees in 2002, and almost half of these have been with the company less than five years. The airline also has flown beyond its Texas roots into other regions of the USA. Ten years ago it served 31 cities, five years ago 45 and today 56. Southwest is finding that it must work differently to make

---

sure its culture endures. In an attempt to address this, a committee focusing on new employees was created. As turnover edges up an internal branding campaign reminds employees of the 'freedoms' that working at Southwest brings. The airline also is in the relatively new position of having to search for applicants rather than waiting for candidates to come to it.

It takes a lot of hard work to maintain the culture but the airline regularly finds a place towards the top of Fortune magazine's annual list of the 100 best companies to work for in America, the rankings for which are partly determined by employee comments. Southwest's charismatic leader, 69-year-old Herb Kelleher, has devoted much time and energy to creating and maintaining the company's distinctive corporate culture.

Southwest, which began operating in 1971, now challenges the major North American airlines such as American, United and Delta. Originally offering flights in a triangle between Dallas, San Antonio and Houston, the idea of offering fares so cheap that people would abandon their cars for jets has proved very attractive to consumers and has been widely copied. The airline's core offering is to offer lots of short flights between pairs of cities, though in recent years it has been offering more long flights. Reinforcing the low fares is a culture of relaxed professionalism which includes flight attendants who might crack jokes or burst into song. The airline also has neither assigned seats nor a meal service.

Southwest's employees appear to understand what's made the airline succeed. This provides a clarity of purpose at Southwest that makes it easy to retain the culture while growing. In recent years, the airline has added between one and three destinations a year while it has continued to increase the number of flights from its existing cities such as Houston.

Employees get four cards a year from the company: for birthdays, a December holiday, Valentine's Day and the company anniversary day. Throughout the company, employees are encouraged to hold 'celebrations' to mark birthdays, engagements and other milestones. Creativity also is emphasized, especially when it comes to finding relief in high-stress jobs. Customer relations workers may come to work in pyjamas for a day. Profit sharing ties employees directly to company performance. Southwest built an infrastructure that ensures that when an employee does something good, the whole organization knows about it. The lives of Southwest employees, along with the company's history, are highlighted on the headquarters' walls.

To help facilitate communications a 'culture committee' was established in 1990 aiming to do what was necessary to create, enhance and enrich the Southwest spirit. In one way or another the committee tries to ensure that fellow workers are appreciated and that people appreciate the difficulties involved with other people's positions. Local culture committees have also been established in cities across Southwest's network. A committee focusing on new employees has also been added in order to make sure that new employees are inducted appropriately and receive proper guidance and mentoring during their early careers. The company is paying more attention to employee retention as turnover creeps up. For a long time it was 5–7%, but it increased to 9.8% in 1999. An internal branding campaign has been established which identifies eight basic freedoms of working at Southwest. Employees, the company says, get the freedom to: pursue good health; travel; learn and grow; stay connected; have financial security; work and have fun; make a positive difference; and be creative and innovative.

References and further reading

Augustyn, M. and Ho, S.K. (1998) Service Quality and Tourism. *Journal of Travel Research*, 37 (August), 71–75.

Baum, T. (1995) *Managing Human Resources in the European Hospitality and Tourism Industry – a Strategic Approach*. London: Chapman Hall.

Baum, T. (1997) Making or Breaking the Tourist Experience: the Role of Human Resource Management, in C. Ryan (ed.), *The Tourist Experience – a New Introduction*. London: Cassell.

Berry L.L. and Parasuraman, A. (1991) *Marketing Services*. New York: The Free Press.

Bruush, R. (1997) Managing Quality Organizations in the US Hospitality Sector, in Foley, M., Lennon, J. and Maxwell, G. (eds), *Hospitality, Tourism and Leisure Management*. London: Cassell.

Bitner, M.J., Booms, B.H. and Mohr, L.A. (1994) Critical Service Encounters: the Employee's Viewpoint. *Journal of Marketing*, 58 (October) 95–106; also reprinted in M. Gabbott and G. Hogg (eds) (1997) *Contemporary Services Marketing Management – a Reader*. London: The Dryden Press, pp 149–170.

Campbell, A. and Goold, M. (1987) *Strategies and Style*. London: Basil Blackwell.

Campbell, A., Goold, M. and Alexander, M. (1994) *Corporate Level Strategy*. London: Wiley.

Carlzon, J. (1987) *Moments of Truth*. Cambridge, MA: Ballinger.

Chandler, A. (1962) *Strategy and Structure*. Cambridge, MA: MIT Press.

Choy, D. (1995) The Quality of Tourism Employment. *Tourism Management*, 16(2), 129–137.

Goold, M. (1996) Parenting Strategies for the Mature Business. *Long Range Planning*, June, p. 395.

Goodale, P.A. and Wood, R.C. (1997) Organizational Culture in Luxury Hotels, in M. Foley, J. Lennon and G. Maxwell (eds), *Hospitality, Tourism and Leisure Management*. London: Cassell.

Handy, C.B. (1996) *Understanding Organizations*, 4th edn. London: Penguin.

Hickson, D.J. and Pugh, D.S. (1995) *Management Worldwide*. London: Penguin.

Hofstede, G. (1980) *Culture and Organizations: Software of the Mind*. London: McGraw-Hill.

Hoque, K. (1999) New Approaches to HRM in the UK Hotel industry. *Human Resource Management Journal*, 9(2), 64–76.

Johnson, G. (1992) Managing Strategic Change: Strategy, Culture and Action. *Long Range Planning*, 25(1), 28–36.

Jones, P. and Davies, A. (1991) Empowerment: A Study of General Managers at Four Star Hotel Properties in the UK. *International Journal of Hospitality Management*, 10(3), 211–217.

Kandampully, J. (1997) Quality Service in Tourism, in M. Foley, J. Lennon and G. Maxwell (eds), *Hospitality, Tourism and Leisure Management*. London: Cassell.

Kay, J. (1993) *Foundations of Corporate Success*. Oxford: Oxford University Press.

Kelliher, C. and Johnson, K. (1997) Personnel Management in Hotels – an Update: a Move to Human Resource Management? *Progress in Tourism and Hospitality Research*, 3(4), 321–331.

Lashley, C. (1995) Towards an Understanding of Employee Empowerment in Hospitality Service. *International Journal of Contemporary Hospitality Management*, 7(1), 27–32.

Leiper, N. (1990) *The Tourism System*. Auckland: Massey University Press.

Lucas, R. (1997) Maximising Labour Flexibility, in M. Foley, J. Lennon, and G. Maxwell (eds), *Hospitality, Tourism and Leisure Management*. London: Cassell.

Lucas, R. (1995) *Managing Employee Relations in the Hotel and Catering Industry*. London: Cassell.

Lynch, R. (2000) *Corporate Strategy*, 2nd edn. London: Pitman.

Maxwell, G.A. (1997) Empowerment in the UK Hospitality Industry, in M. Foley, J. Lennon, and G. Maxwell (eds), *Hospitality,*

Tourism and Leisure Management. London: Cassell, pp 53–68.

Miles, R.E. and Snow, C.C. (1978) *Organizational Strategy, Structure and Process*. New York: McGraw-Hill.

Mullins, L.J. (1995) *Hospitality Management: a Human Resources Approach*. London: Pitman.

Nickson, D. (2000) Human Resource Issues in Travel and Tourism, in L. Moutinho (ed.), *Strategic Management in Tourism*. Wallingford: CABI, pp 169–185.

Pettigrew, A. and Whipp, R. (1991) *Managing Change for Competitive Success*. Oxford: Basil Blackwell.

Riley, M. (1996) *Human Resource Management in the Hospitality and Tourism Industry*. Oxford: Butterworth-Heinemann.

Ryan, C. (1996) Market Research in Tourism: Shifting Paradigms for New Concerns, in L. Moutinho (ed.), *Marketing Research in Tourism*. London: Prentice Hall.

Schein, E. H. (1992) *Organizational Culture and Leadership*, 2nd edn. San Francisco: Jossey–Bass.

Stacey, R. (1996) *Strategic Management and Organizational Dynamics*, 2nd edn. London: Pitman.

Watson, S. (1997) Management Development in the UK Hospitality Industry, in M. Foley, J. Lennon and G. Maxwell (eds), *Hospitality, Tourism and Leisure Management*. London: Cassell, pp 69–98.

Woods, R.H., Heck, W. and Sciarini, M. (1998) *Turnover and Diversity in the Lodging Industry*. American Hotel Foundation.

Worsfold, P. and Jameson, S. (1991) Human Resource Management: a Response to Change in the 1990s, in R. Teare and A. Boer (eds), *Strategic Hospitality Management – Theory and Practice for the 1990s*. London: Cassell, pp 99–121.

WTTC (2000) *Tourism Satellite Accounting Research, Estimates and Forecasts for Governments and Industry*. London: World Travel and Tourism Council.

www.southwestairlines.com

The travel and tourism organization – financial analysis and performance indicators

Introduction and Chapter Overview

The ability to make sense of an organization's financial situation is an important part of strategic analysis. In order to carry out a financial analysis of a company's situation or of an industry, it is necessary to understand some of the fundamentals of finance and its sources. This chapter begins with a discussion of the sources of corporate finance and then goes on to discuss the costs of the various types of capital. This information helps students to make sense of a company's financial structure before the tools of conventional financial analysis are discussed. The various 'tools' for financial analysis are introduced and, finally, the concept of benchmarking is explained and its use in analysis is discussed.

Learning Objectives

After studying this chapter, students should be able to:

- understand what is meant by financial analysis;
- identify the sources of funds available to companies and the relative advantages and disadvantages of each;

- assess a company's potential for further funding based on current position, future prospects and past performance;

- explain the cost and non-cost issues involved in raising and using various forms of capital;

- understand the importance of the cost of capital;

- describe the limitations of a company report and accounts as a source of data for financial analysis;

- describe the major tools that can be used to analyse a company's financial position;

- explain the nature and analysis of foreign exchange risks in travel and tourism;

- understand the nature and analysis of cash flow risks in travel and tourism;

An introduction to financial analysis

The importance of finance

Although the travel and tourism industry covers a diversity of different organizations, including tour operators, airlines, hotels and travel agencies, financial management is important to all of them. Financial management is that part of the total management function concerned with the effective and efficient raising and use of funds. Finance, like a physical resource, has a large number of competing uses; is scarce but can be obtained at a price; and is bought and sold in markets. Financial management is concerned with managing this scarce resource so as to ensure that:

- sufficient *finance is* available at the right time;
- *finance* is obtained at the least possible cost;
- *finance* is used in the most profitable ways.

Most university business courses have an accounting and finance content. You may consequently be familiar with some of the content of this chapter and this will be to your advantage. This chapter develops the material into the context of strategic analysis.

Money, or the lack of it, is central to the strategic development of all organizations, large or small. It is one of the key resource inputs and cannot be ignored. The most original strategies and the most complex plans for the future of a business are meaningless unless management has considered the financial position of the organization at the outset and during the period covered by the strategy. The ability of a company to finance both current and future strategies is central to any analysis of the company's position. A central theme to this chapter will be the ability of the company to finance current strategies – its ability to raise the funding required for future developments.

The success or failure of the organization is judged by its ability to meet its strategic objectives. The financial information (in the form of annual corporate reports) produced by companies provides a quantifiable means of assessing success. It is important to recognize, however, that other quantifiable information, such as efficiency and productivity data, and non-quantifiable data such as the company's image, can also be used to make such judgements. In this chapter we will examine the value of information extracted from corporate reports as a source from which judgements can be made.

Corporate reports are, however, just one source of information about a company's financial state. Managers have a number of ways of gathering information about their own and competitors' finances and we will discuss these later in the chapter. The case of the UK tour operator International Leisure Group (ILG) illustrates the pitfalls that can overcome an organization when management makes strategic errors in the financial management of a company.

International Leisure Group (ILG)
Flying too close to the sun – anatomy of a corporate collapse

The ILG group of companies, like Icarus from Greek mythology, flew too close to the sun, got burnt and fell to earth. We can focus on four aspects of ILG and its demise.

1   The company
ILG was formed in the early 1970s by the extrovert, publicity seeking Harry Goodman. It traded under various brand names, including Intasun, Club 18–30, Lancaster tour operators and the airline Air Europe. The company grew rapidly throughout the 1970s and 1980s, spurred on by Britain's apparently insatiable appetite for package holidays, the number of which trebled during the 1980s. The company was also helped by the collapse of Clarkson's, the UK's second largest tour operator, in 1974 and Laker Airways eight years after, both of which 'Harry' took full advantage of.

The growth in company sales (which in its last published figures for 1989 had a turnover of approximately £722 million) was not matched by a corresponding growth in profits and its gearing levels were extremely high.

After a relatively brief life as a quoted company, the management team led by Harry Goodman took the company 'private' in the spring of 1987. The stock market, it was said, took too short term a view of the company. A Swiss financier took a 49% holding in the company, which was reduced to 29.5% in 1990.

2   The strategy
ILG's financial strategy was simple. It used cash generated from its travel and charter airline businesses to finance the development of a new scheduled airline. The tour operations certainly worked on very tight margins (thanks in part to the price war Goodman himself had started in 1985), but tour operations also produced a good cash flow. Advance payments from customers (which usually stood at about £50 million) provided a source of interest-free funding.

The company was to have been a pan-European airline based on modern fuel-efficient aircraft and taking advantage of European airline deregulation in the 1990s. Cash was also provided by the group's third, less visible business, trading in aircraft. By placing orders for new aircraft several years ahead, the company was at the head of the queue in the mid 1980s when aircraft demand was high. Consequently the company could sell aircraft at a profit. This source provided a third of operating profits in 1989.

3   The faults
Although tour operations provided a good cash flow, it was, nevertheless, fundamentally a high volume, low margin business trying to finance a highly volatile airline development. The costs of developing the airline were considerable and were much higher than had been planned.

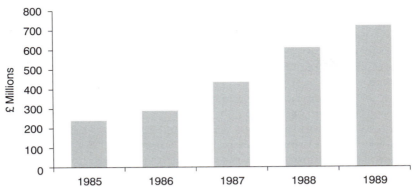

ILG total sales (i.e. turnover), 1985–1989

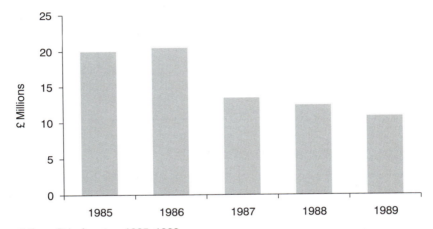

ILG profit before tax, 1985–1989
ILG gearing (debt/share capital + reserves + debt)

1987	74.2%
1988	73.4%
1989	75.6%

To develop the airline, the company negotiated inventive leasing arrangements with a handful of banking syndicates, the largest led by Citibank accounting for 10 of the company's 37 aircraft.

The first apparent weakness, then, was that in return for narrow lending margins, the banks insisted on onerous covenants (financial restrictions) and these were to prove crucial later. A second apparent weakness was an over-commitment by Lloyds Bank. Lloyds began with a £30 million working capital facility but eventually had up to £90 million at risk. A third financial weakness existed in the financial team. Goodman was highly autocratic, but his flair was largely marketing based rather than financial. Beneath him the company appeared to lack an obvious financial strategist. A fourth financial weakness was that the management was also firmly entrenched. They had only 15% of the equity but 100% of ordinary voting shares (Goodman with 53%), giving them a blocking vote.

> **4   The collapse**
>
> By spring 1990 Goodman had already decided that the company should be sold. Some approaches were made but nothing materialized. At the end of October 1990 ILG breached the strict covenants agreed in spite of a £22 million injection of funds by the Swiss investors. The banks gave three months for the company to sort out the problems.
>
> However, bookings in the crucial pre-Christmas period were poor with the onset of recession (down an estimated 20% on the already poor level of 1989). The Gulf War in the New Year was disastrous for package bookings, which were down 40% on a year earlier and scheduled services were operating at 35% of capacity.
>
> The writing seemed to be on the wall, but a last minute deal was agreed at the end of January with £40 million of cash from the Swiss and Lloyds converting £50 million of debt into equity. By mid February it was clear that this would not be enough. The Swiss investors were themselves in trouble. Lloyds then agreed to an additional £20 million with a further £20 million from a German investor. In early March the German investor pulled out and a syndicate of banks led by Citibank took steps to have 10 of Air Europe's aircraft 'arrested'. The following day the company was placed in administration.
>
> The company, bought out largely with funds provided by the banks, found in the end that the banks would not support it, but it was ILG's flawed financial structure that was its real undoing.

Understanding financial structure

At the outset it is necessary to have an understanding of a business's financial structure. A company's annual accounts will contain two key statements: the balance sheet and the statement of profit and loss. We will examine each briefly.

Understanding the balance sheet

Assets are financed (and matched in the balance sheet) by capital and liabilities. Liabilities may be current (less than one year) or long term (over one year).

Capital + Liabilities = Assets

The principles underpinning a balance sheet are shown in Figure 5.1.

In Figure 5.1 the assets of the business are 'funded' by long-term funds (capital), comprising such items as long-term loans, share capital and reserves. Current liabilities comprise items such as overdrafts and trade creditors.

A proportion of the short-term assets are funded by long-term funding, which, unlike short-term funding (current liabilities), is difficult to take away at short notice and consequently represents a more stable form of financing. Overdrafts, for example, can be quickly recalled by banks if they choose to do so.

Long-term (or fixed) assets such as property, land, vehicles and aircraft are financed entirely by more stable financing sources, i.e. long-term funding.

The difference between current assets (stock, debtors and cash) and current liabilities (creditors, overdrafts and short-term loans) is the company's 'working capital' (net current assets).

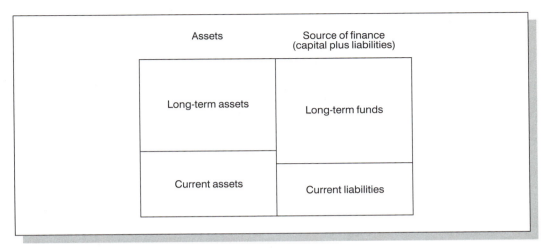

Figure 5.1 A representation of the principles of a balance sheet

A skeleton balance sheet is shown below:

	Item	£	Examples
A	Fixed assets	80	Semi permanent assets – property, plant, vehicles, aircraft etc.
B	Current assets	40	Trading assets – stock, debtors, cash
C	Current liabilities	(20)	Trading liabilities – creditors, overdrafts
	Net current assets (working capital B–C)	20	
	Total capital employed (A + B – C)	**100**	
D	Shareholder finance	75	Share capital, retained profits
E	Long term liabilities	25	Medium- and long-term loans
	Sources of finance (D + E)	**100**	

Understanding the profit and loss account

A profit and loss (P&L) account matches the revenue earned in a period with the costs incurred in earning it. A skeleton profit and loss account is shown below:

	Sales or income received
Less	Cost of sales
Equals	Gross profit
Less	Expenses (such as personnel costs, head office costs, administration and distribution)
Equals	Profit before interest and tax (also called operating, trading or 'net' profit)
Less	Interest and tax
Equals	Profit after interest and tax (also called earnings)
Less	Dividends to shareholders
Equals	Retained profit (which is transferred to the balance sheet)

Sources of corporate funding

Financial resources, as we have already learned, are an essential input to strategic development. Capital for development can be raised from several sources and these are summarized here.

Key concept: Capital

Accountants use the term capital to describe one particular type of 'money'. It is usually contrasted with revenue. *Revenue* is money that is earned through normal business transactions – through sales, rents or whatever the company 'does' through its normal activities. *Capital* is money that is used to invest in the business – to buy new equipment, new capacity, extra aircraft, etc. The investment of capital enables the business to expand and, through that expansion, to increase its revenue and profits in future years. Capital can be raised from shareholders, through retained profits, through rights issues, through loan capital or through the disposal of assets.

Share capital

For limited companies, a sizeable proportion of capital is raised from shareholders (the financial owners of the company) in the form of share capital.

Historically, share capital has comprised the majority of capital for a limited company's start-up and subsequent development. In return for their investment, shareholders receive a return in accordance with the company's performance in a given year in the form of a dividend. The dividend per share is taken as an important measure by shareholders of the company's success in its chosen strategy. Shares also confer on their holders a right to vote on company resolutions at annual or extraordinary company meetings *pro rata* with the proportion of their holding. It follows of course that a shareholding in excess of 50% confers total control over a company's strategy.

Under normal circumstances, share capital is considered to be permanent – it is not paid back by the company. It is thus unlike other forms of capital (e.g. loan capital). The shareholders' only 'payback' is in the form of dividends and through capital growth – an increase in the value of the shares. Shareholders who wish to divest their stock (i.e. shareholding) in a company must usually sell it via a stock exchange (in the case of shares in a public limited company) or through a private sale (in the case of a private company). In exceptional circumstances, some companies offer a 'buyback' of their own shares.

Shareholders can be individuals or 'institutional shareholders'. Some individuals hold their personal share portfolio but the vast majority of shares are held by institutional shareholders such as pension funds, life assurance companies and investment trusts. The profile of shareholders varies from company to company and from country to country.

Key concepts: Share value and share volume

Share value is the price of a given company's shares at a given point in time. Like any other commodity, its value is determined by the forces of supply and demand. Given that in normal circumstances the supply is fixed over the short to medium term, price is determined by how many people want to buy it. If the market has confidence in a company's prospects, demand for the share will rise and so, accordingly, will its price. If a

---

company's prospects are considered poor, investors will sell the share, fewer will want to buy it and the price will fall.

Share volume is the number of shares issued by a company in total. This is usually determined at the foundation or flotation of a company although rights issues and similar events can increase the share volume. It is generally true that larger companies have higher share volumes than smaller concerns.

Rights issue capital

From time to time, a company may seek to increase its capital for expansion by means of a *rights issue*. This is when a company issues new shares to the stock market, normally giving its own shareholders the first refusal *pro rata* with their current proportion of the company's share volume.

The decision to go for a rights issue may well be a strategic decision for management because it can impact on the ownership of the company. If existing shareholders do not exercise their right to buy, then it is likely that ownership will be diluted, i.e. shareholders will find that they own a lower percentage of share volume than they used to.

Those shares not taken up by shareholders, who may be unable or unwilling to buy them, are normally covered by *underwriters* (institutional investors) at a price agreed, in advance. Underwriting is an important technical feature of new share issues and as such is a major cost in the process. A rights issue is sometimes seen as a reward to loyal shareholders.

A variation on a rights issue is *placing*. A placing involves the selling of shares direct to a small number of investors, usually large financial institutions. This may be marginally cheaper than a rights issue, but its major advantage is its flexibility in enabling new shareholders to have significant and possibly strategic holdings. Placings take place, for example, as a part of a joint venture agreement whereby the two companies exchange placed shareholdings as a sign of their mutual commitment to the alliance.

Retained profit as a source of capital

Shareholders provide other funds for development by agreeing *not* to receive all the company's profits in a given year. *Retained profit,* that element of operating profit not paid to shareholders in the form of dividend, is the most common method of funding strategic developments, particularly if the company is quite old in terms of years. By using this form of funding, organizations save on the costs involved in using alternatives such as fees to merchant banks, lawyers and accountants. It also means management do not have to reveal nor justify their strategies to others and risk their plans becoming known to competitors.

It should be recognized that retained profits do not constitute a loss to shareholders as such, because the value of the organization and consequently the share price is normally increased when these funds are used for reinvestment. It is, however, important that companies recognize the need to balance the proportion of profits distributed and retained in order to satisfy those shareholders who need regular funds flow themselves (such as insurance and pension companies).

Loan capital

An important consideration in the use of retained profits to fund corporate development is clearly the ability of the company actually to make a profit that can be, at least in part, distributed to shareholders as dividends. Whilst a company may make a profit from its normal activities after taxation, some profits may be required to meet the cost of other forms of debt finance or loans.

Debt finance is shown in the balance sheet under two headings, *Creditors: amounts following within one year* and *Creditors: amounts falling due after more than one year*. The form of borrowing with most impact on strategic development is that falling due after more than one year – long-term debt. This type of borrowing can take a number of forms. In addition to the use of long-term bank loans, a company can use debentures, convertible loan stock or corporate bonds.

Debt finance is normally for a set period of time and at a fixed rate of interest. The interest must be paid every year, regardless of the level of profit (referred to as *servicing the debt*). The interest rate for this source is normally less than the cost of share capital (when the dividend payable on the shares is taken into account).

Comparing share capital and loan capital.

Each of the types of capital described above has its pros and cons. Share capital has the advantage that the amount paid on the capital is dependent upon company results. A company can decide not to pay a dividend if profits are poor in any given year. Loan capital, by contrast, must be serviced regardless of results in much the same way that a mortgage on a house must be repaid regardless of other commitments.

Offsetting this advantage is the fact that share capital is permanent. As long as the company exists, it has an obligation to repay a dividend to its shareholders. Loan capital has the advantage to the company that it is time-limited. Servicing the capital is restricted to the term of the loan (like a mortgage on a house) and when it is finally repaid in full, the business has no further obligation to the lender.

The fact that the repayment of debt finance takes precedence over dividends on shares means that shareholders bear an increased risk. If the company performs badly, their return on investment will be small or non-existent in a given year. Against this possibility, they usually expect to receive higher returns compared to providers of loan capital in the years when profits are good.

The major advantages and disadvantages of share and loan capital are set out in Table 5.1.

	Advantages	Disadvantages
Share capital	No fixed charge or legal obligation to pay a dividend No maturity date Issue of equity increases credit worthiness Marketable, i.e. can be traded	Extension of voting rights High issue costs May increase average cost of capital Dividends not tax deductible
Loan capital	Known and often lower cost No dilution of equity Interest payable is tax deductible	Increase in risk which may cause value of equity to fall Need for repayment Limit to amount of available funding

Table 5.1 Summary of the major advantages and disadvantages of share and loan capital

In practice, business profits can vary significantly over time. In some years, it is preferable to use loan capital, especially when interest rates are low and profits are high. In other years, when profits are lower and interest rates are higher, share capital works out cheaper. The fact that the benefits are so finely divided means that most companies opt to use an element of both. The relationship of debt capital to shareholder capital is referred to as the company's *gearing ratio*.

Gearing is an indication of how the company has arranged its capital structure. It can be expressed as either:

$$\frac{\text{Borrowed capital (i.e. debt)}}{\text{Total capital employed (i.e. borrowings plus shareholders' capital)}}$$

or, as

$$\frac{\text{Borrowed capital (i.e. debt)}}{\text{Shareholders' capital (i.e. equity)}}$$

Both are usually expressed as percentages by simply multiplying the quotient by 100. It is not important which one is used unless we are comparing the gearing of two or more companies.

Other sources of capital

Whilst the foregoing are the most common mechanisms of raising capital for development, others are available under some circumstances. One such method is to dispose of existing fixed assets. This can range from selling of an aircraft to selling a subsidiary to a third party.

Finally, marginal improvements in a company's capital situation can be achieved by improving the management of working capital. Over the course of a financial year, small savings can accumulate to significant proportions, increasing both profitability and capital for reinvestment. This can be achieved by:

- extending the time taken to pay creditors;
- getting debtors to pay sooner; or,
- spreading payments through leasing rather than purchasing assets.

Key concept: Working capital

Working capital is the amount of money that a company has tied up in the normal operation of its business. Working capital comprises money tied up in:

- stocks;
- debtors (money owed to the business);
- creditors (money the company owes);
- cash or current bank deposits.

A company's objective is usually to minimize this figure, or to manage the working capital in such a way that minimizes financing costs or maximizes earnings on cash balances. This is an important source of earnings for many travel and tourism companies.

Working capital is needed to pay for goods, services and expenses before money can be recovered from creditors. The ability of a business to pay its cash commitments as they fall due shows that it has sufficient *liquidity*.

Inefficient management of working capital can lead to over-investment in working capital – *over-capitalization*. Conversely *under-capitalization*, also known as overtrading, often occurs when a company tries to do too much, too soon with too little long-term capital. A company can be trading profitably but run out of cash to make payments, i.e. it can become *insolvent*. Warning signs of overtrading include: a rapid increase in sales, a rapid increase in current assets, small increase in share capital, a deterioration in liquidity ratios such as the acid test ratio which measures the proportion of current assets less stocks to current liabilities.

Cost of capital

Definitions

Availability of capital (where to get it from) is one issue when examining a company's capital funding, but another equally important consideration is its cost. We learned above that providers of loans or share capital (equity) both require a return on their investments. Management therefore need to know what return (profit) they need to make in order to meet the minimum requirements of capital providers. Failure to achieve this minimum will make the raising of future funds all the more difficult. The cost of capital can be seen as the minimum return required on the company's assets, which in turn may influence the objectives of the company.

At its simplest, the cost of capital can be viewed as the annual amount payable (as a percentage) against the principal amount of money. Most of us will be aware that the return payable on such things as loans varies between lenders and over time as interest rates rise or fall. The cost of loans on a credit card is, for example, much higher than a mortgage loan (where the security against the loan is mainly responsible for the difference). Some fortunate people are able to borrow money interest-free (at zero cost of capital).

Costs of debt capital

The costs of debt capital are relatively easy to calculate as they tend to correspond closely to the prevailing rate of interest. If the loan is to be repaid at a fixed rate, the calculation is even more straightforward. It is generally the case that the rate of interest attached to a loan will be strongly influenced by the risk of default. Unsecured loans attract the highest rates whilst those that can be recovered by the sale of the asset against which the loan is taken out (such as a property) will attract a lower rate. The history of the business in dealing with lenders (its credit rating) will also be a factor.

Costs of share capital

Calculating the cost of share capital is slightly more complex as it contains more variables. Accounting academics spend a great deal of time discussing what should and should not be included in this calculation and how each component should be weighted. Reasons for this complexity include the indefinite nature of the funding, the opportunity cost of undistributed profits and shareholders' expectations. These mean that some models try to include components for inflation, industry averages and attitudes towards risk.

At its simplest, the cost of share capital can be calculated as follows:

$$\text{Cost of share capital (equity) as a percentage} = \frac{\text{Current net dividend per share}}{\text{Current market price of share}} \times 100$$
$$+ \text{ average percentage annual growth rate}$$

Example

If the market price for shares were 400p per share and the annual dividend was 20p. If growth in profits average 10% per annum, this gives

Cost of share capital = 20/400 × 100 + 10%
= 15%

Models of capital costing

The CAPM model • • •

The *Capital Asset Pricing Model* (CAPM) is a more complex but widely used model used for calculating the cost of share capital.

Cost of share capital = Ri + β(Rm – Ri)

The model takes into account the competitor financial products available to potential investors. These range from the percentage return on virtually risk free government bonds (Ri) to a component covering the average interest for the share (equity) markets overall (Rm). The final element of the model represents the company itself, or more correctly its position relative to the market overall. The β coefficient is a measure of the volatility of the company's financial returns.

The CAPM model does have a number of drawbacks, which need to be recognized. First, the shares of the company need to be traded on a stock market. This means that the cost of equity in private companies cannot be calculated using this model. Secondly the volatility of share prices in recent years causes problems in arriving at a date for 'acceptable' returns. The dynamic and complex nature of many industries and markets also suggest that historical data has limited value.

Example: CAPM model

Assume that risk free government bonds were trading at 4% and the average return on the market was 10%. Also assume that the volatility of the company had been calculated at 1.1, (meaning the shares fluctuated slightly more than the market average).

Cost of share capital (equity) = 4% + 1.1(10% – 4%) = 10.6%

The WACC model • • •

Whereas the CAPM model is used to calculate the cost of share capital, the *Weighted Average Cost of Capital* (WACC) can be used to determine the overall cost of funding to a company. The calculation of this information is relatively simple.

WACC = (Proportion of loan finance × Cost of loan finance) + (Proportion of shareholders' funds × Cost of shareholders' funds)

Example: WACC model

Assume that a company had £30 million of loan capital and £70 million equity funding. The cost of each type had been calculated as 5% and 15% respectively, the calculation would be as follows:

Type of capital	Proportion	Cost (after tax)	Weighted cost
Loan finance	0.3	5%	1.5%
Shareholders' funds	0.7	15%	10.5%
Total	1.0		12.0%

Why calculate the cost of capital?

The cost of capital is usually an important figure to calculate because if it works out to be too high, the development that it is intended to fund may not be viable. Given that both debt and share capital attract servicing costs, the profit returns must exceed these servicing costs to the extent that the proposal is economically attractive.

If the projected returns on a strategic development (such as a new factory facility) are not much more than the projected servicing costs, then management will have to make a judgement as to whether the investment is actually 'worth the risk'.

The whole situation is rendered more complex if debt capital is obtained at a variable rate of interest. Interest rates can vary substantially throughout an economic cycle and depend upon such things as government inflation targets, the currency exchange value and the national rate of capital deposition.

There are no guidelines as to the ideal capital structure – the balance between debt and equity finance. The optimal structure will vary from company to company, from industry to industry and from year to year. Some companies will calculate their WACC and include factors which are difficult to quantify, such as the degree of risk faced by the industry, trends in interest rates and even the cost and availability of funds to competitors.

Financial analysis

The basics

We would usually employ an analysis of a company's financial situation as part of an internal strategic analysis. We may wish to understand a company's finances in order to make an assessment of its 'health' or its readiness to undertake a phase of strategic development.

Three key areas of financial analysis are:

- longitudinal analysis (sometimes called trend analysis);
- cross-sectional analysis (or comparison analysis);
- ratio analysis.

A comprehensive analysis of a company's financial situation would normally involve an element of all three of these analyses. The one thing to bear in mind when looking at accounting statements is that they contain numbers in isolation. An accounting number on it own is just that – a number. In order to make any sense of it, we must compare it with other accounting numbers. In the next few sections Air New Zealand will be used to illustrate some of the 'tools' of financial analysis. Air New Zealand is an airline providing services to, from and within New Zealand, Australia, and the South West Pacific. In June 2000 Air New Zealand achieved full ownership of the Australian carrier Ansett, giving the combined Air New Zealand–Ansett Group, which is a member of the 'Star' strategic alliance, the scale of a world top 20 airline. Note, the airline subsequently sold its Ansett stake.

To many organizations in travel and tourism two further areas of finance are key to considering the overall financial situation, namely analyses of the organization's exposure to:

- foreign exchange risks analysis;
- cash flow risk analysis.

Longitudinal analysis

The simplest means of assessing any aspect of a company's finances is to compare the data for two or more years and see what has increased and what has decreased over that time period, and by how much. It goes without saying that the longer back in time we look, then the better idea we will get as to the organization's current position in its historical context (see for example Figure 5.2.). Many company corporate reports provide a five or ten year record and this can help us in constructing a longitudinal analysis.

The easiest way to perform this form of analysis is conduct an initial scan of the figures to identify any major changes between the years. This involves simply looking along each line in turn, and highlighting any larger than normal increases or decreases, for example a scan along five years of fuel expenses shown below clearly indicates that large increases in these costs occurred over the period 1996 to 2000 and particularly between the years 1999 and 2000.

Year	2000	1999	1998	1997	1996
Fuel costs (NZ$000)	464	322	347	356	318

Anomalies like these may need further investigation. The impact of the 'blip' on the year's performance must be assessed as must its impact on current performance. Further investigation of the balance sheet or profit and loss account, together with any notes to the accounts, may provide some clues.

The initial scan may need to be followed by a more detailed analysis, which might, for example, calculate the year on year increase/decrease in percentage terms. It is sometimes

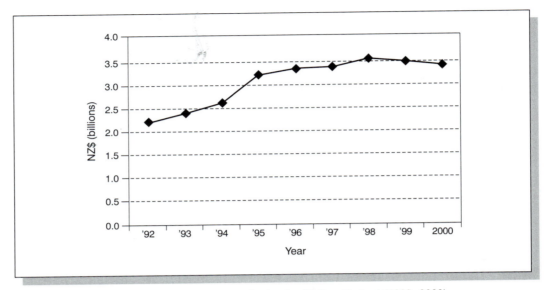

Figure 5.2 A simple longitudinal analysis: annual sales for Air New Zealand (1992–2000)

helpful to plot trends on a graph against time (such as in Figure 5.2). This can help to highlight changes at particular points in time.

The identification of trends, in terms of say turnover, costs or of some items of a balance sheet (such as debtors) can therefore be valuable in our financial analysis. Such trends should, however, be seen in their context. An organization operating in a static or slow growth market may judge a 1% year on year increase in turnover as a great success, whereas for a company in a buoyant market would judge a 1% increase as a failure.

Cross-sectional analysis

Whilst longitudinal analysis helps us to assess performance against a historical trend, it tells us nothing of the company's performance against that of competitors or of companies in other industries. If we were, for example, to identify strong sales growth of 10% a year in a longitudinal analysis of Company A's financial statements, we might be tempted to think that the company was performing well. If we were then to compare this company with one of its competitors only to find that the industry average rate of growth was 15%, then we would wish to modify our initial assessment of Company A's performance.

Inter-company comparison or financial *benchmarking* is a variation on cross-sectional analysis. It usually involves an analysis of 'like' companies, usually in the same industry but it can occasionally be an inter-industry analysis.

In order to make the benchmarking analysis meaningful, the company selection should usually be guided by similarity by:

- company size (i.e. they should be comparable in terms of turnover, market value or similar);
- industry (in that the companies produce similar products);
- market (i.e. the companies share a similar customer base.

In practice, sample selection for benchmarking study always involves some compromise because no two companies are in all respects directly comparable. Many companies, for example, operate in more than one industry and this may render problematic any comparisons with another company that operates in only one industry.

Accountants and financial analysts have undertaken the practice of inter-company (cross-sectional) analysis using financial data for many years. Benchmarking, however, can be used to compare financial and, importantly, non-financial information between two or more companies.

Benchmarking is now used to compare the effectiveness of various processes, products and procedures against others. The objective is to identify where superior performance is found in whatever variable that is being used for comparison. Once the company with the highest performance is identified, the exercise becomes to explore the reasons behind the superior performance.

The benchmarking process therefore involves decisions on:

- What are we going to benchmark? (financial or non financial data)
- Who are we going to benchmark against? (sample selection)
- How will we get the information?
- How will we analyse the information?
- How will we use the information?

The value of benchmarking is in identifying not only which company has the superior performance in a sector but also why this is the case. Our analysis, for example, might highlight the fact that Company X enjoys a return on sales significantly higher than the other companies in the sector. Company X thus occupies the profitability benchmark in the sector. The other companies may then wish to examine the practices within Company X that give rise to this level of performance.

For non-financial indicators, our analysis may highlight the fact that Company Y is able to attract the best-qualified people within a key category of personnel, for example the best scientists or computer programmers. In this case, Company Y demonstrates the benchmark in successful recruitment. Other companies who are unable to attract the best personnel would usually wish to examine Company Y to see why it is so successful in this regard.

Commonly sized accounts are particularly useful in cross-sectional analyses but it can also be used to analyse the same company's accounts from year to year. If we were, for

	Company A		Company B	
	£m	Common size	£m	Common size
Sales	113.4	100	224.6	100
Cost of sales	65.0	57.32	112	49.87
Gross profit	48.4	42.68	112.6	50.13
Administrative and other costs	33.7	29.72	67.0	29.83
Operating profit	14.7	12.96	45.6	20.3

Table 5.2 Simplified profit and loss accounts for two hypothetical companies

example, to examine the P&L or balance sheets of two companies in the same industry, we may at first be unable to make sense of differences between the two. We can sometimes make sense of the two separate accounts by making the totals of both equal 100 and then dividing each entry by the resultant quotient accordingly. A simplified example of commonly sized accounts is shown in Table 5.2.

From Table 5.2, we can make comparisons between the cost structures of the two companies despite the fact that Company B has approximately twice the turnover of Company A. We can tell, for example, that overall, Company B is better at controlling overall costs that Company A evidenced by the fact that its operating profit is 20.3 compared to Company A's figure of 14.7. We could draw comparable conclusions from other commonly sized components of the accounts.

Key concept: Financial statements

One of the conditions placed upon limited companies is the requirement to file an audited annual report and accounts. There are five compulsory components to this document as set out in the UK in the Companies Act (1985 as amended): chairman's statement, auditor's report, profit and loss statement, balance sheet and cash flow statement. The accounting rules by which they are to be constructed are prescribed in financial reporting standards (FRSs) to ensure that all companies mean the same thing when they make an entry in one of the statements. When they are completed (following the company's financial year end), they become publicly available. Each shareholder receives a copy, and a copy is lodged at UK Companies House in Cardiff or London.

It is for the purposes of comparisons of this nature that cross-sectional analyses are important. As well as comparing accounting numbers like turnover, its is often helpful to compare two or more companies' ratios (see next section), such as return on sales or one of the working capital ratios.

Ratio analysis

The third important tool in the analysis of company performance is *ratio analysis*. A ratio is a comparison (by quotient) of two items from the same set of accounts. Given that there are a lot of numbers in a set of accounts, it will not come as a surprise to learn that a large number of ratios can be drawn – some of which are more useful than others.

Ratio analysis is an area of some academic debate, and accordingly, the way in which ratios are expressed may vary between accounting and strategy textbooks. What is important therefore is to employ a consistent approach to ratio analysis, especially in longitudinal and cross-sectional analyses.

For most purposes, we can divide ratios into five broad categories:

1 Performance ratios
2 Efficiency ratios
3 Liquidity ratios
4 Investors' ratios
5 Financial structure ratios

Performance ratios

As their name suggests, performance ratios test to see how well a company has turned its inputs into profits. This usually involves comparing *return* (PBIT or profit before interest and tax) against either turnover or against its capital. This is because the rates of tax and interest payable vary. Using profit after interest and tax would distort the performance figure.

Return on capital employed (ROCE) is perhaps the most important and widely used measure of performance. It indicates the return being made compared to the funds invested. At its simplest, it is this figure that tests the gains of investing in a business as opposed to simply placing capital on return in a bank.

Where an organization can break down its figures by divisions or subsidiaries, individual performance can be measured and decisions relating to continued ownership made.

Return on equity or *Return on ordinary shareholders' funds* gives an indication of how effectively the share capital has been turned into profit (i.e. it does not take account of loan capital). This ratio should be used carefully as the capital structure of the company can affect the ratio.

Return on sales, or *profit margin*, either net or gross, is a popular guide to the profitability of a company. This ratio assesses the profit made per £ (or other currency) sold. Return on sales tends to vary from industry to industry and between companies within an industry. Airlines and tour operators, for example, typically make returns of under 10% whilst companies in the pharmaceuticals sector rarely make less than 20%. Figure 5.3 shows a graphical representation of return on sales for Air New Zealand.

Examples: Performance ratios

Each expressed as a percentage by multiplying the ratio by 100:

$$\text{Return on capital employed} = \frac{\text{PBIT (from P\&L account)}}{\text{Total capital employed (i.e. one side of the balance sheet)}}$$

$$\text{Return on shareholders' funds} = \frac{\text{PBIT}}{\text{Shareholders' funds (from balance sheet)}}$$

$$\text{Net return on sales} = \frac{\text{PBIT}}{\text{Total sales (also called turnover or revenue)}}$$

$$\text{Gross return on sales} = \frac{\text{Gross profit}}{\text{Total sales}}$$

Note: Gross profit is the profit after direct costs (i.e. conversion costs) have been deducted from sales, but before indirect (i.e. administrative) costs. Gross margin is an indication of how effectively a company has managed its wages, energy and stocks.

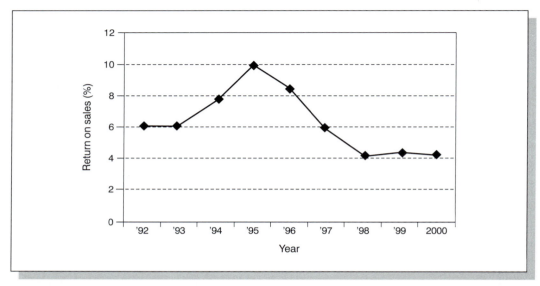

Figure 5.3 A longitudinal analysis of Air New Zealand return on sales, 1992–2000

Efficiency ratios

These ratios show how efficiently a company has used its assets to generate sales. We can use any one of a number of a company's inputs to test against sales or profits. Common efficiency ratios include *sales per employee* and *profit per employee*, both of which test the efficiency with which a company uses its labour inputs.

Key concept: Efficiency

The term efficiency is used in many ways – not just in accounting. We may speak of an efficient engine or the efficiency of a heating system in a house. At its simplest, efficiency is a comparison of a systems output to its inputs with a view to testing how well the input has been turned into output. It follows that a more efficient system will produce more output for a given input than a less efficient one.

It can be expressed mathematically as a quotient.

$$\text{Efficiency} = \frac{\text{Work output}}{\text{Work input}} \times 100 \text{ (to arrive at a percentage)}$$

Other commonly used efficiency ratios are *asset turnover* and a variant of this, *fixed asset turnover*. A high level of asset turnover indicates that the company is using its assets efficiently and, conversely, a low level may indicate that the company is suffering from overcapacity. Stock turnover gives an indication of how well the company controls its stocks. A company that keeps stock moving will generally have a higher stock turnover than one that has piles of unsaleable or obsolete materials.

Examples: Efficiency ratios

$$\text{Sales per employee (£)} = \frac{\text{Total sales (from P\&L)}}{\text{Number of employees (usually found in the notes to the accounts)}}$$

$$\text{Profit per employee (£)} = \frac{\text{PBIT}}{\text{Number of employees}}$$

$$\text{Stock turnover} = \frac{\text{Cost of sales (from P\&L)}}{\text{Value of stock (from balance sheet)}}$$

Note: Stock turnover is measured in *times* – i.e. the number of times the total stock is turned over in a given year.

Liquidity ratios

These ratios test the company's ability to meet its short-term debts – an important thing to establish if we have reason to believe the company is in trouble. Essentially, they ask the question, 'has the company enough funds to meet what it owes?'.

The *current ratio* is the best-known liquidity ratio. It is a measure of a company's total liabilities in comparison to its total assets and is thus calculated entirely from balance sheet figures. It is used to assess the company's ability to meet its liabilities by the use of its assets such as stock, debtors (receivables) and cash.

The *acid test ratio* is a variant of the current ratio and tests the company's ability to meet its short term liabilities using its cash or 'near cash' assets. Many textbooks suggest a ratio of 2:1 should be a target for this ratio and a target of 1:1 should be sought for the acid test ratio. These are simple guides and should not be taken as the norm for all industries. For example, many companies in the travel industry have low levels of stock and, as a result, their current ratio will be well below 2:1, and consequently the acid test ratio provides a better guide in such cases.

Investors' ratios

This family of ratios test for things that are important to a company's investors – usually its shareholders or potential shareholders. There are three that are widely used.

Earnings per share (EPS) are calculated by dividing profit after interest and tax (called earnings) by the number of shares. It shows how much profit is attributable to each share. The *price earnings ratio* (P/E) gives an indication of the stockmarket's confidence in a company's shares. It is the current market price of the company's ordinary shares divided by its EPS at the last year end and it follows therefore that the P/E varies with the share price. Broadly speaking, it is a way of showing how highly investors value the earnings a company produces. A high P/E ratio (where the price is high compared to the last declared EPS) usually indicates growth potential whilst a low P/E suggests static profits. The P/E ratio for quoted companies is regularly published in the financial press.

Dividend yield is the third widely used investors' ratio. Potential shareholders often want to know what the most recent return on the share was in terms of percentage.

Dividend yield is calculated by dividing the dividend per share at the last year end by the current price (and then multiplying by 100 to arrive at a percentage).

Examples: Investors' ratios

$$EPS = \frac{\text{Profit after interest and tax}}{\text{Share volume}}$$

$$P/E = \frac{\text{Price of share (as of 'today')}}{\text{EPS at most recent year end}}$$

$$\text{Dividend yield} = \frac{\text{Gross dividend per share}}{\text{Current price of share}} \times 100$$

Financial structure ratios

We encountered financial structure above when we discussed the relative merits of loan and share capital. The way in which a company 'mixes' these forms of capital is referred to as its financial (or capital) structure.

The *gearing ratio* looks at the relationship between all the borrowings of the company (including short-term borrowings), and all the capital employed by the company. This provides a view of the extent to which borrowing forms part of the total capital base of the company and hence the risk associated with rising interest rates.

The *debt–equity ratio*, a variation on the gearing ratio, uses the shareholders' funds in the calculation rather than the total capital employed. This ratio provides a more direct comparison between the funds attributed to shareholders and liability of the company to loan providers.

Examples: Financial structure ratios

$$\text{Gearing} = \frac{\text{Debt capital (typically borrowings due after one year)}}{\text{Debt capital plus shareholders' funds}}$$

$$\text{Debt/equity ratio} = \frac{\text{Debt capital (borrowings due after one year)}}{\text{Shareholders' funds}}$$

Using ratios in financial analysis

Compared to simply looking at accounting numbers, ratios provide a way of making some sense of published accounts. However, if we place a ratio within its longitudinal or cross-sectional context, its usefulness is maximized.

If we take return on sales as an example, we would usually want to know how Company A's figure this year compares not only with last year's (i.e. is it more or less), but also with Company A's competitors. This enables us to assess how Company A is performing over time and to make a judgement on its competitive position in its industry. This is because profitability is an important indicator of competitive success.

Limitations of financial information

For most purposes in strategic analysis, we can accept the proposition that the data we collect from a company's annual accounts are accurate and provide a truthful statement on its financial position. From time to time, however, we may need to qualify our analysis because of one or more reasons.

First, whilst the financial statements are audited for accuracy, other parts of the annual report are not. If our financial analysis consists of an examination of the entire document and not just the accounting sections, then we would need to be aware of this. Additional disclosures made in corporate reports may serve a number of purposes. Some commentators have suggested that such disclosures may be something of a public relations and marketing exercise.

Second, we should remember that the financial information in a corporate report is historical, often published up to three months after the period they represent. Whilst this historical information can be used to judge past performance, it may have limited use in predicting future performance. The balance sheet shows the financial position at 'a moment in time' (at the year end). It does not (unlike the P&L) summarize a full year's trading and things can sometimes change quickly after the year-end.

In an attempt to avoid this potential problem, Stock Exchange quoted companies are required to produce interim reports, normally half yearly and unaudited, which show their profit and turnover for that period. Quoted companies are also required to provide the Stock Exchange with information that may have a significant impact on its prospects such as changes on the Board or anything that gives rise to a 'profits warning'.

Third, those who prepare a company's financial statements (the financial accountants) sometimes have cause to 'hide' bad news so as to avoid alarming the company's investors. It is possible to employ legal financial restructuring so as to make some figures appear better than perhaps they are. A year on year increase in the value of fixed assets, for example, may appear at first glance to be healthy, but it may be that the company has accumulated a high amount of debt to finance it. It is for this reason that we sometimes need to examine all parts of a company's financial statements to spot any countervailing bad news that has been obscured by the company in its reporting.

Finance and risk in travel and tourism

Foreign exchange risk analysis

The travel and tourism industry operates internationally, producing international flows of funds in various currencies. Tour operators and airlines, for example, typically have a very large exposure to movements in foreign exchange rates, almost certainly far larger than for most companies of a similar size engaged in other areas of the economy (manufacturing companies, for example). The very purpose of these companies implies that they are international in their activities, thereby leaving them exposed to international risks associated with foreign exchange transactions.

The profitability of any company that trades internationally is affected by changes in foreign exchange rates. As Lockwood (1989) stated: 'as a large part of the travel and tourist industry is concerned with persuading and assisting people to cross national boundaries and thus to buy goods and services priced in a foreign currency, the identification and management of exchange rate exposures is vital to the profitable operation of a travel and tourist business.'

Thus foreign exchange management is very significant for many travel and tourism businesses. The lack of stability caused by the continual changes in exchange rates between currencies creates uncertainty. Specifically, uncertainty is created as to:

- what foreign income will be worth when it is received;
- what payments will cost when they have to be made;
- what the value of foreign assets and liabilities might be in the future.

British Airways' foreign exchange exposure

The overall foreign exchange position of a company may be complicated as illustrated by the position of British Airways: 'The group does business in approximately 140 foreign currencies which account for approximately 60% of Group Revenue and approximately 40% of operating expenses. The Group generates a surplus in most of these currencies [i.e. revenues are greater than costs]. The principal exceptions are the US dollar and the pound sterling in which the Group has a deficit arising from capital expenditure and the payment of some leasing costs, together with expenditure on fuel, which is payable in US dollars and the majority of staff costs, central overheads and other leasing costs, which are payable in pounds sterling.'

Source: British Airways Annual Report and Accounts, 1998–99

It is imperative to the profitability of many companies operating in the travel and tourism industry that this exposure to foreign exchange rate movements is recognized and managed appropriately.

In all cases risk attributed to foreign exchange rate movements arises out of uncertainty about the future exchange rate between two currencies. This risk would be minimized if it were possible to predict future rate movements. Unfortunately, it is not possible to do so with any degree of accuracy, and for a company to try to do so can be financially dangerous. If foreign exchange rates cannot be predicted, another option might be to pass on to the customer the effects of any adverse movements in exchange rates, and hence the company would incur no impact. In most cases, however, the highly competitive nature of the travel and tourism business prevents higher costs being passed on to the customer in this way. Clearly then it is prudent to manage these risks, although it is common in the industry for the risks to be ignored, especially by smaller companies.

Types of risk exposure

We can identify three different types of foreign exchange risk or exposure a company may be faced with:

Transaction exposure • • •

Transaction exposure arises, 'because the cost or proceeds (in home currency) of settlement of a future payment or receipt denominated in another currency may vary due to changes in exchange rates' (Buckley, 2000).

Transaction exposure relates to the foreign exchange exposure where contracts have already been entered into. When a company has contracted to receive or pay an amount of money in a foreign currency at some time in the future a risk is incurred. The specific risk is that adverse exchange rate movements between now and the time of the eventual cash receipt/payment will increase the amount to be paid out or decrease the amount to be received.

For example, a UK tour operator selling holidays to America would receive its income in pounds sterling but have to make payments to hoteliers and other suppliers in US dollars. In order to make the payments at some stage the company would have to convert sterling into US dollars. This would entail a risk that the US dollar might rise in value (appreciate) against sterling, thereby making the payments more expensive in sterling terms. Assume, for instance, the company had costed its hotel beds in its American programme at a rate of $1.50 to the pound (i.e. 1 pound buys 1.50 US dollars), and that the total cost to purchase the required bed spaces was $1 500 000. The cost in sterling to the company would be $1 500 000/1.50 = £1 000 000. Now if the rate subsequently fell to $1.40 the cost would increase to $1 500 000/1.40 = £1 071 429.

Translation exposure

As Buckley (2000) states, 'Translation exposure arises on the consolidation of assets, liabilities and profits denominated in foreign currency in the process of preparing consolidated accounts.'

The concept is also known as *accounting exposure*. For example, if a UK hotel company purchases a hotel in Australia, it acquires an asset priced in Australian dollars. Each year when the balance sheet of the business is prepared, the value of the hotel would be translated into sterling at the prevailing rate on the balance sheet date. The hotel might therefore be worth less in sterling terms as shown in the balance sheet of the company.

Economic exposure

Economic exposure (sometimes referred to as political exposure) arises from the effect of adverse exchange rate movements on future cash flows, where no contractual arrangement to receive or pay money has yet been made. This kind of exposure is longer term in nature and often difficult to quantify exactly and forecast accurately.

For instance, suppose a specialist tour operator operates most of its programme to one country, perhaps Gambia for example. The company will have a high economic exposure to that country and its currency. In some countries the political and economic circumstances are very uncertain, and if, for example, the government should be replaced in a violent way, (as occurred in recent years in Gambia), customers will be reluctant to book holidays to that country, thereby severely limiting the revenues of the specialist tour operator.

Thus, movements in foreign exchange rates lead to a number of different problems or exposures for travel and tourism companies. These exposures can be dealt with in a number of ways. The most obvious ways of dealing with such exposures are to avoid the exposures altogether, either by trading in domestic markets only, or by passing the exposure over to suppliers or customers. These alternatives are seldom possible in international travel and tourism, so other management methods such as the use of forward foreign exchange contracts or foreign exchange options have to be employed in order to reduce the risks. For a full discussion of these methods see Samuel, Wilkes and Brayshaw (1995) and Ross (1996).

Cash flow risk analysis

Travel and tourism has one of the most highly seasonal patterns of demand for any product, with less variation than the demand for Christmas cards or air conditioners, but more than nearly all high value individual purchases (Bull, 1995). This seasonality is largely due to climate, but is also related to factors such as school holidays, festivals, and historic travel patterns. Seasonality of demand for the product leads to a highly seasonal pattern of cash inflows and outflows. Consequently, at certain times of the year companies may have large cash balances to invest and at other times of the year many companies need to borrow money in order to maintain payments to suppliers (creditors). The industry is also *cyclical* in nature, in that cash flows are very responsive to changes in the general level of economic activity.

In terms of cash management, tour operators, travel agents and airlines are typically low margin businesses, deriving important parts of their income, not from operating profits (through the selling of travel arrangements), but from interest income derived from investing cash surpluses they may be holding at certain times of the year.

Seasonality of cash flow for a UK tour operator

If we take as an example a typical UK outbound tour operator selling mass-market package holidays largely to Europe, it is greatly affected by the seasonality of the product and this directly affects its cash flow and in turn its management.

Such an operator may have a number of operating characteristics:

- The bulk of holidays sold would be summer sun, with the season lasting from April to September, but with the peak months being July and August during school holidays.
- Summer sun holidays are typically booked in three distinct periods:
  (i) T*he early booking period starting in August or September*, when a significant number of people book. This applies especially to families, and those who are tied to taking holidays between certain dates, or are trying to take advantage of particular offers such as 'free child places', or low deposits.
  (ii) *The post Christmas period from January to March*, which is usually the largest booking period, and during which customers may be targeted with a second edition of the brochure.
  (ii) *The late booking period, from April onwards*, which has become increasingly significant in recent years, and may be a time of intense competition as operators try to sell remaining capacity and vary prices in order to do so.
- Many tour operators have attempted to widen their range of activities, and reduce the effects of seasonality, by, for instance, introducing winter sun and skiing programmes. The winter sun season normally lasts from October to April, whilst the skiing season normally lasts from December to April with peaks in February and at Easter. In most cases the combined size of these programmes is far smaller than the summer programme, representing perhaps 25% of the summer programme in terms of receipts. Bookings for the winter sun and skiing programmes are taken throughout the summer and autumn, but the winter ski programme in particular is subject to a great deal of late booking in late autumn and early winter as customers wait to see what snow conditions are likely for the season.

- The tour operator will have a number of seasonal costs such as airline fuel, staff working at resorts, and accommodation charges. However, the tour operator will also have a high level of costs that have to be met throughout the year, such as the costs of head office staff, aircraft maintenance, and computer facilities.

The characteristics of the tour operating business outlined in the box entitled 'Seasonality of cash flow for a UK tour operator' have certain implications for cash flow analysis and cash management. Cash builds up and declines in a seasonal way. During certain times of the year, particularly in the spring, large surplus cash balances are free to be invested until the cash is needed to pay bills during the summer season and for the remainder of the year. The size and timing of the cash balances, and the interest to be earned from the invested balances will vary from year to year, since the profile of bookings and level of interest rates also vary from year to year.

The period of greatest risk for many travel and tourism companies, however, usually comes in the autumn and winter. Cash balances have been run down as seasonal payments have been made during the preceding summer season and the bulk of bookings for the subsequent season have yet to be made. The position is often exacerbated by companies offering favourable payment terms to customers whereby a low initial deposit is required. Companies often have to rely on bank support to help them through this period.

The problems of cash flow may be compounded, however, if the early summer booking period for the forthcoming season and winter ski and sun bookings are poor, and post Christmas bookings are delayed.

In a case where a bank (or other party) fails to lend the necessary support, insolvency is the inevitable result. Insolvency (the inability to pay bills as they become due), has often befallen companies in this sector when revenue from expected bookings has failed to materialize.

When a company reaches an insolvent position it normally leads to the company's failure and liquidation. A company can sometimes survive for many years without making profits or making very low levels of profit, but if they run out of cash it is difficult for them to survive, because employees and creditors must be paid. Many travel and tourism companies routinely rely on banks to provide short-term finance for a part of the year, but it is when these negative cash balances are larger or more prolonged than usual and banks feel unable to provide finance that problems occur.

Figure 5.4 illustrates the cash flow problems described above for Interjet, a fictional small outbound UK tour operator with ambitious plans. The company plans to increase its sales turnover by around 25% each year. However, like many tour operators, travel agents and other tourism businesses, the company experiences annual seasonal cash flow difficulties. A cash flow forecast has been prepared for the following financial years and this is shown in Figure 5.4.

On analysing the cash flow, the following may be necessary.

- Insert all known income and payments for each period on to a cash flow schedule (as illustrated in the case of Interjet, Figure 5.4).
- Income and payments should be totalled to produce a balance carried forward to next period.
- Forecast future cash flow using available information.

	1 Apr	2 May	3 Jun	4 Jul	5 Aug	6 Sep	7 Oct	8 Nov	9 Dec	10 Jan	11 Feb	12 Mar	Total
Inflows													
Receipts from debtors	230	250	120	50	60	75	80	90	110	150	220	320	1744
Dividend on investment							45						45
Total inflows	230	250	120	50	60	75	125	90	110	150	220	320	1800
Outflows													
Payments to creditors	102	80		80	79	88		88		88		92	516
Wages and others expenses		77	58	103	10	59	105	80	62	108	83	63	979
Payments for fixed assets				70		15					5		100
Dividend payable			80										80
Corporation tax									120				120
Total outflows	102	157	138	253	89	162	105	168	182	196	88	155	1795
Net in/out	128	93	–18	–203	–29	–87	20	–78	–72	–46	132	165	5
Bank balance													
Opening	30	158	251	233	30	1	–86	–66	–144	–216	–262	–130	
Closing	158	251	233	30	1	–86	–66	–144	–216	–262	–130	35	

Notes:

a. As a tour operator, most funds are received by customers as a deposit and subsequent payment of balance. On average this results in 3 months' credit being granted to customers.

b. On average 6 weeks' credit is taken from customers.

c. Capital expenditure budget:

New computer facilities	Month 4	40 000
Routine replacement of motor vehicles	Month 4	30 000
Computer software and programming costs	Month 5	10 000
Progress payment on building extensions	Month 7	15 000
Office furniture and equipment	Month 11	5 000

d. Negotiated overdraft facilities currently stand at 60 000

Figure 5.4 Interjet – cash flow forecast (£000s)

- Produce 'sensitivity' analyses, i.e. what if, for instance sales were 10% lower/higher than expected or jet fuel prices rose by 50%?
- Produce a graph showing monthly or weekly balances may help indicate trends.

Analysis of the cash flow should prompt certain questions such as :

- How easily predictable are the cash flows?
- How seasonal or cyclical are the cash flows?
- Can the company keep within its borrowing limits?
- Is the company generating enough cash to ensure its survival?
- Does the company require further credit facilities?
- How long does it take customers to pay the company?
- How quickly does the company pay suppliers and others?

There are a number of actions a company may wish to consider to alleviate perceived cash flow problems including:

- Postponing capital expenditure.
- Accelerating cash inflows.
- Postponing or reducing cash outflows.
- Selling assets.
- Negotiating new lines of credit.
- Leasing rather than buying equipment.

References and further reading

Allen, D. (1997) *An Introduction to Strategic Financial Management*. London: CIMA/Kogan Page.

Atkinson, H., Berry, A. and Jarvis, R. (1995) *Business Accounting for Hospitality and Tourism*. London: Thomson International Business Press.

Air New Zealand (2000) *Air New Zealand Data Handbook* (September).

British Airways (1999) *British Airways Annual Report and Accounts, 1998–99.*

Buckley, A. (2000) *Multinational Finance*, 4th edn. Harlow: Financial Times/Prentice Hall.

Bridge, J. and Moutinho, L. (2000) Financial Management in Tourism, in L. Moutinho (ed.), *Strategic Management in Tourism*. Wallingford: CABI.

Bull, A. (1995) *The Economics of Travel and Tourism*. Melbourne: Longman Australia.

Burgess, C. (2000) Financial Structures and Practices, in B. Brotherton (ed.), *An Intro-duction to the UK Hospitality Industry*. Oxford: Butterworth-Heinemann.

Camp, R.C. (1994) *Business Process Benchmarking*. ASQC Quality Press.

Department of Trade and Industry (1992) *Best Practice Benchmarking*. London: HMSO for DTI.

Ellis, J. and Williams, D. (1993) *Corporate Strategy and Financial Analysis*. London: Pitman.

Evans, N. (2002) Financial Management in Travel and Tourism, in Sharpley, R. (ed.) *The Tourism Business*, 2nd edn. Sunderland: Business Education Publishers.

Franks, J.R. and Broyles, J.E. (1979) *Modern Managerial Finance*. London: John Wiley.

Harris, P.J. and Brown, J.B. (1998) Research and Development in Hospitality Accounting and Financial Management. *International Journal of Hospitality Management*, 1(2): 161–181.

Higson, C. (1995) *Business Finance*. Oxford: Butterworth-Heinemann.

Lockwood R.D. (1989) Foreign Exchange Management, in S.F. Witt and L. Moutinho (eds), *Tourism Marketing and Management Handbook*. London: Prentice Hall.

Mott, G. (1991) *Management Accounting for Decision Makers*. London: Pitman Publishing.

Owen, G. (1998) *Accounting for Hospitality, Tourism and Leisure*, 2nd edn. Harlow: Longman.

Ross, D.A. (1996) *International Treasury Management*, 3rd edn. London: Euromoney Publications.

Samuels, J.M., Wilkes F.M. and Brayshaw, E. (1995) *Management of Company Finance*, 5th edn. London: Chapman and Hall.

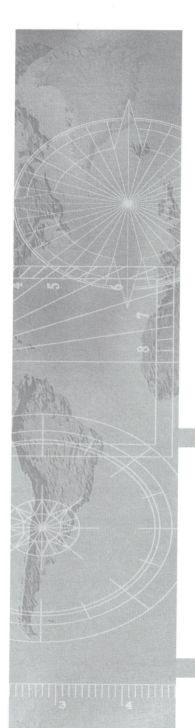

The travel and tourism organization – products and markets

The way in which an organization relates to its markets is one of the most important aspects of competitive strategy. The idea of a market as a place where buyers and sellers come together can apply to both inputs and outputs. Product markets are those in which an organization competes for sales whilst resource markets are those in which an organization competes for its resource inputs.

In this chapter, we discuss the key elements of this system – the nature of markets and the nature and importance of products. The way in which an organization configures itself in respect to these elements is crucial to the success of business strategy.

After studying this chapter, students should be able to:

- explain the term *market* and describe three ways by which markets can be defined;

- describe market segmentation and explain the ways that markets can be segmented;

- describe ways of approaching market segmentation in tourism;
- understand the concepts of targeting and positioning in tourism;
- explain the term product and describe Kotler's five levels of product benefit;
- understand the stages in and uses of the product life cycle;
- explain the concept of portfolio;
- understand the composition and limitations of the Boston matrix;
- explain how the GEC matrix works.

Ways of defining and understanding markets

The importance of understanding markets

Economists refer to a market as a system comprising two 'sides'. The demand side comprises buyers or consumers of a product and the supply side produces or operates the products.

In strategy, we often use the term slightly differently. By market, we usually mean a group of actual or potential customers with similar needs or wants (the demand side). We usually refer to the supply side as an industry.

The definition and boundaries of an organization's markets represent a key starting point for the formulation of strategy, and this provides a basis for measuring competitive performance. The analysis and definition of markets will also provide key information concerning the threats and opportunities facing an organization.

A distinctive capability becomes a competitive advantage only when it is applied in a market or markets (Kay, 1995) so it is of critical importance that managers are able to define and understand the markets in which they are operating. Specifically, an understanding of markets is important for several reasons:

- It gives managers an indication of the demand and potential demand for an organization's products.
- It allows mangers to assess the potential for market growth and gaining market share over competitors.
- It enables managers to recognize and evaluate the number, type and capabilities of competitors.
- It enables managers to position products in the market so that they are able to develop and sustain their competitive advantage.

Market attractiveness

Managers often consider the attractiveness of a market in that they consider whether products offered in a particular market will deliver returns on investment that are attractive to the organization and its investors. A number of factors contribute to market attractiveness, including market size, market growth and supplier concentration.

- *Market size:* In general terms the larger the size of a market the more attractive it will be in that it will offer wider opportunities for a larger number of organizations. Such a market, however, will also attract powerful suppliers who will attempt to dominate it

by gaining a high market share. The market for mass holidays to Spain for example is large and consequently it is supplied by a large number of tour operators whereas the market for activity holidays for teenagers is far smaller and is consequently supplied by fewer companies.

- *Market growth rate:* A growing market is normally more attractive than a static or declining market since growing markets allow opportunities for businesses to expand in line with the growth of the market. In static or declining markets, growth for individual organizations can only be achieved by taking market share away from competitors, which can be expensive and may lead to lower margins. The market for fast travel between Europe's major capital cities has been growing quickly in recent years and consequently state airlines, low cost airlines and rail services have all been able to add capacity whereas overall hotel capacity in English seaside resorts has been falling.

- *Supplier concentration:* Concentration refers to the extent to which a market is dominated by its largest suppliers and is usually measured by the percentage market share of the top four or five organizations in the industry. Thus in year 2000 the top four UK based tour operator groups (MyTravel, Thomson, Thomas Cook and First Choice) accounted for 56% of licensed tour operating capacity from the UK out of over 1800 licences issued. Large organizations, which dominate the industry, will tend to have advantages over smaller organizations in terms of costs, available promotional budgets and power over customers and suppliers in terms of setting prices and minimizing costs respectively. However, large organizations may find it difficult to increase their market share beyond a certain point due to regulatory restrictions and smaller organizations may compensate for their disadvantages. For example, they may be more flexible in their approach, know their customers' preferences more thoroughly, have access to a market niche (which is too small to attract larger organizations) and be less bureaucratic than larger competitors. In such circumstances it may be that medium-sized organizations find their competitive position is difficult to defend since they possess neither the advantages of scale nor the benefits that small organizations may be able to exploit.

Defining markets

We can also define the boundaries of markets in different ways. If different companies define a market in different ways, it is not surprising that the sum of their claimed market share may add to more or less than 100 per cent. The 'overseas holiday' market, for example, may mean different things to different companies. One might include all holidays taken abroad whilst another company might only include such holidays taken by air or sold as part of a package.

It is clearly important, therefore, that market share measures are stated explicitly, with the market boundaries clearly defined. Market share is a measure of an organization's performance with regard to its ability to win and retain customers relative to other organizations. It can be measured either by volume or by value. Volume measures concern the organization's share of units sold to the market (e.g. number of air inclusive holidays sold by a tour operator in relation to the total number of air inclusive holidays sold over a period). Value measures concern the sales turnover of one company in proportion to the total value of the market (e.g. the sales turnover of one air inclusive tour operator relative to the turnover for all air inclusive tour operators).

Market definitions

There are three ways in which markets are commonly defined:

- definition based on product;
- definition based on need satisfaction or function performed;
- definition based on customer identity.

We will briefly examine each of these in turn.

Definition based on product

If someone working for an organization is asked what market the company is in, a common reply will be to describe the products that are sold. Thus, we would have examples like 'holidays' or 'conferences and exhibitions'. If the product definition is wide, this type of definition is close to describing an industry. Since government economic statistics are often produced on this basis, markets defined in this way often have the advantage of ease of measurement.

A drawback of this approach is that it sometimes fails to take into account that a product may provide a range of different benefits, and different products often derived from completely different sources might meet the same need. This can lead to a failure to recognize threats that may come from a different industry altogether. Holidays and watching sport appear to be entirely different products with different markets, but they both may compete for customers' discretionary income and time (the income and time left over when essentials have been dealt with). They can also both be considered as part of the wider 'leisure' market.

An advantage of a product-based definition of markets can be that economies of scale in operations may be gained by the sharing of particular processes. This can lead to a view of a market as the market for the products that a company happens to produce even where they appear to have little in common. For example, Saga is a UK-based company which sells services directly to the public which are exclusively targeted at the over-55 age group. Within this age group the company, which initially offered only holiday products, has built up a sizeable market share and an enviable reputation. Using its database of clients it has been able to diversify selling other products such as financial services to the same target market.

Definition based on need satisfaction or function performed

The reason why consumers purchase a good or service is to gain *utility*. The concept of utility infers that whenever a consumer makes a purchase, they make a cost–benefit calculation wherein they make the judgement that the benefit they will get from the product is of higher value than the price paid.

This understanding enables the organization to understand its markets according to customers' perceptions. Horner and Swarbrooke (1996) considered success in the development of tourism, leisure and hospitality products to depend upon 'the ability to match the product which is offered with the benefits sought by the customers'. The authors concede, however, that the matching of the two is a challenging process. Swarbrooke (1995) considered the benefits being sought by visitors to various types of attraction, as shown in Table 6.1.

Type of attraction	Main benefits sought
Theme park	Excitement, variety of on-site attractions, atmosphere, the company of other users, value for money, light-hearted fun
Beach	Sun tan, sea bathing, economy, company of others *or* solitude
Cathedral	History, aesthetic pleasure derived from architecture, atmosphere – sense of peace or spirituality
Museum	Learning something new, nostalgia, purchasing souvenirs
Theatre	Entertainment, atmosphere, status
Leisure centre	Exercise, physical challenges and competing against others, status

Source: adapted from Swarbrooke (1995)

Table 6.1 Main benefits sought in types of tourist attraction

Whilst need satisfaction definition can lead to a more open minded approach to the formulation of strategy, its weakness can be that very broad definitions can lead to a view of markets that does not allow a practical approach to decision-making. A restaurant chain, for example, might define itself as being in the 'leisure' market, but it is probably wise for restaurant companies to also consider threats and opportunities that might arise from competing sources such as television, bars, computer games, holidays, etc. Opportunities only arise from leisure activities that the company's competences would allow it to enter (see Chapter 3), and threats would come from activities that would be likely to provide substitution for a company's products.

Key concept: Needs and wants

Whenever a customer makes a purchase decision, he or she expects to gain a benefit from the product purchased. This benefit satisfaction is usually expressed as a *need* or a *want*. The difference between the two is in the perception of the consumer – one customer's want is another's need.

The practical use of the distinction is in the price responsiveness of the product. Generally speaking, customers who need – or who believe they need – a product will be less price sensitive than those who merely want it. Hence, the greater the felt need, the more price inelastic the demand.

Definition based on customer identity

Groups of customers have requirements in common, and differ from other groups of customers. In this way, the *identity* of customers can be used to define markets. We could, for example, consider the 'business travel market' a quite distinct market. The market might be for products as diverse as airline flights, hotel rooms, meeting and exhibition spaces, car hire etc. But the market could clearly be seen as the market for types of travel and ancillary services needed by those travelling away from their offices for business purposes.

In terms of strategy formulation, the advantage of this approach is that it allows accurate targeting of the customer so that efficient use can be made of advertising, mail shots, personal selling, etc. Its main disadvantage is that whilst marketing economies may be made, a number of different suppliers might need to be used to service the various requirements so that the control of the quality of these suppliers becomes an issue of concern.

Combined definition

In practice, most businesses serve several markets with a range of products. They will define their markets with a combination of the ways listed here, and to the extent that one or other approach is uppermost, the advantages and disadvantages that we have already encountered will apply. A key task for management at the strategic level is to produce combinations that gain synergistic benefits and that enable opportunities to be best chosen and exploited. In cases where change in aspects of the technology of supply or the characteristics of markets takes place (so that synergies previously thought achievable may be no longer available), a case exists for restructuring an organization to divest itself of some activities and/or to acquire new ones.

In terms of working out competitive success in markets, a key concept is that of the *served market* – that part of a market that the company is in. It is on that basis that the measure of market share is most meaningful.

STP marketing

To Kotler (1997), the heart of modern strategic marketing can be described as 'STP' marketing, namely segmenting, targeting and positioning. In STP or 'target marketing' the seller distinguishes the major *segments* (identifiable parts) of the market, *targets* one or more of these segments and *positions* products and marketing programmes so that they will appeal to the needs and wants of these chosen target segments.

Companies are increasingly adopting such an approach. Target marketing helps sellers:

- to identify marketing opportunities better;
- to develop the right product features to attract each target market;
- they can adjust their prices, distribution channels, and promotional activities to 'reach' the target market efficiently.

The approach can be seen as focusing marketing efforts on those customers that the organization has the greatest chance of satisfying. Underpinning this strategic process are two important information requirements:

- an organization needs to understand the process by which potential purchasers arrive at a decision to purchase a particular product, i.e. 'buyer behaviour;
- in order to understand buyer behaviour and to gain an understanding of the structure of the market attention needs to be given to the importance of detailed marketing research.

We will explore the themes of STP in the next three sections of this chapter.

S – market segmentation

Markets are rarely completely homogeneous. Within markets there are groups of customers with requirements that are similar, and it is this similarity of needs and wants that distinguishes one market segment from another. These 'sub-markets' are known as *market segments*. By considering the extent to which the segments should be treated differently from others, and which ones will be chosen to serve, organizations can develop *target markets* and gain a focus for their commercial activity. As Moutinho (2000) states, 'the concept of market segmentation arises from the recognition that consumers are different. Market segmentation is a strategy of allocation of marketing resources given a heterogeneous tourist population.'

This process of segmentation represents a powerful competitive tool. It is true to say that a business will prosper by giving the customer what the customer wants. Since not all customers are likely to want the same thing, then identifying sub groups and attending to their requirements more exactly is a way of gaining competitive advantage. We might say that it is better to be hated by half of potential customers and loved by the other half than to be quite liked by them all. The latter is a recipe for being everyone's second choice, and underlines the dangers of placing too much reliance on averages in market research.

By identifying a specific market segment and concentrating marketing efforts at the segment, many organizations can build a degree of *monopolistic power* (a mini-monopoly)

Travel and tourism sector	Principal consumer segments
Hotels	Corporate/business clients Visitors on group package tours Independent vacationers Visitors taking weekend/midweek package breaks Conference delegates
Tour operators	Young people, singles and couples, 18–30-year-olds Families with children Retired/senior citizens/empty nesters Activity/sports participants Culture seekers
Transport operators	First-class passengers Club-class passengers Standard-class passengers Charter groups APEX purchasers
Destination attractions	Local residents in the area Day visitors from outside local area Domestic tourists Foreign tourists School parties

Source: adapted from Middleton and Clarke (2001)

Table 6.2 Consumer segments in the main sectors of travel and tourism

in the segment and thereby achieve higher profit margins than would otherwise be achievable. Many organizations that have each identified a highly specific segment can each succeed and gain reasonable profits by configuring their internal activities to precisely meet the needs and wants of the customer group.

For the most part, we can assume that segments exist naturally in most markets, and it is up to organizations as to how to exploit the differences that exist in the sub-markets. We do, however, have to recognize that activities of companies can also shape the segments to some extent. We could expect, for example, that men and women may buy differently. If, in those markets, suppliers offer and promote different products to men and women, then this tendency will be reinforced.

Before considering the ways in which markets segments might be identified and specific segments targeted, it is useful to consider the range of subgroups that exist within the different sectors of the travel and tourism industry. In Chapter 2 (Figure 2.1), following Middleton and Clarke (2001) we considered a framework for the industry, which identified five main sectors. These authors went on to identify five broad consumer segments for four of the industry segments, as shown in Table 6.2. Destination organizations are excluded since most are seen as having regard to all the segments identified.

Four approaches to segment marketing

Four broad approaches are recognized in respect to the ways that an organization can approach marketing to market segments (or sub-markets)

Undifferentiated marketing • • •

The first approach in relating to segmentation is called *undifferentiated* marketing. This means that the organization denies that its total markets are segmented at all and relates to the market assuming that demand is homogeneous in nature. The economies of a standardized approach to marketing outweigh any advantages of segmenting the market. Undifferentiated marketing is appropriate when the market the organization serves is genuinely homogeneous in nature.

Differentiated marketing • • •

Companies that adopt *differentiated* marketing recognize separate segments of the total market and treat each segment separately. Different segments need not always be different in every respect – it could be that some standard products can be promoted differently to different segments because of certain similarities or common characteristics. In other cases the product will be substantially or completely different and marketing to each segment will necessitate a distinctive approach to each one.

Concentrated marketing • • •

An extreme form of differentiated marketing is *concentrated* marketing, where an organization's effort is focused on a single market segment. In return for giving up substantial parts of the market, an effort is made to specialize in just one niche, and so we may see this referred to as *niche marketing*. This approach offers the advantage that the organization can gain a detailed and in-depth knowledge of its segment, which in turn can enable an ever-improving match between the product and the customer requirement.

The disadvantage relates to the extent to which the company may become dependent upon the one segment it serves. Any negative change in the demand pattern of the segment will leave the supplier vulnerable because of the narrowness of its market portfolio (see below).

Customized marketing • • •

Customized marketing occurs in cases where a market is viewed as being so diverse that an organization has to focus its marketing efforts on the needs of each individual customer. Such an approach enables the organization to modify its product or they way in which it is delivered, promoted or priced in order to satisfy individual requirements. However, such an approach is costly since any potential economies of scale are lost.

A company operating with a large product range in many markets will typically use a multi-focus strategy – a combination of the above.

Criteria for segmentation

The reason why market segmentation occurs lies in the fact that organizations can no longer regard markets as being uniform, where all consumers wish to purchase the same product. Thus each organization has to divide the market into clearly defined segments where each segment represents a discreet body of consumers, each of whom will have clearly defined needs, which warrant a separate marketing strategy.

However, the method by which the marketer or strategist divides the market into segments is extremely important. One method might be to divide the population into groups according to eye colour. We might end up with people with blue eyes, people with brown eyes and people with mixed eye colours. This would be a perfectly valid method of classifying people into groups whose members were similar to each other and dissimilar from members of other groups. But what use would it be to the marketing of a tourist destination for instance? Very little.

In travel and tourism there are perhaps two major problems to consider when segmenting the market:

1 The travel and tourism product itself, is, in many cases very inflexible. The basic attraction of the product (sun, sea, mountains, etc.) are to a great extent given.
2 In many cases resources are extremely limited. Destinations, attractions, and national or regional tourism authorities often have very small promotional budgets.

The most important aspect of market segmentation is the choice of criteria used to divide customers into groups. These criteria selected must be relevant to the customers' needs and/or their behaviour in the market concerned.

Bases for segmentation

There is no single way of segmenting a market. Each organization has to choose *bases*, or variables, that it thinks are appropriate in respect of its consumers. It must never be forgotten that there is not only a great variety of tourist products – countries, regions cities, agencies, airlines, tour operators, etc. – but that the cost of promoting and distributing these products is extremely high. This forces each provider to consider critically all expenditure and to define clearly groups of customers that are most likely to purchase the products.

Furthermore, various writers have differentiated between bases in various ways. For example, Middleton and Clarke (2001) referred to seven bases:

- Purpose of travel.
- Buyer needs, motivations and benefits sought.
- Buyer behaviour/characteristics of product usage.
- Demographic, economic and geographic characteristics.
- Psychographic characteristics.
- Geo-demographic profile.
- Price.

In the literature and in practice a distinction is often made between two groups of variables:

- Demographic variables ⎫
- Geographic variables ⎬ *Consumer characteristics*
- Psychographic variables ⎭
- Behaviouristic variables } *Consumer responses*

Kotler (1997) pointed out that there is a basic distinction between geographic, demographic and psychographic variables on the one hand and behaviouristic on the other in that behaviouristic variables represent the responses that consumers exhibit to various marketing stimuli whereas the other categories of variable represent character-istics of the consumers themselves.

We will look briefly at each of these means of segmentation and add a fifth variable category, that of *'geo-demographic segmentation'* which is really a combination of geographic and demographic segmentation. For a detailed examination of the more common bases to segment markets in a tourism context see Moutinho (2000), Middleton and Clarke (2001) and Pender (1999).

The various bases should generally be regarded, not as alternative choices for segmentation but as overlapping and complementary ways of sub-dividing a total market. In most cases the actual segments chosen by organizations represent a combination of bases or sometimes referred to as *matrix segmentation*.

Demographic segmentation

This form of segmentation addresses the question of 'Who buys'? Perhaps the most common means of segmenting the market, particularly where the major travel agents and tour operators are concerned, is by using demographic data. Some tour operators for example specialize in providing packages for specific demographic groups. By way of example, Contiki Tours specializes in coach tours in Europe, Australia and New Zealand and North America aimed at the 18–30 age groups located in many countries while Saga specializes in tours for the over-55s predominantly located in the UK.

There are a number of demographic characteristics, which may be of relevance to different markets. These characteristics usually refer to the age, sex, income, socio-economic group and stage in the family life cycle of the consumer.

- *Age* – Segmenting customers according to age bands is very common since, for example, children are clearly different to retired people in their needs.

- *Sex* – is a relevant segmentation criterion for many markets. Some travel and tourism products are largely designed for either males or females while others appeal to both sexes.
- *Income* – The personal disposable income of the consumer can be used as a segmentation variable. Some products are targeted at consumers with high disposable incomes – cruises, flights on Concorde. Other products are aimed at consumers with relatively low disposal incomes, such as camping holidays.
- *Level of education* – The age at which people leave full time education is used as a segmentation variable in some cases. This criterion has obvious value with products requiring a certain level of intellectual application, such as books, but has also been found to influence other products as well. For example, people with lower levels of education often opt for the 'safety' of well-known destinations whilst those with higher levels of education are sometimes more likely to have the confidence to try more diverse locations.
- *Family life cycle* – Another demographically based variable is the stage that consumers have reached in their family development. Two married couples with identical jobs and income levels, one with four children and the other childless, will exhibit significant differences in their spending patterns. Family life cycle segments might include:
  (i) young single people;
  (ii) young couples with no children;
  (iii) families with young children;
  (iv) families with older children;
  (v) middle aged couples with no children or whose children now live away from home;
  (vi) retired couples;
  (vii) retired single people.

Geographic segmentation

This form of segmentation addresses the question of 'Where do they buy'? An organization may segment its market according to the geographic location of its consumers. A visitor attraction will need to know where its customers are coming from in order to plan its strategy for attracting repeat custom and for targeting new geographical areas. Similarly it is useful to be able to make distinctions between affluent and poor areas, and between various types of urban and rural areas.

Psychographic segmentation

In psychographic segmentation, consumers are divided into different groups on the basis of social class, lifestyle and/or personality.

The majority of people do not regard holidays as status symbols. Rather, they are merely seeking to spend two weeks in the sun having as much fun and enjoyment as they can at the best possible price. When choosing holiday destinations therefore, these tourists might not be motivated by the local culture, but others might be seeking destinations that are less demanding and remind them of home.

Thus Plog (1977) divided tourist consumers into five different psychographic traits: allocentrics, near allocentrics, midcentrics, near psychocentrics and psychocentrics. At the two extremes, allocentrics seek cultural and environmental differences from their norm, belong to higher income groups, are adventurous and require little in the way of tourism infrastructure. Psychocentrics seek familiar surroundings, belong to lower income groups, are unadventurous and require a high level of tourism infrastructure. A psychocentric New Yorker might favour Coney Island (a New York beach resort) whilst an allocentric New Yorker might favour an African Safari.

Attitudes and motivations, together with beliefs and perceptions, form the 'psychographic' profile of a consumer. Once the provider of tourism products can understand this profile, they can infer a person's buying behaviour and devise the appropriate tourist products to cater for these segments of the market.

People's product interests are influenced by their lifestyle. It covers people's day to day habits, work patterns, leisure interests, attitudes and values. Lifestyle segments would be based on distinctive ways of living and social values portrayed by certain types of people. This approach is sometimes felt to offer a more complete picture of the consumer than other approaches. Lifestyle market segmentation divides the market up according to the consumer's way of life. It is this which has resulted in the marketing world labelling segments with acronyms such as 'Yuppies' (standing for young, upwardly mobile professionals), 'Dinkies' (double income, no kids), 'Wooppies' (well-off old people) and 'Glammies' (the greying, leisured, affluent, middle-aged sector of the market). A travel or tour company which has taken a lifestyle approach can develop products that will appeal specifically to people with a particular way of life.

Lifestyle segmentation – Saga Holidays

Tour operators such as Saga Holidays are well placed to serve the special needs of senior citizens. Saga Holidays, based in Folkestone, Kent, have been very successful in marketing specifically to senior citizens using 'direct sell' techniques. A growth area in recent years has been the market for extended winter holidays in the Mediterranean for senior citizens. In order to cater for the specialized needs of this group, tour operators have had to build up a complete picture of customers' lifestyles so as to ensure that all requirements can be met. As part of the package offered to senior citizens, British nurses are on hand to provide them with health care, non-denominational religious services are held by British clergy, special leisure activities are organized for them such as whist drives and old-time dancing, and facilities are arranged so that they can obtain their state pensions.

Source: Adapted from P. Callaghan, P. Long and M. Robinson (1994)

Geo-demographic segmentation

Geo-demographic segmentation seeks to combine geographic and demographic principles of segmentation. For example *ACORN* (A Classification Of Residential Neighbourhoods), developed in the UK in the late 1970s, classifies households according to the neighbourhood in which they are found. The underlying philosophy is that certain types of neighbourhood will not only display similar housing but also will have residents with similar demographic and social characteristics who will share common lifestyles and will tend to display similar purchasing behaviour.

For example, a new visitor attraction in a particular area aimed at families with young children in the local vicinity could use an 'ACORN map' of the town. This will inform the managers of the attraction of the types of residential areas in the vicinity and hence those most likely to include the target customers.

Behaviour segmentation

In behavioural segmentation, 'buyers are divided into groups on the basis of their knowledge, attitude, use, or response to a product' Kotler (1997).

In the case of behaviouristic segmentation, unlike the use of other variables, we are concerned with consumer responses rather than consumer characteristics. Behaviour in the product field answers the question of 'how people buy' and what do they buy. Consumers can be classified according to the brands they choose or company loyalty, whether they are price-conscious, and whether they are frequent or infrequent purchasers of travel or tourism products. Many markets can be segmented in terms of benefits sought by customers.

Travel and tourism consumers are often attracted not by the product features but by the benefits they perceive they are likely to derive from their purchase. Consumers may be encouraged to buy a product if they recognize that they will benefit from it. For example, customers who purchase an inclusive tour to the Australian Outback are not buying their package holiday simply for the flight on the aeroplane, the accommodation provided, and the excursions that are arranged for them (which we could describe as the features of the holiday). Rather, the tourists are buying the complete package in order to enjoy the benefits of going away on holiday: a chance to experience a different lifestyle, the opportunity to sample different forms of culture, a break from normal everyday routine, and encounter wildlife not encountered in the home environment.

In order to take advantage of this knowledge, tour operators, for example, would have to identify the specific benefits that consumers in a particular market segment look for when going on holiday. When identified, the tour operator can devise holiday packages providing the specific benefits that are attractive to market segments.

T – targeting

When the possible range segments have been identified and the characteristics of each of the segments has been analysed, the tourism organization then has to decide which market segments to target.

When deciding which segments to target a number of considerations should be borne in mind in relation to the segments. Each segment should reflect the following important characteristics.

Market size and market growth

Each segment should be large enough, or demonstrate growth potential, to justify further investment of time and money by the company. As part of this evaluation an organization might consider the number and type of competitors in each segment. For example, it would probably be possible to construct and promote hotels solely for people in wheelchairs but would this be a substantial enough segment of the population to ensure success?

Accessibility

Each segment should be 'reachable', in the sense that it should be possible to give the consumers in that segment appropriate information about the company's products. For example, a coach operator finds that most customers are single and aged between 18 and 35, but unless they live in certain geographical areas they may be difficult to reach cost-effectively.

Measurability

Each segment should be measurable so that the likely demand for travel and tourism products in that segment can be identified. Research is very expensive and certain variables are very difficult to measure. For example, many people in deciding upon their holiday do so in the expectation of receiving certain benefits such as peace and relaxation or a lively night life, but it is difficult to measure such 'motivations', especially when sometimes people are unwilling to answer personal questions in an honest manner. Some young people's true motivations for travel may be a desire to meet members of the opposite sex and to consume alcohol but they may be reluctant publicly to acknowledge such motivations.

Actionability

Each segment should be 'actionable' in that effective programmes can be formulated for servicing the segments. For example, a small airline might identify seven market segments, but its staff and financial resources are too small to develop separate cost-effective marketing programmes for each segment identified. However, some of the long-held assumptions suggesting that the smallest segments cannot be economically reached are likely to change. Flexible technology is enabling products to be tailored to individual requirements more cheaply, thereby increasing choices available to consumers. In advertising we are used to the concept of broadcasting. In the future we shall have to become used to the concept of 'narrowcasting', as a revolution in media takes place. At present, if a company advertises on television and its product is only of interest to city dwellers, it is also paying to reach all the rural viewers. Cable technology allows organizations to direct adverts much more accurately at prospective customers. The same process is taking place in mail shots, where most mail shots can now be very accurately aimed and the Internet allows people to select what they want to see. The result of this process will be that very great rewards will be available to organizations that can come up with sophisticated segmentation strategies, as opposed to straightforward old-style mass marketing.

P – product positioning

What is positioning?

All organizations need to differentiate themselves and their products from competing organizations and products. Product positioning is the way in which a product or a brand is perceived in relation to preferences of segments of the market and in relation to competitive products. The perceptual image that a consumer holds about an organization or product is important because a positive and favourable image can lead to the consumer purchasing products from the organization in question whereas a negative image inevitably results in consumers looking elsewhere for their product purchases. Thus tourism strategists and (marketers) must seek to match the attributes of their product and buyers' perceptions of those attributes with the needs and priorities of customers in that segment. A number of authors have considered positioning in a travel and tourism context. See for example, Dev *et al*. (1999), Lovelock *et al*. (1999), Connell (1994) and Harris (1988).

By way of example, assume that market research has been carried out which has identified that the two key attributes on which consumers rate specific airlines are price

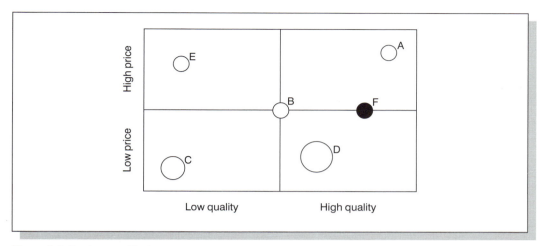

Figure 6.1 Product positioning

and quality. This enables the market position of all the main competing products in that segment to be analysed by asking customers to rate each airline according to the two attributes of quality and price. The customer may be asked to rate each on a ten-point scale. The results can then be plotted on a scatter diagram where the position of each response can be accurately marked (see Figure 6.1).

The five competitors A,B,C, D and E differ in sales volume as reflected by the sizes of the circles. The competitors' positions on the map are as follows:

- Competitor A occupies the high quality/high price position, sometimes termed a 'premium' position.
- Competitor B is perceived by the market as offering an average quality product at an average price.
- Competitor C sells a low quality product at a low price, sometimes termed a 'budget' position.
- Competitor D sells a high quality product at a low price, sometimes termed a 'value-for-money' position.
- Competitor E sells a low quality product at a high price, sometimes termed a 'cowboy' position.

The best position for a particular product can be determined. If a company is very lucky the survey will have revealed an 'ideal' position not occupied by any existing product. If so, the objective of locating a group of customers with an unsatisfied need will have been achieved. In Figure 6.1 a newcomer to the market might give consideration to locating at position F, where a high quality product is provided at an average price. However, in reality in today's very competitive markets the product-positioning map will probably not reveal such an obvious opportunity. The ideal product may be close to or identical to an existing or several existing products. If so two basic positioning choices are possible:

- Introduce a *me too* product, replicating the attributes of existing products occupying a similar position.
- Move into a gap on the product-positioning map, introducing a product bearing little similarity to any of the existing leading products.

If an organization finds a group of customers with a particular requirement for a combination not currently offered, it will literally have discovered a *gap* in the market (see the 'gap' on the bottom right of the chart). More likely, it will have to make the best of subtle differences in position, since all major combinations may be filled.

Product positioning: the case of Courtyard by Marriott

The development of the Courtyard brand by the US based Marriott corporation provides an example of product positioning. Research allowed Marriott to identify a niche in the mid-level market, which was not being filled by any hotel concept at that time. From its launch with three test hotels in 1983, the Courtyard chain has expanded rapidly in several countries and several hotel chains have attempted to duplicate the format.

Marriott management identified three criteria, which had to be met in the design of the Courtyard concept:

- To assure that the new concept offered consumers good value for money.
- To minimalize cannibalization (taking business away) from their other hotel offerings.
- To establish a market position that offered management a substantial competitive advantage.

Marriott developed a product positioning statement for the hotel concept, which stated that the Courtyard product was to serve business travellers who wanted moderately priced hotels of consistent high quality, and pleasure travellers who wanted an affordable room that was a safe base of operations. A basic conceptual framework for the product was then developed. The product would have the following features:

- It would be tightly focused for the transient mid-priced market segment.
- It would be relatively small (150 rooms or fewer) to project a residential image.
- It would serve a limited menu, and it would offer less than competitors in the way of public space and amenities.
- It would be a standardized product managed in clusters (i.e. five to eight hotels in one area).
- The Marriott name would be attached for recognition and a 'halo effect'.

Source: Adapted from Crawford-Welch (1994)

Tourism destination positioning

The principles of positioning and repositioning can also be applied to destinations and a large literature has developed around the subject area (see for example Ahmed, 1994; Alford, 1998; Aswood and Voogd, 1994; Bramwell and Rawding, 1996; McKercher, 1995; Morgan and Pritchard, 1998; Scott *et al*, 2000; Walmesley and Young, 1998). However, destinations differ from organizations in that the assumptions of strong leadership and clear goal-driven decisions to which all participants adhere may be lacking since destinations may be viewed as conglomerates of attractions, operators and agencies which each have individual objectives (Scott *et al.*, 2000).

Tourism destination positioning: the case of Queensland, Australia

Tourism Queensland, a state government owned enterprise charged with the promotion of Queensland as a tourist destination, has in recent years promoted five key destination areas to visitors as distinctive destinations. This positioning strategy was initiated as a response to the emergence of a number of Queensland tourist nodes, each having distinctive attributes, target markets and a sufficiently developed tourist industry to warrant a portfolio approach to their management as destinations. The approach reflects the diversity and scale of Queensland (and its tourism industry) and translates into different destination images, target markets, positional and promotional programmes for each destination. These can be summarized thus:

Destinations	Positioning elements	Brand personality	% domestic visitors
Tropical North Queensland (TNQ)	Great Barrier Reef and tropical rainforest	Relaxed, friendly, natural, adventurous, active	57
Brisbane	Stimulating subtropical capital city experience	Plenty to see and do, relaxed fresh outdoors	75
Gold Coast	Beach and excitement, nightlife and entertainment	Exciting, fast-paced, fun	70
Sunshine Coast	Beach and relaxation	Relaxed, simple, the way things used to be	90
Whitsundays	Aquatic playground	Relaxed, fresh, friendly, vibrant, natural	75

Source: Adapted from Scott *et al.* (2000)

Once an organization has decided how it wants to position itself relative to its competitors, it adapts its marketing 'mix' to achieve such a differentiation. The marketing mix comprises those variables that an organization can control which stimulate consumer demand. Traditionally marketers have viewed the marketing mix as being concerned with the '4 Ps' of product, promotion, price and place (distribution). However, it is common for those managing in the service sector to also include personnel, physical environment and processes, thereby recognizing the importance of these aspects in a service setting. A full consideration of the marketing mix is beyond the scope of this text since the issues are concerned with more detailed implementation issues often dealt with by marketers. Here we will, however, consider the product, since achieving a balance between products at different stages of development can be viewed as a strategic issue affecting resource allocation, cash flow and risk.

Products

Product definition

According to Kotler, a product is 'anything that can be offered to a market for attention, acquisition or consumption that might satisfy a want or a need. It includes physical objects, services, persons, places, organizations and ideas' Kotler (1997).

Importantly of course it is the sale of the product which provides sales revenue for the company. If a consumer buys a package from one tour operator and is satisfied with that holiday, then he or she may decide to book again with the same tour operator in the future. Therefore, the company must pay careful attention to all facets of the product to make sure that it lives up to consumers' expectations and leads to brand and or company loyalty. When thinking about travel and tourism products it must be recognized that the 'product' does not just include the actual holiday or travel that is purchased, or the visit to the tourist attraction, for example. The product is in fact all those elements that make up the experience enjoyed by the customer. Indeed, Kotler (1997) recommended that marketers recognize the product as being made up of five levels:

- the core product
- the generic product
- the expected product
- the augmented product
- the potential product.

Core product • • •

The core product is the main benefit, which the customer gains when purchasing the product. For example, when a holidaymaker goes on a holiday to Majorca, the core product may be one representing rest and relaxation whereas the core product for a holidaymaker going to Vietnam might be somewhat different. In this instance the core product might be to explore a newly developed tourist destination.

Generic product • • •

The generic product is a basic version of the product. It refers to the features of the holiday that are purchased. For example a holiday in Majorca might include a flight to Spain, 14 nights self-catering accommodation in apartments, and transfers to and from the airport. All the standard features that comprise the holiday, including the holiday brochure, are part of this generic product.

Expected product • • •

The expected product represents a set of attributes and conditions that buyers normally expect and agree to when purchasing a product. In our example, for instance, customers might normally expect certain features at the apartments, which might form a part of the package arrangements such as, clean rooms, bed linen, towels, plumbing fixtures, hanging space for clothes, and privacy.

Augmented product ◦ ◦ ◦

The augmented product goes beyond the customer's expectations to provide something extra and desirable. The levels of service provided by staff in the travel agency who arrange the booking and the way that tour operators deal with customer complaints are examples. These other services all 'add value' to the holiday.

Kotler saw this augmented level as being the level at which most competition takes place in the increasingly competitive market now faced by companies. To be successful in business, companies have continually to review their products to make sure that they are superior to competitors. However, each augmentation costs the organization resources in time or money and consequently questions must be asked as to whether customers will pay enough to cover the extra cost. Augmented benefits soon become expected benefits. *En suite* rooms, for instance, have moved from being the exception to the norm in most European hotels in the past 30 years. Similarly, what is contained in the expected product in one market may be in the augmented product in another. Air conditioning might be a bonus in a temperate climate, but a necessity in a tropical one. This means that competitors have continually to search for still further features and benefits to add to their products. Sometimes, after a period of rivalry where competitors try to compete by adding more and more features and cost, a market segment emerges for a basic stripped down low cost version that just supplies the expected benefits. Thus the emergence of the low cost airline sector in recent years can be seen in this way.

Potential product ◦ ◦ ◦

The potential product includes all the augmentations and transformations that the product might ultimately undergo in the future. Whereas the augmented product describes product features included in today's product, the potential product represents the possible evolution of the product. Successful companies will therefore manage their products very carefully. They will appreciate that some additional benefits must be provided to attract customers in competitive markets. Farsighted companies will therefore put much effort into research and development because the potential product is the product that is likely to be successful in tomorrow's markets.

All companies need to decide on an optimum number of different products to offer consumers. Should the tour operator offer only inclusive air tours to Greece, or should packages also be developed for Cyprus and Turkey? Should the travel agent specialize in high value cruise and long haul specialized products, or products that will have more of a mass market appeal? The organization, however, must not only consider the present situation since changing consumer tastes can change tourist destinations. The organization must therefore also consider the future situation and specifically new products that could be launched onto the market.

The answers to these questions will depend upon factors such as:

- the resources available to the business;
- the market segments to be targeted;
- the needs of the consumers.

Controlling the company's range of products, the so-called 'product portfolio', and phasing in new products as established ones decline, is an important function of a strategic manager as distinct from the marketing manager, who has also to take decisions concerning the features that will be included in each product.

The product life cycle

What is the product life cycle?

The product life cycle concept is based on the analogy with living things, in that they all have a finite life. All products would be expected to have a finite life, whether it is long or short. The life cycle can operate at an individual product level, or a product type, or at a product class level, where arguably a market life cycle would be a more appropriate title. At individual product level, the product life cycle is a useful tool in product planning, so that a balance of products is kept in various stages of the life cycle.

Key concept: The human life cycle metaphor

The concept of life cycle can apply to humans (or animals) just as it can to products and tourist destinations. Human beings undergo a life cycle that has a huge bearing, not just on our biological changes, but also on behaviour.

We undergo *introduction* when we are conceived and grow inside our mothers. After birth, we begin to *grow* – a process that continues until, after puberty, we reach our full height and weight. Our *maturity* phase is the longest. For most people, it will last from our mid-teens until the time when our faculties begin to fail us – perhaps in our sixties or seventies. When we reach old age, we begin to *decline*. Our eyesight may begin to deteriorate, we slow down and we may lose some of our intellectual sharpness. Finally, when decline has run its course, life is no longer viable, and we *die*.

At the product class level, we can use the product life cycle concept to analyse and predict competitive conditions and identify key issues for management. It is conventionally broken into a number of stages as shown in Figure 6.2. We shall explore the key issues posed by the different stages.

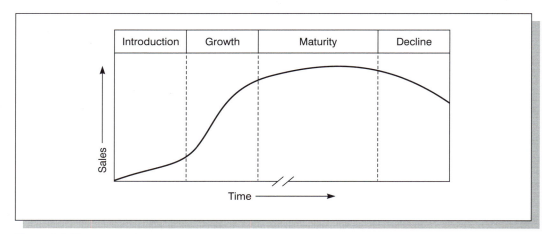

Figure 6.2 The product life cycle

The introduction stage

The introduction stage follows the product's development. It is consequently new to the market, will be bought by 'innovators', a term used to describe a small proportion of the eventual market. The innovators may not be easy to identify in advance and there are likely to be high launch and marketing costs. Because production volumes are likely to be low (because it is still at a 'pilot' stage), the production cost per unit will be high.

The price elasticity of demand will strongly influence whether the product is introduced at a high 'skimming' price, or a low 'penetration' price. Price skimming is appropriate when the product is known to have a price inelastic demand, such as with new exclusive resort developments or supersonic Concorde flights serving a new destination. Penetration is appropriate for products with price elastic demand and when gaining market share is more important than making a fast recovery of development costs. A low cost airline launching a new route might provide an example of such a product.

'Pioneer' companies (those who are first to the market with a particular product) are usually forced to sell the product idea in addition to an existing brand, and the early promotion may help competitors who enter the market later with *me too* versions of the product idea.

Entering the market at an early stage is usually risky. Not only will the company be incurring a negative cash flow for a period, but also many products fail at this stage. Against this risk is the prospect of increasing market share in the new product area faster than the me toos and consequently achieving *first mover* advantage such that the first product becomes the established provider and establishes a *barrier to entry* for subsequent entries to the market.

The growth stage

During the growth stage, sales for the market as a whole increase and new competitors typically enter to challenge the pioneer for some of the market share. The competitors may develop new market segments in an attempt to avoid direct competition with the established pioneering market leader.

The market becomes profitable, cash flow becomes positive and the funds generated can be used to offset the development and launch costs. This is an important time to win market share, since it is easier to win a disproportionate share of new customers, than later on to get customers to switch brands. As new market segments emerge, key decisions will need to be made as to whether to follow them or stay with the original.

The maturity stage

Maturity is reached when a high proportion of people who will eventually purchase a product have already purchased it once. It is likely to be the longest stage, but depending on the market, this could range from days or weeks to many decades or even centuries. It is important at this stage either to have achieved a high market share, or to dominate a special niche in the market. It can be expensive and risky to achieve large market share changes at this time, thus many companies prefer to concentrate their competitive efforts on retaining existing customers and competing very hard for the small number of new customers appearing. In this phase it is likely that large positive cash flows are being generated which can be reinvested in new products or in products at an earlier stage of their evolution.

It has been pointed out that market shares amongst leading competitors are often very stable over extremely long periods of time (Mercer, 1993), and this may be used as a criticism of the product life cycle concept. However, in order to maintain and protect their position in a mature market, companies have to be vigilant in detecting changes taking place. In response to changes, organizations have to be ready to modify or improve products and how customers perceive them and to undertake product repositioning.

The decline stage

It is part of product life cycle theory that all markets will eventually decline, and therefore companies have to be ready to move to new markets where decline is felt to be inevitable, or to be ready with strategies to extend the life cycle if this is felt to be feasible. Appropriate extension strategies could include developing new uses for the product, finding new users, and repositioning the product to gain a presence in the parts of the market that will remain after the rest of the market has gone. Even where markets have reached an advanced stage of decline, there may remain particular segments that can be profitable for organizations able to anticipate their existence and dominate them.

Companies that succeed in declining markets usually adopt a 'milking' strategy, wherein investment is kept to a minimum, and take up any market share that may be left by competitors that have left the market because of the decline. There is a certain recognition that death will come eventually and thus any revenues that can be made in the interim are something of a bonus.

The tourist area life cycle (TALC)

The ideas of the product life cycle have been applied in a tourism destination context through the Tourist Area Life Cycle (TALC). According to TALC (Butler, 1980, 2000; Haywood, 1986; Agarwal, 1994; Cooper et al., 1998) destinations go through a similar evolution to that of products, but visitor numbers are substituted for product sales. Destinations move from evolution (similar to introduction in the PLC), through involvement, development, consolidation (similar to growth in the PLC) before reaching stagnation (similar to maturity in the PLC). As with the PLC, decline will inevitably follow unless actions are taken which result in rejuvenation of the destination. The shape of the curve, the length of each stage and the length of the cycle itself are variable. For example, Cooper et al. (1998: 114) pointed to 'instant' resorts such as Cancun in Mexico which moved almost immediately to growth. In contrast, well-established resorts such as Scarborough on England's east coast have taken three centuries to move from exploration to rejuvenation.

Criticisms of the product life cycle

The product life cycle appears to be both widely understood and used (Greenley and Bayus, 1993). Despite this, some important criticisms have been made.

Whilst it is easy to go back into history and demonstrate all the features of the concept, it is hard to forecast the future, and in particular it is hard to forecast turning points. Not to try to do so at all, however, would seem to avoid confronting hard strategic issues.

Another criticism is that life cycles may sometimes not be inevitable, as dictated by the market, but created by the ineptitude of management. If management assume that decline will come, they will take the decision to reduce investment and advertising in anticipation of the decline. Not surprisingly, decline does come, but sooner than it otherwise would have done had the investment not been withdrawn.

Moutinho (2000: 143) detailed several criticisms of the concept in a tourism context. For the tourist area life cycle, decline relates to visitor numbers failing to fill capacity levels at the destination, but Moutinho pointed out that capacity is a notoriously difficult concept to operationalize as it is possible to envisage different forms of capacity threshold. Physical, environmental and psychological capacity may vary and it may be possible to 'manage' capacity.

New product development

The importance of new products

Change in society, markets, economies and society has led to a shortening of life cycles, and this has intensified the need for most organizations to innovate in terms of the products that they offer. New products can provide the mechanism whereby further growth can take place. Increasing competition, often itself coming from new or modified products, means that innovation is frequently not an option, but a necessity.

'Newness' can vary from restyling, or minor modification such as the introduction of restyled brochures or new aircraft liveries, to producing products that are *new to the world* that lead to new markets. The rise of international tourism to Cuba is an example of a new market having been created over recent years. The higher the degree of newness, the more likely it is that major gains in sales and profits may be made, but at the same time, the risks of incurring high costs and market failure are also increased. A single new product failure, if big enough, could bankrupt an organization. It is generally accepted that a very large proportion of new products fail, although precise quantification is impossible as many new products may be kept on the market despite not meeting their original objectives.

Organizations are faced with a dilemma in the management of new product development: new product development is essential, but is also fraught with risks. The successful management of the dilemma is often to produce a large number of new product ideas, most of which will never reach the market because they have been weeded out by an appropriate screening process.

New product idea generation

Ideas for new products can come from many sources. The greater the range of sources used, the more likely it is that a wide range and large number of new ideas will be produced (Sowrey, 1990).

For most organizations, the most important source of new ideas will be the customers. Obtaining ideas from customers is a good way of ensuring that ideas are produced that will produce products as a result of 'market pull'. This means that there will be a market for the products that result because they are specifically requested by the customers. Surveys and focus groups can help to produce ideas. The more straightforward approaches may give ideas for improvements, but more subtle approaches may reveal new needs.

Eric von Hippel (von Hippel, 1978) showed that a very successful approach for new ideas in industrial markets was to work with lead customers (respected, technically advanced buyers) to overcome their particular problems, and then to use the resulting new products to sell to other customers. Sometimes the products may require modification for the other customers at some cost, but the products then have unique value for these customers and price inelasticity of demand (Coates and Robinson, 1995).

It is impossible to construct a comprehensive list of sources of new products but the following have proved themselves to be useful in the past:

- advertising agencies (who sometimes have their 'finger on the pulse' of market requirements);
- consultants (who may carry out market research on a company's behalf);
- universities and other academic institutions;
- competitors (where an organization copies a competitive product);
- suppliers (who may have devised a way to use a component or material);
- employees, sometimes through 'employee idea' schemes;
- distributors and agents.

Screening

Once the idea for a new product has been generated, a company must then sift through them to develop only those with genuine potential – a process known as *screening*. As far as possible, the screening process has to attempt to avoid two potential types of errors – GO errors, where products are developed that ultimately fail, or do not meet objectives, and DROP errors, where ideas are abandoned that would ultimately have succeeded. GO errors are recognizable, at least by the organization that makes them, but most DROP errors are unrecognized because the project has not gone ahead (unless of course a competitor makes a success of an idea that has been abandoned).

In practice, the screening process is normally multi-stage, with at least some kind of review at several points in the process. Since risks may be high, and organizational politics may play a part, it is usually recommended that in at least one of the stages, a formal process is undergone where the idea is evaluated against predetermined objective criteria.

Development

The stages in development will vary according to the nature of the product and the work required to develop a new version, but it is important to include stages of the screening process before activities that involve the commitment of large amounts of finance, and it would not make sense to spend large amounts in developing a new product without producing evidence that there would be some demand for it. Stages in the process are typically as follows:

1 initial appraisal;
2 detailed business analysis and investment appraisal;
3 technical development;
4 market testing;
5 launch.

A traditional view of the development process is that one stage should precede another. With increasing competition, reducing time to market has become very important in many industries. To reduce the time to market, some of the activities may go on at the same time, sometimes known as *parallel processing*. This puts a premium on good communications in the company between functions such as operations, finance and marketing. To avoid the delays and complications that might be involved in handing a project from one function in the organization to another, multi-disciplinary teams known as *venture teams* may be created, and in some circumstances the team may be given the new product to manage when it is on the market. If such a team is created, it is likely that higher management will make the GO or DROP decisions to avoid the risk of the bias of an enthusiastic but optimistic team taking over.

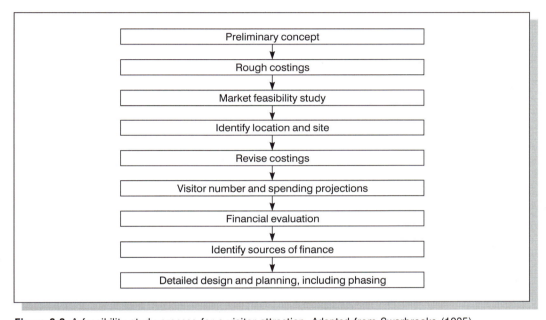

Figure 6.3 A feasibility study process for a visitor attraction. Adapted from Swarbrooke (1995)

In some areas of travel and tourism, such as the development of new hotels, resort development or the creation of visitor attractions, new product development requires significant capital investment. Consequently it is common to carry out a feasibility study prior to deciding whether to go ahead in order to test the viability of the proposed project. Swarbrooke (1995), for example, identified a nine-stage feasibility study process when assessing the viability of a visitor attraction. The stages are summarized in Figure 6.3.

Key points of the study include:

- Assessing the 'penetration factor' – predictions of the proportion of people in each market segment who may visit the attraction.
- Analysis of where the visitors will come from and when they will come.
- Analysis of capital costs, estimated likely income and estimation of the breakeven level of visitors.

Product portfolio theory

What is a portfolio?

The notion of portfolio exists in many areas of life, not just for products. Underpinning the concept is the need for a business to spread its opportunity and risk. A broad portfolio signifies that a business has a presence in a wide range of product and market sectors. Conversely, a narrow portfolio implies that the organization only operates in few or even one product or market sector.

A broad portfolio offers the advantage of robustness in that a downturn in one market will not threaten the whole company. Against this advantage is the problem of managing business interests that may be very different in nature – the company may be said to lack strategic focus. An organization operating with a very narrow portfolio (perhaps in just one sector) can often concentrate wholeheartedly upon its sector, but it can become vulnerable if there is a downturn of demand in the one sector it serves.

The BCG matrix

The Boston Consulting Group (BCG) matrix offers a way of examining and making sense of a company's portfolio of product and market interests. As with other models and matrices used in strategic analysis, the BCG matrix is a simplifying tool. It selects one parameter, relative market share, as an indicator of the strength of the competitive position and one parameter, growth, as indicating the potential and attractiveness of the market (Morrison and Wensley, 1991). A key point of the matrix is that market share and market growth provide approximations of the company's ability to generate cash. Cash flow is important in that it represents the most important determinant of a company's ability to develop its product portfolio.

Also implicit in the use of the matrix are the benefits to be gained from the *experience effect*. It is well recognized that companies (as with people) carry out their activities more efficiently with greater experience. Lessons are learned and adjustments to processes and systems are made. The experience effect is linked to market share through a virtuous cycle (Hooley and Saunders, 1993) where:

- A company with high market share gains more experience than its competitors.
- The experience results in lower costs.
- The lower costs mean that, at a given price, the company with the highest market share has the highest profits.
- The company with the highest profits or contributions from sales has more to spend on research and development or marketing, which allows it to maintain its high market share.

Applying this cycle to a tour operator in its dealings with travel agents:

- A high market share enables the tour operator to have greater experience of dealing with travel agents than its competitors.
- The experience represented by the large market share allows the tour operator to be able to reassure the agents that large volumes will be sold through the agents' branches.
- As a consequence of the high volumes, lower commission rates will be paid by the tour operator to the agent.
- The lower costs enable the tour operator with the highest market share to achieve the highest profits.

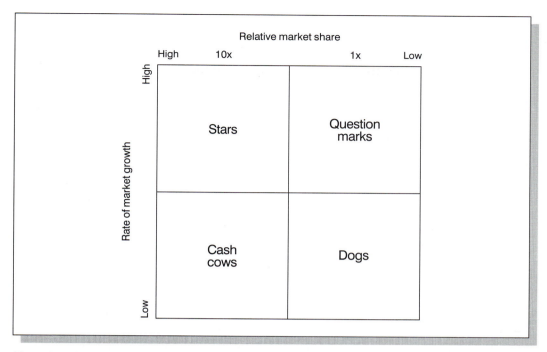

Figure 6.4 The Boston Consulting Group matrix

- The tour operator with the highest profits has more to spend on research and development or marketing, which allows it to maintain its high market share.

A large empirical study by the Profit Impact of Market Strategy (PIMS) provides further justification for the BCG approach. Perhaps the most important finding from the PIMS study is that there is a strong correlation between a high market share and the level of profitability (Buzzell and Gale, 1987). Thus a high market share is not an end in itself but something that is desirable since it leads (on average) to higher returns being achieved. The BCG matrix is used to analyse the product range with a view to aiding decisions on how the products should be treated in an internal strategic analysis. Figure 6.4 shows the essential features of the Boston matrix.

The axes of the BCG matrix

The market share measure

The horizontal axis is based on a very particular measure of market share. That measure is share relative to the largest competitor. A product with a share of 20% of the market, where the next biggest competitor had a share of 10%, would have a relative share of 2, whereas a product with a market share of 20% and the biggest competitor also had 20%, would have a relative share of 1. The cut-off point between high and low share is one, so high market share products in this analysis are market leaders. This arrangement of scale is sometimes described as being logarithmic in nature.

The market growth measure ◦ ◦ ◦

The vertical axis is the rate of market growth, with the most relevant definition of the market being served. A popular point used to divide high and low growth in the market is 10% year on year growth, but the authors have found it useful in practical situations to use growth that is faster than the rate of growth in the economy as a whole, which, after inflation is usually between 1% and 2.5% a year.

Using the BCG matrix

Cash cows ◦ ◦ ◦

A product with a high market share in a low growth market is normally both profitable and a generator of cash. Profits from this product can be used to support other products that are in their development phase. Standard strategy would be to manage conservatively, but to defend strongly against competitors. Such a product is called a cash cow because profits from the product can be 'milked' on an ongoing basis. This should not be used as a justification for neglect.

These are products associated with high positive cash flows and consequently can be used to support stars and selected question marks.

Dogs ◦ ◦ ◦

A product that has a low market share in a low growth market is termed a dog in that it is typically not very profitable. To cultivate the product to increase its market share would incur cost and risk, not least because the market it is in has a low rate of growth. Accordingly, once a dog has been identified as part of a portfolio, it is often discontinued or disposed of.

More creatively, opportunities might be found to differentiate the dog and obtain a strong position for it in a niche market. A small share product can be used to price aggressively against a very large competitor as it is expensive for the large competitor to follow suit.

The matrix does not have an intermediate market share category, but there are large numbers of products that have large market share, but are not market leaders. They may be the biggest profit earners for the companies that own them. They usually compete against the market leader at a disadvantage that is slight, but real. Management need to make very efficient use of marketing expenditure for such products and to try to differentiate from the leader. They should not normally compete head on, especially on price, but to attempt to make gains if the market changes in a way that the leader is slow to exploit.

These are products associated with modest positive or negative cash flow.

Stars ◦ ◦ ◦

Stars have a high share of a rapidly growing market, and therefore rapidly growing sales. They may be the sales manager's dream, but they could be the accountant's nightmare, since they are likely to absorb large amounts of cash, even if they are highly profitable. It is often necessary to spend heavily on advertising and product improvements, so that when the market slows, these products become cash cows. If market share is lost, the product will eventually become a 'dog' when the market stops growing.

These are products associated with modest positive or negative cash flow.

Question marks • • •

Question marks are aptly named as they create a dilemma. They already have a foothold in a growing market, but if market share cannot be improved, they will become dogs. Resources need to be devoted to winning market share, which requires bravery for a product that may not yet have large sales, or the product may be sold to an organization in a better position to exploit the market. These products will be high users of cash because they are trying to establish themselves in a growth market.

These are products associated with large negative cash flow.

BCG and strategy

In summary, portfolio management is concerned with balancing products and hence cash flow so that one category of products can support the development of other categories and risks can thereby be diminished. Specifically, companies should be looking to develop question marks into stars and stars into cash cows. Using the terminology that is usually applied to the matrix, portfolio management is concerned with:

- *harvesting* surplus cash generated by cash cows;
- using the cash generated in *maintaining* stars and *investing* in selected question marks; and
- *withdrawal* from dogs (if profitable niche positions cannot be established.

Limitations of the BCG matrix

Accurate measurement and careful definition of the market are essential to avoid misdiagnosis when using the matrix. Critics, perhaps unfairly, point out that there are many relevant aspects relating to products that are not taken into account, but it was never claimed by the Boston Consulting Group that the process was a panacea, and covered all aspects of strategy. Above all, the matrix helps to identify which products to push or drop, and when. It helps in the recognition of windows of opportunity, and is strong evidence against simple rules of thumb for allocating resources to products. However, the information needed to apply the matrix might be difficult and time consuming to obtain and to update and some tourism managers might feel that the effort is not worthwhile.

A composite portfolio model – the GEC matrix

The limitations of the BCG matrix have given rise to a number of other models that are intended to take a greater number of factors into account, and to be more flexible in use. A leading example is the General Electric matrix, developed by McKinsey and company in conjunction with the General Electric company in the United States. It is mainly applied to strategic business units such as the subsidiaries of a holding company. The model rates *market attractiveness* as high, medium, or low; and *competitive strength* as strong, medium, or weak. Strategic business units are placed in the appropriate category, and although there is no automatic strategic prescription, the position is used to help devise an appropriate strategy.

Market attractiveness criteria will be set by the user, and could include factors such as market growth, profitability, strength of competition, entry/exit barriers, legal regulation, etc. Competitive strength could include technological capability, brand

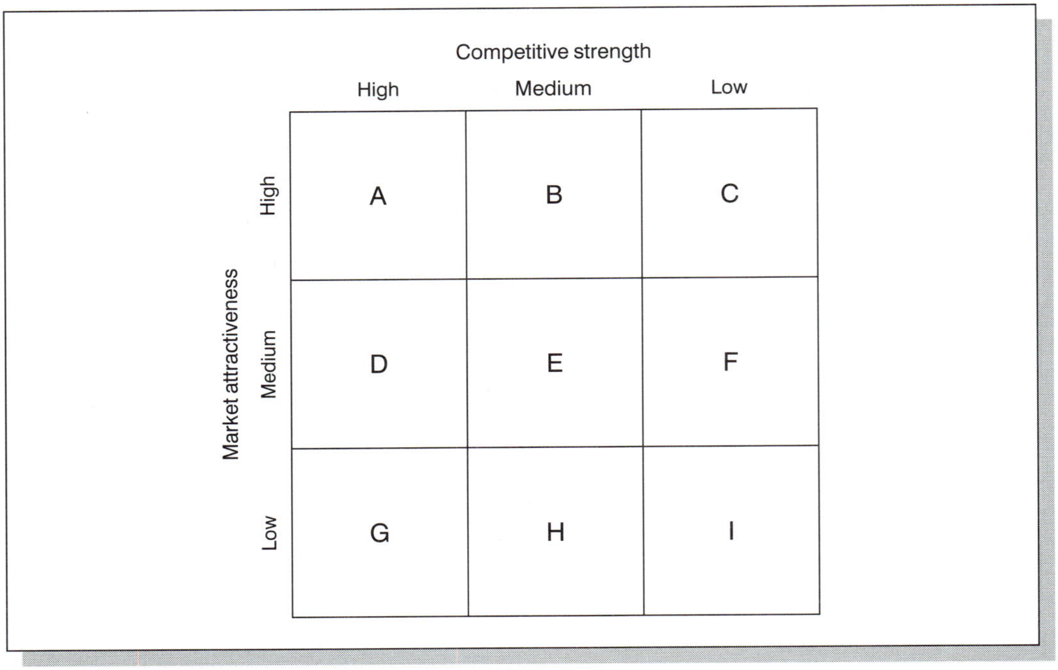

Figure 6.5 The GEC matrix

image, distribution channel links, production capability and financial strength. The flexibility to include as many variables as required is useful, but could lead to over-subjectivity. Most users of the model recommend that the variables be given a weighting to establish their relative importance, which will, in turn, reduce the potential for bias. In practice, managers tend to be aware that the tool is likely to be used as a basis for resource allocation and, consequently, they may attempt to influence the analysis in the favour of their own product or strategic business unit. The analysis gives rise to a three by three matrix (Figure 6.5).

For products in cell A, the company would invest strongly, as this is potentially in an attractive strategic position, where distinctive competences can be harnessed to good opportunities. In B, the company could be aggressive and attempt to build strength in order to challenge, or it could build selectively. In C, there are real dilemmas, in that there is the difficulty of competing well against stronger competitors – most plausible options would be to divest, as the opportunity might be attractive to others, or to specialize around niches where some strength could be built. D would indicate investment and maintenance of competitive ability. E and F would indicate risk minimization and prudent choices for expansion. G and H would indicate management for earnings, whilst I would require divestment or minimizing investment.

Extreme care is required in the judgments that would place products or strategic business units into any one category, and the model does not take directly into account synergies between different products or business. The astute reader will recognize that the model represents a means of relating competences to the external environment, and that it is also a means of taking SWOT a stage further.

References and further reading

Aaker, D.A. (1995) *Strategic Market Management*, 4th edn. New York: John Wiley and Sons Inc.

Agarwal, S. (1994) The Resort Cycle Revisited: Implications for Resorts, in C.P. Cooper and A. Lockwood (eds), *Progress in Tourism, Recreation and Hospitality Management*, Vol. 5. Chichester: John Wiley.

Ahmed, I.S.Z. (1994) Determinants of the Components of a State's Tourist Image and Their Marketing Implications. *Journal of Leisure and Hospitality Marketing*, 2(1), 55–69.

Alford, P. (1998) Positioning the Destination Product – Can Regional Tourist Boards Learn from Private Sector Practice? *Journal of Travel and Tourism Marketing*, 7(2), 53–68.

Aswood, G. and Voogd, H. (1994) Marketing of Tourism Places: What Are We Doing?, in M. Uysal (ed.), *Global Tourist Behaviour*. New York: Haworth Press.

Bramwell, B. and Rawding, L. (1996) Tourism Marketing Images of Industrial Cities. *Annals of Tourism Research*, 23(1), 201–221.

Brown, R. (1991) The S-curves of Innovation. *Journal of Marketing Management*, 7(2), pp 189–202.

Brownlie, D. (1985) Strategic Marketing Concepts and Models. *Journal of Marketing Management*, 1, 157–194.

Buzzell, R.D. and Gale, B.T. (1987) *The PIMS Principles*. New York: The Free Press.

Butler R.W. (1980) The Concept of the Tourist Area Life Cycle of Evolution and Implications for Management. *The Canadian Geographer*, 24, 5–12.

Butler, R.W. (2000) The Resort Cycle Two Decades On, in B. Faulkner, G. Moscardo and E. Laws (eds), *Tourism in the 21st Century: Lessons from Experience*. London: Continuum.

Civil Aviation Authority (2000) *ATOL Business*. London: CAA.

Coates, N. and Robinson, H. (1995) Making Industrial New Product Development Market Led. *Marketing Intelligence and Planning*, 13(6), 12–15.

Connell, J. (1994) Repositioning Forte Hotels Portfolio. *English Tourist Board Insights*, March, London: English Tourist Board, C43–51.

Cooper, C., Fletcher, J., Gilbert, D., Shepherd, R. and Wanhill, S. (1998) *Tourism Principles and Practice*, 2nd edn. Harlow: Longman.

Copeland, M.T. (1923) Relation of Consumers' Buying Habits to Marketing Methods. *Harvard Business Review*, 1 (April), 282–289.

Crawford-Welch, S. (1994) The Development of Courtyard by Marriott, in R. Teare, J.A. Mazanec, S. Crawford-Welch and S. Calver (1995), *Marketing in Hospitality and Tourism: a Consumer Focus*. London: Cassell.

Dev, C.S., Morgan, M.S. and Shoemaker, S. (1999) A Positioning Analysis of Hotel Brands, in T. Baum and R. Mudambi (eds), *Economic and Management Methods for Tourism and Hospitality Research*, Chichester: John Wiley.

Dickman, S. (1999) *Tourism and Hospitality Marketing*. Melbourne: Oxford University Press.

Doyle, P. (1994) *Marketing Management and Strategy*. Englewood Cliffs, NJ: Prentice Hall.

Greenley, G.E. and Bayus, B.L. (1993) Marketing Planning Decision Making in UK and US Companies: an Empirical Comparative Study. *Journal of Marketing Management*, 9, 155–172.

Harris, M. (1988) Economical Positioning. *Cornell Hotel and Restaurant Administration Quarterly*, 31(2), August, 97–115.

Haywood, K.M. (1986) Can the Tourist Area Life Cycle be Made Operational? *Tourism Management*, 7, 154–167.

Hind, D. (1994) *Tourism Marketing*, in P. Callaghan, P. Long and M. Robinson (eds), *Travel and Tourism*, 2nd edn. Sunderland: Business Education Publishers.

Hooley, G.J. and Saunders, J. (1993) *Competitive Positioning: The Key to Marketing Strategy*. London: Prentice Hall.

Horner, S. and Swarbrooke, J. (1996) *Marketing Tourism, Hospitality and Leisure in Europe*. London: International Thomson Business Press.

Jobber, D. (1995) *Principles and Practice of Marketing*. New York: McGraw-Hill.

Kay, J. (1995) *Foundations of Corporate Success*. Oxford: Oxford University Press.

Kotler, P. (1997). *Marketing Management Analysis, Planning, Implementation, and Control*, 9th edn. Englewood Cliffs, NJ: Prentice Hall.

Kotler, P., Bowen, J. and Makens, J. (1996) *Marketing for Hospitality and Tourism*, 2nd edn. Englewood Cliffs, NJ: Prentice Hall.

Kotler, P., Haider, D.H. and Rein, I. (1993) *Marketing Places*. New York: Free Press.

Lancaster, G. and Massingham, L.(1993) *Marketing Management*. London: McGraw-Hill.

Lovelock, C., Vandermerwe, S. and Lewis, B. (1999) *Services Marketing: A European Perspective*. London: Prentice Hall Europe.

Lumsden, L. (1997) *Tourism Marketing*. London: International Thomson Business Press.

McKercher, B. (1995) The Destination-Market Mix: a Tourism Market Portfolio Analysis Model. *Journal of Travel and Tourism Marketing*, 4(2), 23–40.

Mercer, D. (1993) Death of the Product Life Cycle, *Admap*, (September), pp. 15–19.

Middleton, V.T.C. and Clarke, J. (2001) *Marketing in Travel and Tourism*, 3rd edn. Oxford: Butterworth-Heinemann.

Morgan, N. and Pritchard, A. (1998) *Tourism Promotion and Power: Creating Images, Creating Identities*. Chichester: John Wiley.

Morrison, A. and Wensley, R. (1991) Boxing Up or Boxed In?: A Short History of the Boston Consultancy Group Share/Growth Matrix. *Journal of Marketing Management*, 7: 105–129.

Moutinho, L. (2000) *Strategic Management in Tourism*. Wallingford: CABI.

Pender, L. (1999) *Marketing Management for Travel and Tourism*. London: Stanley Thornes.

Plog, S. (1977) Why Destination Areas Rise and Fall in Popularity, in Kelly, E. (ed.), *Domestic and International Tourism*. Wellesley, MA: Institute of Certified Travel Agents.

Scott, N., Parfitt, N. and Laws, L. (2000) Destination Management: Co-operative Marketing, a Case Study of the Port Douglas Brand, in B. Faulkner, G. Moscardo and E. Laws (eds), *Tourism in the 21st Century: Lessons from Experience*. London: Continuum.

Seaton, A.V. and Bennett, M.M. (1996) *Marketing Tourism Products: Concepts, Issues and Cases*. London: International Thomson Business Press.

Sowrey, T. (1990) Idea Generation: Identifying the Most Useful Techniques. *European Journal of Marketing*, 42(5), pp 20–29.

Swarbrooke, J. (1995) *The Development and Management of Visitor Attractions*. Oxford: Butterworth-Heinemann.

Teare, R., Mazanec, J.A., Crawford-Welch, S. and Calver, S. (1995) *Marketing in Hospitality and Tourism: a Consumer Focus*. London: Cassell.

von Hippel, E. (1978) Successful Industrial Products from Customer Ideas. *Journal of Marketing*, 42(1), 39–49.

Walmesley, D. and Young, M. (1998) Evaluative Images and Tourism: The Use of Personal Constructs to Describe the Structure of Destination Images. *Journal of Travel Research*, 36 (Winter), 65–69.

Wearne, N. and Morrison, A. (1996) *Hospitality Marketing*. Oxford: Butterworth-Heinemann.

Part Three

External analysis

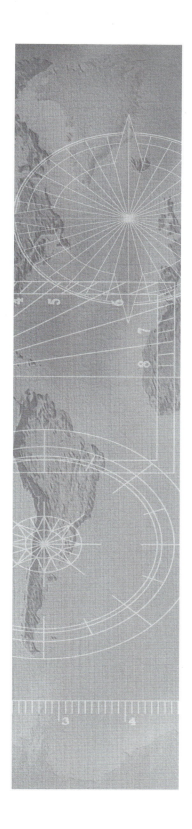

Introduction

The analysis of the internal environment (which provides the analytical underpinning for the strengths and weaknesses of the SWOT) was considered in Part Two of this book. Part Three now turns to the analysis of the external environment facing travel and tourism organizations. The analysis provides a rigorous underpinning for the 'opportunities' and 'threats' components of the SWOT. In some ways this form of analysis can be viewed as being more complicated than internal analysis since by definition it includes everything that is happening outside the travel and tourism organization's control. Since such analysis potentially covers a vast array of factors; the problems lie in deciding the relevant factors to include and in categorizing them in a useful and meaningful way.

We can view external analysis on two levels. First the macroenvironment (sometimes called the broad or general environment) contains a number of factors that affect not only an organization itself, but also all others in the industry. Most strategy textbooks use the STEP (or PEST) approach. In this book in recognition of the key influence of environmental (in terms of the built and natural environments) factors in a travel and tourism context the STEP framework is widened to STEEP.

The socio-demographic, technological, economic, environmental and political factors are certainly beyond an individual organization's control, although in some cases an organization may be able to exert some influence over some of the factors. Consequently, strategic management rests upon an organization's ability to cope with any changes in the macroenvironment through the formulation and implementation of appropriate strategies. The macroenvironment is considered in Chapter 7.

Second, the 'micro' or 'near' environment is the sphere in which the organization interacts most often – usually on a day-to-day basis. Any changes in the microenvironment can affect a travel and tourism organization very quickly and sometimes dramatically. In the case of most organizations, the microenvironment comprises influences from the competitive environment – its industry and markets. In Chapter 8 two models are discussed for making sense of these important strategic influences – Porter's five forces model and the resource or core competence based model.

Chapter 9 provides the culmination of the analytical phase by bringing together and summarizing the results of the internal and external analyses in the form of a SWOT. The SWOT provides a position statement of where the organization is now. Having understood the present position of the travel and tourism organization, the SWOT provides a firm platform for going on to consider the future in terms of the strategic options to be pursued. Part Four will consider strategic choices: the formulation, evaluation and selection of strategic options.

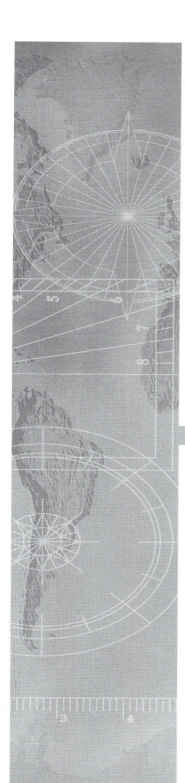

The external environment for travel and tourism organizations – the macro context

The most widely used technique for analysing the macro-environment is known as STEEP analysis. STEEP analysis divides the influences in the macroenvironment into five categories:

> *Socio-demographic* – social, cultural and demographic forces.
> *Technological influences* – products, processes, IT, communications, and transport.
> *Economic influences* – fiscal and monetary policy, incomes, living standards, exchange rates etc.
> *Environmental influences* – waste disposal, pollution, and energy consumption.
> *Political influences* – governmental, legal and regulatory influences.

It is worth noting that in some texts the STEEP acronym is replaced by STEP with environmental influences omitted. In other texts the STEP acronym is turned around and presented as PEST. However, the framework for analysis is essentially the same in both cases. It is this popular framework which is explained and explored in this chapter.

After studying this chapter, students should be able to:

- Explain what is meant by the macroenvironment.

- Explain Ginter and Duncan's mechanisms of carrying out macroenvironmental analysis.

- Describe the components of each of the four STEEP influences.

- Describe how the STEEP factors are interlinked and interrelated.

The macroenvironment

What is the macroenvironment?

We refer to the macroenvironment as the broad environment outside of an organization's industry and markets. It is generally beyond the influence of the individual organization but can have significant impact on the microenvironment (industry and market) in which the organization operates. The macroenvironment is sometimes referred to as the *far* or *remote* environment because it tends to exert forces from outside the organization's sphere of influence and the forces are usually beyond control.

Changes in the macroenvironment can be of immense importance to an organization. They can bring about the birth or death of an entire industry, they can make markets expand or contract, they can determine the level of competitiveness within an industry and many other things. It is therefore essential that managers are alert to actual and potential changes in the macroenvironment and that they anticipate the potential impacts on their industry and markets. In many ways analysis of the macro environment is more difficult than internal analysis since it involves everything that occurs outside the organization. The problems when dealing with such a vast amount of information are, first, assessing what should be included and what should be left out; and second, how the information should be organized in a rational and meaningful way. As Lynch (2000: 109) made clear, 'there are no simple rules governing an analysis of the organization. Each analysis [of the macroenvironment] needs to be guided by what is relevant for that particular organization.' This is to say that although analytical frameworks can be suggested for sorting and organizing pertinent information, the key issues are likely to be highly specific to each organization's circumstances.

Conducting macroenvironmental analysis

Ginter and Duncan (1990) listed the following activities as components of macroenvironmental analysis:

- *Scanning* macroenvironments for warning signs and possible environmental changes that will effect the business.
- *Monitoring* environments for specific trends and patterns.
- *Forecasting* future directions of environmental changes.
- *Assessing* current and future trends in terms of the effects such changes would have on the organization.

The same authors went on to identify the potential benefits of macroenvironmental analysis as:

- Increasing managerial awareness of environmental changes.
- Increasing understanding of the context in which industries and markets function.
- Increasing understanding of multinational settings.
- Improving resource allocation decisions.
- Facilitating risk management.
- Focusing attention on the primary influences on strategic change.
- Acting as an early warning system, providing time to anticipate opportunities and threats and devise appropriate responses.

Limitations of macroenvironmental analysis

We should be careful to note that macroenvironmental analysis has its limitations and pitfalls. At its root, the macroenvironment can be extremely complex and at any one time there may be conflicting and contradictory changes taking place. The pace of change in many macroenvironment situations is increasing and becoming more turbulent and unpredictable. This degree of uncertainty has, to some extent, cast some doubt over the value of carrying out a macroenvironmental analysis at all. By the time that an organization has come to terms with one major change in the macroenvironment, another change may have occurred that requires even more attention and action.

Accordingly, managers that are concerned with strategic analysis must:

- be aware of the limitations and inaccuracies of macroenvironmental analysis;
- carry out the analysis continuously (because it changes so frequently);
- constantly seek to improve sources of information and techniques for its analysis;
- use the information as one source of organizational learning;
- use the information to inform future strategy.

With these points in mind, macroenvironmental analysis is a valuable mechanism for increasing strategic awareness of managers.

STEEP analysis

Overview of the STEEP influences

The complexity of the macroenvironment makes it necessary to divide the forces at work into the five broad categories we have already encountered. It is important to remember that the four categories are interrelated and constantly interact with each other. In the process of STEEP analysis (sometimes called STEP or PEST analysis) it is therefore important to explore and understand the relationships between the forces at work. It is equally important to identify the relative importance of the influences at work for the organization, its industry and its markets. Finally, because of the uncertainty of the effects of macroenvironmental change on the microenvironment, it is essential that a range of possible outcomes of the changes are identified and considered.

In carrying out a STEEP analysis it should be pointed out that some of the factors may be generic in that they affect all industrial sectors, whilst others are specific to travel and tourism, or a particular sector within the industry. Peattie and Moutinho (2000) provided a review of some of the major environmental influences in travel and tourism using an extended framework, which they termed SCEPTICAL analysis. In this case the acronym stands for:

Social
Cultural
Economic
Physical
Technical
International
Communications and infrastructure
Administrative and institutional
Legal and political

Other texts such as Lockwood and Medlik (2001), Buhalis (2001), Vogel (2001), Cooper and Gilbert (1998) and Vanhove (2001) also give some interesting insights in discussing the key macroenvironmental factors affecting the travel and tourism industry.

In her analysis, Auliana Poon (1993) pointed to the radical changes that were changing the travel and tourism industry. She suggested that a 'new tourism' was developing to replace the 'old tourism' based on mass tourism. The five key forces (consumers, technology, production, management and 'frame conditions') which had served to create mass tourism in the first place were themselves changing to create the new tourism. Figure 7.1 summarizes some of the changes taking place.

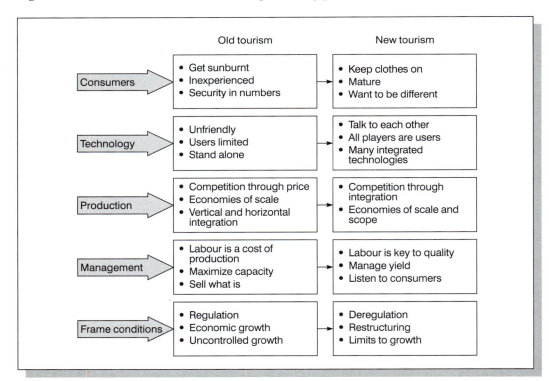

Figure 7.1 Old and new tourism compared (adapted from Poon, 1993)

Some texts use the STEP or PEST acronym, thereby omitting explicit recognition of physical environmental influences but considering these as part of the other influences. The approach adopted here, however, is to explicitly recognize the central importance of physical environmental influences in a tourism context by considering them under a separate heading. It is clearly the case that there can be few industries where the interdependence between the physical environment and economic activity is so clearly visible (Peattie and Moutinho, 2000).

In the following sections the component parts of STEEP are considered systematically. The approach adopted here is to list some of the generic factors and to provide illustrations of the industry specific factors by using the airline industry for purposes of illustration.

Socio-demographic influences

Analysis of the social environment is concerned with understanding the potential impacts of society and social changes on a business, its industry and markets.

For most analyses, analysis of the social environment will require consideration of:

- *Social culture* (values, attitudes and beliefs) – its impact on demand for products and services, attitudes to work, savings and investment, ecology, ethics, etc.
- *Demography* – the impact of the size and structure of the population on the workforce and patterns of demand.
- *Social structure* – its impact on attitudes to work and products and services.

Social culture

The cultures of countries in which a business operates can be of particular importance. The culture of a country consists of the values, attitudes and beliefs of its people, which will affect the way that they act and behave (or, put simply, its 'personality'). There are important cultural differences between all countries. Culture can affect consumer tastes and preferences, attitudes to work, attitudes to education and training, attitudes to corruption and ethics, attitudes to credit, attitudes to the social role of a business in society and many other things.

Demography

Demographic trends are similarly important. Demography is the social science concerned with the charting of the size and structure of a population of people. The size of the population will obviously be a determinant of the size of the workforce and the potential size of markets. Just as important will be the structure of the population. The age structure will determine the size of particular segments and also the size of the working population. The size and structure of the population will constantly be changing and these changes will have an impact on industries and markets.

Social structure

Social structure is strongly linked to demography and refers to the ways in which the social groups in a population are organized. There are a number of ways of defining social structure, such as by socio-demographic groupings, by age, sex, location, population density in different areas, etc. The social structure will affect people's lifestyles and expectations and so will strongly influence their attitudes to work and their demand for particular products and services.

Among the most important general changes in recent years in the social environment has been the change in people's attitudes to the physical environment. Increasing awareness of the problems caused by pollution and the exhaustion of non-renewable resources have caused travel and tourism organizations to rethink (in many cases) the way that they produce their products and the composition of the products themselves. Similarly, changes in social structure (upward mobility), lifestyle (increased leisure) and demography (ageing populations in developed countries) have significantly altered many market and industry structures.

Socio-demographic influences – airline sector

A number of demographic factors point towards a greater use of air travel. Thus an increasing proportion of the population being relatively healthy and prosperous, increasing numbers of retired people, a decline in average family size, increasing amounts of paid holidays and larger numbers of double income families all point to higher usage of air services. Leisure travel (which accounts for about 80% of trips) has grown more rapidly than business based travel.

Other factors that might be considered are lifestyle trends and attitudes of society towards air travel and associated airport development. An increasingly mobile society where people take safe, reliable and affordable air transportation for granted is challenged by a critical society which assesses the contribution of air travel to air and noise pollution (Holloway, 1998). This dichotomy, in which the competing needs and interests of airline stakeholder groups need to be considered, represents a challenge to airlines, regulators and governments.

Technological influences

Analysis of the technological environment involves developing an understanding of the effects of changes in technology on all areas of a business and its activities, including:

- Goods and services.
- Operational processes.
- Information and communications.
- Transport and distribution.
- Society, politics and economics.

Developments in information and communications technology (ICT), like the development of personal computers (PCs), networks, satellite, cable, Internet and digital communications together with rapid advances in software, have all contributed to revolutionizing the way that business is conducted in many industries. Activities are now better co-ordinated, research and development is speeded up, thus making businesses more flexible and responsive. For example, many activities previously carried out by middle layers of managers, which often involved collating and analysing data from operational activities, and reporting to senior managers can now be more effectively carried out using ICT solutions. As a result, many companies such as British Airways have cut costs through reducing the numbers of people employed particularly at middle levels of the organization in a process referred to as *de-layering*.

Similarly, changes in transport technology have revolutionized business and have changed societies and cultures. It is possible to transport tourists as well as materials, components and products with far greater speed and at much lower cost as a result of developments in road, rail, sea and air transport. These improvements in transport have also increased the total amount of personal and business travel that people undertake and this has led to profound societal changes both in tourist 'exporting' and 'importing' regions. Increasing wine consumption and more varied culinary tastes in the UK are responses (at least in part), to wider participation in international travel.

As a consequence, it is important that organizations monitor changes in the technologies that can affect their operations or their markets. In most industries, organizations must be flexible and be ready to innovate and adopt new technologies as they come along. The way in which (and the extent to which) organizations do or do not employ the latest technology can be an important determinant of competitive advantage.

Technological influences – airline sector

The Computer Reservation Systems (CRS) such as Sabre developed by American Airlines are powerful tools of travel marketing technology. The systems developed largely in the 1960s and 1970s have attained global reach and hence they are now often referred to as Global Distribution Systems (GDS). The recent development of Internet search and booking engines developed by CRS providers allow for diversified distribution and communication channels to be utilized thus creating new opportunities for airline marketing. Allied to the use of CRS are the Revenue Management Systems that have been developed. These systems, which utilize the CRS accumulated databases, allow for the yield realized to be optimized by varying prices and altering the mix between classes of tickets that are issued.

In relation to the aircraft themselves, technological innovations continue to drive costs down and influence route structures. The 380 (*Megaliner*) currently being developed by Airbus Industries, for example, will have a capacity of some 550 passengers with operating costs about 17% lower than the Boeing 747 (Brown, 2001). Route patterns and airport infrastructures are two aspects which may well have to change in response to the aircraft's introduction. Additionally, a number of short to medium range jet aircraft models with twin fuel efficient lean burn engines have been introduced over recent years and further such developments are planned. Such aircraft allow the airlines to consider introducing routes which were previously considered to be unviable.

Economic influences

Analysis of the economic environment will centre on changes in the macro-economy and their effects on business and consumers. It is important to remember that because governments intervene (to varying extents) in the operation of all countries' economies, many factors classed as political in this chapter will have important economic implications.

Broadly speaking, the regulation of a national economy is brought about by two key policy instruments – fiscal policy and monetary policy. These policy instruments, alongside influences from international markets, determine the economic climate in the country in which a business competes. From these, a number of other, vital economic indicators 'flow' and it is these that organizations experience – either for good or ill.

Key concepts: Fiscal and monetary policy

Fiscal policy is the regulation of the national economy through the management of government revenues and expenditures. Each fiscal year, a government raises so much in revenues (such as through taxation) and it spends another amount through its various departments (such as on health, education, defence, etc.). The government is able to influence the economic climate in a country by varying either or both of these sides of the fiscal equation.

Monetary policy is the regulation of the national economy by varying the supply and price of money. Money supply concerns the volume of money (in its various forms) in the economy and the 'price' of money is the base rate which determines the interest rate that banks and other lenders charge for borrowings.

In the UK, the Chancellor of the Exchequer is in charge of fiscal policy whilst monetary policy is overseen by the Monetary Policy Committee of the Bank of England.

When the effects of fiscal and monetary pressure work themselves out in the economy, they can affect any or all of the following economic factors:

- Economic growth rates (the year to year growth in the total size of a national economy, usually measured by gross domestic product).
- Levels of income in the economy.
- Levels of productivity (i.e. output per worker in the economy).
- Wage levels and the rate of increase in wages.
- Levels of inflation (i.e. the year to year rise in prices).
- Levels of unemployment.
- Balance of payments (a measure of the international competitiveness of one country's economy against its international competitor countries).
- Exchange rates (the exchange value of one currency against another).

Economic growth, exchange rates, levels of income, inflation and unemployment will all affect people's ability to pay for goods and services and, accordingly, they can affect levels and patterns of demand. Similarly, levels of productivity, wage levels, levels of inflation, and exchange rates will affect costs of production and competitiveness. All of these indicators must be monitored in comparison to those faced by competitors abroad to provide indications of changes in international competitiveness.

Economic influences – airline sector

The economic environment of the airline sector has been characterized by growth in relation to most key figures. Air travel demand has closely mirrored the cyclical pattern shown by gross domestic product (GDP) figures in that it responds to cyclical upswings and downswings. However, air travel growth has far exceeded GDP growth over the period. Between 1960 and 1995 the total world economy, measured by GDP, grew by a factor of just over three, while air transport, measured by tonne-kilometres, grew by a factor of nearly 20 (Hanlon, 1999). The airline industry also has a high level of fixed costs and consequently average load factors and revenue measures per passenger are crucial in maintaining profitability. Furthermore, fuel and aircraft prices are major expenditure items subject to fluctuations and the international orientation of the industry means that movements in foreign exchange rates can have major effects upon industry profitability. Holloway (1998) maintained that aviation managers face the need to pursue strategies capable of sustaining profitability throughout entire economic cycles.

Environmental influences

The environmental influences here refer to the influence of concerns for the physical environment (both the natural environment and the built environment) on travel and tourism organizations. In recent years increasing concerns about ecology and 'green issues' has been an important social trend and this has changed people's attitudes towards the effects of products and operational processes on the environment. Issues such as global climate change, ozone layer depletion, deforestation, extinction of species, soil erosion, desertification, acid rain, toxic wastes and water pollution have become important concerns with regard to the natural environment (Peattie and Moutinho, 2000). To such concerns regarding the natural environment might be added others concerning the built environment such as traffic congestion, deteriorating buildings and historic sites, poor urban planning, and visually intrusive buildings. The problems and issues identified have certain unifying characteristics. First, they all have international dimensions and second they are not exclusively tourism related but nevertheless have important implications for tourism managers amongst others.

Whereas twenty years ago most consumers showed little concern for the long-term effects of products and processes on the natural environment, today people are increasingly aware of the need to protect it. Following various developments such as the publication of the Brundtland Report in 1987 (WCED, 1987) and the Earth Summit in Rio de Janeiro in 1992, there has been increasing commitment to the principles of sustainable development in many industries, including tourism.

This has led to pressure on governments to introduce legislation and other measures to control pollution. The combined desire of consumers for products which are themselves environmentally friendly and which have been produced by 'green' methods has resulted in the realization by business that there are profits to be made by being environmentally friendly or at least appearing to be environmentally friendly. British Airways, for example, has developed a series of environmental awareness programmes for its managers and sponsored the 'Tourism for Tomorrow' awards in recognition of tourism organizations that have attempted to create products that have a positive environmental impact.

Scandic Hotels – environmental programme as a source of competitive advantage

Scandic Hotels (which is now part of Hilton plc.) is the leading hotel brand in Scandinavia, a region in which consumers traditionally are highly environmentally conscious. The group, which employs some 7500 people, has 155 hotels of which 133 are in the Scandinavian countries with others located around Europe. The brand, which positions itself as offering 'value for money', places great emphasis on continual competence development of employees at all levels of the organization and on its environmental programme.

Scandic's environmental programme was launched in 1994 following consultation with staff, and the hotel group is an active member of the International Hotel Environment Initiative (IHEI). The programme involves the continuing education of all employees and includes initiatives such as:

- The introduction in 1995 of eco-rooms, which are 97% recyclable. More recently, the company has also developed 'eco-hotels', in which the entire construction of the hotels is guided by environmental principles. To date, more than 8000 eco-rooms and six eco-hotels have been built.
- The achievement of 'Swan' certification for four hotels. The Swan is the official eco-label in Scandinavia and verifies that the hotels have met stringent environmental standards.
- The abolition of individual soap and shampoo packages in 1994 reduced emissions of soap and shampoo by 40 metric tonnes and eliminated 10 million packages annually.
- The introduction of the 'resource hunt', a programme promoting the efficient use of resources. Initially carried out in the Scandinavian hotels between 1997 and 1999, the programme reduced carbon dioxide emissions by more than 15% and energy costs by 20%.

During 2000, Scandic also introduced, following staff consultation, a community involvement programme called 'Scandic in Society' which aimed to define the company's role in society by engaging in local issues that were important to each community in which Scandic hotels were located. Through such a programme the company aimed to demonstrate its corporate citizenship and contribute to societal changes and improvements.

Source: adapted from www.scandic-hotels.com

The issues of the sustainability of tourism development for tourist destinations and attractions has been widely addressed in the tourism literature over recent years by authors such as Hawkins and Holtz (2001), Weaver (2000), Berry and Ladkin (1997), Clarke (1997) and Mowforth and Munt (1998). A number of authors have also traced the environmental impacts of particular sectors of travel and tourism.

Graham (2001), for example, traced environmental policies and practices at a number of airports including Oslo, Manchester, London Heathrow and Amsterdam. Cartwright and Baird (1999) traced the environmental impacts of cruising and reported on the ways in which attempts have been made to reduce the polluting effect of cruise ships. The traditional method of removing rubbish from ships was to dump it overboard. Now such practices are outlawed and large fines are imposed on shipping companies found guilty of such pollution, partly in response to consumer pressures. A modern cruise ship such as P&O's *Oriana* contains four sewage plants so that as much rubbish as possible is retained and disposed of safely into containers at ports. There is also a worldwide ban on the discharge of fuel oil into the sea (Cartwright and Baird, 1999).

Environmental influences – airline sector

Environmental concerns in the airline sector include the effects of noise and aircraft emissions, and the impacts of developing airport and ground transportation infrastructure. Public tolerance of aircraft noise has been diminishing in spite of the reduction in noise levels due to the development of less noisy aircraft types (Graham, 2001). The problems associated with aircraft noise have led to ever more stringent and sophisticated noise abatement measures being introduced at most major airports. Some of these gases emitted by aircraft in flight, primarily carbon dioxide and water vapour, are greenhouse gases which contribute to global warming and climate change. However, it is thought that aviation's contribution to global human-made carbon dioxide emissions amounts to only around 2% of the total (Graham, 2001). The infrastructure of creating airports and ground transportation to support airlines has often proved controversial. Thus the agreement to proceed with a fifth terminal for London's Heathrow Airport was secured only after ten years of public consultations whilst Manchester Airport proceeded with building a second runway in the face of strong lobbying by environmental pressure groups.

Political, governmental, legal and regulatory influences

The political environment is defined as that part of the macroenvironment, which is under the direct control, or influence, of the government. Governments have direct control or influence over:

- *Legislation and regulation* – this covers laws that influence employment, consumer protection, health and safety at work, contract and trading, trade unions, monopolies and mergers, tax, etc.
- *Economic policy* – particularly over fiscal policy. Governments usually set policy over the levels of taxation and expenditure in the country.
- *Government-owned businesses* – nationalized industries. Some governments retain control over key strategic industries (such as airlines) and the way in which these are controlled can have 'knock-on' effects to other parts of the economy.
- *Government international policy* – government intervention to influence exchange rates, international trade, etc.

The objectives that a government may have towards the regulation of business will depend in large part upon the political leaning of the governing party. Most governments have, however, sought to construct policy over a number of key areas of business activity.

- Control of inflation (such as to improve international competitiveness).
- Promotion of economic growth and investment.
- Control of unemployment.
- Stabilization of exchange rates.
- Control of balance of payments.
- Control of monopoly power, both by businesses and trade unions.
- Provision of public and merit goods like health, education, defence, etc.
- Control of pollution and environmental protection.
- Redistribution of incomes (to varying degrees).
- Consumer protection.
- Regulation of working conditions.
- Regulation of trade.

To varying degrees, all businesses will be affected by political influences. Accordingly, it is important for managers to monitor government policy to detect changes early so as to respond effectively.

Another important aspect of the political environment is *political risk* and its potential effects on business. Political risk is particularly important in international business. Whilst Western Europe and North America are comparatively politically stable, other parts of the world like Eastern Europe, South America, sub-Saharan Africa and parts of the Middle East have undergone periods of political instability. It is therefore necessary to monitor closely the political situation in these areas when trading with them, as the political risks are large. Even in more stable areas, political uncertainty can be higher at, for example, election times or when other political crises arise.

Political environment – airline sector

The political environment of the airline sector has been characterized by an extended network of national and international rules and regulations, many of which date back to the Chicago Convention of 1944 and the Bermuda Agreement of 1946 (Sampson, 1984). Based on the acknowledgement of the sovereignty of nations over their airspace and of the equal right for every nation to participate in air travel, the so-called *five freedoms of the air* were established:

- *First Freedom* The right to fly over another country without landing
- *Second Freedom* The right to make a landing for technical reasons (e.g. refuelling) in another country without picking up/setting down revenue traffic.
- *Third Freedom* The right to carry revenue traffic from your own country (A) to the country (B) of your treaty partner.
- *Fourth Freedom* The right to carry revenue traffic from country B back to your own country A.
- *Fifth Freedom* The right of an airline from country A to carry revenue traffic between country B and other countries such as C or D on services starting or ending in its home country A. (This freedom cannot be used unless countries C or D also agree.)

(Source: Doganis, 2001)

The five freedoms were followed by a complex web of bilateral inter-governmental agreements that allowed national governments involved to maintain control over national interests related to air travel. A more liberal approach is reflected in the so-called *open skies* agreements granting carriers of the states involved unlimited access to the routes between airports in these states. The concept of open skies reflects a development of major importance for the airline industry: liberalization unfolding around the globe (Doganis, 2001).

In the USA (which accounts for over 40% of the world's airline industry), the strict regulations governing the domestic air travel market were swept away by the Airline Deregulation Act of 1978. The act abolished regulations specifying the carriers that were allowed to fly on particular routes and impose controls on air fares. After deregulation many new carriers entered the market (and many subsequently folded), but most of the largest carriers, such as United, American, Delta and Northwest, survived but undoubtedly competition in the US domestic market has increased in the longer term by the emergence of low cost carriers such as Southwest Airlines.

Subsequently, similar deregulation occurred in Europe. A different approach towards implementation was selected, however, owing to the complexity of achieving deregulation in the fragmented political landscape of the European Union. Consequently, a step by step process towards liberalization took place which culminated in 1997. Another major trend among European governments was the privatization (in whole or in part) of former state-owned carriers such as British Airways, Air France and Lufthansa.

Heavy regulation over the ownership of airlines remains, however. In many cases, such as the USA, airlines must still be 'substantially owned' or effectively controlled' by nationals of the designated states. Thus airlines continue to be treated in a different manner to most other industries, reflecting its strategic significance, and as Doganis (2001) pointed out, paradoxically the most international of industries remains almost exclusively national in terms of ownership and control.

The relationships between the STEEP influences

The example of environmental influences

A temptation when carrying out a STEEP analysis is to think of each influence as separate when in fact they are often interlinked. The effects of environmental influences on organizations provide an example. The environmental concerns themselves (such as the use of water resources for golf course developments or the building of visually intrusive hotels in scenic areas) are issues to be dealt with within the 'environmental' category of the STEEP analysis. However, such concerns might also involve social, political and technological factors in the analysis. Thus, social factors (increased awareness) have impacted on political factors (legislation and regulation) and the two forces together have produced technological change (products and processes which are less damaging to the environment). Accordingly, a macroenvironmental analysis should recognize the ways in which the four STEEP factors might be linked to each other.

Using the STEEP analysis

How to carry out a STEEP analysis

Now that we know what the STEEP influences are and how they are interrelated, we turn to actually using the framework in strategic analysis. The analysis is generally considered as falling into four stages.

1 Scanning and monitoring the macroenvironment for actual or potential changes in social, technological, economic and political factors.
2 Assessing the relevance and importance of the changes for the market, industry and business.
3 Analysing each of the relevant changes in detail and the potential relationships between them.
4 Assessing the potential impact of the changes on the market, industry and business.

What to analyse

When managers carry out a STEEP analysis as part of a strategic analysis (and the same is true of students examining a case study), they would normally examine how each factor might impact upon:

- *The internal parts of an organization* – the effects of STEEP factors on the organization's core competences, strategies, resources, and value system.
- *An organization's markets* – the effects of STEEP factors on product markets (e.g. market size, structure, segments, customer wants, etc.) and resource markets.
  The industry in which the organization competes – the effects of STEEP factors on the five competitive forces (buyer power, supplier power, threat of entry, threat of substitutes, competitive rivalry – see Chapter 8).

References and further reading

Berry, S. and Ladkin, A. (1997) Sustainable Tourism: a Regional Perspective. *Tourism Management*, 18(7), 433–40.

Buhalis, D. (2001) The Tourist Phenomenon: The New Tourist and Consumer, in S. Wahab and C. Cooper (eds), *Tourism in the Age of Globalisation*. London: Routledge.

Brown, S.F. (2001) How to Build a Really Big Plane. *Fortune*, No. 5, pp. 76–82.

Cartwright, R. and Baird, C. (1999) *The Development and Growth of the Cruise Industry*. Oxford: Butterworth-Heinemann.

Chakravarthy, B. (1997) A New Strategy Framework for Coping with Turbulence. *Sloan Management Review*, Winter, pp. 69–82

Clarke, J. (1997) A Framework of Approaches to Sustainable Tourism. *Journal of Sustainable Tourism*, 5(3), 224–233.

Cooper, C. and Gilbert, D. (1998) Models and Patterns of Tourism Demand, in C. Cooper, J. Fletcher, D. Gilbert, R. Shepherd and S. Wanhill, *Tourism Principles and Practice*. Harlow: Longman.

Doganis, R. (2001) *The Airline Business in the 21st Century*. London: Routledge.

Elenkov, D.E. (1997) Strategic Uncertainty and Environmental Scanning: the Case for Institutional Influences on Scanning Behaviour. *Strategic Management Journal*, 18(4), 287–302.

Fahey, L. and Narayanan, V.K. (1986) *Macroenvironmental Analysis for Strategic Management*. St Paul, MN: West Publishing.

Ginter, P. and Duncan, J. (1990) Macroenvironmental Analysis. *Long Range Planning*, December.

Graham, A. (2001) *Managing Airports: an International Perspective*. Oxford: Butterworth-Heinemann.

Hanlon, P. (1999) *Global Airlines*, 2nd edn. Oxford: Butterworth-Heinemann.

Hawkins, D.E. and Holtz, C. (2001) Environmental Policies and Management Systems Related to the Global Tourism Industry, in S. Wahab and C. Cooper (eds), *Tourism in the Age of Globalization*. London: Routledge.

Helms, M.M. and Wright, P. (1992) External Considerations: Their Influence on Future Strategic Planning. *Management Decision*, 30(8), 4–11.

Holloway, S. (1998) *Changing Planes: A Strategic Management Perspective on an Industry in Transition*. Aldershot: Ashgate.

Johnson, G. and Scholes, K. (2002) *Exploring Corporate Strategy*. Harlow: Pearson Education.

Levitt, T. (1983) The Globalisation of Markets. *Harvard Business Review*, May/June.

Lockwood, A. and Medlik, S. (2001) *Tourism and Hospitality in the 21st Century*. Oxford: Butterworth-Heinemann.

Lynch, R. (2000) *Corporate Strategy*, 2nd edn. Harlow: Pearson Education.

Makridakis, S. (1990) *Forecasting, Planning, and Strategy for the 21st Century*. New York: Free Press.

Mintzberg, H. (1991) *The Strategy Process – Concepts, Contexts, Cases*. Englewood Cliffs, NJ: Prentice Hall.

Moutinho, L. (ed.) (2000) *Strategic Management in Tourism*. Wallingford: CABI.

Mowforth, M. and Munt, I. (1998) *Tourism and Sustainability: New Tourism in the Third World*. London: Routledge.

Peattie, K. and Moutinho, L. (2000) The marketing environment for travel and tourism, in L. Moutinho (ed.), *Strategic Management in Tourism*. Wallingford: CABI.

Poon, A. (1993) *Tourism Technology and Competitive Strategies*. Wallingford: CABI.

Sampson, A. (1984) *Empires of the Sky: The Politics, Contests and Cartels of World Airlines*. London: Hodder and Stoughton.

Sanchez, R. (1995) Strategic Flexibility, Firm Organization, and Managerial Work in Dynamic Markets: A Strategic Options Perspective. *Advances in Strategic Management*, 9, 251–91.

Sanchez, R. (1995) Strategic Flexibility in Product Competition. *Strategic Management Journal*, 16 (Summer), 135–159

Stonehouse, G.H., Hamill, J. and Purdie, A. (1999) *Global and Transnational Business – Strategy and Management*. London: John Wiley.

Strebel, P. (1992) *Breakpoints*. Cambridge, MA: Harvard Business School Press.

Turner, I. (1996) Working with Chaos. *Financial Times*, 4 October.

Vanhove, N. (2001) Globalisation of Tourism Demand, Global Distribution Systems and Marketing, in S. Wahab and C. Cooper (eds), *Tourism in the Age of Globalisation*. London: Routledge.

Vogel, H.L. (2001) *Travel Industry Economics*. Cambridge: Cambridge University Press.

WCED (World Commission on Environment and Development) (1987) *Our Common Future*. Oxford: Oxford University Press.

Weaver, D. (2000) Sustainable Tourism: Is it Sustainable?, in B. Faulkner, G. Moscardo and E. Laws (eds), *Tourism in the 21st Century: Lessons from Experience*. London: Continuum.

www.scandic-hotels.com

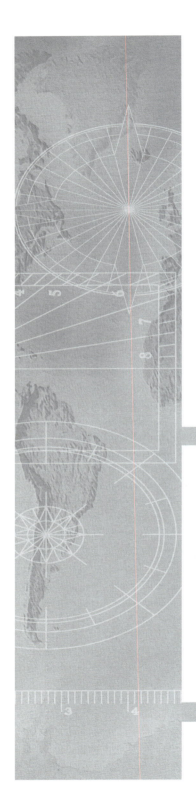

The external environment for travel and tourism organizations – the micro context

Introduction and Chapter Overview

In the introduction to Part Three, we encountered the idea that an organization's external environment comprises two strata – the macro environment and the micro environment. Chapter 7 has considered the macroenvironment (using the STEEP framework) and in this chapter we turn to an analysis of the microenvironment.

The microenvironment comprises those influences that the organization experiences frequently. For most businesses, it concerns the industries in which they operate. Within this arena, business may compete with each other or, in some circumstances, collaboration may be more appropriate. We discuss two models for industry analysis in this chapter. Then we discuss the scope of collaborative behaviour, before considering the way in which competitors in an industry fall into strategic groups.

Learning Objectives

After studying this chapter, students should be able to:

■ explain the importance of industry and market analysis;

- describe the construction and application of Porter's five forces framework;
- explain the limitations of Porter's five forces framework;
- describe how competitive analysis can be used for a nation or region;
- define and distinguish between competitive and collaborative behaviour in industries;
- describe and explain the limitations of the resource-based model of industry analysis;
- define strategic groups and describe their usefulness in competitive analysis.

Industries and markets

The importance of industry and market identification

Some strategic management texts wrongly use the terms *industry* and *market* interchangeably. Kay (1995) pointed out that to confuse the two concepts can result in a flawed analysis of the competitive environment and, hence, in flawed strategy. Modern organizations such as vertically integrated travel companies may operate in more than one industry (or industrial sector) and in more than one market. MyTravel plc (formerly Airtours), for example, is a vertically integrated UK based travel group that operates in the airline, travel intermediary (tour operator and travel distribution), accommodation and cruising sectors of the travel industry. It also has major markets in Scandinavia, continental Europe, the UK and North America. Each industry (or industrial sector) and market has its own distinctive structure and characteristics which have particular implications for the formulation of strategy. Industries are centred on the supply of a product while markets are concerned with demand. It is important, therefore, to understand and analyse both industries and markets to assist in the process of strategy selection.

Key concept: Micro- and macroenvironments

The most commonly used frameworks for analysing the external business environment distinguish between two levels or strata of environmental influence:

- The *micro- (or near) environment* is that which immediately surrounds a business, the parts of which the business interacts with frequently and over which, it may have some influence. For most purposes, we can identify competitors, suppliers and customers as comprising the main constituents of this stratum of the environment.
- The *macro- (or far) environment* comprises those influences that can affect the whole industry in which a business operates. The macro environment comprises influence arising from political, economic, sociodemographic and technological factors. The nature of these factors normally means that individual businesses are unable to influence them – strategies must usually be formulated to cope with changes in the macroenvironment.

It is sometimes difficult to define a particular industry precisely. Porter (1980) defined an industry as a group of businesses whose products are close substitutes, but this definition can be inadequate because some organizations and industries produce a range of products for different markets.

While an industry is centred upon producers of a product, a market is centred on customers and their requirements (needs and wants). A particular market consists of a group of customers with a specific set of requirements which may be satisfied by one or more products. Analysis of a market will therefore involve gaining understanding of customers, their requirements, the products which satisfy those requirements, the organizations producing the products and the means by which customers obtain those products (distribution channels).

As well as selling their products in markets, businesses also obtain their resources (labour, materials, machinery, etc.) in markets – referred to as resource markets. Additionally, most businesses are interested in markets for substitute products and they will also be keen to investigate new markets for their products.

Ways of defining and understanding markets, industries and strategic groups in strategy

Kay (1995) considered the differences between markets, industries and strategic groups. A core competence (or distinctive capability) becomes a competitive advantage only when it is applied in a market, an industry or a strategic group. Competitive advantage is a relative term in that an organization can enjoy a competitive advantage by reference to other suppliers to the same market, other organizations in the same industry, or other competitors in the same strategic group. Demand factors determine the market, while supply factors determine the industry. By way of example Kay cited Eurotunnel and P&O Ferries. Both serve the same market as they represent alternative options customers might choose in order to cross the English Channel. However, they are in very different industries in that one is a shipping company whilst the other is the manager of a large infrastructure project. The strategic group is viewed as the competitive battleground and is determined by classifying companies with similar strategies. Thus Lufthansa and British Airways are part of the same strategic group, Southwest Airlines, a low cost airline operating only domestic services in the USA, would be in a different strategic group.

It is important for organizations to identify the relevant market, industry and strategic group and to understand that they are not the same. The case of Bass, the country's largest brewer, was discussed in Chapter 3, page 61. In attempting to reposition the company through the purchase of a tour operator, the company failed to successfully distinguish between an industry and a market. A later attempt at repositioning its core business has been more fundamental and ultimately more successful. The company's core business is now firmly in the branded hotel sector and the company, now renamed SixContinents plc, owns a number of brands including: Holiday Inn, Intercontinental Hotels and Crowne Plaza.

Source: Adapted from Kay (1995)

Key concepts: Industry and market

- Industries *produce* goods and services – the supply side of the economic system.
- Markets *consume* goods and services that have been produced by industries – the demand side of the economic system.

The relationship between a business organization, its industry and markets

Analysis of its industry and markets allows an organization to:

- identify other industries where it may be able to deploy its core competences;
- understand the nature of its customers and their needs;
- identify new markets where its core competences may be exploited (see Chapter 3 for a discussion of core competences);
- identify threats from existing and potential competitors in its own and other industries;
- understand markets from which it obtains its resources.

Analysis of the competitive environment (industry and market) is important to the development of an organization's future strategy, as is analysis of the macro environment (covered in Chapter 7) and internal analysis (which was the subject of Part Two of this book). The industry and market context will play an important role in shaping an organization's competences and core competences. The core competences of a business must continually be reviewed in relation to changing customer needs, competitors' competences, and other market opportunities.

Competitive analysis

What is competitive analysis?

Competitive analysis aims to establish the nature of the competition in the industry and the competitive position of the business in relation to its product and resource markets. Industry dynamics, in turn, are affected by changes in the macroenvironment (see Chapter 7). For example, ageing populations in many developed countries have significantly affected the demand for tourism products, with the growth in cruising and long-stay holidays being but two industry responses to the trend. There is a danger that competitive analysis can be seen as a 'one off' activity, but like all components of the strategic process, it should be undertaken on an ongoing basis. The competitive analysis framework developed by Porter (1980) is the most widely used and is explained in this section.

Porter's five forces framework of competitive analysis

Porter (1980) developed a framework for analysing the nature and extent of competition within an industry. He argued that there are five competitive forces, which determine the degree of competition within an industry. Understanding the nature and strength of each of the five forces within an industry assists managers in developing the competitive strategy of their organization. The five forces are:

- The threat of new entrants to the industry.
- The threat of substitute products.
- The power of buyers or customers.
- The power of suppliers (to businesses in the industry).
- Rivalry among businesses in the industry.

By determining the relative 'power' of each of these forces, an organization can identify how to position itself to take advantage of opportunities and overcome or circumvent

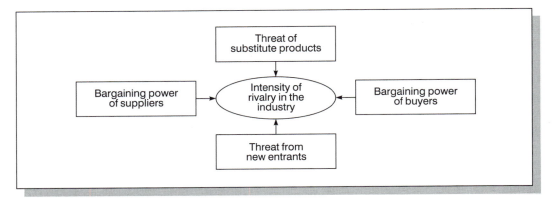

Figure 8.1 Porter's five forces framework (adapted from Porter, 1980)

threats. The strategy of an organization may then be designed to exploit the competitive forces at work within an industry.

Before considering the detailed aspects of the five forces framework, a number of points should be noted:

1 Although originally developed with commercial businesses in mind, the framework can provide valuable insights for most organizations, destinations or attractions.
2 When using Porter's framework it is important to identify which of the five forces are the key forces at work in an industry. In many cases, it transpires that one or more of the five forces prove to be 'key forces' and the strategic analysis must focus on these if it is to use the framework fruitfully.
3 The dynamic nature of the competitive environment (meaning that it is constantly changing) means that the relative strength of the forces in a particular industry will change over time. It is therefore important that the five forces analysis is repeated on a regular basis so as to detect such changes before competitors and allow an early adjustment of strategy.
4 Before any conclusions can be drawn about the nature of competition within an industry each of the five forces must be analysed in detail.
5 The framework should be based at the level of the *strategic business unit* (SBU) rather than at the level of the entire organization. That is to say, when considering the five competitive forces facing an organization it is not the entire organization that should be considered (except where the organization is simple and consists of one SBU only) but the forces should be considered in relation to constituent SBUs. This is because individual organizations may be diverse in their markets and operations. A vertically integrated travel company such as Thomson, for example (a UK subsidiary of Tui, a German company), operates tour operations, travel agents and an airline. In each of these sectors the company faces different sets of competitors, suppliers and substitutes and also faces varying regulatory processes. As Johnson and Scholes (2002) pointed out, an airline might compete simultaneously in several different arenas such as long haul, domestic and European. In each of these the airline might target different target groups, such as leisure, business and freight, and the competitive forces are different in each of these.
6 The five forces are not independent of each other, with pressures from one competitive force having the potential to trigger off changes in the other forces. For example,

potential new entrants to a market finding their route to be blocked may find new routes to the market by bypassing traditional distribution channels using agents or intermediaries and sell directly to consumers. Thus easyJet, the UK-based low cost airline, rejected distribution through travel agents and did not feature prominently on GDS systems. Instead tickets were sold directly to consumers (at first through a telephone call centre and more recently through the Internet), thereby cutting out the travel agents and the commission, which would ordinarily have been paid to them. Thus the bargaining power of one set of buyers (the travel agents) was reduced by the introduction of a new market entrant whilst the bargaining power of another set (consumers) was increased as a result of increased competition provided by the new entrant. EasyJet now sell over 90% of their flights over the Internet.

We will now discuss each of the five forces in turn in the context of various forms of travel and tourism organization.

Force 1: The threat of new entrants to the industry

The threat of entry to an industry by new competitors depends upon the 'height' of a number of entry barriers. Barriers to entry can take a number of forms.

The capital costs of entry

The size of the investment required by a business wishing to enter the industry (or industry sector) will be an important determinant of the extent of the threat of new entrants. The higher the investment required, the less will be the threat from new entrants. The lower the required investment, the greater the threat. In some areas of tourism such as the building of a hotel or a visitor attraction, starting a cruise line or launching an airline, the capital costs are clearly quite high. However, in some cases it might be possible to avoid or defer some capital costs by separating ownership from the management of the assets or by leasing. Separating ownership and management is common in the hotel sector where a property company may own the physical assets but a hotel operator manages the hotel. Leasing aircraft and ships is common in the airline and cruising sectors and allows high up-front costs to be spread out over a period of time. In other areas of travel and tourism such as starting up a tour operator or travel agency, the capital costs might be relatively low since neither require the purchase of expensive assets.

Brand loyalty and customer switching costs

If the companies in an industry produce differentiated products and customers are brand loyal, then potential new entrants will encounter resistance in trying to enter the industry. Brand loyalty will also be an important factor in increasing the costs for customers of switching to the products of new competitors. In some instances, tourism destination products are able to differentiate their products fully. There is only one Louvre art gallery in Paris where the Mona Lisa can be viewed, and the Emperor penguin can only be viewed in extreme southern latitudes. Thus customers cannot switch to new entrants if they want to experience these attractions. However, in many cases tourism consumers are driven by price and exhibit little brand loyalty. Thus consumers may switch from existing tour operators, travel agents, hotel groups, and airlines to new entrants on the basis of a more competitive offering. In some cases, however, switching costs are imposed through customer loyalty schemes such as the 'Frequent Flyer' programmes operated by the airlines.

Economies of scale or scope available to existing competitors ● ● ●

If existing competitors are already obtaining substantial economies of scale it will give them an advantage over new competitors who will not be able to match their lower unit costs of production. A new entrant offering package holidays to Spain from the major European markets (Germany, the UK and Scandinavia) would face strong competition from large entrenched operators such as TUI, First Choice and Thomas Cook. These operators often have long-standing arrangements with accommodation suppliers in Spain and, given their ability to contract bed spaces in bulk, are able to negotiate highly favourable terms which may not be available to a smaller new entrant.

Access to input and distribution channels ● ● ●

New competitors may find it difficult to gain access to channels of distribution, which will make it difficult to provide their products to customers or obtain the inputs required. In the case of the tour operator cited previously, such is the shortage of some categories of accommodation in Spain that existing operators have often contracted all the available capacity, thereby excluding new entrants to access to the necessary inputs. Furthermore, the existing large tour operators have established distribution channels (such as travel agents, call centres and the Internet) in their major markets which they have developed over the years in order to provide the most cost-efficient means of distribution. A new entrant would require heavy investment in order to secure such access.

The resistance offered by existing businesses ● ● ●

If existing competitors choose to resist strongly it will make it difficult for new organizations to enter the industry. For example, if existing businesses are obtaining economies of scale it will not be possible for new entrants to undercut prices. In some cases, existing competitors may make price cuts or increase marketing expenditure in order to deter new entrants. It has sometimes been claimed that such 'predatory' pricing behaviour has sometimes been undertaken by the large airlines in order to deter new low-cost carriers.

If barriers to entry make it difficult for new competitors to enter the industry then this will limit the amount of competition within it. As a result, competitors within the industry will attempt to seek to strengthen the barriers to entry by cultivating brand loyalty, increasing the costs of entry and 'tying up' input and distribution channels as far as is possible. Potential new entrants will lobby for the removal or reduction of such barriers in order to allow them to enter the industry and compete for business. In other words, they will try to make the industry 'contestable'.

Force 2: The threat of substitute products

A substitute can be regarded as something which meets the same needs as the product of the industry. For example, an individual wishing to cross the English Channel can choose to travel by cross channel ferry, by hovercraft or by the train service through the Channel Tunnel. These products all provide the benefit to the customer of crossing to France, despite the fact the ferry and rail services are provided by different industries. The extent of the threat from a particular substitute will depend upon two factors.

The extent to which the price and performance of the substitute can match the industry's product ● ● ●

Close substitutes whose performance is comparable to the industry's product and whose price is similar will be a serious threat to an industry. The more indirect or materially different the substitute, the less likely the price and performance will be comparable. Since most travel products are of high cost and the expenditure is usually seen as a luxury rather than a necessity, the products compete for disposable income with other high cost items such as cars and 'white goods' (refrigerators and washing machines).

The willingness of buyers to switch to the substitute ● ● ●

Buyers will be more willing to change suppliers if switching costs are low or if competitor products offer lower price or improved performance. This is also closely tied in with the extent to which customers are brand loyal. The more loyal customers are to one supplier's products (for whatever reason), then the threat from substitutes will be accordingly reduced.

Key concept: Switching costs

One of the key strategic manoeuvres in maintaining customer loyalty is to increase the cost – to the customer – of changing to a new supplier. If switching costs are high, then customers will have an economic disincentive to switch and hence will tend to stay with the existing supplier.

Competitors in an industry will attempt to reduce the threat from substitute products by improving the performance of their products, by reducing costs and prices, and by differentiation.

Force 3: The bargaining power of buyers

The extent to which the buyers (customers) of a product exert power over a supplying organization depends upon a number of factors. Broadly speaking, the more power that buyers exert, the lower will be the transaction price. This has obvious implications for the profitability of the producer.

The number of customers and the volume of their purchases ● ● ●

The fewer the buyers and the greater the volume of their purchases the greater will be their bargaining power. A large number of buyers each acting largely independently of each other and buying only small quantities of a product will be comparatively weak. Thus the major cruise lines operating in the Caribbean (of which there are relatively few) have power over the many competing small Caribbean island destinations when deciding on their cruise schedules and negotiating port charges, but individual travel agency customers have limited bargaining power when dealing with large travel agency chains which have multiple branches.

The number of businesses supplying the product and their size ● ● ●

If the suppliers of a product are large in comparison to the buyers, then buying power will tend to be reduced. The number of suppliers also has an effect – fewer suppliers will tend to reduce the bargaining power of buyers as choice and the ability to 'shop around' is reduced. Thus individual airlines wanting to serve London are faced with a situation where they have to deal with a situation where the three largest airports (Heathrow, Gatwick and Stansted) are owned and operated by a single company, BAA plc.

Switching costs and the availability of substitutes ● ● ●

If the costs of switching to substitute products are low (because the substitutes are close in terms of functionality and price), then customers will accordingly be more powerful. Customers will not be financially penalized for moving their business from one Spanish resort to another.

We should bear in mind that buyers are not necessarily those at the end of the supply chain. At each stage of a supply chain, the bargaining power of buyers will have a strong influence upon the prices charged and the industry structure.

In the supply chain for hotel rooms at destination, for example, the buyers include consumers, tour operators, airlines and other transportation groups, and event promoters. The amount of power which each buyer exerts can differ substantially. Tour operators might be able to exert far greater pressure on hotels than can individual consumers.

Force 4: The bargaining power of suppliers

Organizations must obtain the resources that they need to carry out their activities from resource suppliers. These resources fall into the five categories we have previously encountered: human, financial, operational, physical and intellectual.

Resources are obtained in resource markets where prices are determined by the interaction between the organizations supplying a resource (suppliers) and the organizations from each of the industries using the particular resource in question. It is important to note that many resources are used by more than one industry. As a result, the bargaining power of suppliers will not be determined solely by their relationship with one industry but by their relationships with all of the industries that they serve.

The major factors determining the strength of suppliers are discussed below.

The uniqueness and scarcity of the resource that suppliers provide ● ● ●

If the resources provided to the industry are essential to it and have no close substitutes then suppliers are likely to command significant power over the industry. If the resource can be easily substituted by other resources, then its suppliers will have little power. It is for this reason, for example, that people with rare or exceptional skills can command higher salaries than lesser skilled people. Similarly, the limited number of aerospace suppliers gives them considerable power. The worldwide suppliers of large jet aircraft are limited to two (Boeing of the USA and Airbus, a collaboration between France, Germany, the UK and Spain) whilst the large scale suppliers of jet aircraft engines are limited to four (General Electric and Pratt and Whitney of the USA, Rolls-Royce of the UK and SNECMA of France).

How many other industries have a requirement for the resource • • •

If suppliers provide a particular resource to several industries then they are less likely to be dependent upon one single industry. Thus, the more industries to which they supply a resource, the greater will be their bargaining power. Thus in some developed markets such as London and New York, hotels often find it difficult to recruit an adequate supply of staff as they have to compete for labour with many other industries.

Switching costs between suppliers • • •

In some cases switching between suppliers may be difficult and costly. Close working relationships may have been built up over a protracted period of time so that any new supplier would not have the necessary knowledge or experience required or systems and services may have been tailored towards the requirements of a particular supplier. Thus an airline which operated an all-Boeing fleet of aircraft would find it difficult to switch quickly to supply from Airbus since pilots would have been trained for Boeing aircraft, capacity would have been calculated using Boeing seat configurations, engineers would have been trained to maintain Boeing aircraft and parts would have been stored only for the Boeing aircraft.

The number and size of the resource suppliers • • •

If the number of organizations supplying a resource is small and the number of buyers is large, then the greater will be the power of the suppliers over the organizations in any industry. If the suppliers are small and there are a large number of them, they will be comparatively weak, particularly if they are small in comparison to the organizations buying the resource from them. For example, most of the suppliers of food and services to an international hotel group such as Sheraton are weak because they are small in comparison to the hotel company. Sheraton has a number of suppliers at its various locations and is able to switch suppliers if necessary to gain lower input costs or higher quality.

In summary, therefore, suppliers to an industry will be most powerful when:

- the resource that they supply is scarce;
- there are few substitutes for it;
- switching costs are high;
- they supply the resource to several industries;
- the suppliers themselves are large;
- the organizations in the industry buying the resource are small.

When the opposite conditions apply then suppliers will be relatively weak.

Force 5: The intensity of rivalry among competitors in the industry

Businesses within an industry will compete with each other in a number of ways. Broadly speaking, competition can take place on either a price or a non-price basis.

Price competition involves businesses trying to undercut each other's prices, which will, in turn, be dependent upon their ability to reduce costs of production. Non-price competition will take the form of branding, advertising, promotion, additional services to customers, and product innovation. In some sectors of travel and tourism competitive rivalry is fierce, while in others it is less intense or even non-existent since concentrated oligopolies or monopolies are formed. The competition amongst upscale hotels in many parts of Southeast Asia, for example, has been intense over recent years. A building boom during the 1980s and 1990s was followed by economic slowdown after 1997 which severely affected occupancy rates and led to heavy discounting of room rates. This can be contrasted with rail services in many countries such as France, Italy and Germany where state controlled enterprises hold monopoly positions.

In highly competitive markets, companies engage in regular and extensive monitoring of key competitors. Lynch (2000) cited four examples:

- examining price changes and matching any significant move immediately;
- examining any rival product change in great detail and regularly attempting new initiatives in one's own organization;
- watching investment in new competing operations;
- attempting to poach key employees.

In Figure 8.1 it can be seen that the other four forces point inwards towards this fifth force. This representation is intentionally to remind us that the strength of this force is largely dependent upon the contributions of the other four that 'feed' it. However, there are also some conditions within the industry itself that may lead specifically to a higher degree of competitive rivalry. These specific factors include the following.

The relative size of competitors

When competitors in a sector are of roughly equal size, rivalry will tend to be increased as the competing companies try to gain a greater degree of market dominance but profits will usually fall as a result of this increased rivalry. The UK outbound tour operating industry might be such a sector. Four large tour operators (Thomson, MyTravel, First Choice and Thomas Cook) have, for a number of years, jostled each other in the fight for market share and profits in the industry have proved to be somewhat volatile. Where there is a dominant organization, there may be less rivalry (and consequently higher levels of profitability) because the larger organization is often able to stop or curtail moves by smaller competitors. Air fares between Britain and South Africa, for example, have traditionally been very high as long established airlines (British Airways and South African Airways) have, with the support of national governments, kept most competition away from these particular routes, thus making them highly profitable.

The nature of costs in industry sectors

If sectors of an industry have high fixed costs in that they are capital intensive, rivalry amongst competitors may become more intense as price-cutting becomes a way of filling capacity and thus helping to dilute the high fixed costs. Thus, in the cruise sector and amongst hotels and airlines, discounting during the period close to departure or when the accommodation is required is commonplace. This is as a result of the inherent perishability of the product and the high level of fixed costs.

The maturity of the markets served

If the market is mature and thus only growing slowly, competition is likely to be more intense than a market that is still growing vigorously. This is because, in a mature market, the only way for an organization to achieve higher sales is by taking market share from competitors. This, in turn, intensifies rivalry in the industry. In markets which are still growing vigorously, however, new opportunities open up for organizations and thus sales can be increased without taking market share from competitors.

The degree of brand loyalty of customers

If customers are loyal to brands then there is likely to be less competition and what competition there is will be non-price. If there is little brand loyalty then competition will be more intense. Cruise passengers, for instance, have traditionally been very loyal to a particular cruise line and even to their preferred ship whereas North European package tourists taking Mediterranean holidays have shown themselves to be willing to switch brands freely, lured by a high level of price competition. Such brand loyalty is closely linked to a further factor – that of differentiation.

The degree of differentiation

Where products can be easily differentiated, rivalry is likely to be less intense, whereas where differentiation is difficult to achieve, rivalry is likely to be more intense. Continuing the example from above, it is relatively easy to differentiate a cruising product through the type, size, quality and crew of a ship, whereas in a package holiday to the Mediterranean, tour operators may use similar types of aircraft, accommodation, ground handling agents and distribution channels, and offer the same destination choice and consequently the opportunities to differentiate their product offerings are more limited.

Government regulation

The degree of government regulation will have an influence over the extent of competitive rivalry in a sector. The international airline industry has traditionally been heavily regulated, with governments taking direct roles in setting inter-governmental agreements in order to exert control. Accordingly, international air travel between many countries is regulated through a complex web of bilateral treaties negotiated between the governments at either end of air routes. Similarly, in the UK, the government acting through the Civil Aviation Authority's Air Travel Organizers' Licence (ATOL) system seeks to control the capacity of air inclusive tour operators. In both these cases rivalry might be more intense if government regulation ceased to exist. By contrast, government controls over the international hotel sector are rare other than through normal planning restrictions.

The height of exit barriers

The height of exit barriers (the ease with which organizations can leave an industry) will have an impact upon competitive rivalry. Where high capital costs have been incurred by the purchase of high value fixed assets such as aircraft, cruise liners or the construction of hotels or visitor attractions, it may be difficult to exit from these sectors as such assets cannot easily be put to other uses and may be difficult to sell, particularly in times of economic downturn. Consequently, overcapacity may persist in such sectors for a period of time, leading to increased rivalry between competitors. For example, overcapacity in some Asian hotel markets, such as Kuala Lumpur, Singapore and Bangkok, resulted in heavy discounting in the late 1990s and this, in turn, reduced profit margins and returns on investment.

A high degree of rivalry will usually reduce the potential profitability of an industry and may lead to innovations that serve to stimulate consumer demand for the travel and tourism products. In recent years, many sectors of the travel and tourism industry have become more competitive as the result of the influence of several factors, including technology advances, government deregulation (and in some cases privatization) and limits on supply. Thus the competition amongst European tour operators to secure hotel rooms and self catering accommodation rooms at prime Spanish resorts, the competition between European cities as short break destinations and the increased competition in the European and North American air travel markets are all examples of increasingly competitive sectors of travel and tourism.

The five forces framework and profitability – a summary

As has been discussed, a relationship can be established between an industry's or company's position in respect to the five forces and its potential profitability. Table 8.1 shows a summary of how the five forces can help to determine company and industry profitability.

Force	Profitability is likely to be higher if there is/are:	Profitability is likely to be lower if there is/are:
Bargaining power of suppliers	weak suppliers	strong suppliers
Bargaining power of buyers	weak buyers	strong buyers
Threat of new entrants	high entry barriers	low entry barriers
Threats from substitute products	few possible substitutes	many possible substitutes
Competitive rivalry	little rivalry	intense rivalry

Table 8.1 Porter's five forces and profitability – a summary

Limitations of the five forces framework

Porter's five forces framework represents a good starting point for the understanding of competitive forces and has obvious value as a tool for managers seeking a better understanding of such forces. However, the framework has been subject to several important limitations. The major limitations of the framework are as follows.

It implies that suppliers, buyers and competitors are threats • • •

The framework is built on the premise that suppliers, buyers and competitors represent threats that need to be tackled. However, some organizations have built successful strategies on the basis of building close working relationships with suppliers, buyers and competitors. *Collaborative strategy* or *partnering* has become an important part of the overall travel and tourism competitive landscape and is discussed by a number of authors, including Bennett (1997), Donne (2000), Oum and Park (1997), Rhoades and Lush (1997), and Evans (2001a) in relation to airlines; Evans (2001b) in relation to travel businesses; Dev and Klein (1993), Olsen (1993) and Go and Pine (1995) in relation to hotels; and, Buhalis and Cooper (1998) and Go and Appelman (2001) in relation destination enterprises.

It claims to assess industry profitability • • •

Porter (1980) argues that the framework makes it possible to assess the potential profitability of a particular industry. While there is some evidence to support this claim, there is also strong evidence to suggest that company-specific factors are more important to the profitability of individual businesses rather than industry factors (Rumelt, 1991).

It implies that the five forces apply equally to all competitors in an industry • • •

In reality, the strength of the forces may differ from business to business. The framework implies that if, for example, supplier power is strong then this will apply to all the businesses in the industry. In fact, supplier power may differ from business to business in the industry. Larger businesses will face less of a threat from suppliers than will smaller ones. Similarly, businesses with strong brand names will be less susceptible to buyer power and substitutes than those with weaker brands.

The European airline industry – forces driving competition

New entrants
- Relatively high entry barriers
- High capital costs for start-ups
- Well-established brands
- Some examples of tacit government support for 'flag carriers'
- Shortages of airport take-off and landing slots
- Corporate jets, low cost carriers, and regional airlines challenging larger more established airlines

Buyers
- Decreasing customer loyalty
- Airline frequent flyer programmes
- Greater choice on some routes
- Complicated and confusing fare structures
- Competition from charter carriers on some routes
- Consolidation amongst travel intermediaries

Substitutes
- Development of high speed trains, particularly in France, Italy Germany and Spain
- Extensive motorway network for car usage
- New telecommunication technologies, such as teleconferencing

Suppliers
- Oligopoly of aircraft and aircraft engine suppliers
- Oligopoly of aircraft leasing companies
- Local monopolies of infrastructure providers (airports and surface transport)
- National monopolies and undercapacity of air traffic control providers

---

Rivalry among competitors
- Varies on different routes but increasing generally
- Increasing price competition and continuing quality and service competition
- Extensive use of GDS systems and increasing use of Internet distribution
- Sophisticated yield management systems in widespread use enabling *price discrimination* to take place
- Collaboration through strategic alliances and code sharing
- Charter, regional and new low cost entrants providing increased competition for established carriers
- Established carriers adding to service quality or dropping service features to compete with new entrants
- Market liberalization during the 1990s and continuing privatization of state owned airlines
- Failure of some established airlines (Swissair and Sabena) in late 2001

In discussing the increasing rivalry amongst Europe's competing airlines, Holloway (1998) noted that the nature of competition is changing as market liberalization has enabled access for new entrants to the market. New operational practices, lower service levels, Internet distribution and operation of a single aircraft type keep costs at low levels in a manner pioneered by Southwest Airlines in the USA. New entrants to the European airline market such as Ryanair and easyJet operate highly profitable networks (Donne, 2000) and have induced new demand for air travel among the population. Intense competition among airlines has also been triggered by overcapacity resulting from over-ordering aircraft in the mid-1990s and expansion policies pursued by several major airlines. An environment of deregulation and privatization has resulted in a somewhat more open market but, congestion at several major airports, air traffic control limitations, and strong entrenched airlines have limited competition on some routes. The turbulent environment has placed a high degree of pressure on airlines to adapt in order to survive. As a sign of adaptation the formation of strategic alliances has become a defining characteristic of the global air transport sector.

The competitive analysis of nations or regions

Porter's 'diamond'

Porter's five force analysis was developed during the 1980s and has proved to be highly influential in providing a framework for the analysis of a wide variety of organizations, including those in the public and not for profit sectors. In a later work, Porter (1990) developed his ideas relating to competition and related them to countries in trying to explain why some nations are more competitive than others and some regions within countries are also more competitive than others. For a full discussion of the contribution of this framework to strategic thinking, see Stonehouse *et al.* (2000). Tourism greatly contributes to wealth creation, as it did to Spain in the 1960s and 1970s, to Greece since the early 1970s and to Turkey since the mid-1980s (Wahab and Cooper, 2001). Porter developed his 'diamond' analysis to assess the competitive advantage of nations. The diamond represents a framework consisting of four factors which individually and through the linkages between them can be used to assess the degree to which a country or region enjoys a relative competitive advantage. The four factors are:

- Factor conditions (physical resources, human resources, capital resources, infrastructure and knowledge resources).
- Market structures, organization and strategies.
- Demand conditions.
- Related and supporting industries.

In addition, Porter identified two further factors: government (which can influence any of the four factors) and chance events (which can shift competitive advantage in unpredictable ways).

In Porter's analysis each of these factors should be analysed and the relative strengths or weaknesses evaluated. An important aspect of Porter's work relates to the importance of *clusters*. Clusters are geographic concentrations of interconnected companies and institutions in a particular field. They encompass an array of linked industries and other entities which are important to competition. Thus where such clusters can be identified, a mutually supportive set of enterprises exists that compete and collaborate in such a way that may give rise to competitive advantage being established.

The Porter diamond is shown in Figure 8.2.

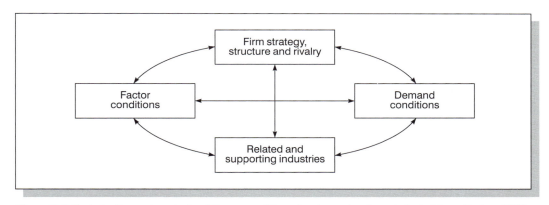

Figure 8.2 Porter's diamond analysis of the competitive advantage of nations (adapted from Porter, 1990)

In their paper, which is based on an earlier work (ECES, 1998), Wahab and Cooper (2001) discussed Porter's diamond in a tourism context and applied the analysis to Egypt. The authors concluded that whilst Egypt clearly has great potential as a tourist destination, some of the potential has yet to be realized and, consequently, the country has not yet reached a position of comparative advantage.

Improving the competitiveness of a tourist destination

A list of guidelines for improving the competitiveness of a tourist destination were produced by Smeral (1996) building on the work of Porter (1990) and reported by Wahab and Cooper (2001). The guidelines set out below include factor conditions (which are background considerations), but of specific importance to the tourism sector are market structures, organization and strategies, demand conditions and government.

1 Market structures, organization and strategies:
- Image building within the context of global competition.
- Aggressive and innovative marketing to foster growth and expansion of tourism's value-added through special interest motivations.
- Information coordination and intensification of knowledge pertaining to a destination's strengths and weaknesses within a competitive environment at the international, national and regional levels.

2 Demand conditions
- Expanding the destination's share of quality tourism movement from primary, secondary and opportunity markets, offering them quality facilities and services.
- Reducing demand seasonality through strategies aiming at guaranteeing a steady flow of tourist traffic from various markets.
- Enhancing tourist receipts by concentrating mostly on higher spending tourist arrivals.
- Encouraging repeat visitors through offering them diversified attractions separately presented or in combined forms.
- Holistically oriented local, regional and national policy.

3 Government
- Encouragement of systematic and continuous research into tourism market trends, demand changes and innovations in leisure and tourism activities.
- Serious and systematic control of and guidance to the travel and tourism industries to keep total quality at its most appropriate to face global competition.
- Improving academic and professional education and intensifying quality training in tourism to meet industry requirements.
- Eliminating 'red tape' and avoiding all administrative hurdles including any conflict or overlapping of jurisdictions.
- Ameliorating environmental quality.
- Proactive management of change and better usage of state commitments under the Free Trade in Services Agreement.

An alternative approach to competitive and collaborative analysis

Competitive and collaborative arenas

It is not always the case that businesses in an industry compete with each other – they might, from time to time, have reasons to collaborate with each other. Accordingly, in some 'arenas', businesses compete whilst in others, they may work together.

At the root of this understanding is the fact that organizations and industries are open systems – they interact with many environments. The 'arenas' in which the organization operates are described below.

- *The industry* – the industry within which the organization currently deploys its resources and competences in producing products.
- *Resource markets* – the markets from which the organization, its competitors and other industries obtain their resources.
- *Product markets* – markets where the organization sells its products. These can be subdivided into markets for the organization's products, markets for substitute products, and new markets to which the organization may be considering entry.
- *Other industries* – where businesses possess similar competences to those of the organization. Such industries are important for two reasons. The first is that the

business may be considering entry to them. The second is that the organizations in these industries are potential competitors who may enter the business's industry and markets.

Each of these arenas must be analysed as they directly affect an organization's competitive positioning and hence its chances of outperforming competitors.

The competitive and collaborative arena framework builds upon Porter's five forces framework but explicitly recognizes that the competitive environment is divided into four separate but interrelated arenas.

A resource-based approach to environmental analysis

Limitations of existing frameworks of analysis

This chapter has so far concentrated on explaining the traditional strategic management frameworks employed in the analysis of the competitive environment. The resource-based approach to strategic management, which emphasizes the importance of core competence in achieving competitive advantage, employs a different approach to analysis of the competitive environment. There are several limitations to existing (traditional) frameworks:

- they do not sufficiently integrate external and internal analysis;
- they presuppose that businesses are naturally competitive and not collaborative in their behaviour;
- they tend to emphasize product and service markets rather than those where organizations obtain their resources;
- they do not adequately recognize the fact that organizations themselves may alter their own competitive environments by their competence leveraging and building activities;
- they do not adequately recognize the fact that organizations currently outside a company's industry and market may pose a significant competitive threat if they possess similar core competences and distinctive capabilities;
- similarly, they do not recognize that the leveraging of existing competences and the building of new ones may enable businesses to compete outside their current competitive arenas.

The resource-based framework

A resource based framework for analysis of the business and its competitive environment is shown in Figure 8.3. Analysis is divided into five interrelated areas:

- the organization;
- its industry;
- product markets (existing markets, markets for substitutes, potential new markets);
- resource markets;
- other industries.

The significance of each area is considered below.

The organization · · ·

'The organization' concerns the configuration of the internal value chain, its competences, resources and core competences and is discussed in Part Two of this book (particularly in Chapter 3).

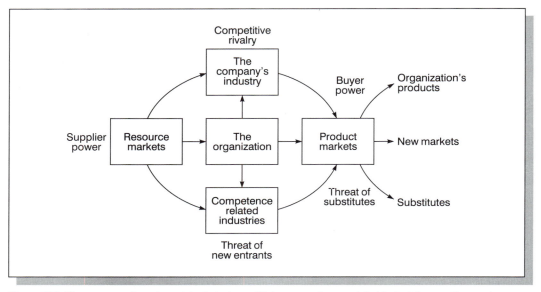

Figure 8.3 The resource based model of strategy. (Note: competence related industries are those where businesses possess similar competences to those of competitors)

The organization's industry • • •

The organization's industry consists of the business and a group of companies producing similar products, employing similar capabilities and technology.

Analysis of the industry therefore examines over time (for each player in the industry):

- the skills and competences of the competitors;
- the configuration of value adding activities;
- the technologies employed;
- the number and relative size of competitors in the industry;
- the performance of competitors (particularly in financial terms);
- ease of entry to and exit from the industry;
- strategic groupings (see later in the chapter for a discussion of this concept).

This analysis will assist the organization in gaining greater understanding of its core competences, its major competitors and their core competences, and competitive and collaborative opportunities and threats.

Product markets • • •

Product markets are those where businesses deploy their competences and sell their products and services. A business may operate in one or more product markets. In addition, a business will be interested in understanding markets to which it is considering entry on the basis of its core competences and also markets for substitute products. Each of these markets will have its own characteristics and each market can be analysed in terms of:

- customer needs and motivations;
- unmet customer needs;
- market segments and their profitability;
- the number of competitors to the market and their relative market shares;
- the number of customers and their relative purchasing power;
- access to distribution channels;
- potential for collaboration with customers;
- ease of entry;
- potential for competence leveraging;
- need for new competence building.

Unless an organization's products and services are sold at a profit, the business will ultimately fail. Market driven businesses, which set out to meet existing customer needs, anticipate their currently unmet needs and actually seek to shape the needs of their customers are likely to be the most successful.

Market leading products – the case of Center Parcs

Center Parcs (originally a Dutch company), in developing a new holiday and short break concept for northern European climates, was able to take advantage of the shift away from coastal holidays, the trend towards more activity based holidays and the commercial requirement to lengthen the season. In responding to these factors Center Parcs developed large inland sites with a variety of activities from aromatherapy to orienteering. The activities include swimming in a large enclosed sub-tropical swimming complex and indoor sports such as badminton and squash. The activities can be undertaken in all weather conditions thereby making the destination resort into an all year round attraction. The product proved innovative and attracted both high occupancy rates throughout the season and a number of imitators, such as Oasis (in the UK) which was developed by the Rank Organization as a me too product and was subsequently taken over by Center Parcs. The high quality and diversity of the facilities and the siting in scenic rural retreats away from the perceived tackiness of the seaside allowed the company to attract largely high spending middle class customers. Such customers are often taking a second holiday in traditionally non-peak periods of the year for northern European climates.

Market subgroups

An important part of understanding the market is identifying subgroups within the market that share common needs. Such shared characteristics will cause specific customer groups to have different needs and to act and behave differently to other customer groups (or *segments*). Fundamentally, segmentation means subdividing the total market into customer subgroupings, each with their own distinctive attributes and needs. Customer groups are commonly segmented according to demographic variables (or 'people dividers'), like age, sex, occupation, socio-economic grouping, race, lifestyle, buying habits, geography (i.e. where they live). When customers are other businesses, they can be grouped by the nature of the business, organization type and by their size. Each segment is then analysed for its size and potential profitability, for customer needs and for potential demand, based on ability and willingness to buy. Segmentation analysis assists in the formulation of strategy by identifying particular segments and consumer characteristics, which can be targeted. The concept of market segmentation was discussed in greater depth in Chapter 6.

Customer motivations • • •

Once market segments have been identified, they must be analysed to reveal the factors that influence customers to buy or not buy products. It is particularly important to understand factors affecting customer motivations such as:

- sensitivity to price;
- sensitivity to quality;
- the extent of brand loyalty.

Differences in customer motivations between market segments can be illustrated by reference to the market for air travel. The market can be segmented into business and leisure travel. Customers in each group have very different characteristics and needs. Business travellers are not particularly price-sensitive but are sensitive to standards of service, to scheduling, and to availability of connections. Leisure travellers on the other hand are generally much more price rather than service conscious and are less sensitive to scheduling and connections. Market research has an important role to play in building understanding of customer needs so that they can be targeted by appropriate product or service features.

Potential new markets are those where the product or service bought by customers is based upon similar competences to those of the organization or where customer needs are similar to those of customers in the business's market. If conditions are favourable the organization may consider using its current competences to enter new markets. Of course it may also have to build new competences in order to be able to meet new customer needs.

Resource markets • • •

Resource markets are those where organizations obtain finance, human resources, materials, equipment, services, etc. It is evident that businesses will normally operate in several such markets, each with its own characteristics, depending upon the company-specific resources that are required. Resource markets can be analysed in terms of:

- resource requirements;
- number of actual and potential resource suppliers;
- size of suppliers;
- supplier capabilities and competences;
- potential for collaboration with resource suppliers;
- access by competitors to suppliers;
- the nature of the resource and the availability of substitutes.

By analysing each of its resource markets, the managers of a business can identify the extent of competition that they face from suppliers of resources, the competition that they face from other competitors using the same resources, and the potential for collaboration with suppliers (if appropriate).

Competence related industries ● ● ●

Other industries comprising businesses possessing similar competences and which often produce products which are substitutes for those of the business in question must also be analysed. This analysis is necessary for three reasons. First, the organization may face a threat from other competitors possessing similar competences, which may seek to enter its industry and markets. Second, the organization may be able to enter industries where competences are similar to those which it already possesses. Third, the organization may be able to enter the markets currently served by competitors in the competence related industry.

Competence related industries can be analysed for:

- key competences of the businesses in the industry;
- the number and size of the businesses in the industry;
- the threat from competitors in such industries who may leverage their competences to enter the markets of the business;
- opportunities for the business to leverage its existing competences and build new ones in order to enter competence related industries and their markets;
- substitutability of the products of the industry for those of the business – how close the substitute product is to satisfying the same consumer demands as the business's product or service.

A summary of the resource-based model

The competence/resource-based model is more complex than the five forces framework but offers a more comprehensive analytical framework. It enables an organization to establish the extent of competition within its own industry and market. It also enables the organization to assess the threat of competition from competitors in industries where similar competences to their own are employed. Equally, based on this model, the organization is able to identify other markets, which it may be able to enter by leveraging its existing competences and by adding new ones.

Once adapted the framework enables managers to:

- understand the nature of competition within the industry and markets (both product and resource) in which they operate;
- understand the threat from competitors in other industries;
- understand potential opportunities in new industries and markets.

Strategic group analysis

What are strategic groups?

A business can rarely confine its analysis to the level of the industry and markets in which it operates. It must also pay particular attention to its closest competitors who are known as its 'strategic group' (Porter, 1980). Strategic groups cannot be precisely defined but they consist of organizations possessing similar competences, serving customer needs in the same market segment and producing products or services of similar quality. Such analysis allows the managers of a business to compare its performance to that of its closest competitors in terms of profitability, market share, products, brands, customer loyalty, prices and so on. In this way managers are able to *benchmark* the performance of their organization against their closest rivals.

In the accommodation industry, for example, we can observe a number of important strategic groupings. Although the London Ritz Hotel and a small Blackpool guesthouse both provide the same service (providing accommodation and meals for guests) – and hence are technically competitors – they operate in quite different strategic groups. They are unlikely to appeal to the same customers and their products, distribution channels, identities and prices are quite different. The Ritz strategic group will include other luxury hotels in London and key world capitals, whereas the Blackpool guesthouse strategic group will include other Blackpool guesthouses and those at competing resorts.

Strategic group analysis (sometimes called competitive group analysis) is an interesting way of analysing the competitive structure in an industry and assessing the positioning of key competitors. By plotting how the major organizations in an industry (or a sub-sector within it) compete along two competitive dimensions, managers start to understand the relative position of their company and its products or services relative to major competitors.

There are three steps involved in the analysis and graphical representation of strategic groups.

1 Identify the important competitive dimensions in an industry, taking into account the information available. Competitive dimensions are the specific factors the firms are using to compete within the industry. The competitive dimensions might include factors such as quality (perceived or actual), price, geographical scope or typical customer types.
2 Construct two-dimensional plots of the competitive dimensions.
3 Analyse the firm's position relative to competitors.

Competitor profiling

Strategic group analysis enables an organization to identify its key competitors. A useful further step is to profile these key competitors in order to gain a more detailed insight as to how and where the competitors might pose a threat or under what circumstances might collaboration be sought. Such an analysis might be carried out using the following headings:

- Overview
- Objectives
- Resources
- Past record of performance
- Current products and services
- Present strategies.

Competitor profiling – Whitbread plc

A hotel operator seeking to expand in the UK hotel industry would need to profile existing key competitors. One of these would certainly be Whitbread plc which holds the master franchise for Marriott hotels in the UK and has developed the leading brand of 'Lodge' hotels which offer 'value for money' accommodation with few 'add-ons'.

Overview: The UK Company Whitbread plc was a major brewer founded in the middle of the nineteenth century. The end of the twentieth century and the start of the twenty-first marked a watershed in the company's history, as Whitbread sold its breweries and then exited its pubs and bars business. After several decades of diversification, during which the beer and pubs giant branched out into new markets, Whitbread re-focused its business on the growth areas of hotels, restaurants and health and fitness clubs. The reinvention of Whitbread as a leading UK leisure business naturally coincided with the end of the brewing and pub-owning tradition which Samuel Whitbread had begun so many decades before.

Objectives: The priorities, on behalf of shareholders, are to grow the business and to achieve annual improvements in the return on their capital. The business is focused on growth sectors of the UK leisure market – lodging, eating out and active leisure.

Resources: The company has a turnover of some £3.5 billion a year with profits standing at over £300 million. Approximately 60 000 people are employed by the company, of which about 20 000 are employed by the hotel businesses.

Past record of performance: The company has consistently recorded adequate levels of profitability but in recent years some variability in profits has been apparent. The repositioning of the company to move away from brewing and bars to focus on three core areas in which it possesses strong brands has started to show results. Between 1993 and 2001 Whitbread was Britain's fastest growing hotel company, developing more hotels and more rooms than any other operator and the Whitbread Hotel Company accounts for approximately 59 per cent of the group's profits.

Current products: In the hotel sector the company has a two-pronged assault, based on consistent value for money budget hotels and internationally branded four-star hotels in the fast growing UK hotel market.

Present strategies: The company is trying to achieve its stated objectives through:

- Growing the profitability, scale and market share of the company's leading brands.
- Seeking new brands that have the potential to reach significant scale.
- Managing the business so that economic value is added by each of the activities.
- Ensuring that each of the brands is a leader in its field for customer service.
- Becoming the employer of choice in the UK leisure industry.
- Working to meet responsibilities to the wider stakeholders in the business, including commercial partners and the communities in which the company's brands operate.

Adapted from: www.whitbread.co.uk

References and further reading

Arthur, W.B. (1996) Increasing Returns and the New World of Business. *Harvard Business Review*, 74, July/August, 100–111.

Aaker, D.A. (1992) *Strategic Market Management*. New York: John Wiley.

Abell, D.F. (1980) *Defining the Business: The Starting Point of Strategic Planning*. Englewood Cliffs, NJ: Prentice Hall.

Baden-Fuller, C. and Stopford, J. (1992) *Rejuvenating the Mature Business*. Oxford: Routledge.

Bennett, M.M. (1997) Strategic Alliances in the World Airline Industry. *Progress in Tourism and Hospitality Research*, 3, 212–223.

Buhalis, D. and Cooper, C. (1998) Competition or Co-operation? Small and Medium Sized Tourism Enterprises at the Destination, in E. Laws, B. Faulkner and G. Moscardo (eds), *Embracing and Managing Change in Tourism – International Case Studies*. London: Routledge.

Campbell, D., Stonehouse, G. and Houston, B. (1999) *Business Strategy: An Introduction.* Oxford: Butterworth-Heinemann.

Chakravarthy, B. (1997) A New Strategy Framework for Coping with Turbulence. *Sloan Management Review,* Winter, pp 69–82.

D'Aveni, R.A. (1994) *Hypercompetition: Managing the Dynamics of Strategic Manoeuvring.* New York: Free Press.

Dev, C.S. and Klein, S. (1993) Strategic Alliances in the Hotel Industry. *Cornell Hotel and Restaurant Administration Quarterly,* February, pp 43–45.

Donne, M. (2000) The Future of International Airline Alliances. *Travel and Tourism Analyst,* 6, 3–21.

ECES, Egyptian Center for Economic Studies (1998) Egypt: The Tourism Cluster, Final Report, Phase 1.

Evans, N. (2001a) Collaborative Strategy: an Analysis of the Changing World of International Airline Alliances. *Tourism Management,* 22, 229–243.

Evans, N. (2001b) Alliances in the International Travel Industry: Sustainable Strategic Options? *International Journal of Hospitality and Tourism Administration,* 2(1), 1–26.

Ginter, P. and Duncan, J. (1990) Macro-environmental analysis. *Long Range Planning,* December, 91–100.

Go, F M. and Pine, R. (1995) *Globalisation Strategy in the Hotel Industry.* London: International Thomson Business Press.

Go, F.M. and Appelman, J. (2001) Achieving Global Competitiveness in SMEs by Building Trust in Interfirm Alliances, in S. Wahab and C. Cooper (eds), *Tourism in the Age of Globalisation.* London: Routledge.

Hamel, G. and Prahalad, C.K. (1989) Strategic intent. *Harvard Business Review,* 67(3), 63–76.

Hamel, G. and Prahalad, C.K. (1994) *Competing for the Future.* Cambridge, MA: Harvard Business School Press.

Heene, A. and Sanchez, R. (1997) *Competence-based Strategic Management.* New York: John Wiley.

Helms, M.M. and Wright, P. (1992) External Considerations: Their Influence on Future Strategic Planning. *Management Decision,* 30(8), 4–16.

Holloway, S. (1998) *Changing Planes: A Strategic Management Perspective on an Industry in Transition.* Aldershot: Ashgate.

Johnson, G. and Scholes, K. (2002) *Exploring Corporate Strategy,* 6th edn. Harlow: Pearson Education.

Kay, J. (1993) *Foundations of Corporate Success.* Oxford: Oxford University Press.

Lynch, R. (2000) *Corporate Strategy,* 2nd edn. Harlow: Pearson Education.

McGahan, A.M. and Porter, M.E. (1997) How Much Does Industry Matter, Really? *Strategic Management Journal,* 18 (Summer special issue), 15–30.

Olsen, M.D. (1993) International Growth Strategies of Major US Hotel Companies. *Travel and Tourism Analyst,* 3, 51–64.

Oum, T.H. and Park J.H. (1997) Airline Alliances: Current Status, Policy Issues, and Future Directions. *Journal of Air Transport Management,* 3(3), 133–144.

Porter, M.E. (1979) How Competitive Forces Shape Strategy. *Harvard Business Review,* March/April.

Porter, M.E. (1980) *Competitive Strategy: Techniques for Analysing Industries and Competitors.* New York: Free Press.

Porter, M.E. (1985) *Competitive Advantage.* New York: Free Press.

Porter, M.E. (1990) The *Competitive Advantage of Nations.* London: Macmillan.

Prahalad, C.K. and Hamel, G. (1990) The Core Competence of the Organization. *Harvard Business Review,* 68(3), 79–93.

Rhoades, D.L. and Lush, H. (1997) A Typology of Strategic Alliances in the Airline Industry: Propositions for Stability and Duration. *Journal of Air Transport Management,* 3(3), 109–114.

Rumelt, R.P. (1991) How Much Does Industry Matter? *Strategic Management Journal,* 12(3), 167–186.

Simonian, H. (1996) Star Parts for Bit Players. *Financial Times,* 28 October.

Smeral, E. (1996) Globalisation and Changes

in the Competitiveness of Tourism Destinations, in *Globalisation and Tourism, Editions AIEST*, St Gallen, Switzerland: Editions AIEST.

Stonehouse, G., Hamill, J., Campbell, D.J. and Purdie, A. (2000) *Global and Transnational Business – Management and Strategy*. Chichester: John Wiley.

Strebel, P. (1992) *Breakpoints*. Cambridge, MA: Harvard Business School Press.

Turner, I. (1996) Working with Chaos. *Financial Times*, 4 October.

Wahab, S. and Cooper, C. (2001) Tourism, Globalisation and the Competitive Advantage of Nations, in S. Wahab and C. Cooper (eds), *Tourism in the Age of Globalisation*. London: Routledge.

www.whitbread.co.uk

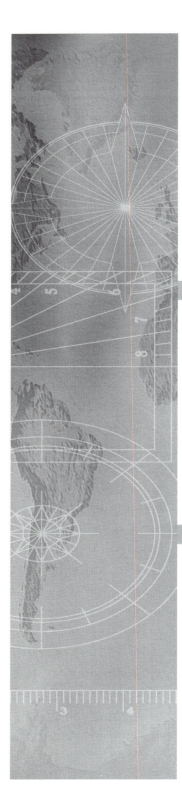

CHAPTER 9

SWOT analysis

SWOT analysis (sometimes referred to as TOWS analysis, particularly in the USA), is an acronym where the letters stand for Strengths, Weaknesses, Opportunities and Threats. The analysis has become a major analytical tool and has become firmly established in the literature. Although it is the most widely used technique for summarizing the results of the various types of analysis described in the previous chapters, it nevertheless can be undertaken in various ways. Consequently, different approaches are advocated in the many texts which cover this analytical technique, but here a structured and logical approach is suggested. The chapter first covers the general principles of SWOT analysis before going on to consider how the analysis should be carried out.

After studying this chapter, students should be able to:

- explain what is meant by SWOT analysis;

- understand the relationship between the SWOT presentation and detailed internal and external analyses;

- describe how a SWOT should be constructed;

- consider the way in which points can be presented in a SWOT;

- apply the SWOT analysis principles to travel and tourism organizations;

- understand the relationship between the SWOT analysis and strategic formulation.

General principles

Some basics

The strengths and weaknesses are based on the internal analysis of an organization (which was covered in Chapters 3 to 6) and the opportunities and threats are based on analysis of the environment that is external to the organization (which was covered in Chapters 7 and 8). The key distinguishing characteristic between the strengths and weaknesses on the one hand and the opportunities and threats on the other is the degree of control that managers may have. With the internal strengths and weaknesses managers can exert control whereas with regard to the opportunities and threats, managers may not be able to control such factors. If, for instance, the organization has a strong balance sheet (a strength) this will have resulted from managerial decisions. If, instead, the organization is seen as being overstaffed (a weakness), managers can address the issue through reducing staff numbers. However, by way of example, changing government policies, product changes by competitors or a war breaking out (all of which might produce opportunities or threats to an individual organization depending on the circumstances) are beyond the control of managers.

Key concept: SWOT

SWOT is the key technique for presenting the results of strategic analysis, which provides a platform for going on to formulate the strategy for the future. The strengths and weaknesses should be based upon the internal analysis of the organization whilst the opportunities and threats should be based upon an analysis of the organization's external environment.

Although it is very common in practice to begin the process of formulating strategy by asking the participants in a rather informal way to draw up a SWOT for their organization, such a process represents a limited use of the technique. It is, however, useful for getting the participants to become quickly and fully engaged in the process of strategy formulation (Finlay, 2000). It can also help identify the wide range of factors that might warrant further more detailed investigation. The final SWOT presented should however be based on a thorough, wide-ranging and detailed audit and assessment of an organization and its environment so that points presented are evidence based and thus can be fully justified. Thus the SWOT should be seen primarily as representing the end point of the analysis (rather than the starting point) in which findings can be presented in a clear, concise manner.

The SWOT represents a *position statement,* stating where the organization is at the time of the analysis in relation to its environment. It is not the strategy itself and should not involve making statements about what should be done next. Instead it provides a firm platform for planning for the future of the organization, i.e. formulating the strategy which is the next stage in the strategic process.

SWOT implementation

How it is constructed

The SWOT is often presented in a table. Figure 9.1 shows a SWOT and its underlying logic.

	Factors which help the organization achieve its objectives	Factors which prevent the organization achieving its objectives
Internal factors under the control of managers	Strength	Weakness
External factors outside the control of managers	Opportunity	Threat

Figure 9.1 The logic of SWOT analysis (adapted from Wickham, 2000)

The SWOT should have a strategic focus in that it concentrates on those factors which have:

- A major impact on past performance.
- A major impact on future performance.
- Distinguish the organization from its competitors.

In presenting the SWOT table, a number of rules should be followed.

- Too much detail should be avoided so that the key points can be clearly seen. Each point should be kept short and to the point, so that an overview can quickly be gained. The detailed justifications for the points presented in the table should be presented separately.
- Many of the points presented in the SWOT may be relative rather than absolute and consequently a matter of some judgement. Thus it is difficult to say at exactly what level a high level of financial gearing becomes a weakness or a share of a particular market becomes a strength.
- The SWOT should not concentrate solely on 'hard' facts (such as financial measures or market growth statistics) that can be measured or proved. Softer factors such as organizational culture or the leadership skills exhibited by managers may be more difficult to measure but they are nevertheless important for organizational performance.
- The analysis should prioritize and combine points. The most important points should be shown first and points that are not key or strategic in nature should be excluded. In some

cases it may be necessary to combine smaller points to make one large overarching point. For example, if a SWOT is partly based on a financial analysis of an organization which indicates a strong financial position, the SWOT should not have individual points on high level of profitability, low gearing, adequate liquidity, etc. for to do so would confuse the presentation. The point presented in the SWOT should be that the organization has a strong financial position. The justification for making such a point would be provided by the assessments relating to profitability, gearing liquidity and so on.

- The presentation should be specific, avoiding blandness and be realistic in its assessment.

Typical contents

In his analysis of the problems of presenting a valid SWOT, Lynch (2000) stated that 'probably the biggest mistake that is commonly made in SWOT analyses is to assume the analysis is bound to be "correct" if it contains every conceivable issue and is truly comprehensive'. This is not the case: 'it merely demonstrates a paucity of real thought and

Internal	
Strengths	*Weaknesses*
• Market dominance • Core strengths • Economies of scale • Low-cost position • Leadership and management skills • Financial and cash resources • Operational ability and age of equipment • Innovation processes and results • Organizational structure • Reputation • Differentiated products • Good balance of products • Product or service quality	• Share weakness • Few core strengths and low on key skills • Old equipment with higher costs than competition • Weak finances and poor cash flow • Management skills and leadership lacking • Poor organizational structure • Low quality and reputation • Products not differentiated • Dependent on few products • Products concentrated in mature or declining PLC stages • Low market share
External	
Opportunities	*Threats*
• New markets and segments • New products • Diversification opportunities • Market growth • Competitor weaknesses • Strategic space • Demographic and social change • Change in political and economic environment • New take-over or partnership opportunities • Economic upturn • International growth	• New market entrants • Increased competition • Increased pressure from customers and suppliers • Substitutes • Low market growth • Economic cycle downturn • Technological threat • Change in political or economic environment • Demographic change • New international barriers to trade • Environmental impacts of activities • New destinations

Figure 9.2 Some possible factors in a SWOT analysis (adapted from Lynch, 2000)

Internal	
Strengths	*Weaknesses*
• Airports used are more convenient than those used by other no-frills airlines • Management flexibility • Lower costs than established airlines • Ease of booking flights • Recognized logo and corporate image • Use of IT facilities • Better than average employee relations	• Airports used have poorer facilities and are less convenient than those used by big carriers • Poor reputation for punctuality • Cash flows • No long term safety record • Poorer than average customer service
External	
Opportunities	*Threats*
• Strong business demand for cheap air fares • Strong leisure demand for cheap air fares • Increasing use of the Internet • Many secondary airports underused	• The further entry of subsidiaries of the big carriers • Existing carriers changing to 'no-frills' mode of operations • Higher airport charges • Increasing competition from charter carriers

Figure 9.3 A SWOT analysis for a 'no frills' airline (adapted from Finlay, 2000)

a lack of strategic judgement about what is really important for the organization' have been employed in its preparation.

'Another common error is to provide a long list of points but little logic, argument and evidence. A short list with each point well argued is more likely to be convincing' (Lynch, 2000). In order to keep the SWOT focused it is suggested that a maximum of seven points should be presented under each of the SWOT headings. However, it might be the case that in some circumstances the overriding importance of certain points mean that far fewer than six points are presented.

In Figure 9.2 a number of issues are presented for possible inclusion in a SWOT presentation. It should be noted that this list is indicative since the issues will vary enormously depending upon individual circumstances.

In presenting an example of implementing a SWOT, Finlay (2000) applied the concept to a fictitious 'no frills' airline, which has newly entered the airline market. The example is shown in Figure 9.3.

Summary

Although it has been supplemented by more recent techniques, SWOT is a tool that is widely used and understood by students and managers. It should represent a solid foundation for moving on to strategic formulation but care has to be taken in implementing the SWOT so as to ensure it is not bland, and is fully supported by the evidence that is available. Crucially, as Haberberg and Rieple (2001) point out in their comprehensive treatment of the subject area, the SWOT analysis should not be viewed as the start of the analysis. Instead, 'in order to arrive at a proper SWOT appraisal, other analyses need to be carried out first'.

References and further reading

Coulter, M. (2002) *Strategic Management in Action*, 2nd edn. Englewood Cliffs, NJ: Prentice Hall.

Finlay, P. (2000) *Strategic Management: An Introduction to Business and Corporate Strategy*. Harlow: Pearson Education.

Haberberg, A. and Rieple, A. (2001) *The Strategic Management of Organizations*. Harlow: Pearson Education.

Knowles, T. (1996) *Corporate Strategy for Hospitality*. Harlow: Longman.

Lynch, R. (2000) *Corporate Strategy*. Harlow: Pearson Education.

Middleton, V.T.C. and Clarke, J. (2001) *Marketing in Travel and Tourism*, 3rd edn. Oxford: Butterworth-Heinemann.

Stevenson, H.H. (1989) Defining Corporate Strengths and Weaknesses, in D. Asch and C. Bowman (eds), *Readings in Strategic Management*. Basingstoke: Macmillan in association with The Open University.

Wickham, P.A. (2000) *Financial Times Corporate Strategy Casebook*. Harlow: Pearson Education.

Part Four

Strategic choices

Introduction

The previous two parts of this book have been concerned with strategic analysis and culminated in the bringing together of available information in order to present a clear view of the current position of the organization being considered. Establishing the current position is a necessary prerequisite for moving on to consider the options available to travel and tourism organizations for future development. In Part Four we turn towards the future by considering the strategic choices travel and tourism organizations have to make. Strategic choices are concerned with making the decisions about an organization's future and the way in which it needs to respond to the many pressures and influences (Johnson and Scholes, 2002), which were discussed in previous chapters.

Specifically strategic choice is concerned with three stages:

1 Formulating options for future development.
2 Evaluating between available options.
3 Selecting which options should be chosen.

Many travel and tourism organizations are complex in terms of the scope and scale of their operations and in the way that they are managed. The nature of the industry is such that many such organizations may:

• be operating internationally;
• comprise many different departments or divisions;
• have operations that are geographically scattered;
• have a large centralized head office or a small head office with dispersed authority.

As a result of this complexity it is common to distinguish between various levels of strategic choice, although textbooks often vary in their definition and scope of these levels. The approach adopted in this text broadly follows the approach adopted by Johnson and Scholes (2002). Three levels of organizational strategy are discernible: corporate level, business level and the operational level. However, it must be said at the outset that the boundaries between the levels are often unclear, particularly in smaller organizations where frequently the levels will effectively merge together.

A full discussion of the corporate level is beyond the scope of this text. The reader is referred to Johnson and Scholes and (2002), Finlay (2000) and Haberberg and Rieple (2001) for a more detailed coverage. The operational level strategy issues are concerned with the more detailed implementation issues, which are considered in Part Five. The reader is also referred to Johnson and Scholes (2002), Bennett (1996) for a generic discussion and Moutinho (2000) and Phillips and Moutinho (1998) for a discussion in a tourism and hospitality context. The focus of this section of the text is thus primarily at the business level of strategy.

Corporate level strategy

Strategy at this level is concerned with the overall purpose and scope of an organization. This might include the broad determination of which business areas or geographical areas the organization might want to be involved with. Clearly this area of strategic choice is thus closely involved with the organization's mission and its manifestation in the form of a mission statement. Thus in the 1990s Bass plc (once the UK's largest brewer and bar operator), sold its brewing interests and most of its pubs. The proceeds raised from these disposals were used to invest in hotels primarily through the purchase of the Holiday Inn and Inter Continental chains. This was clearly a corporate level decision to entirely refocus the business, which culminated in 2001 with the renaming of the company as Six Continents plc, recognition that the company had been transmogrified from a largely domestic brewer into a global hotel operating company.

Business level strategy

Strategy at this level is concerned with how to compete successfully in certain markets. The focus is not upon the entire organization (as in corporate level strategy) but upon breaking the entire organization down into its constituent parts, i.e. its strategic business units (SBUs). The concerns at this level of strategy include:

- How can advantage over competitors be achieved?
- Which products or services should be developed in which markets?
- What methods can be used to achieve competitive advantage and to develop products and services?

These three concerns of business level strategy can be addressed by considering:

- The bases of competition – *Competitive strategy.*
- The direction of development – *Strategic direction.*
- The methods of development – *Strategic methods.*

These three aspects of strategic formulation (which are summarized in Figure 1) will be covered in this part of the book. Competitive strategy and strategic direction are considered in Chapter 10, while strategic methods are discussed in Chapter 11.

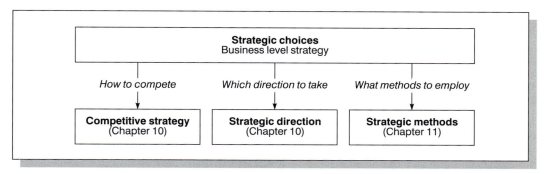

Figure 1 The three aspects of business level strategy

Operational level strategy

Strategy at this level is concerned with the more detailed implementation issues relating to how the proposed corporate and business level strategies can successfully be put into practice. The concern here is how the changes arising from the adoption of corporate and business level strategies can be managed effectively and on the detailed decisions that have to be made in each area of the organization to implement the higher order decisions.

Once strategic options for the future have been identified it is necessary for them to be evaluated and the most appropriate strategies should be selected. The evaluation and selection of strategies are considered in Chapter 12.

References and further reading

Bennett, R. (1996) *Corporate Strategy and Business Planning*. London: Pitman.

Finlay, P. (2000) *Strategic Management: an Introduction to Business and Corporate Strategy*. Harlow: Pearson Education.

Haberberg, A. and Rieple, A. (2001) *The Strategic Management of Organizations*. Harlow: Pearson Education.

Johnson, G. and Scholes, K. (2002) *Exploring Corporate Strategy*, 6th edn. Harlow: Pearson Education.

Moutinho, L. (2000) *Strategic Management in Tourism*. Wallingford: CABI.

Phillips, P.A. and Moutinho, L. (2000) *Strategic Planning Systems in Hospitality and Tourism*. Wallingford: CABI.

Competitive strategy and strategic direction for travel and tourism organizations

Introduction and Chapter Overview

This chapter is concerned with two aspects of strategic formulation:

- The bases of competition – *competitive strategy.*
- The direction of development – *strategic direction.*

An important point is that the focus of strategy at this level is not upon the entire organization (as in corporate level strategy) but upon breaking the entire organization down into its constituent parts, i.e. its strategic business units (SBUs). The concerns at this level of strategy include:

- How can advantage over competitors be achieved?
- Which products or services should be developed in which markets?

The study of strategic management offers several explanations of how competitive advantage can be achieved and sustained. This chapter focuses on two of the major explanations of competitive advantage: competitive positioning and core competence.

The *competitive positioning* approach is based largely upon Porter's generic strategy framework (Porter, 1980, 1985). The *core competence* or *resource-based* approach explains competitive advantage in terms of the development and exploitation of an organization's core competences (see Chapter 3). These two approaches can be seen as complementary and mutually enriching rather than mutually exclusive. The two frameworks are first explored separately and then the linkages between them are developed.

The chapter ends with a discussion of the general mechanisms that organizations employ to grow and develop in order to sustain and develop their competitive advantage strategic directions. We use the Ansoff matrix as a starting point for this discussion.

Learning Objectives

After studying this chapter, students should be able to:

- explain the concept of competitive advantage;
- describe and evaluate Porter's generic strategy framework;
- describe and evaluate the strategy clock and Poon's tourism competitive strategy concepts;
- explain the concept of hybrid strategy;
- explain the role of core competences and distinctive capabilities in building competitive advantage;
- explain the role of the value chain in linking core competences and generic strategies;
- identify the strategic direction available to organizations;
- identify where core competences and strategies can be exploited;
- provide illustrative examples from travel and tourism of competitive strategy and strategic directions.

Competitive strategy

Competitive strategy is concerned with the bases on which a strategic business unit might achieve competitive advantage in its chosen market or markets. For public service or publicly funded organizations such as tourist offices, museums and art galleries or historic monuments, the concern is with an equivalent issue. Here the concern can be expressed in terms of the bases on which the organization chooses to sustain the quality of its services within agreed budgets or, as it is often expressed; how it provides 'best value'.

Michael Porter's generic strategies

Introduction

Perhaps the oldest and best-known explanation of competitive advantage is given by Porter in his *generic strategy* framework. Although this framework has been increasingly called into question in recent years, it still provides useful insight into competitive behaviour. The framework and its limitations are considered in this section. Perhaps its main use is that it provides a framework that forces managers to think about the underlying basis upon which they are attempting to compete.

According to Porter (1985), competitive advantage arises from selection of the generic strategy which best fits the organization's competitive environment and then organizing value adding activities to support the chosen strategy. There are three main alternatives:

- *differentiation* – creating a customer perception that a product is superior to those of competitors so that a premium price can be charged;
- *cost leadership* – being the lowest cost producer of a product so that above-average profits are earned even though the price charged is not above average;
- *focus* – utilizing either a differentiation or cost leadership strategy in a narrow profile of market segments (possibly just one segment).

Any organizations that fail to make a strategic decision to opt for one of these strategic stances is in danger of being 'stuck in the middle' (to use Porter's terminology). In other words, the organization in failing to decide, tries both to be the cost leader and the differentiator and achieves neither, and in the process confuses consumers.

Porter's generic strategy framework

Porter argues that an organization must make two key decisions on its strategy:

- Should the strategy be one of differentiation or cost leadership?
- Should the scope of the strategy be broad or narrow?

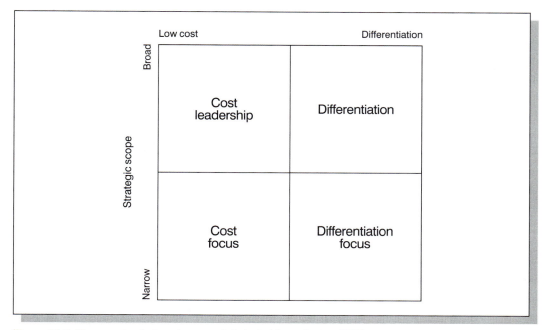

Figure 10.1 The generic strategy framework (adapted from Porter, 1985)

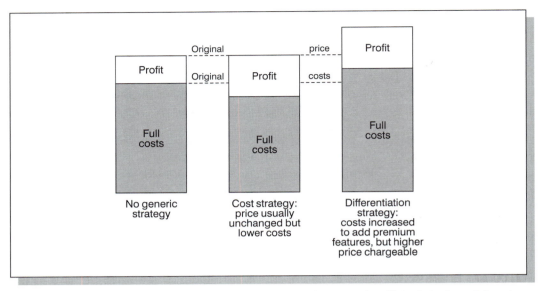

Figure 10.2 A simplified understanding of cost and differentiation strategies. (Note that price = full costs plus profits)

In other words, the organization must decide whether to try to differentiate its products and sell them at a premium price or whether to gain competitive advantage by producing at a lower cost than its competitors. Higher profits can be made by adopting either approach. Second, it must decide whether to target the whole market with its chosen strategy or whether to target a specific segment or niche of the market.

Cost leadership strategy

A cost leadership strategy is based upon a business organizing and managing its value adding activities so as to be the lowest cost producer of a product (a good or service) within an industry.

There are several potential benefits of a cost leadership strategy:

- The business can earn higher profits by charging a price equal to, or even below that of competitors because its costs are lower.
- It allows the business the possibility to increase both sales and market share by reducing price below that charged by competitors (assuming that the product's demand is price elastic in nature).
- It allows the business the possibility to enter a new market by charging a lower price than competitors.
- It can be particularly valuable in a market where consumers are price sensitive.
- It creates an additional barrier to entry for organizations wishing to enter the industry.

Value chain analysis is central to identifying where cost savings can be made at various stages in the value chain and its internal and external linkages (see Chapter 3).

A successful cost leadership strategy is likely to rest upon a number of organizational features. Attainment of a position of cost leadership depends upon the arrangement of value chain activities. Examples of how costs savings might be achieved include the following.

- Reducing costs by copying rather than originating product design features. For example, a tour operator might copy the design and functions of an existing web site developed by a competitor.
- Using less expensive resource inputs. For example, easyJet, the 'no frills' airline, lowers costs by substituting operational resources in the form of computer technology for more expensive labour inputs by using the Internet as its primary source of bookings.
- Producing products with 'no frills', thus reducing labour costs and increasing labour productivity. For example the low cost so-called no frills airlines such as Southwest Airlines in the United States and Ryanair, easyJet, Go and Buzz in the UK have removed additional product features thus leading to reduced staffing and other costs.
- Achieving economies of scale by high volume sales perhaps based on advertising and promotion, allowing high fixed costs of investment in modern technology to be spread over a high volume of output. For example, LastMinute.com promoted their late booking website heavily in the early stages, allowing it to raise investment capital and achieve market leadership in its area of operations which has allowed the company to invest heavily on developing its Internet technology.
- Using high volume purchasing to obtain discounts for bulk buying of resource inputs such as accommodation or transportation requirements. For example Tui has grown to a pre-eminent position in European tour operations allowing it to demand lower prices for resource inputs than might be available to smaller competitors.
- Locating activities in areas where costs are low or government help, such as grant support, is available. For example, British Airways has located call centres at peripheral locations in the UK such as Newcastle and Glasgow where abundant fairly cheap labour is available and where government aid in the form of tax savings is available for incoming investors.
- Obtaining 'experience curve' economies. For example, the operator of an established theme park may be able to operate the park with lower costs than a new entrant since they might have experience of staff scheduling, minimizing power costs, purchasing new rides, waste disposal, etc.
- Standardizing products or resource inputs. For example, Holiday Inn is able to franchise its concept internationally to franchisers because it is fairly standardized throughout the world. Southwest Airlines is able to achieve economies in maintenance, purchasing and crew training because it operates only one aircraft type (albeit in various versions), the Boeing 737.

Cost leadership at Southwest Airlines and easyJet

(A) The Southwest Airlines low cost, no frills model of cost leadership

Product features
Fares   Low
                Simple, unrestricted
                Point-to-point services
                No interlining

Distribution	Direct sales and travel agents
	Ticketless
In-flight	Single class, high density
	No set assignment
	No meals
	Snacks and light beverages only
Frequency	High
Punctuality	Very good

Operating features

Aircraft	Single type (Boeing 737), four variants
	High utilization (over 11 hours/day)
Sectors	Short to average – below 800 km (500 miles)
Airports	Secondary or uncongested
	15–20 minute turnarounds
Growth	Target 10% per annum
	Maximum 15% per annum
Staff	Competitive wages
	Profit-sharing since 1973
	High productivity

Source: Adapted from Doganis (2001)

(B) Cost comparison of low cost easyJet and conventional short haul airline British Midland in 1998

Cost category	easyJet (pence per seat-km)	bmi British Midland (pence per seat-km)
Direct operating costs		
Cabin/flight crew salaries	0.43	0.92
Fuel	0.35	0.55
Airport charges	0.55	1.20
Maintenance	0.39	0.41
Depreciation	0.58	0.75
En-route	0.02	0.26
Aircraft rentals	0.80	1.23
Insurance		0.02
TOTAL DIRECT	3.14	5.34
Indirect operating costs		
Station costs	0.01	1.36
Handling	0.31	0.40
Passenger services	0.04	0.63
Sales/reservations	0.18	0.47
Commission	0.01	0.78
Advertising/promotion	0.27	0.31
General and administration	0.17	0.44
Other	0.06	0.14

Cost category	easyJet (pence per seat-km)	bmi British Midland (pence per seat-km)
TOTAL INDIRECT	1.05	4.52
TOTAL OPERATING COSTS	4.19	9.86
Other operating comparisons	easyJet	British Midland
Average aircraft size	122 seats	148 seats
Passenger load factor	67.1%	69.2%
Fleet comparison	4 Airbus 321 7 Boeing 737–300 5 Boeing 737–400 12 Boeing 737–500 6 Fokker 100 3 Fokker 70	9 Boeing 737–300

Source: Adapted from Doganis (2001) based on Civil Aviation Authority data and company annual reports

A cost leadership strategy coupled to low price is best employed in a market or segment where demand is price elastic. Under such circumstances sales and market share are likely to increase significantly thus increasing economies of scale, reducing unit costs further, so generating above average profits.

Key concept: Price elasticity of demand

Economists use the term *price elasticity* to describe the extent to which the volume of demand for a product is dependent upon its price. The coefficient of elasticity is expressed in a simple equation.

$$Ep = \frac{\text{Percentage change in quantity}}{\text{Percentage change in price}}$$

The value of Ep (price elasticity) tells us the price responsiveness of the product's demand. If, for any given price change, Ep is more than −1, it means that the change in price has brought about a higher proportionate change in volume sold. This relationship between price change and quantity is referred to as price elastic demand.

Demand is said to be price inelastic if the quantity change is proportionately smaller than the change in price (resulting in an Ep of less than −1). The larger the value of Ep, the more price elastic the demand and conversely, the nearer Ep is to 0, the more price inelastic the demand.

The price elasticity of demand (the value of Ep) is dependent upon the nature of the market's perception of a product. Products tend to be price elastic if the market sees a product as unnecessary but desirable. Products will have price inelastic demand if the customer perceives a *need* for a product rather than a *want* (such as the demand for most medicines, tobacco, etc.)

Alternatively, if a price similar to that of competitors is charged accompanied by advertising to boost sales, similar results will be obtained.

Differentiation strategy

A differentiation strategy is based upon persuading customers that a product is superior in some way to that offered by competitors. Differentiation can be based on premium product features or simply upon creating consumer perceptions that a product is superior. The major benefits to a business of a successful differentiation strategy are:

- Its products will command a premium price.
- Demand for its product will be less price elastic than demand for competitors' products.
- Above average profits can be earned.
- It creates an additional barrier to entry to new businesses wishing to enter the industry.

A business seeking to differentiate itself will organize its value chain activities to help create differentiated products and to create a perception among customers that these offerings are worth a higher price.

Differentiation can be achieved in several ways:

- by creating products that are superior to competitors' by virtue of design, technology, performance etc. For example, only two airlines, Air France and British Airways, are able to offer flights which cross the Atlantic in under four hours since they are the only airlines featuring Concorde supersonic aircraft in their fleets.
- by offering a superior level of service. For example, an upscale hotel chain such as Mandarin–Oriental (which operates largely in Southeast Asia) differentiates by offering a very high level of service, which is achieved by having a high ratio of staff to guests.
- by having access to superior distribution channels. For example, a multiple chain of travel agents which has been established for some time may have been able to develop a network of branches in prime retail locations (especially important in the retail sector) which it would take a newcomer some time and expense to accumulate.
- by creating a strong brand name through design, innovation, advertising, frequent flyer programmes and so on. For example, the development by American Airlines of the world's largest frequent flyer programme (American Advantage) creates a loyalty for its brand among passengers.
- by distinctive or superior product promotion. For example, the 'I ♥ New York', 'Glasgow's Miles Better' and British Airways' 'The World's Favourite Airline' were successful examples of promotion which highlighted the distinctive features of the respective products or destinations concerned.

A differentiation strategy is likely to necessitate emphasis on innovation, design, research and development, awareness of particular customer needs and marketing. To say that differentiation is in the eyes of the customer is no exaggeration. It could be argued that it is often brand name or logo which distinguishes a product rather than real product superiority. For example, prices of holidays at fashionable St Tropez in the south of France, or Marbella on Spain's Costa del Sol command prices well above those of similar local resorts because their 'brand' status is superior.

A differentiation strategy is employed in order to reduce price elasticity of demand for the product so that its price can be raised above that of competitors without reducing sales volume, so generating above-average profits.

Differentiation at Hyatt Regency Hotels

Hyatt Corporation, based in Chicago, opened its first hotel in 1957. The hotel management company now manages over 200 hotels in the USA and in many other countries. The company's core brand, Hyatt Regency, operates in the crowded deluxe category of international hotels vying for custom with others in this category such as Ritz-Carlton, Shangri-La and Regent International Hotels. It was in 1967 that Hyatt first received significant international attention when it opened the world's first 'atrium' hotel. The Hyatt Regency in Atlanta featured a 21-storey atrium lobby tower, which was a significant and dramatic departure from traditional hotel architecture. The challenge for hotel architects was no longer to eliminate extra space but instead to create grand, wide-open public spaces. The atrium idea (which has often been copied subsequently) has been taken on by other Hyatt Regency Hotels ranging from Kota Kinabalu (Sabah, Malaysia) to Chicago O'Hare Airport and San Francisco. Although not all Hyatt Regency hotels now feature atriums in their design, the hotel chain retains a reputation for creative and innovative architectural design. Thus in this case design acts as a means of differentiating the product from those of competing product offerings in a crowded sector of the market.

Source: Adapted from www.Hyatt.com

Focus strategy

A focus strategy is aimed at a segment of the market for a product rather than at the whole market. A particular group of customers is identified on the basis of age, income, lifestyle, sex, geography, other distinguishing demographic characteristics or on the benefits sought from travel and tourism products. Within the segment a business employs either a cost leadership or a differentiation strategy.

The major benefits of a focus strategy are:

- It requires a lower investment in resources compared to a strategy aimed at an entire market.
- It allows specialization and greater knowledge of the segment being served.
- It makes entry to a new market less costly and simpler.

A focus strategy will require:

- identification of a suitable target customer group which forms a distinct market segment;

- identification of the specific needs of that group;
- establishing that the segment is sufficiently large to sustain the business;
- establishing the extent of competition within the segment;
- production of products to meet the specific needs of that group;
- deciding whether to operate a differentiation or cost leadership strategy within the market segment.

Focus strategies can be developed in travel and tourism in a range of different circumstances by:

- focusing on a particular group of buyers. Contiki, for example, markets its coach-based holidays to customers in many parts of the world. The company founded by a New Zealander as a safe and secure means for Australians and New Zealanders to see Europe now offers tours (which combine activities and sightseeing) in North America, Australia, New Zealand and Europe targeted at the 18–35 age group.
- specializing in particular geographic destinations. For example Sunvil Holidays, a small specialist UK-based tour operator, was founded, and is still owned by, an entrepreneur from a Greek Cypriot background. Although it has now diversified into other areas, the company is able to compete with larger rivals in the market for holidays to Cyprus by utilizing in-depth knowledge of the destination and a network of contacts.
- catering for the benefits sought by a particular group of buyers. For example, PGL Adventure Holidays in the UK provide holidays for children offering a large range of organized activities at an all-inclusive price.
- resort destinations targeting particular market segments. La Manga in Spain has, for example, successfully targeted sports enthusiasts particularly golfers.

Many organizations use a focus strategy to enter a market before broadening their activities into other related segments.

Table 10.1 provides a summary of the key features of generic competitive strategies.

Criticisms of Porter's generic strategy framework

A critical evaluation of the framework

In recent years Porter's generic strategy framework has been the target of increasing criticism (see for example Cronshaw *et al.*, 1990; Mintzberg, 1991; Baden-Fuller and Stopford, 1992; Miller, 1992; Johnson and Scholes, 2002; and, in a travel and tourism context, Poon, 1993). At least six objections to Porter's model have been advanced.

A business can apparently employ a successful 'hybrid' strategy without being 'stuck in the middle'

Porter argued that a business must choose between a differentiation and cost leadership strategy. To be 'stuck in the middle' between the two, he argued, will result in sub-optimal performance. There is evidence to suggest, however, that some companies with lower than industry-average costs can nevertheless sell their products on the basis of differentiation. That is, they employ a combined or 'hybrid' strategy. The effects of innovations or economies of scale may allow a successful hybrid strategy to be employed. An airline flying a new fuel-efficient aircraft type for example may achieve the benefits of

	Differentiation	Cost leadership	Focus
Aim	Ability to charge a premium price	To be lowest cost supplier	Either to charge a premium price or to be lowest cost supplier in particular segments of the market
How?	Superior product/service Advertising and promotion Branding Distribution channels Different locations Customer care Technology Licences/regulation	High volume sales Economies of scale New technology High productivity Low cost inputs Low distribution costs Low location costs	As for differentiation or cost leadership applied to particular segments
Strategy entails	Changed perception Higher price than rivals Quality Innovation	Price equal to or below rivals Acceptable quality Advertising to sell high volume	Identifying market segments and consumer needs Choose differentiation or cost leadership strategy for a segment or niche
When to use	Price insensitive Established position in the market	Price sensitive market Market entry	For firms not large enough to target whole market Firms possessing specialist skills

Table 10.1 Key features of generic competitive strategies

cost leadership and differentiation simultaneously. A successful hybrid strategy will be based upon a conscious decision by senior mangers to combine differentiation with price and cost control. Under such circumstances a business can be successful. When a business slips into the situation unconsciously it can still be regarded as being 'stuck in the middle' but is less likely to be successful.

Are low cost airlines really pursuing cost leadership competitive strategies?

It could be argued that none of Porter's categories should be regarded as alternatives and that in reality to categorize competitive strategy in this way is simplistic and possibly misleading.

In the case of the low cost European airlines, for example, they clearly need to control their costs strictly and be *cost leaders* (in order to offer the lowest priced products). However, they also choose to *focus* on highly price sensitive customer groups whilst *differentiating* their products by providing a limited range of added service benefits. Additional cost savings are becoming more difficult to achieve. As easyJet chairman Stelios Haji-Ioannou has stated 'there are only so many frills you can cut' (Doran, 2002). The airline is now considering the purchase Airbus aircraft alongside its existing Boeing fleet. The easyJet chairman remarks that 'it is time we look at contestable markets to reduce our costs. This has never been done [by a low cost carrier] with the purchase of aircraft' (Doran, 2000).

Cost leadership does not, in and of itself, sell products • • •

Buying decisions are made upon the basis of desirable product features or upon the price, not on the basis of the unit cost itself, which may not be known by consumers.

Differentiation strategies can be used to increase sales volumes rather than to charge a premium price • • •

Porter's work does not consider the possibility that a business employing a differentiation strategy might choose not to charge a premium price, but rather to increase sales and market share by foregoing the premium price for an introductory period. This criticism, however, does not fundamentally undermine Porter's thinking.

Price can sometimes be used to differentiate • • •

Porter does not consider the possibility that price may be used to differentiate a product. Mintzberg (1991) argues that price, along with image, support, quality and design, can be used as the basis of differentiation.

A 'generic' strategy cannot give competitive advantage • • •

It is evident that in order to outperform competitors a business must do things better than and differently to them. The word 'generic' could be construed to imply that Porter is arguing that there are general recipes by which competitive advantage can be achieved. This, however, is not the case. Porter's framework is merely a framework by which competitive strategies can be grouped to assist in understanding and analysis.

The resource/competence based strategy has arguably superseded the generic strategy framework • • •

The resource based approach argues that it is the core competences of the individual business which give it competitive advantage and not generic strategies. In fact the two approaches do not preclude each other. The relationships between the two approaches are discussed in a later section of this chapter.

Despite these criticisms, Porter's work can, in modified form, constitute the basis of a useful framework for categorizing and understanding sources of competitive advantage. One such approach is the 'strategy clock' framework developed by Bowman in 1995 and reported by Haberberg and Rieple (2001), and Johnson and Scholes (2002).

Other competitive strategy frameworks

The strategy clock framework

The strategy clock framework develops and adds to Porter's original model, and consequently some aspects are open to similar criticisms. However, it is a more sophisticated approach, which recognizes and deals with some of the criticisms of Porter and in particular recognizes that in certain circumstances a 'hybrid' combined strategy can be successful. The model is shown in Figure 10.3, with brief explanations of the categories used.

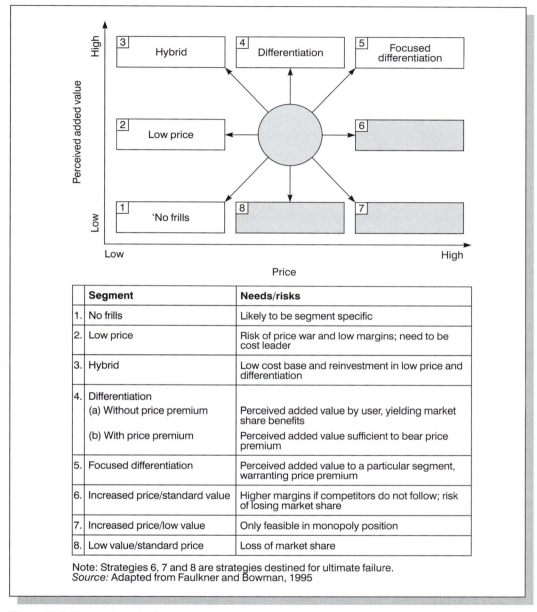

	Segment	Needs/risks
1.	No frills	Likely to be segment specific
2.	Low price	Risk of price war and low margins; need to be cost leader
3.	Hybrid	Low cost base and reinvestment in low price and differentiation
4.	Differentiation (a) Without price premium	Perceived added value by user, yielding market share benefits
	(b) With price premium	Perceived added value sufficient to bear price premium
5.	Focused differentiation	Perceived added value to a particular segment, warranting price premium
6.	Increased price/standard value	Higher margins if competitors do not follow; risk of losing market share
7.	Increased price/low value	Only feasible in monopoly position
8.	Low value/standard price	Loss of market share

Note: Strategies 6, 7 and 8 are strategies destined for ultimate failure.
Source: Adapted from Faulkner and Bowman, 1995

Figure 10.3 The strategy clock

In concluding this section, it is possible to say that the extent of differentiation, price and cost control will depend upon the nature of the market in which the business is operating. In markets where consumers show a preference for quality then the emphasis be less on price and costs whilst in markets where demand is price sensitive the emphasis will be on keeping both price and costs as low as possible. Of course, organizations may also seek to shape customer attitudes by advertising and promotion so as to modify market conditions.

Competitive strategies for travel and tourism – Poon's framework

The approaches to competitive strategy outlined in this chapter up to this point have not been developed in a travel and tourism context specifically, although the approaches can be applied to the industry. Poon (1993), conscious of the limitations and criticisms levelled at the approach of Porter, developed a rather different approach, which, she argued, takes into account the realities of the industry. The key realities identified by Poon were:

1 The service orientation of the industry and its need to focus on the quality of service delivery which in turn is inextricably linked with the development of human resources.
2 The increasing sophistication of travel and leisure consumers.
3 The industry-wide diffusion of information technology.
4 The radical transformation of the industry, which requires continuous innovation to ensure competitive success, is achieved.

In order successfully to respond to these industry realities Poon postulates that travel and tourism organizations need to apply four principles in developing their competitive strategies:

• Put customers first.
• Be a leader in quality.
• Develop radical innovations.
• Strengthen the organization's strategic position within the industry's value chain.

The principles of competitive success in travel and tourism (according to Poon) are outlined in Figure 10.4.

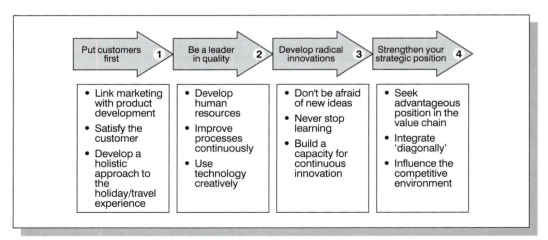

Figure 10.4 The principles of competitive success in travel and tourism. Note: Diagonal integration – a process whereby firms use information technologies logically to combine services for best productivity (adapted from Poon, 1993)

Competence based competitive advantage

The generic strategy model is not the only one that seeks to provide an explanation of the sources of competitive advantage. The *competence* or *resource based model* emphasizes that competitive edge stems from attributes of an organization known as *competences* or *capabilities*, which distinguishes it from its competitors allowing it to outperform them (see Chapter 3).

Core competence and distinctive capabilities

Chapter 3 explained the ways in which internal analysis makes it possible to better understand core competences by a process of deconstructing them into the component resources and competences that act as their foundation. This chapter builds upon this analysis to explore the ways in which existing competences can be extended and new ones cultivated. It goes on to examine how and where these core competences can be exploited so as to acquire and prolong competitive advantage. Much of the recent attention to the concept of core competence is based upon the work of Prahalad and Hamel (1990), Stalk, Evans and Shulmann (1992), who advocated the idea of competing on the basis of capabilities, and Kay (1993), who advances the idea that competitive advantage is based upon distinctive capability.

Core competences

Perhaps the best known explanation of core competence is that provided by Prahalad and Hamel (1990):

> Core competences are the collective learning of the organization, especially how to co-ordinate diverse production skills and integrate multiple streams of technologies.

Prahalad and Hamel specified three tests to be applied in the identification and development of core competence. A core competence should:

- equip a business with the ability to enter and successfully compete in several markets;
- add greater perceived customer value to the business's products and services than that perceived in competitor's products;
- be difficult for competitors to imitate.

According to Prahalad and Hamel (1990), there are many examples of core competence resulting in competitive advantage. They argued that competitive advantage is likely in practice to be based upon no more than five or six competences. These competences will allow management to produce new and unanticipated products, and to be responsive to changing opportunities because of operational skills and the harnessing of technology. Given the turbulent business environment in many sectors of travel and tourism, such adaptability is essential if competitive advantage is to be built and sustained.

Application of core competences at Novotel

Founded by two French entrepreneurs in 1967, the Novotel chain of hotels (now a part of Accor, one of the world's leading hospitality groups) expanded steadily during the 1960s and 1970s. The expansion first in France, then in the rest of Europe followed by other parts of the world owed much to the exploitation of a core competence in reliability. The company developed a standard format for hotel room designs, for furnishing and for standards of service allowing a uniform standard of service to be delivered (particularly to business customers) throughout the group. The reliability core competence was underpinned by a competence in control that enabled the company to ensure that standards were maintained.

In 1987 Novotel went a step further in developing a rigid set of rules and procedures, the '95 Bolts' that specified every aspect of the operation of the hotels in minute detail. Even the personal greeting to guests was standardized. The strategy was not a success as the new systems made it difficult for staff to show personal warmth or to act spontaneously in meeting customer requirements and managers were unable to vary prices in order to match those of local competitors. The core competence (control) had been turned into a core rigidity and in 1992 a new strategy was developed. The new strategy gave hotel general managers greater autonomy whilst supporting them through new systems which enabled them to learn from one another and to share best practices.

Source: Adapted from Haberberg and Rieple (2001)

Distinctive capabilities

Kay (1993) took the concept of capability, initially identified by Stalk, Evans and Shulmann (1992), to develop a framework which explains competitive advantage in terms of what he defines as *distinctive capability* (see also Chapter 3). This idea of distinctive capability has much in common with that of core competence in that it views competitive advantage as being dependent upon unique attributes of a particular business and its products.

According to Kay (1993), distinctive capability results from one or more of the following sources.

- *Architecture* – the unique network of internal and external relationships of an organization which produces superior performance. These can be unique relationships with suppliers, distributors or customers which competitors do not possess. Equally, the unique relationships may be internal to the business and based upon the way that it organizes its activities in the value chain.
- *Reputation* – this stems from several sources including superior product quality, characteristics, design, service and so on.
- *Innovation* – the ability of the business to get ahead and stay ahead of competitors depends upon its success in researching, designing, developing and marketing new products. Equally it depends upon the ability of the business to improve the design and organization of its value adding activities.
- *Strategic assets* – businesses can also obtain competitive advantage from assets like natural monopoly, patents and copyrights which restrict competition.

Core competence, distinctive capability and competitive advantage

So what do the concepts of core competence and distinctive capability add to our understanding of competitive advantage?

1 They provide us with insight into how an organization can build attributes which can deliver superior performance.
2 They inform the process of determining where such competence and capabilities can be exploited.
3 A core competence becomes competitive advantage when it is applied in a particular market or markets.

The process of building new core competences or extending existing ones must take into account the following considerations:

- *Customer perceptions* – competences, capabilities and products must be perceived by customers as being better value for money that those of competitors. The organization's reputation (although difficult to measure) can be particularly important in this regard.
- *Uniqueness* – core competences must be unique to the organization and must be difficult for competitors to emulate. Similarly there must be no close substitutes for these competences.
- *Continuous improvement* – core competences, products and services must be continuously upgraded to stay ahead of competitors. Product and process innovation are particularly important.
- *Collaboration* – competitive advantage can result from the organization's unique network of relationships with suppliers, distributors, customers and even competitors. There is the potential for 'multiplier effects' resulting from separate organizations' complementary core competences being combined together.
- *Organizational knowledge* – competences must be based upon organizational knowledge and learning. Managers must improve the processes by which the organization learns, builds and manages its knowledge. Knowledge is, today, potentially the greatest source of added value.

Sustainable competitive advantage

It is a worthy cause for travel and tourism organizations to strive to achieve a competitive advantage. However, if the position cannot be maintained over a period of time then it may not be worth the effort and investment that are necessary to achieve such a position in the first place. Sustainable competitive advantage will have been achieved 'when an organization receives a return on investment that is greater than the norm for its competitors, and when this enhanced return persists for a period long enough to alter the relative standing of the organization among its rivals' (Finlay, 2000). Sustainability in this sense depends on three factors.

1 *Durability* – no advantage is sustainable for ever, as competitors will seek to imitate it. Reputation has the potential, however, for providing long-lasting advantage as the standing of well known long-lasting market leaders such as British Airways, Thomson and American Express testifies.

2 *Transparency* – the harder it is for outsiders to understand how an organization does what it does the harder it will be for imitators. Disney has long been admired for the way in which it successfully manages and operates its theme parks, and competitors have found it difficult to exactly replicate the successful formula.

3 *Replicability* – once a rival has understood the competences needed to copy a rival, they will need to obtain the resources necessary to replicate the rival's product. If the resources are freely available in markets then this might not pose a problem but in some circumstances they may be limited. Thus airport take off and landing slots, hotel rooms in popular resorts, specialist staff such as pilots, access to airline routes and access to distribution channels are all examples of resources which might be restricted for some reason.

Core competence, generic strategy and the value chain – a synthesis

How the different approaches 'agree'

It has been argued (see for example Heene and Sanchez, 1997) that the resource or competence-based approach is largely incompatible with the competitive positioning or generic strategy approach advocated by Porter (1980, 1985). Mintzberg, Quinn, and Ghoshal (1995), however, make the case that the two approaches are in many respects complementary rather than mutually contradictory. Perhaps the best way of illustrating the linkages between the approaches is through the value chain of the organization.

As competitive advantage is based upon the unique approach of the individual organization to its environment, it is not possible to identify a one-for-all prescription, which will guarantee superior performance in all situations. Both the competitive positioning and the resource based approach, however, provide frameworks which allow broad sources of competitive advantage to be categorized for the purposes of analysis and development of future strategy.

A differentiation strategy, for example, will be likely to be dependent upon core competences in areas of the value chain like design, marketing and service. Similarly a cost or price based strategy may well require core competences in value chain activities like operations, procurement and perhaps in marketing. It is much less likely that a cost leader will have core competences based on design and service. Possible relationships between core competences, generic strategies and the value chain are shown in Table 10.2.

Where to exploit core competences and strategies

As core competences and business strategies are developed, it is necessary to decide where they can be exploited. Core competences and strategies can be targeted on existing customers in existing markets or it may be possible to target new customers in existing markets. Alternatively it may be possible to target new customers in new markets. These markets may be related to markets currently served by the organization or they may be unrelated markets. The organization may also consider employing its competences in a new industry.

These decisions, on where to deploy core competences, are concerned with determining the *'strategic direction'* of the organization. Once this decision has been made then decisions must be made on the *methods* to be employed in following the chosen strategic direction.

Value chain activity	Areas of competence associated with differentiation strategies	Areas of competence associated with cost/price based strategies
Primary activities		
Inbound logistics	Control of quality of inputs	Strict control of the cost of inputs. Tendency to buy larger volumes of standard inputs
Operations	Control of quality of output, raising standards	Lowering operational costs and achieving high volume operations
Marketing and sales	Sales (and customer relations) on the basis of quality technology, performance, reputation, outlets etc.	Achieving high volume sales through advertising and promotion
Outbound logistics	Ensuring efficient distribution	Maintaining low distribution costs
Service	Adding to product value by high quality and differentiated service	Minimal service to keep costs low
Support activities		
The business's infrastructure	Emphasis on quality	Emphasis on efficiency and cost reduction
Human resource development	Training to create a culture and skills which emphasize quality, customer service, product development	Training to reduce costs
Technology development	Developing new products, improving product quality, improving product performance, improving customer service	Reducing production costs and increasing efficiency
Procurement	Obtaining high quality resources and materials	Obtaining low cost resources and materials

Table 10.2 Possible relationships between generic strategies and core competences in relation to the value chain

The process of exploiting existing core competences in new markets is known as competence leveraging. In order to enter new markets it is often necessary for the organization to build new core competences, alongside the existing core competences, which are being leveraged, so as to satisfy new customer needs. Identification of customer needs to be served by core competences is based upon analysis of the organization's competitive environment using the resource based framework developed in Chapter 8. The remainder of this chapter considers the alternative strategic directions an organization can pursue. The methods that can be employed in following these strategic directions are considered in Chapter 11.

Strategic directions

Introduction

Just as every product or business unit must determine an appropriate competitive strategy in order to achieve an enhanced competitive position relative to rivals so every organization must also decide upon its attitude towards growth or alternative *directions* of strategic development. That is, should the direction taken be to expand, cut back or continue operations unchanged?

As with the other key business level decisions (relating to the competitive stance and strategic methods) decisions related to strategic direction are usually taken at the strategic business unit or product level since conditions in one part of the organization may be different from those in another part. A vertically integrated travel company might want to expand its airline activities whilst at the same time reducing the size of its tour operations because of the market conditions pertaining to these two parts of the business. In this case there might be over-capacity in tour operating but under-capacity in airline capacity.

At the overall organizational (or 'corporate') level however, managers must be mindful of the overall *balance* between the directions taken by individual business units since available resources will be finite. Necessary resources may not be available to invest in all aspects of the organization simultaneously so that resources may be taken from one area to invest in another area in order to allow it to develop and grow. These principles of selective investment and growth are consistent with the thinking embodied in the product life cycle and portfolio models (such as the Boston Consultancy Group matrix) which were explained in Chapter 6.

In general terms, three orientations are possible with regard to directional strategy:

- Growth strategies – expanding the activities of the SBU.
- Stability strategies – maintain the activities of the SBU.
- Retrenchment strategies – reduce the activities of the SBU.

Having chosen the general orientation (such as growth), the management of an organization can then choose more specific strategies. Growth for example can be broken down according to Ansoff (1987) into four distinct categories. We will now turn to look briefly at three strategic directions of growth, stability and retrenchment.

Growth – Igor Ansoff's product–market framework

The most commonly used model for analysing the possible strategic *growth* directions which an organization can follow is the Ansoff matrix, shown in Figure 10.5. This matrix, which has two variables (products and markets), shows potential areas where core competences and generic strategies can be deployed. There are four broad alternatives:

- *market penetration* – increasing market share in existing markets utilizing existing products;
- *market development* – entering new markets and segments using existing products;
- *product development* – developing new products to serve existing markets;
- *diversification* – developing new products to serve new markets.

It should be emphasized that the matrix is related to the level of risk that managers are prepared to accept. Entering new markets or producing new products present areas of risk

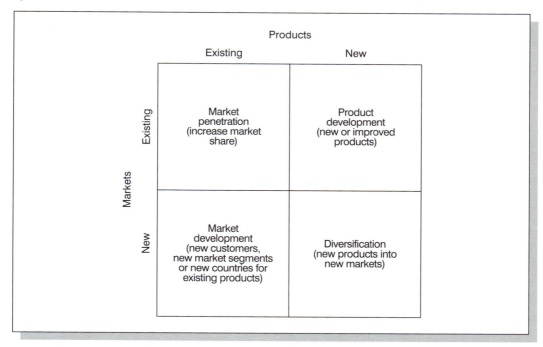

Figure 10.5 The Ansoff matrix (growth vector components) (adapted from Ansoff, 1987)

since many new products fail and managers will not have precise knowledge of market conditions when they enter new markets. Thus the lowest risk option is market penetration, with diversification representing the highest risk category.

Market penetration

The main aim of a market penetration strategy is to increase market share using existing products within existing markets. This may involve taking steps to enhance existing core competences or building new ones. Such competence building may be intended to improve service or quality so as to enhance the reputation of the organization and differentiate it from its competitors. Equally, competence development may be centred on improving efficiency so as to reduce costs below those of competitors.

Mature or declining markets are more difficult to penetrate than those which are still in the growth phase, which provide more opportunities. In the case of a declining market, the organization may also consider the possibility of retrenchment or withdrawal so as to re-deploy resources to more lucrative markets.

Market penetration is likely to be appropriate when:

- The existing market has growth potential.
- Other competitors are leaving the market.
- The organization can take advantage of its acquired experience and knowledge in the market.
- The organization is unable for some reason (such as lack of resources or regulatory restrictions) to enter new markets.

When a business's current market shows signs of saturation then it may wish to consider alternative directions for development.

Market penetration at Travelodge

The concept of 'lodge' hotels has taken root in the UK over the past ten to fifteen years. The hotels, often located at convenient roadside locations, offer good quality standardized rooms capable of accommodating a family at a reasonable price. The growth of these hotels has placed pressure on older 'three and four star' properties and on the traditional bed and breakfast establishments. The Travelodge chain (which was developed by the Forte Group before its acquisition by Granada plc in the mid-1990s) was bought by the Compass Group of companies in 2000.

Travelodge, which was overtaken by the Travel Inn brand (owned by Whitbread plc) in the late 1990s as the largest UK lodge brand, announced ambitious growth plans in late 2001. The chain, which has 213 hotels and over 12 000 rooms in the UK, intends to add a further 5000 rooms to its portfolio over five years and aims to have a presence at every major travel hub in the UK. Part of the growth will be achieved through deploying the strategic method of franchising after a deal was signed with Jarvis Hotels plc. The Travelodge managing director commented that franchising 'fits perfectly with our business as it will enable us to extend the portfolio while still protecting our brand standards'.

Market development

Market development is based upon entry to new markets, employing essentially unchanged products (although they may be modified in detail). The new markets may be new geographical areas or new segments of existing markets. In either case the strategic option attempts to attract new customers for the existing range of products. The key to success in market development is the transferability of the product as it is *repositioned* in new markets. McDonald's fast food restaurants, for instance, have advanced inexorably from country to country with only minor amendments to the overall product concept in order to take into account national cultural differences and purchasing habits. Entering new markets is likely to be based upon leveraging existing competences but may also require the development of new competences (see the key concept in Chapter 3 for a definition of leveraging). Entering new segments of existing markets may require the development of new competences, which serve the particular need of customers in these segments.

Internationalization and globalization are commonly used examples of market development. It is likely that an organization will need to build new competences when entering international markets to deal with linguistic, cultural, logistical and other potential problems.

Market development is likely to be appropriate when:

- the existing market has little or no growth potential;
- regulatory or other restrictions prevent an increase in an organization's market share in its current market;
- other geographic markets or market segments offer good growth potential;
- existing products are easily transferable.

The major risk associated with market development is that it centres on entry to markets of which the organization's managers may have only limited experience and consequently costly mistakes may be made.

Market development at Holidaybreak plc

Holidaybreak plc was founded in 1973 as Eurocamp Travel Limited – a family run business, based in Cheshire, UK offering camping holidays in Brittany. From modest beginnings the business grew steadily, benefiting from the growing interest in France as a holiday destination. In the early 1980s mobile homes and destinations outside France were added to the product range. The 1980s were years of innovation and growth as the UK market to France expanded rapidly and the company's Eurocamp brand took over leadership of the camping sector.

In 1984 the core Eurocamp brand was launched on the Dutch market followed by Germany in 1988. Since the floatation of the company on the London Stock Exchange in 1991 the business has continued to develop and the corporate name was changed from Eurocamp to Holidaybreak plc to reflect the diversity of the company's expanding activities. In recent years the marketing reach of the Eurocamp brand has been extended into several new territories, notably Switzerland, Belgium, Denmark and most recently Poland, whilst customers have increasingly opted for mobile home rather than tent accommodation.

Product development

Product development centres on the development of new products for existing markets. As with the previous two growth directions, the intention is to attract new customers, retain existing ones and to increase market share. Providing new products will be based upon exploiting existing competences but may also require that new competences are built (such as in product research and development).

Product development offers the advantage to a business of dealing with customer needs of which it has some experience because they are within its existing market. In a world of shortening product life cycles, product development has become an essential form of strategic development for many organizations.

Product development is likely to be appropriate when:

- an organization already holds a high share of the market and could strengthen its position by the launch of new products;
- the existing market has good potential for growth providing opportunities of good economic returns for new product launches;
- customer preferences are changing and they are receptive to new product ideas or new destinations;
- competitors have already launched their own new products.

Although when mentioning product development 'new' products are considered, it is possible to consider new products in several different ways. There are very few products that are totally new. Holidays to the moon might be such an example. Many new products are variations on existing products or products that are new to a particular organization. Thus new products might be:

- completely new to a particular organization as for example when a tour operator launches an airline;
- developments of additional lines of existing products, as for example when tour operators launch new destinations;
- creations of differing quality versions of the same product, as for example when British Airways added an additional airline class in 2000 for those paying 'full economy' (as opposed to discounted fares).

Introducing new products is, however, highly risky because many new products fail. Johnson and Scholes (2002) cited four factors, which could reduce the risks of failure. New products should:

- have a market focus;
- build on existing core competences;
- involve cross-disciplinary teams in their development;
- involve good internal communications so that all within the organization are kept informed.

Product development at Club Med

In the 1990s, after two decades of spreading the gospel for all-inclusive resort vacations and their easy lifestyle, Club Med took its formula to sea in the world's largest sailing ships that have all the facilities of a cruise ship. Stretching the length of two football fields and rigged with five 164-foot masts and seven computer-monitored sails, the two Club Med ships marry twentieth-century technology with the romance of large ocean-going sailing ships. They sail with little in the way of listing while the officers are on the bridge watching their computers.

Club Med cruises are basically a product of French culture and traditions, with the same informal, carefree ambience that Club Med has developed at its resort villages which are situated around the world.

Diversification

Diversification is growth achieved through new products and new markets. Diversification can be achieved by developing in a number of directions (which will be discussed in subsequent sections) and by utilizing a number of different methods (which will be discussed in the following chapter). Figure 10.6 summarizes the directions and methods of diversification available to managers.

It is an appropriate strategic option when:

- Current products and markets no longer provide an acceptable financial return.
- The organization has underutilized resources and competences.
- The organization wishes to broaden its portfolio of business interests across more than one product/market segment.

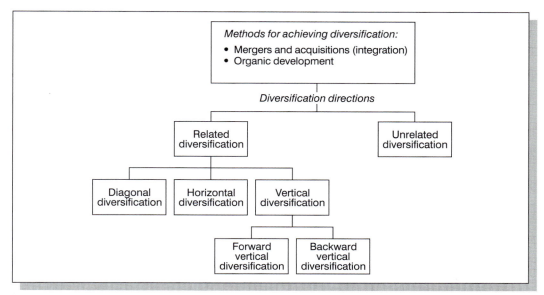

Figure 10.6 Directions and methods of diversification

- The organization wishes to make greater use of any existing distribution systems in place, thus diluting fixed costs and increasing returns.
- The organization wants to spread risks.
- There is a need to even out the cyclical effects in a given sector.

Related diversification is said to have occurred when the products and/or markets share some degree of commonality with existing ones. This 'closeness' can reduce the inherent risks (since managers are dealing with both new markets and new products) associated with diversification. In practice, related diversification usually means growth into similar industry sectors or *forward* or *backward* in an organization's existing supply chain.

Unrelated diversification is growth into product and market areas that are completely new and with which the organization shares no commonality at all.

Related diversification (sometimes termed *concentric* diversification) can follow four main patterns, as shown in Figure 10.7.

Vertical backward diversification occurs when an organization seeks to operate in markets from which it currently obtains its resources (i.e. extending the value chain in an *upstream* direction). A tour operator developing a hotel chain or an airline would be an example of this. Upstream diversification provides greater control over supplies of resources. The benefits of vertical backward diversification are that:

- supplies are guaranteed;
- the costs of supplies are internalized, i.e. brought within the organization's control;
- supplies may be denied to competitors or made more expensive to acquire;
- the portfolio of activities is broadened giving protection against risk;
- potential problem areas with regard to supplies are identified and dealt with quickly.

Vertical forward diversification describes the situation in which an organization seeks to operate in markets currently served by its customers or distributors (i.e. extending the value chain in a *downstream* direction). In this case an example would be a tour operator

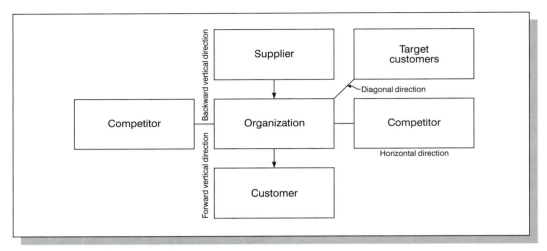

Figure 10.7 Patterns of related diversification

developing a distribution network such as a chain of travel agents and/or call centres. This form of diversification gives an organization closer contact with customers and can give significant marketing advantages in that it gives an organization market intelligence that might not be forthcoming when dealing through an intermediary such as an independently owned chain of travel agents. The benefits of vertical backward diversification are that:

- guaranteed outlets are provided for products to be distributed;
- the costs of distribution are internalized;
- distribution outlets are denied to competitors;
- information is gathered regarding consumer purchasing behaviour both for one's own products and for competing products;
- the portfolio of activities is broadened giving protection against risk.

Vertical diversification should not be confused with *vertical integration*, which concerns mergers or takeovers in order to integrate existing organizations. That is a further decision regarding the *method* of diversification to be employed. Rather than purchase an existing travel agency chain, for example, a tour operator might choose to develop such a chain from scratch.

Horizontal diversification involves an organization entering complementary or competing markets. An example of this would be a tour operator working with or taking over another tour operating organization or an airline strategic alliance when two or more airlines work in a complementary manner to achieve common objectives. This should not be confused with *horizontal integration*, which is the acquisition of a competitor. Diversification may be achieved by integrating a competitor that had been acquired but it might also be achieved through joint developments (such as alliances), or by developing internally (see Chapter 11 on strategic methods). The benefits of horizontal diversification are that:

- market share is increased;
- greater purchasing power leads to more favourable rates being negotiated with suppliers and distributors;

- economies of scale are derived from the enlarged organization;
- opportunities to increase market share are denied to competitors;
- competitors may become collaborators.

Related diversification has the benefit of leveraging existing competences as well as requiring the building of some new competences. In other words, it draws upon existing organizational knowledge as well as requiring the building of some new skills and knowledge.

Related diversification at First Choice plc

First Choice is a leading European leisure travel company comprising mainstream and specialist tour operations, travel retail and aviation businesses. First Choice employs over 14 000 people, operating from 13 countries worldwide. The business was formed in 1973 and for many years traded as Owners Abroad plc. In 1994 the company was restructured and rebranded as First Choice Holidays plc.

In recent years the group has diversified both horizontally and vertically, largely through acquisitions. The UK travel industry rapidly began to consolidate in the late 1990s and First Choice played an active role, acquiring in June 1998 two key UK tour operators – the Unijet Travel Group and Hayes & Jarvis. In the same year, other acquisitions included the retail agencies Bakers Dolphin and Intatravel to complement the opening of new travel shops under the name of Travel Choice and an initial stake (25%) in Holiday Hypermarket (out-of-town travel superstores). UK acquisitions in 1999 were of premium niche market operators: Meon (Meon Villas and Longshot Golf Holidays), Flexigroup (ski holidays and conferences) and Sunsail International (leading yacht charter and water-sports club operator). Within retail, Ferrychoice, a small regional agency chain, and a number of small Irish agents were also acquired. In May 2000 the remaining outstanding interest in Holiday Hypermarket was acquired.

The year 2000 saw the commencement of the anticipated consolidation within the European tour operating industry. In particular there was a convergence of a small number of European participants principally in the UK and Germany, the two most dominant markets in Europe. First Choice did not participate in this mass market consolidation; instead it chose clearly to set out a strategy to differentiate itself from the traditional main competitors, acquiring smaller more specialized companies than its competitors. In 2000 two key acquisitions marked the start of First Choice's expansion into European markets: the European tour operating businesses of the Ten Tour Group, which provided an immediate presence in six important markets in mainland Europe, and Barceló Travel of Spain, which involved the purchase of three principal businesses: – tour operations, retail travel and destination management services. In particular the Barceló Travel acquisition also contained the ability to create a hotel joint venture with its former parent company Barceló Travel Group.

Through these and further acquisitions during 2001 within Continental Europe, First Choice now has a presence in France, Spain, Italy, Portugal, Germany, Belgium, The Netherlands, Austria and Switzerland. A strategic alliance with Royal Caribbean Cruise Lines initiated in 2000 strengthened the group's position in the growing cruise sector whilst providing an investment of £200 million in First Choice by the cruise line.

Poon (1993) referred to the a fourth pattern of related diversification as *diagonal diversification*. This form of diversification(common in service industries) utilizes a common platform of information-utilizing technology to target a group of customers with a closely related set of products. Thus banks use their customer databases to target their customers with offers of insurance, mortgages, financial planning services and possibly travel products. In a similar way Saga, a UK company that developed travel products for the over-55 age categories, has more recently targeted its customers with a range of financial services. Another example would be provided by American Express, which is involved in travel related and financial services. Many of its sales in leisure travel are to its American Express credit card holders. Diagonal diversification offers the following benefits:

- It allows organizations to get close to their customers and lower costs for each product by sharing overheads across several product categories.
- It allows organizations to benefit from economies of scope and systems savings.
- It is cheaper for one organization to produce a combination of services rather than for many organizations to produce each separately.

Diagonal diversification is illustrated in Figure 10.8.

Unrelated diversification (sometimes termed *conglomerate* diversification) carries greater risk than related diversification as it involves producing new products for markets with which the organization is unfamiliar. Businesses tend to take this option when they see serious restrictions on growth potential in their existing markets, and in related markets, or when they see significant opportunities for growth in new market areas. In addition, there are potential economies of scale, opportunities to build on existing competences and the possibility of synergy.

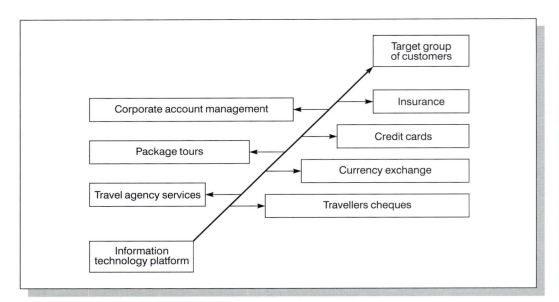

Figure 10.8 Diagonal diversification in travel and tourism (adapted from Poon, 1993)

Unrelated diversification at Tui AG

Tui is a leading integrated tourism and services group. The tourism companies that are part of the Tui Group includes the German-based TUI Travel Group and the British-based Thomson Travel Group which are active in 15 European source markets. Familiar brand names to European travellers, such as TUI, Thomson Holidays and Fritidsresor, well-known travel agency chains such as FIRST, Holland International and Lunn Poly, and airlines Britannia and Hapag-Lloyd-Flug are all part of the Tui Group. Through strategic alliances with Nouvelles Frontières and Alpitour, the Group has also gained access to the French and Italian travel markets. The logistics and energy divisions complete the group's portfolio of activities. In the 1999/2000 financial year the group achieved a turnover of some 22 billion euros, 50 per cent of which was generated in the field of tourism. However the group intends to increase this proportion amount to 80 per cent in future years.

Although Tui is now best known for its travel and tourism activities, this strategic focus represents a radical diversification away from its industrial roots. The company was originally called the Prussian Mining and Iron and Steel and was formed by the state of Prussia in 1923. In addition to coal, non-ferrous metals and energy, logistics also soon came to play an important role in the company, and during the economic boom of the 1950s and 1960s the consumer goods industry was of importance. Nevertheless, with the structural changes in the economy and the growing difficulties on the European raw and basic materials markets, Preussag as it was called was eventually confronted with the question of what future direction the company should take. Consequently Preussag decided to give up its industrial activities to concentrate on new fields of growth. Since 1997 the entire face of the Group has changed. The companies now focus their attentions on the services sector, and with the acquisition and integration of TUI and Thomson Travel, particularly on the core business sector of tourism. The corporate name changed to Tui in 2002.

Stability strategies (maintain the activities of the SBU)

An organization's SBUs may choose stability over growth by continuing current activities without any significant change in direction. Stability strategies are not the same as 'doing nothing', for to remain stable actions have to be taken to defend the current market position from competitors. There may be several reasons for opting for such a strategic direction.

- The current environment is hostile or unpredictable making investment required for growth unattractive.
- A balance has to be maintained in the organization so that finite resources have to be deployed in other SBUs which provide greater opportunities.
- A position of maturity has been reached where further growth is difficult and emphasis is placed on defending the current position.
- Many small business owners opt for this strategy as they are happy with their position having found a niche that they understand and which they are able to defend.

Stability strategies can be very useful in the short to medium term but can be dangerous in the longer term as competitors start to make inroads into market share. The Thomson

Travel Group (now a part of Tui AG), for example, was the market leader in the UK outbound holiday market from its entry to the market in 1965. It grew rapidly during the 1960s and 1970s and defended its market leadership position aggressively through discounting and other methods when necessary. However, its market share steadily decreased in the 1980s and early 1990s and Airtours (now MyTravel plc) was viewed as being consistently a step ahead of the UK number one (Bywater, 2001).

Wheelan and Hunger (2002) identified three variants of stability:

1 *Pause/proceed with caution* – is an opportunity to rest and reflect before continuing a growth or retrenchment strategy. It represents a deliberate attempt to make only incremental improvements until the environment changes. Such a strategy may be the result of excessive growth in the past, which has led to pressures on the organization, or from the need to stabilize after a period of decline.
2 *No change* – is a decision to do nothing new, choosing to continue current operations for the foreseeable future. Returns are adequate in the current position so why put these returns at risk by going after growth?
3 *Profit* – is a decision to do nothing new in a worsening environmental position but instead to act as though the organization's problems are only temporary. The profit strategy attempts to support profits when an organization's sales are declining by reducing investment and reducing unnecessary expenditure.

Retrenchment strategies (reduce the activities of the SBU)

An organization's SBU may pursue a retrenchment strategy when it is in a weak competitive position and the environment remains hostile for the alternative stability or growth strategies. For example, in the period following the 11 September 2001 terrorist attacks in America, travel companies around the world chose to reduce the scale of their operations in response to the severe drop in demand. Aer Lingus, the Irish airline, for example, which relied on the Transatlantic trade (which was particularly badly hit) for about 70% of its revenues, scaled back a large parts of its operations in the wake of the attacks, looked for potential partners and sought additional sources of finance. Swissair and the Belgian airline Sabena both went bankrupt.

Wheelan and Hunger (2002) identified four variants of retrenchment:

1 *Turnaround* – emphasizes the improvement in operational efficiency when an organization has problems which whilst serious are not critical. Analogous to a weight reduction diet, Pearce and Robbins (1994) view such a strategy as a two-stage process involving contraction followed by consolidation. Contraction is the initial effort to 'stop the bleeding' with general cutbacks in size and costs followed by consolidation which implements a programme to stabilize the now leaner organization.
2 *Captive company* – involves giving up independence in return for security whereby management offers the company to one of its largest customers to ensure survival. The customer guarantees the survival of the company by offering a long-term contract.
3 *Sell out/divestment* (see also strategic methods chapter) – if a an organization or SBU is in a weak competitive position it may choose to retrench through selling the entire organization or divesting those SBUs that are in a weak position in order to provide finance for those that are stronger.
4 *Bankruptcy/liquidation* – occurs when the organization finds itself in a very poor competitive position with few prospects. Bankruptcy (sometimes called administration)

involves giving up the management of the company to the courts in return for some settlement of the corporation's obligations. The court appointed managers would attempt to keep the organization going as a 'going concern'. By contrast liquidation is the termination of the organization the organization is too weak to be sold to others as a going concern and any assets are sold in order to pay as much as possible to the organization's creditors.

Strategic development and risk

There are risks associated with all forms of strategic development. The risks are smallest when development is largely based upon existing core competences and when it takes place in existing markets. The risks are greatest when development requires entry to unrelated markets. Whether or not the risks are worth taking will depend upon the current position of the organization and the state of its markets and products. Entry to new markets, whether related or unrelated, will depend upon the business's assessment of the opportunities in new markets compared to opportunities in its existing markets.

References and further reading

Ansoff, I. (1987) *Corporate Strategy.* London: Penguin.

Baden-Fuller, C. and Stopford, J. (1992) *Rejuvenating the Mature Business.* Oxford: Routledge.

Barney, J.B. (2002) *Gaining and Sustaining Competitive Advantage.* Upper Saddle River, NJ: Prentice Hall.

Bywater, M. (2001) Who Owns Whom in the European Travel Distribution Industry, in D. Buhalis and E. Laws (eds), *Tourism Distribution Channels: Practices, Issues and Transformations.* London: Continuum.

Cravens, D.W., Greenley, G., Piercy, N.F. and Slater S. (1997) Integrating Contemporary Strategic Management Perspectives. *Long Range Planning*, 30 (4), August, 493–506.

Cronshaw, M., Davis, E. and Kay, J. (1990) On Being Stuck in the Middle or 'Good Food Costs Less at Sainsburys'. Working paper, *Centre for Business Strategy*, London School of Business.

Doganis, R. (2001) *The Airline Business in the 21st Century.* London: Routledge.

Doran, R. (2000) EasyJet Plans Price War. *The Times*, London, p. 29.

Finlay, P. (2000) *Strategic Management: An Introduction to Business and Corporate Strategy.* Harlow: Pearson Education.

Grant, R.M. (1991) The Resource Based Theory of Competitive Advantage: Implications for Strategy Formulation. *California Management Review*, 33 (Spring), 114–35.

Haberberg, A. and Rieple, A. (2001) *The Strategic Management of Organizations.* Harlow: Pearson Education.

Hall, R. (1992) The Strategic Analysis of Intangible Resources. *Strategic Management Journal*, 13, 135–44.

Hamel, G. and Prahalad, C.K. (1989) Strategic Intent. *Harvard Business Review*, 67 (3), 63–76.

Hamel, G. and Prahalad, C.K. (1994) *Competing for the Future.* Cambridge, MA: Harvard Business School Press.

Heene, A. and Sanchez, R. (eds) (1997) *Competence-Based Strategic Management.* New York: John Wiley.

Johnson, G. and Scholes, K. (2002) *Exploring Corporate Strategy*, 6th edn. Hemel Hempstead: Prentice Hall.

Kay, J. (1993) *Foundations of Corporate Success.* Oxford: Oxford University Press.

Kay, J. (1995) Learning to Define the Core Business. *Financial Times*, 1 December.

Miller, D. (1992) The Generic Strategy Trap. *Journal of Business Strategy*, 13(1), 37–42.

Mintzberg H. (1991) *The Strategy Process –*

Concepts, Contexts, Cases. Englewood Cliffs, NJ: Prentice Hall.

Mintzberg, H., Quinn, J.B. and Ghoshal, S. (1995) *The Strategy Process: Concepts, Contexts and Cases, European Edition.* Englewood Cliffs, NJ: Prentice Hall.

Pearce II, J.A. and Robbins, D.K. (1994) Retrenchment Remains the Foundation of Business Turnaround. *Strategic Management Journal,* June, 313–323.

Poon, A. (1993) *Tourism, Technology and Competitive Strategies.* Wallingford: CABI.

Porter, M.E. (1980) *Competitive Strategy: Techniques for Analysing Industries and Competitors.* New York: Free Press.

Porter, M.E. (1985) *Competitive Advantage.* New York: Free Press.

Prahalad, C.K. and Hamel, G. (1990) The Core Competence of the Corporation, in *Harvard Business Review,* reprinted in Segal-Horn, S. (1998) (ed.), *The Strategy Reader.* Oxford: Blackwell in association with The Open University.

Stalk, G., Evans, P. and Shulmann, L.E. (1992) Competing on Capabilities: The New Rules of Corporate Strategy. *Harvard Business Review,* March/April, 57–69.

Wheelen, T.S. and Hunger, J.D. (2002) *Strategic Management and Business Policy,* 8th edn. Upper Saddle River, NJ: Prentice Hall.

www.compass-group.co.uk

www.cruise2.com

www.holidaybreak.com

Strategic methods of development for travel and tourism

Introduction and Chapter Overview

The decision as to which method of strategic development to adopt is critical to the success of strategy. We encountered the idea of growth as one of the main business objectives in Chapter 1. Chapter 10 discussed the theory of competitive and directional strategies and their contribution in achieving growth objectives. The theories developed in these earlier chapters underpin much of the discussion undertaken here. The variety of methods used for development will be considered, together with a critical appraisal of the success or failure of these methods.

The chapter briefly considers internal (or organic) growth, and then discusses the various mechanisms of external development. The recent trend in collaborative arrangements such as the strategic alliance is discussed and finally, the chapter looks at 'downsizing' strategies such as demerger.

Learning Objectives

After studying this chapter, students should be able to:

- define and distinguish between internal and external business growth;

- describe the various types of merger and acquisition;

- explain the motivations behind mergers and acquisitions and the reasons why they succeed or fail;

- describe what is meant by the various forms of joint development such as strategic alliances, and why organizations enter into them;

- explain what is meant by a disposal and describe why organizations pursue this pathway;

- understand the regulatory and legal frameworks that influence business growth.

Alternative strategic methods

Having considered the direction of development and aspects of competitive strategy in the previous chapter we can now turn to a consideration of the strategic methods that can be employed to achieve the strategic objectives that have been set. In determining the methods by which strategic development will take place the management of a travel and tourism organization is faced with making a choice between three basic options:

- to develop internally (or organically as it is sometimes called), utilizing existing available resources;
- to merge with or acquire other companies, or;
- to develop some form of joint development with other organizations by making some form of collaborative arrangement.

Clearly many organizations use each of the alternative strategic options in different circumstances. The same company may, for instance, choose to grow organically in one market, acquiring another company in a second market and form a collaborative venture in a third market in recognition of the differing market characteristics that exist.

Organic (internal) growth

The commonest mechanism of growth

Organic growth is the most straightforward mechanism of business growth. Most companies have used internal growth as their main method of growth at some time, and so its 'popularity' is obvious. The essential feature of organic growth is the reinvestment of previous years' profits in the existing business, together with finance provided by shareholders and banks. By increasing capacity (by, say, offering a larger number of holidays for sale), the organization takes on more employees to cope with the extra demand. In so doing, turnover increases and so does the capital (balance sheet) value of the business.

Organic growth is common during the early stages of corporate development as companies build markets and develop new products. However, large companies may use it alongside external growth to consolidate market position. The introduction of an additional cruise ship by a cruise line is an example of internal growth. Earlier years' retained profits, possibly enhanced by additional funding provided by banks or shareholders, are channelled into the development and the organization benefits from the increased market share and increased turnover.

Organic growth offers a number of potential advantages over other methods of development:

- It is usually a lower risk option, in that the increase in capacity remains fully under the control of the existing management thereby avoiding the risks of dealing with other organizations.
- Core competences can usually be exploited and existing expertise can be capitalized upon.
- The problems associated with the integration of differing organizational cultures are avoided.
- Disruption to cash flows is likely to be less than in the case of mergers or acquisitions and to a lesser extent with the various forms of joint development.

On the other hand, organic growth is also associated with a number of potential disadvantages:

- It is usually a slower mechanism compared to the external growth methods where the 'bolting on' of a new company or cooperation with other organizations is a faster route to growth than gradual growth by internal means.
- Relying on the competences and resources of a single organization may lead to shortages and might mean that important opportunities are not exploited.

Many large companies have used this method extensively in reaching their present size, but few have used the method exclusively. Thus when British Airways developed a low cost subsidiary airline ('Go Airlines') in the late 1990s, the airline chose to develop the airline internally from scratch rather than purchase an existing low cost airline, such as perhaps Ryanair or easyJet, or to collaborate in the development with an existing airline. Similarly, the Marriott hotel corporation developed its Courtyard hotels concept organically during the 1990s, from the drawing board through to its current international market penetration in major business cities (Crawford-Welch, 1994).

This method tends to be chosen in circumstances where:

- suitable partners for joint development are unavailable;
- merger or acquisition is prevented on the grounds of cost, unavailability of suitable targets or regulatory disapproval;
- directors want to maintain control;
- the necessary resources and competences are available internally.

Key concept: Internal growth

Internal growth is expansion by means of the reinvestment of previous years' profits, loan and share capital in the existing business. This results in increased capacity, increased employment and ultimately, increased turnover.

- *Advantages*: lower risk, within existing area of expertise, avoids high exposure to costs of alternative growth mechanisms (e.g. by debt servicing).
- *Disadvantages*: slower than external growth, little scope for diversification, relies upon the skills of existing management in the business.

External mechanisms of growth – mergers and acquisitions (M&As)

Definitions

It is difficult to open the business press without encountering details of a proposed or progressing merger or acquisition. The term *merger* is however sometimes replaced in such text with the word *takeover* or by *acquisition*. The same news story may use all three terms as though the words meant the same thing. For the purposes of a strategy text such as this, it is important to clarify the main terms generally used in connection with this process.

In a *merger* the shareholders of the organizations come together, normally willingly, to share the resources of the enlarged (merged) organization, with shareholders from both sides of the merger becoming shareholders in the new organization.

For example in November 2001, in the business downturn following the September 2001 terrorist attacks on the USA, P&O Princess Cruises and the Royal Caribbean cruise line announced plans to merge. The merger, which was announced as a 'merger of equals', would form the world's largest cruise company with 41 ships offering 75 000 berths. The top jobs would be shared between managers of the two companies and the merger it was stated would lead to the saving of US dollars 100 million in annual operating economies.

An *acquisition* is a 'marriage' of unequal partners with one organization buying and subsuming the other party. In such a transaction the shareholders of the target organization cease to be owners of the enlarged organization unless payment to the shareholders is paid partly in shares in the acquiring company. The shares in the smaller company are bought by the larger.

For example, over the past few years the leading UK outbound tour operators have been very active in acquiring smaller rivals. The leading tour operator, the Thomson Travel Group, for example acquired tour operators such as Austravel, Crystal Holidays and Tropical Places in the late 1990s. However Thomson was itself acquired during 2000 by Preussag (now renamed Tui) a leading German industrial conglomerate based in Hanover, which included tour operating, airlines and travel distribution in its portfolio of activities under brand names such as TUI, Hapag-Lloyd and Fritidsresor.

A *takeover* is technically the same as an acquisition, but the term is often taken to mean that the approach of the larger acquiring company is unwelcome from the point of view of the smaller target company. The term *hostile takeover* describes an offer for the shares of a target public limited company which the target's directors reject. If the shareholders accept the offer (despite the recommendation of the directors) then the hostile takeover goes ahead.

For example, an attempted takeover of First Choice plc by Airtours plc (now renamed MyTravel plc), which would have involved the takeover of the UK's third largest integrated travel business by the second, was resisted by the board of First Choice and was eventually blocked after intervention by the European Commission in 1999. A further example is provided by an acrimonious battle in the cruise sector. In 2000 Carnival Corporation of the USA, the world's largest cruising company, and Star Lines, the world's fourth largest cruise line which is based in Hong Kong, both tried to take over the Norwegian Cruise Line based in Miami. After an expensive and hard fought battle Star Lines succeeded in wresting control of the takeover target.

Whichever of these routes is taken, the result is a larger and more financially powerful company. The word *integration* is the collective term used to describe these growth mechanisms.

A brief history of M&As

All public limited companies have a market value. Market value equals the number of shares on the stock market (the *share volume*) multiplied by the share price. It is taken to be a good indicator of the value of a company because it accounts for the company's asset value plus the 'goodwill' that the market attaches to the share. It follows that the combined market value of a merger or acquisition is the two companies' values added together. It is an indication of what the company will be valued at after the integration goes ahead.

Whilst the M&A process is a well-used mechanism in strategic development, recent history has shown that UK based companies have used it rather more than those based in mainland Europe. Only in the USA have companies used the mechanism to a similar extent. However, recent figures show increased merger and acquisition activity in the global economy generally as companies feel the need to increase in size to become more internationally competitive.

One of the consequences of M&A activity is that many of the well-known 'names' of yesteryear have disappeared while some of today's best-known companies are relatively young in their current form: examples are C&N Touristik (now renamed Thomas Cook AG) owned jointly by Lufthansa, the German airline, and Karstadt, a leading German department store group, operated Condor a large charter airline and a large tour operation operating several brands including Neckermann. In December 2000 the company completed the acquisition from Preussag (another German company) of Thomas Cook, the well-known travel and travellers cheque brand which is usually credited with having been the world's first tour operator, having started operations in the UK during the 1840s.

A common misunderstanding surrounding the integration process is that two organizations always come together in their entirety. In practice, many integrations are the result of one organization joining with a divested *part* of another. That is to say that one company has made a strategic decision to withdraw from an industry or market and in an attempt to maximize the value of the resources it no longer wants (i.e. an unwanted part of the previous company structure), it sells them to another company. The reasons why companies demerge and sell subsidiaries in non-core elements is addressed later in this chapter.

Explanations and motivations for M&As

There are a number of potential reasons for pursuing an external growth strategy. We have already encountered the overall objective of growth, but growth is seldom a stand-alone objective. The question is *why is growth a desired objective?* The following is a summary of these motivations.

- To *increase market share* in order to increase pricing power in an industry.
- To *enter a new market*, possibly to offset the effects of decline in current markets or to broaden market portfolio.
- To *reduce competition*, possibly by purchasing a competitor.
- To *gain control of valuable brand names* or pieces of intellectual property like patents.

- To gain preferential *access to distribution channels* (to gain factor inputs on preferential terms or to secure important supplies) by purchasing a supplier.
- To *broaden product range* in order to exploit more market opportunities and to spread risk.
- To *develop new products* for the market faster than internal research and development could do.
- To *gain access to new production or information technologies* in order to reduce costs, increase quality or increase product differentiation.
- To *gain economies of scale*, such as by increasing purchasing power so that inputs can be purchased at lower unit cost.
- To *make productive use of spare or underused resources*, such as finance that is sitting on deposit in a bank.
- To *'asset strip'* – the practice of breaking up an acquired company and recovering more than the price paid by selling the parts separately.
- To *enhance corporate reputation* (appropriate if the existing company name has been associated with an alleged misdemeanour).

The precise nature of the integration selected will depend upon the specific objectives being pursued. If, for example, market share is the most important objective, then it is likely that a company will seek a suitable horizontal integration. On the other hand, a vertical integration would be more appropriate if supply or distribution concerns are uppermost amongst a company's threats.

External growth is usually expensive and it therefore has significant financial resource implications, not to mention sizeable bills presented by lawyers and merchant (investment) bankers who are inevitably brought in to advise on the process. Accordingly, it is entered into for specific strategic purposes that cannot be served through the normal progression of organic development.

Synergy – the main objective of M&As

Overriding all other purposes served by integration is that of synergy. Synergy refers to the benefits that can be gained when organizations join forces rather than work apart. An integration can be said to be synergistic when the *whole is greater than the sum of the parts*. More popularly, synergy can be expressed as '2 + 2 = 5.' If the integration is to achieve synergy, the 'new' company must perform more efficiently than either of the two parties would have done had they remained separate.

On a simple level, we can conceptualize synergy using a human example. When two people work *together* performing a task like lifting heavy logs onto a lorry, they can achieve far more work than two people lifting logs separately. A rally team of two enables the team to win a race if they work together with one driving and one navigating. If the two were to work separately, then each person would have to drive and navigate at the same time.

Synergy is measured in terms of increased added value. Kay (1993) made the point that, 'Value is added, and only added [in an integration] if distinctive capabilities or strategic assets are exploited more effectively. A merger adds no value if all that is acquired is a distinctive capability which is already fully exploited, as the price paid will reflect the competitive advantage held.' Accordingly, integrations that do not enable the 'new' organization to produce higher profits or consolidate a stronger market position are usually deemed to have been relatively unsuccessful. The next section describes why failures sometimes occur.

Potential problems with M&A – why do they sometimes go wrong?

The fact that mergers and acquisitions are undoubtedly popular as methods of business growth may lead us to conclude that they are always successful. In practice, this is not always true. A number of studies have analysed the performance of companies after integrations and the findings are not very encouraging (see for example Kay, 1995; Porter, 1985; Ravenscraft and Scherer, 1987).

These studies found that many corporate 'marriages' failed to work and ended in divorce. Of those that did survive, Kay (1995) found that when profitability before and after the integration were compared, a 'nil to negative effect' was achieved.

The main failure factors • • •

There are a number of reasons why integrations do not work. We can summarize these 'failure factors' under six headings.

1 *Lack of research* into the circumstances of the target company (and hence incomplete knowledge). Failure in this regard can result in some nasty surprises after the integration.
2 *Cultural incompatibility* between the two parties.
3 *Lack of communication* within and between the two parties.
4 *Loss of key personnel* in the target company after the integration.
5 *Paying too much for the acquired company* and hence overexposing the acquiring company to financial risk.
6 *Assuming that growth in a target company's market will continue indefinitely.* Market trends can fall as well as rise.

Government policy and integrations • • •

Government policy on mergers may have contributed to some integration failures. Corporate growth can be restricted by government (which in the UK is represented by the Competition Commission, formerly the Monopolies and Mergers Commission), as companies are only allowed to establish a certain market share. In the UK an integration which would result in the new organization controlling over 25% of the market is generally subject to government scrutiny which often results in such a merger being blocked. Being prevented from expanding in a related area may force some companies to take the more risky route of diversification (acquiring a company making different products in different markets).

Success factors for M&A

History has shown that mergers and acquisitions work best when the initiator company follows a number of intuitively obvious 'rules'. They are designed to offset the failure factors we identified above. The chances of success might be increased by:

- The *identification of a suitable 'target' candidate* with whom to merge or acquire. The emphasis on the word *suitable* is expanded upon below.
- A preparation for an approach should involve a detailed evaluation of the target company's *competitive position*. This would typically comprise a survey of its profitability, its market share, its product portfolio, its competitiveness in resource markets and so on.

- Consideration being given to the *compatibility of the two companies' management styles and culture*. Because integrations often involve the merging of the two boards of directors, it is usually important that the directors from the two companies are able to work together. In addition, the cultures, if not identical in character, should be able to be brought together successfully.
- The possibility of a successful marriage between the two *corporate structures* (see the discussion of this in Chapter 13). If one is, for example, very tall and centralized and the other is shorter and decentralized, problems may occur in attempting to bring the two together.
- Retaining key personnel. If the target company has key personnel (say a key manager or a distinctive research capability resident within a number of uniquely qualified scientists), then measures should be taken to ensure that these *key people are retained after the integration*. This can often be achieved by holding contractual talks with these people before the integration goes ahead.
- The initiating company ensuring that the *price paid for the target* (of the valuation of its shares) *is realistic*. A key calculation of any investment is the return made on it and this is usually measured as the profit before interest and tax divided by the price paid for it. It follows that the return on investment (as a percentage) will depend upon the price paid for the target company. The valuation of a company is a complex accounting calculation, which depends the balance sheet value, the prospects and performance of the company, and the value of its intangible assets (such as its brands, patents, etc.)

Accordingly, the importance of detailed information-gathering before the integration cannot be overemphasized.

External growth without M&A – joint development

A joint development is where two or more organizations share resources and activities to pursue a strategy (Johnson and Scholes, 2002). The development method has been increasingly popular over recent years as organizations seek help and support from other organizations. Increasingly complex environments (such as globalization) has meant that organizations often cannot cope through using their own resources and competences alone. Joint developments enable organizations to avoid some of the limitations of mergers and acquisitions, such as regulatory restrictions, whilst still gaining the benefits of collaboration.

Collaborative strategy (or cooperative strategy as it is often termed) is rapidly becoming the counterpart to competitive strategy as a key strategic management tool (Faulkner and Bowman, 1995). In rapidly globalizing world markets, collaborative strategy is the engine driving companies that are deficient in certain competences, resources or assets, to link together with other companies in a similar predicament in order to derive jointly the competitive advantages they lack on their own. As Ohmae (1989) observed in comparing commercial organizations with the foreign policies of national governments, 'companies are just beginning to learn what nations have always known: in a complex, uncertain world filled with dangerous opponents, it is best not to go it alone'.

In categorizing these collaborative agreements theoretical bases have been advanced. Contractor and Lorange (1988), for instance, viewed interorganizational collaboration in terms of the degree of interdependency between the parties involved. Faulkner (1995) categorized collaborative relationships in relation to their degree of integration ranging from markets to hierarchies, with the market end of the spectrum being dominated by the

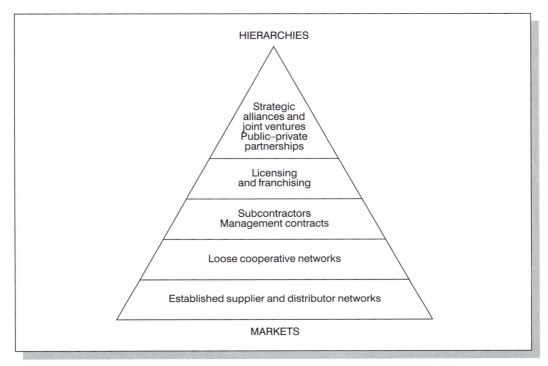

Figure 11.1 The intermediate organizational forms between markets and hierarchies (based on Faulkner, 1995)

price mechanism and the hierarchy being dominated by organizational decisions. Between the two extremes a range of interorganizational forms exist with ascending levels of integration. Strategic alliances and joint ventures represent the most integrated form of interorganizational collaboration. Further integration represents a single corporate form subject to fully integrated decision-making. Figure 11.1 illustrates Faulkner's categorization of interorganizational forms.

Here we will focus on those aspects of joint development of most relevance to travel and tourism namely:

- Strategic alliances and joint ventures
- Public–private partnerships
- Franchising
- Management contracts
- Cooperative networks

Strategic alliances

Defining alliances

The literature is far from clear as to just what constitutes a 'strategic alliance' and many definitions have emerged such as those of French (1997), Bennett (1997) and Glaister and Buckley (1996). There is some consensus that strategic alliances represent a high level of collaboration between partner organizations and that alliances form a subset of collaborative activity that excludes a number of other forms of interfirm cooperation that are not alliances (Glaister and Buckley, 1996). Most writers would agree that the term strategic alliance applies largely to 'horizontal' interorganizational relationships between companies engaged in similar types of activity at the same level. Thus we can define a strategic alliance as:

A particular 'horizontal' form of inter-organizational relationship in which two or more organizations collaborate, without the formation of a separate independent organization, in order to achieve one or more common strategic objectives.

Bennett (1997) distinguished between 'tactical' alliances, which are loose forms of collaboration that exist to gain marketing benefits and 'strategic' alliances, which are characterized by being longer, and wider in their scope and level of commitment. A strategic alliance also involves, in many cases, a demonstration of commitment by way of *equity swaps* in which the partner companies purchase minority equity stakes in each other thereby having a vested interest in ensuring the financial success of partners. In categorizing strategic alliances, most writers would exclude buyer–seller relationships, subcontracting, franchising, and licensing, where to some degree the parties involved may have opposing goals and the relationships are 'vertical' between organizations along the channel of distribution.

The distinction between *joint ventures* and *strategic alliances* is one of emphasis rather than fundamental distinguishing characteristics. A joint venture normally implies joint ownership of assets by the parties involved, the formation of separate independent operating companies for the management of the shared activities, and collaboration on a relatively narrow range of activities. In practice the distinction between the two terms is often blurred.

The major Global Distribution Systems (GDS) operating in the travel industry (such as Sabre and Galileo) would be termed joint ventures since separate independent operating entities have been formed by the collaborating airlines and other investors which own these systems. These companies operate in a relatively autonomous fashion having their own offices, infrastructure and access to capital. Illinois based Galileo, for instance, was floated on the New York stock exchange in 1997. As a British Airways spokesman stated on the sale of the company's remaining 6.7% stake in the GDS in June 1999, 'Galileo is in a non-core area for us.' By way of contrast, strategic alliances have been formed between some airlines and these have been at the heart of the strategic development for the airlines involved. Although there have been some cross-equity holdings, most participants' core assets are directly owned and managed by the constituent airlines. Furthermore, the organizations established to manage the alliances are subject to the direct involvement of the airline alliance partners involved, only having minor devolved responsibilities.

Strategic alliances in the travel industry

The formation of strategic alliances has been evident in many industries including pharmaceuticals, vehicle manufacture and chemicals, and this process has been replicated in the international travel industry where alliances have come to form a central feature of the developing industrial structure. Alliances have been growing between airline and accommodation companies (with ancillary services such as car rental often also involved). It is clear that collaborative arrangements of various types have become an increasingly important strategic method of development in the travel industry, although statistical data indicating success or otherwise is often lacking. Many writers, including Gialloreto (1989),

Dev *et al.* (1996), Garnham (1996), Alamadari and Morell (1997), Bennett (1997), French (1997) and Oum and Park (1997), have pointed to the high level of activity in the field of travel industry alliance formation.

However, the alliances differ in:

- their motives;
- their scope;
- their structures;
- their objectives;
- the ways in which they are managed.

The motivations for forming strategic alliances in the travel industry are numerous and complex, and a full discussion of these motivations is beyond the scope of this chapter. It is clear, however, that the recent economic history of the international travel industry has been characterized by the emergence of many alliances, some of which have subsequently failed and new realignments of companies have been forged. Long-standing 'natural' alliances between travel companies and accommodation providers which saw the ownership of hotels by railway, shipping and airline companies, have been replaced by other arrangements as inter-company and inter-modal competition has increased (Garnham, 1996). Throughout the 1980s, alliance formation in the global travel industry increased until the position was reached in the early 1990s at which most of the world's major airline, hotel and car rental firms were linked by a web of cross-shareholdings, joint ventures, and joint sales and service arrangements (Dev *et al.*,1996).

Many examples of alliances exist in the airline and hotel sectors, although many fall short of being 'strategic' in the true sense. Some are probably best described as 'tactical' in their orientation, focusing primarily on marketing and information technology collaboration, rather than wider collaboration. In distinguishing between three levels of alliance on the basis of short-term, medium-term or long-term (strategic) relationships, Dev and Klein (1993) argued that in such a hierarchy of relationships, partners often progress from the simple short-term relationships through to complex strategic relationships, but that only at the strategic level do alliances offer companies the ability to respond to the pressures of global competition and illiquidity. Potential benefits, they argued, accrue from enhanced market coverage both geographically and by segment; greater economies of scale in advertising, sales, distribution and purchasing; and complementary strengths in operations and marketing.

Strategic alliances – examples from the hotel and tour operating sectors

Radisson Hotels, part of the Carlson group of travel companies, has expanded through an international strategy based on strategic alliances with local hotel groups around the world such as Edwardian Hotels in the UK and Movenpick based in Switzerland (Olsen, 1993). Hilton Hotels also provide a case study illustrating the benefits to be derived from a collaborative approach. The two arms of Hilton, Hilton Hotels Corporation (HHC) of the USA and Hilton Hotels International, a subsidiary of Hilton plc which is based in the UK, were separated under different ownership in 1964, some 45 years after Conrad Hilton opened the first hotel to bear his surname in Chicago. Since that time the relationship between the two chains bearing the Hilton name has frequently been acrimonious and was never close until 1996 when both chains appointed chairmen committed to capitalizing fully on the strength of the Hilton brand. Negotiations culminated in 1997 with an agreement to form a wide-ranging strategic alliance between the two chains, covering a joint reservations system (boosted by $100 million spending on new technology), the extension of HHC's loyalty rewards to Hilton International, the adoption of joint brand identities including a new logo and joint marketing campaigns. To operationalize the strategic alliance the management of the two chains meet four times a year (Nissé, 1998).

In the tour-operating sector, examples of strategic alliances are less common as the preferred strategic method. One example is provided by the British based tour operator MyTravel which entered into a significant strategic alliance with the world's largest cruise line, Carnival Cruises, in April 1996 whereby Carnival acquired 29.5% of Airtours' ordinary share capital. The relationship was discontinued in 2001. Another British based tour operator, First Choice, however, entered a strategic alliance with Royal Caribbean Cruise Lines (RCCL) in 2000 whereby RCCL acquired an equity stake in First Choice plc.

A conceptualization of the collaborative process for international airlines

Figure 11.2 (Evans, 2001a) provides a conceptual model of the strategic management processes involved in the formation of strategic alliances using the airline sector as an example. It can be argued that a four-stage process takes place. The process involves first, the strategic analysis of the internal organizational and external environmental 'drivers' which act as the underlying motivating reasons for alliance formation. Second, alternative strategic options are postulated and evaluated and the option of strategic alliance formation (either with or without equity) participation is chosen. Third, implementation issues have to be considered including the choice of appropriate partners and issues relating to the structure and scope of the alliance. Finally, the strategic alliance is evaluated against selected criteria purporting to measure the success of the alliance. The evaluation of the alliance is fed back into the analytical phase so that any changes based upon experience can be incorporated.

Motivations for strategic alliance formation

Identifying 'driving' forces

A number of studies have sought to identify the underlying motivations for the formation of strategic alliances (Glaister and Buckley, 1996; Bennett, 1997) and it is generally accepted that some types of external driver need to be present (Faulkner, 1995). Two well-known authors in this field (Child and Faulkner, 1998) have suggested that there may be six key external driving forces and four key internal needs acting as motivational forces in the formation of alliances.

External driving forces for alliance formation are:

1 Turbulence in world markets and high economic uncertainty.
2 The existence of economies of scale and/or scope as competitive cost-reducing agents.
3 The globalization or regionalization of a growing number of industries.

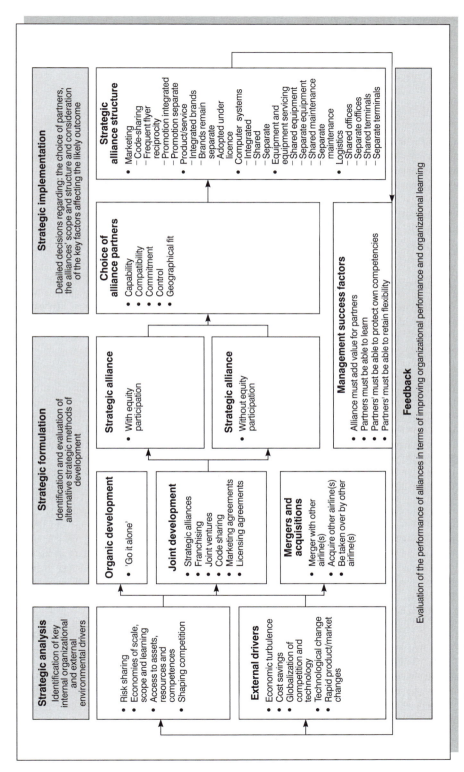

Figure 11.2 Conceptualization of the collaborative strategy process for international airlines (adapted from Evans, 2001a)

4 The globalization of technology.
5 Fast technological change leading to ever-increasing investment requirement.
6 Shortening life cycles.

Internal drivers for alliance formation are:

1 To achieve economies of scale and learning with one's partner.
2 To get access to the benefits of the other firms' assets, be these technology, market access, capital, operational capacity, products or personnel.
3 To reduce risk by sharing it, notably in terms of capital requirements, but also in respect of research and development expenditure.
4 To help shape the market.

The nature of the internal needs and external drivers will of course vary between industries and industry sectors, and the emphasis may alter in different markets and may shift over time.

Potential difficulties with strategic alliances

Despite the surge in their popularity, international strategic alliances are often viewed as inherently unstable organizational forms (Beamish and Inkpen, 1995). It has been noted by Porter and Fuller (1986), for instance, that alliances involve significant costs in terms of coordination, reconciling goals with an independent entity, and creating competitors. These associated costs serve frequently to make alliances transitional rather than stable organizational forms and therefore rarely can they be viewed as a sustainable means of creating competitive advantage. The failure rate associated with alliance arrangements is high, often resulting in significant costs to one or both parties concerned. This high failure rate has been reported in a number of studies. Bleeke and Ernst (1991), in their study of cross-border alliances, found that some two-thirds had run into serious managerial or financial trouble within the first two years, resulting in a high rate of failure.

In a travel industry context, alliances, it can be argued, are usually a second best option, often necessary only as result of regulatory and legal restrictions which frequently make mergers and acquisitions problematic. In the airline sector, for example, most countries have legal restrictions limiting airline ownership by foreign nationals. This view of alliances as being the second best option that is pursued in cases where mergers or takeovers are prevented is illustrated by the case of the Star airline alliance which includes United Airlines and Lufthansa. This alliance has no fewer than 24 committees that endeavour to reach agreement on matters such as network connectivity, purchasing and customer relations. The chairs of these committees are spread around the partners so as to involve fully all the parties to the agreement. Such an organizational structure can hardly be viewed as a model of business efficiency and its long-term sustainability therefore must be questionable.

However, in the travel industry where full ownership of travel companies by foreign based nationals is often prohibited, and which is often characterized by a high degree of consumer loyalty to 'national champions', alliance formation has in many cases been viewed as the only viable market entry mechanism, at least in the short to medium term. Thus, alliances, it can be argued, are rarely stable sustainable entities, for they commonly represent the only viable market entry mechanism when regulatory and other barriers to entry effectively block other market entry modes (such as full acquisition). Additionally, many of the alliances that are formed appear in a constant state of flux, altering their shapes, sizes and partners in response to changes in the competitive environment with partners being added or dropped and partners falling out amongst themselves. Evidence to support the notion that travel industry alliances are not sustainable in the longer run is provided by the many examples of alliances that have been formed and subsequently dissolved or changed in some way and others that have been discussed but have failed to be implemented (see the airline alliances case study later in this book).

Cultural problems in strategic alliances – the case of Inter-Continental Hotels

Alliances often create tension between the partners involved and this can ultimately force the partners apart. Cultural forces can create differences in perception and interpretation of phenomena as evidenced by the break up of the alliance between Inter-Continental and SAS Hotels (Dev and Klein, 1993). The Inter-Continental chain of hotels had been built up by Pan American World Airways (PanAm), and was established in major world business centres served by the airline. After several ownership changes, 40% of the hotel group was bought by Scandinavian Airways System (SAS) in 1989, with the remaining ownership residing with Japanese property group Saison. The two groups represented divergent corporate cultures, SAS being entrepreneurial in its style, with a small executive staff and a flat organizational hierarchy whereas Saison was traditional in its approach, and concerned primarily with property investments. The alliance was ended in 1991 when Saison took full control of the group before its sale to the British company, Bass, during 1998.

One further point to note is that alliances can fail not because of the partners' failure to agree on substantive points but, on the contrary, the alliance leads to the delivery of a high degree of collaboration and agreement between the partners. In cases where the results of successful collaboration are apparent, partners may be forced towards merging their activities providing regulatory and legal restrictions do not stand in the way. Collaboration, though often financially beneficial, nevertheless may imply that the partners are operating sub-optimally, since the need for communication and management duplication imposes higher cost levels. In the case of Hilton Hotels Corporation and Hilton Hotels International, for example, there is an obvious benefit in combining the brands and since management changes took place during 1996 the managerial will has been in place to ensure that a wide-ranging strategic alliance has emerged. The very success of the alliance in this case may make it unsustainable in the longer term since operational and marketing efficiencies could be achieved through the merger of the two companies. Indeed City of London analysts have postulated that the benefits of the alliance can only be maximized by a move towards a full merger of the two chains (Nissé, 1998).

Partner selection in strategic alliances

The many heavily publicized alliance failures in the travel industry are well known, but the underlying reasons for failure are not well understood. Despite the evident instability demonstrated by many of the travel industry alliances, there may be ways in which companies can form and manage alliances to ensure a longer life expectancy and a higher degree of stability. Although there are, no doubt, many complex reasons for alliance failures, many writers (such as Kanter, 1994; Mason, 1993; Stafford, 1994; Medcof, 1997) agree that poor initial selection of alliance partners is a key variable.

Medcof (1997), for example, postulated that the first imperative in partner selection is to ensure that the proposed partner represents a good *strategic fit*, that is the weaknesses of one partner are complemented by the strengths of the other partner and vice versa. In the case of the Hilton Hotel Corporation and Hilton Hotels International strategic alliance, one partner is clearly strong in one geographical area, North America whilst the other is strong internationally.

Four further criteria determine whether a proposed partnership is likely to be workable at an operational level. These criteria referred to conveniently as the four Cs: Capability, Compatibility, Commitment and Control. It should be noted that these partner selection criteria vary from the 'four C's' previously put forward by Brouthers *et al* (1993).

Capability

The capability criterion questions whether the prospective partners have the ability successfully to carry out their respective roles in the alliance. The alliance partnership between British Airways and US Airways, for instance, broke down partly because US Airways was incapable of offering the access to a comprehensive US route network that British Airways desired.

Compatibility

The compatibility criterion concerns the ability of the partners to work together effectively. It therefore relates to the respective corporate cultures of the partner organizations and to the working relationships between staff and management at the partners. The cases of SAS Hotels/Saison, and arguably the often difficult relationahsips in the longstanding alliance between KLM/Northwest Airlines illustrate the need for compatibility among partners.

Commitment

The commitment criterion concerns the willingness of partners to commit resources, effort and know-how to an alliance. In a worst case scenario, a partner might expend only the minimum effort required to keep the alliance alive whilst opportunistically leaving others to bear the brunt of the responsibilities and at the same time receiving know-how and market intelligence from alliance partners. The level of financial commitment by KLM in its alliance was out of proportion in comparison with the commitment made by Northwest. This factor can be viewed as having exacerbated the cultural compatibility problems that have been evident in the alliance.

Control

The control criterion concerns the appropriateness of the arrangements for the coordination of the alliance activities. In some cases one partner may be dominant thereby suppressing the aspirations of others. In other cases a dominant partner may ensure the effectiveness of the alliance owing to that partner's superior expertise or market position.

The key question with regard to control is whether the system of control allows all partners to achieve their strategic objectives. The need to ensure fairness and equity in the control of the Star airline alliance has made the management structure highly bureaucratic which will surely be unsustainable in the longer term when competitive flexibility will be required.

Public–private partnerships

Another form of joint development common in travel and tourism is what are often referred to as *public–private partnerships* which are a response to the nature of the industry. As Long (1997) stated, 'the fragmented nature of the tourism industry comprised, in most areas, of large numbers of small to medium-scale enterprises, together with a wide range of interest groups from public sector agencies to community groups in destinations, is increasingly recognized'. As a response to the fragmentation and range of public sector, private sector and community stakeholder groups, various types of arrangements are now widespread in the UK and elsewhere to bring the interests together through collaborative arrangements in the form of public–private partnerships.

Public sector involvement in tourism is commonplace and has been brought about by a variety of factors (Heeley, 2001). These include the need to:

- regulate private sector activities;
- provide non-remunerative infrastructure and superstructure;
- remove obstacles to more effective private sector performance;
- redress market failures;
- provide industry leadership and promotion.

Increasingly, though, it has been recognized in many countries that in terms of government spending (at national, regional and local levels) spending on tourism rates well down on the order of priorities. Such spending is insignificant both in scale and in terms of need when compared with spending on health, social welfare and education. Tourism is, however, recognized by governments as a significant and growing contributor to revenues and as a contributor to the viability of other activities and investments such as cultural venues and transportation improvements. Although governments may see an advantage to be gained from supporting tourism through public–private partnerships, such support must be balanced against other state-funded areas of expenditure. One way in which some governments have shown limited support for tourism is by *pump priming* to *lever* larger private sector financial contributions once a project or destination has been shown to have potential.

A feature of the past 40 years has been the creation of 'hybrid' public–private sector mechanisms that have been premised on the public sector letting go of some or all of its traditional intervention and leadership accountabilities (Heeley, 2001). The World Tourism Organization (1996) cited numerous examples of such partnerships ranging from Amsterdam to Penang and including Partnership Australia, the Polish Tourist Authority, the Canadian Tourist Commission and US State Tourism departments.

In the UK these joint development initiatives were pioneered by Plymouth in 1978 with the formation of the Plymouth Marketing Bureau. British cities such as Birmingham, Liverpool, Glasgow, Sheffield and Manchester followed in the 1990s. Heeley (2001) stated that both Destination Sheffield and Marketing Manchester were notable as prototypes of what he termed 'the integrated destination marketing communications exercise'. In these cases and in subsequent British examples (such as Leicester Promotions in 1993, Coventry and Warwickshire Promotions in 1997 and Birmingham's re-emergence as Birmingham Marketing Partnerships in 1997) normal visitor and convention bureaux activities, i.e. tourism, were supplemented by the related fields of city imaging and festivals management (Heeley, 2001).

Franchising

Franchising is one of the most popular methods of growth in parts of the travel and tourism industry. Leading industry brands such as Avis, Hertz (car rental companies), Marriott, Holiday Inn, Radisson (hotels), McDonald's, Burger King, Kentucky Fried Chicken (fast food outlets), British Airways, Lufthansa and Air France (airlines) have made franchising an important element of the strategic methods they have employed.

Franchising is a method involving two parties: the franchisor and the franchisee. In return for gaining access to the brand attributes, image, marketing and other support from the franchisor, the franchisee usually takes a substantial portion of the financial risk (providing the capital investment) and pays fees to the franchisor. The franchise method can vary in its detailed implementation. It may involve fairly simple arrangement whereby one franchisee develops one unit or a single territory from the franchisor. Many Avis or McDonald's franchisees for example, operate one or a limited number of franchise locations. A more complex arrangement may exist when a large company purchases a *master franchise* from the franchisor, which gives the company exclusive rights to the franchise name for a region or country. Thus, Whitbread expanded the Marriott chain of hotels in the UK through the operation of a master franchise from the Marriott Corporation.

The reasons for the popularity of franchising for the franchisor include (Olsen *et al.*, 1991):

- seldom having to provide the capital;
- not having to endure alone the problems associated with regulations and licensing required in some countries;
- not having to engage in extensive site selection.

However the franchisor has to be careful in respect of its franchisees. Specifically the franchisor needs to:

- scrutinize the structure, organization and financial viability of the franchisee;
- ensure that safeguards are in place so as to control standards and operational procedures of the franchisee.

Franchising at Holiday Inn Hotels and British Airways

Holiday Inn
An American entrepreneur named Kemmons Wilson opened the first Holiday Inn hotel in 1952 in Memphis, Tennessee, after he returned from a family holiday discouraged over the lack of family- and value-oriented lodgings. Children stayed free, and the hotel offered a swimming pool, air conditioning and restaurant on the property. Telephones, ice and free parking were standard as well. Although commonplace today, these services were revolutionary at the time and set a standard for the hotel industry.

The company became a pioneer of franchising and rapidly expanded the Holiday Inn system, primarily through utilizing this method of strategic growth. The brand was almost literally rolled out across the USA, following the US interstate highway system's growth across the country. On the heels of this domestic success, the brand soon found investor interest in Europe and Asia, becoming the largest single hotel brand in the world. By the late 1980s, the Holiday Inn brand could be found in many parts of the world.

In 1990, Six Continents plc, which had its corporate headquarters in London (then known as Bass plc), acquired Holiday Inn and moved the hotel headquarters from Memphis to Atlanta in the summer of 1991. Atlanta offered the corporate infra-structure, worldwide transportation access and international presence Six Continents felt was necessary for the company to succeed as a global business. Holiday Inn together with its complementary brands (which include Holiday Inn Express, Crowne Plaza and Intercontinental Hotels) now operate approximately 3100 hotels accounting for about 500 000 rooms. Approximately, 2700 of the hotels are franchised.

Go and Pine (1995) suggested that the franchise strategy pursued by Holiday Inn 'is among the greatest success stories in US business'. In operating franchises, Holiday Inn sought to apply strict operating standards and supplied franchisees with almost everything, apart from the land upon which the hotel would be built, in order to ensure that there were 'no surprises' (Lundberg, 1969; Nickson, 1997).

British Airways
A passenger on a scheduled flight from Newcastle to London's Gatwick Airport might well be forgiven for reaching the conclusion that they have caught a normal British Airways flight. The British Airways name, livery and flight codes are used, while inside the aircraft British Airways cabin interior designs are familiar to regular travellers and cabin staff are dressed in standard British Airways uniforms. Only a close inspection of tickets, travel documents or the side of the aircraft reveals the fact that this service (in common with many others) is in fact operated by one of several British Airways franchisees. In this case the flight is operated by British Regional Airlines, which is based at Manchester Airport. The franchise partners enable British Airways to extend their network, offer 'feeder' services to the airline and offer passengers greater choice.

Management contracts

Management contracts are a popular joint development method of international growth in the hospitality sector. Utilizing this method the ownership of the physical asset (the hotel or other accommodation) is separated from its management. The management contract is thus 'an agreement between a hotel owner [or other form of accommodation] and a hotel operating company, by which the owner employs the operator as an agent to assume full responsibility for the management of the property' (Olsen *et al.*, 1991).

As an agent, the operator usually pays, in the name of the owners, all property and operating expenses from the cash flow generated through operations. It also retains its management fees and remits surpluses, if any, to the property owner. The property owner on the other hand usually provides the hotel land, building furniture, furnishings equipment and working capital, while also assuming full legal and financial responsibility for the hotel (Olsen *et al.*, 1991). Many well-known upscale international hotel chains (such as Sheraton, Sofitel, le Meridien, Marriott, Hilton International, Hyatt, Radisson, Nikko and Shangri-La) have successfully utilized this method of expansion. Large international food-service companies such as Compass have also used this method.

For the operating company, the management contract allows for rapid expansion and relatively easy market penetration with little or no capital investment. The operating company is therefore not prone to speculative risks associated with falling property prices (and also does not benefit from rises in property values). In some cases the operating company will, however, invest some of its own capital in the project alongside the property developer. The operating company also has an agreed rate of return built into its contractual terms. The disadvantage of the management contract for the operating company is the associated insecurity. From time to time the management contracts come up for renewal. It is usual for the workings of the relationship to be reviewed and its success judged at this time. In practice a change in the operating company is quite common so that when the management contract is renewed, the company operating an hotel under a management contract might change from say le Meridien to Sheraton.

Cooperative networks

Various types of cooperative networks or consortia have been developed in travel and tourism. The hotel sector (where the method is most frequently evident), for example, is characterized by a high degree of fragmentation with a large number of individual or family owned enterprises. These independently operated businesses face increasing competitive pressures from hotel chains operating branded products which enjoy marketing economies and sophisticated systems.

In response to these threats the individually operated businesses have increasingly joined together in networks or consortia in order to achieve the marketing, branding and systems advantages of larger rivals whilst maintaining their independence. In return for the payment of a fee the individual hotel receives a range of benefits. Knowles (1996) distinguished between four basic types of international hotel consortium:

1 *Full consortia*, which provide not only marketing expertise but also assistance in human resources and purchasing. An example of such a consortium is Best Western.
2 *Marketing consortia*, which provide largely marketing and promotional expertise. An example of this type of consortium is Small Luxury Hotels of the World.
3 *Reservation systems*, which provide a central reservations system, usually based around freephone telephone numbers and Internet sites. Utell provides an example of this category.
4 *Referral consortia*, which usually involve hotel chains rather than individual hotels affiliating their brand, loyalty schemes and reservation systems with certain airlines. Golden Tulip Worldwide Hotels and their affiliation with KLM and other airlines is an example of such a relationship.

Disposals

What are disposals?

We should not assume that business strategies are always designed to cause business growth. There are times when organizations may wish to become smaller. As with growth strategy, size reduction can be achieved by organic reduction (by winding down production of a product area), by divestment – the opposite of acquisition – or by demerger – the opposite of merger.

Demergers and divestments (which together are referred to as *disposals*) involve taking a part of a company and selling it off as a 'self-contained' unit with its own management, structure and employees in place. The unit may then be sold on to a single buyer (for whom it will be an acquisition) or it may be floated on the stock market as a public limited company.

Reasons for disposal

There are a number of reasons why a company may elect to dispose of a part of its structure. The most prominent reasons include:

1 under-performance of the part in question (e.g. poor profitability), possibility due to negative synergy;
2 a change in the strategic focus of the organization in which the candidate for disposal is no longer required;
3 the medium- to long-term prospects for the disposal candidate are poor;
4 the disposal candidate is an unwanted acquisition (or an unwanted subsidiary of an acquired company that is otherwise wanted);
5 the need to raise capital from the disposal to reinvest in core areas or to increase liquidity in the selling company;
6 the belief that the disposal candidate would be more productive if it were removed from the seller's structure;
7 in some circumstances, disposal may be used as a tactic to deflect a hostile takeover bid, particularly if the predatory company is primarily interested in acquiring the company to gain control over the disposal candidate;
8 as part of a programme of 'asset stripping' – the process of breaking a company up into its parts and selling them off for a sum greater than that paid for the whole.

Shareholders and disposals

The most common method of corporate disposal is a 'private' transaction between two companies, which is intended to be of benefit to both parties. The seller gains the funds from the transaction, and is able to focus on its core areas. The buyer gains the product and market presence of the disposal, which, in turn, will be (we assume) to its strategic advantage.

Disposals are designed to create synergy to the shareholders in the same way as are integrations. We should not lose sight of the fact that business organizations are owned by shareholders and it is the role of company directors (as the shareholders' agents) to act in such a way that shareholder wealth is maximized. If this can be achieved by breaking a part of the company off, then this option will be pursued.

Other methods of disposal

In addition to divestments and demergers, two other disposal methods are noteworthy.

Equity carve-outs • • •

Equity carve-outs are similar to demergers insofar as the spin-off company is floated on the stock exchange. However, in this form of disposal, the selling company retains a shareholding in the disposal, with the balance of shares being offered to the stock market. In this respect, equity carve-outs can be seen as a semi-disposal – part of the disposal is kept, but not as a wholly owned subsidiary.

The decision of the Thomson Corporation of Canada to float the Thomson travel group in 1998 is an example of such a policy. In this case the Thomson family retained 20% of the new company's equity, in order to gain an ongoing return on the stock, albeit without strategic control over the company. Ultimately the group was bought by Preussag AG (now Tui) of Germany in 2000.

Management buy-outs • • •

A management buy-out (MBO) is said to have occurred when a company that a parent company wishes to dispose of is sold to its current management. MBOs are often a mutually satisfactory outcome when the disposal candidate is unwanted by its parent but when it has the possibility of being run successfully when the existing management have the requisite commitment and skills.

The advantages of MBOs can be summarized as follows.

- The selling parent successfully disposes of its non-core business and receives a suitable price for it, which it can then re-invest in its main areas of activity.
- The divested organization benefits from committed managers (who become its owners). When the management team finds itself personally in debt as a result of the buy-out (having had to find the money for the purchase), their motivation and commitment tends to be maximized. In some MBOs, some of the capital for the purchase is provided by venture capital companies.
- If part of the MBO capital is met by the company's existing employees, the organization benefits from the commitment of people who have part-ownership, and who therefore share in the company's success through dividends on shares and through growth in the share price.

The regulatory framework of external growth

The purpose of regulation

Most governments have taken the view that there is some need to put in place a regulatory framework for external business growth because of the implications for competition in markets. There is a careful balance to be struck in this regard. Governments are usually keen to encourage business activity in their countries because of their beneficial effects upon employment, tax revenues, exports and standard of living. At the same time, it is generally true that the larger organizations become, the more difficult it is for smaller competitors to make headway against them in terms of pricing and market share. Regulation is therefore a matter of some discretion.

National and supranational regulators

In the UK, regulation arises from two sources – from the national level and from the European level. They have in common two areas of concern – company size and, more specifically, market share.

European Union regulation • • •

Since Britain joined the European Community in 1973, it has been subject to EU regulations and directives. European competition regulations are provided for in the Treaty of Rome, 1957 (the primary legislation of the European Union), in the form of two 'articles' that regulate integration between companies resident within two or more EU states. Both articles are designed to stimulate competition between companies in member states. They can be used by authorities within the EU to influence the behaviour of business that may seek to enter into integrations that may reduce competition in a market. One of these, Article 86, refers particularly to mergers and acquisitions.

Article 86 is designed to prohibit the abuse of a dominant market position (i.e. a high market share). It does not prohibit monopoly as such, but seeks to ensure that large businesses do not use their power against consumer and competitor interests. This indirectly acts against large companies seeking to acquire a high market share by integration.

The administrative part of the EU – the European Commission – has the responsibility to implement Article 86. It can prohibit mergers or acquisitions resulting in a combined national market share of 25% or when the combined turnover in European Union markets exceeds a certain financial figure. On a more operational level, the way that integrations are conducted is also regulated. Rules are in place regarding the transparency of approach (i.e. how it should be announced) and how shareholders should be informed of proposed integrations.

Integrations in the UK • • •

Integrations between companies based in the UK are subject to possible scrutiny by the Office of Fair Trading (OFT) and the Competition Commission (formerly the Monopolies and Mergers Commission). Their activity is governed by two major pieces of British legislation: the Fair Trading Act 1973 and, to a lesser extent, the Competition Act 1980. The Fair Trading Act 1973 targets three areas in pursuit of maintaining healthy levels of competition in markets:

1 monopoly practices;
2 restrictive practices;
3 mergers and acquisitions.

Under its provisions to review mergers and acquisition, this Act allows the Government's regulatory bodies to review an integration if the combined market share exceeds 25%. In this regard, it is in agreement with Article 86.

The OFT and the Competition Commission

The two bodies in the UK that exist to regulate integrations activity are provided for under the terms of the above-mentioned Acts of Parliament. Both act independently of the Government under the instruction of the Secretary of State for Trade and Industry and exist in the legal form of *quangos*.

The Office of Fair Trading • • •

The Office of Fair Trading (OFT) was established in 1973 and is headed by the Director General of Fair Trading (DGFT) – an individual charged, among other things, with the enforcement of the terms of the Fair Trading Act. The OFT is also required to act as a central bureau which collects and publishes information on competition and anti-competitive practices in the UK.

The DGFT has six broad areas of responsibility: The first and most important of these is to collect information on business activities that are potentially harmful to competition or the public interest, including mergers and acquisitions (the DGFT has the power to refer cases to other authorities for review).

The Competition Commission ● ● ●

The role of the Competition Commission is to look into proposed mergers and acquisitions when instructed so to do by the Secretary of State for Trade and Industry. The Competition Commission is unable to act on its own initiative, and its recommendations after an investigation, are advisory only. The Secretary of State may elect to adopt or reject its findings.

References and further reading

Airline Business (1999) Annual Alliances Survey. *Airline Business*, July, 33–65.

Alamadari, F. and Morell, P. (1997) Airline Alliances: a Catalyst for Regulatory Change in Key Markets. *Journal of Air Transport Management*, 3(1), 1–2.

Ansoff, H. (1987) *Corporate Strategy*. London: Penguin.

Baumol, W.J. (1982) Contestable Markets: an Uprising in the Theory of Industry Structure. *American Economic Review*, 72(1), 1–15.

Beamish, P.W. and Inkpen, A.C. (1995) Keeping International Joint Ventures Stable and Profitable. *Long Range Planning*, 28(3), 26–36.

Bennett, M.M. (1997) Strategic Alliances in the World Airline Industry. *Progress in Tourism and Hospitality Research* 3, 213–223.

Bleeke, J. and Ernst, D. (1991) The Way to Win in Cross-border Alliances. *Harvard Business Review*, Nov/Dec, 127–135.

British Airways (1999) www//britishairways.com

Brouthers, K.D., Brouthers, L.E. and Wilkinson, T.J. (1993) Strategic Alliances: Choose Your Partners. *Long Range Planning*, 28(3), 18–25.

Campbell, A. and Luchs, K.S. (eds) (1992) *Strategic Synergy*. London: Butterworth-Heinemann.

Child, J. and Faulkner, D. (1998) *Strategies of Cooperation: Managing Alliances, Networks and Joint Ventures*. Oxford: Oxford University Press.

Contractor, F. and Lorange, P. (1988) Why Should Firms Cooperate? The Strategy and Economic Basis for Cooperative Ventures. In F. Contractor and P. Lorange (eds), *Cooperative Strategies in International Business*, Lexington, MA: Lexington Books, 3–30.

Crawford-Welch (1994), The Development of Courtyard by Marriott, in R. Teare, J.A. Mazanec, S. Crawford-Welch and S. Calver (eds), *Marketing in Hospitality and Tourism: a Consumer Focus*. London: Cassell.

Dev, C.S. and Klein, S. (1993) Strategic Alliances in the Hotel Industry. *The Cornell H.R.A. Quarterly*, February, 43–45.

Dev, C.S. Klein, S. and Fisher, R.A. (1996) A Market-based Approach for Partner Selection in Marketing Alliances. *Journal of Travel Research*, Summer, 11–17.

Doz, Y. and Hamel G. (1998) *Alliance Advantage*. Cambridge MA: Harvard Business School Press.

Evans, N. (2001a) Collaborative Strategy: an Analysis of the Changing World of International Airline Alliances. *Tourism Management*, 22, 229–243.

Evans, N. (2001b) Alliances in the International Travel Industry: Sustainable

Strategic Options?, *International Journal of Hospitality and Tourism Administration*, 2(1), 1–26.

Faulkner, D. (1995) *Strategic Alliances: Cooperating to Compete.* New York: McGraw-Hill.

Faulkner, D. and Bowman C. (1995) *The Essence of Competitive Strategy.* London: Prentice Hall.

French, T. (1997) Global Trends in Airline Alliances. *Tourism Analyst*, 4, 81–101.

Garnham, B. (1996) Alliances and Liaisons in Tourism: Concepts and Implications. *Tourism Economics*, 2(1), 61–77.

Gialloreto, L. (1989) *Strategic Airline Management: 'The Global War Begins.* London: Pitman.

Glaister, K.W. and Buckley, P.J. (1996) Strategic Motives for International Alliance Formation. *Journal of Management Studies*, 33(3), 301–32.

Go, F. and Pine, R. (1995) *Globalization Strategy in the Hotel Industry.* London: Routledge.

Haspeslagh, P., Jemison, D. (1991) *Managing Acquisitions: Creating Value through Corporate Renewal.* New York: Free Press.

Heeley, J. (2001) Public–Private Sector Partnerships in Tourism, in A. Lockwood and S. Medlik (eds), *Tourism and Hospitality in the 21st Century.* Oxford: Butterworth-Heinemann.

Johnson, G. and Scholes, K. (2002) *Exploring Corporate Strategy*, 6th edn. Harlow: Pearson Education.

Kanter, R.M. (1994) Collaborative Advantage: The Art of Alliances. *Harvard Business Review*, July/August, 96–108.

Kay, J. (1993) *Foundations of Corporate Success: How Business Strategies Add Value.* Oxford: Oxford University Press.

Knowles, T. (1996) *Corporate Strategy for Hospitality.* London: Longman.

Long P.E. (1997) Researching Tourism Partnership Organizations: From Practice to Theory to Methodology, in P.E. Murphy (ed.), *Quality Management in Urban Tourism.* London: John Wiley, pp. 235–252.

Lundberg, D.E. (1969) *The Tourism Industry.* Van Nostrand Reinhold.

Mason, J.C (1993) Strategic Alliances: Partnering for Success. *Management Review*, May, 10–15.

Medcof, J.W. (1997) Why too Many Alliances End in Divorce. *Long Range Planning*, 30(5), 718–732.

Nickson (1997)

Nissé, J. (1998) Happening Hilton Rewrites the Hotel Advertising Book. *The Times*, 29 September, p. 33.

Ohmae, K. (1989) The Global Logic of Strategic Alliances. *Harvard Business Review*, March/April, 143–154.

Olsen, M.D., Crawford-Welch, S. and Tse, E. (1991) *The Global Hospitality Industry of the 1990s*, in R. Teare and A. Boer (eds), *Strategic Hospitality Management.* London: Cassell.

Olsen, M.D. (1993) International Growth Strategies of Major US Hotel Companies. *Travel and Tourism Analyst*, 3, 51–64.

Oum, T.H. and Park, J.H. (1997) Airline Alliances: Current Status, Policy Issues, and Future Directions. *Journal of Air Transport Management*, 3(3), 133–144.

Porter, M.E. (1985) *Competitive Advantage.* New York: Free Press.

Porter, M.E. and Fuller, M.B. (1986) Coalitions and Global Strategy. In Porter M.E. (ed.), *Competition in Global Industries.* Boston, MA: Harvard Business School Press.

Ravenscraft, D.J. and Scherer, F.M. (1987) *Mergers, Sell-offs and Economic Efficiency.* Washington, DC: Brooking Institution.

Shaughnessy, H. (1995) International Joint Ventures: Managing Successful Collaborations. *Long Range Planning*, 28(3), 10–17.

Shleifer, A. and Vishny, R. (1986) Large Shareholders and Corporate Control. *Journal of Political Economy*, 94, 461–488.

Stafford, E.R. (1994) Using Co-operative Strategies to Make Alliances Work. *Long Range Planning*, 27(3), 64–74.

Stiles, J. (1994) Strategic Alliances: Making Them Work. *Long Range Planning*, 27(3), 133–137.

Sudarsanam, P.S. (1995) *The Essence of Mergers and Acquisitions.* Englewood Cliffs, NJ: Prentice Hall.

The Economist (1998) Airline Alliances: Mergers in Mind. *The Economist*, 26 September, p. 96.

World Tourism Organization (1996) *Towards New Forms of Public–Private Sector Partnerships: The Changing Role, Structure and* *Activities of National Tourism Administrations*. A Special Report for The World Tourism Organization, Madrid: WTO.

Zajac, E.J. (1998) Commentary on 'Alliances and Networks' by R. Gulati. *Strategic Management Journal*, 19, 319–321.

Strategic evaluation and selection

Introduction and Chapter Overview

Important decisions are never easy. In order to ensure that we make the right choice in any given situation, we must first of all be in possession of all relevant information. This is the purpose of the strategic analysis stage – to ensure that the management of a business is fully aware of the internal strengths and weaknesses, and of the external opportunities and threats.

The next stage in making an important decision is to be aware of *all* of the options available. In Chapters 10 and 11 various options relating to competitive strategy, strategic directions and strategic methods were considered. The most obvious choice is not necessarily the right one. Following the generation of options, the next stage is to evaluate each option using consistently applied criteria. The purpose of evaluation is to ensure that all options are assessed with equal thoroughness. Finally, strategic selection involves actually making a decision based upon the evaluation of the options.

This chapter considers each of these stages in turn.

Learning Objectives

After studying this chapter, students should be able to:

- describe the nature of strategic options;

- explain the key areas that strategic decisions concern;

- describe the four criteria that are applied to strategic options;

- understand the financial tools that can be used to evaluate strategic options;

- understand a number of other tools that can be used to evaluate strategic options;

- understand a worked examples of the tools and techniques in relation to travel and tourism organizations;

- explain the limitations of an emergent approach to strategy when it comes to strategic evaluation and selection.

Identifying strategic options

The nature of strategic options

At the start of this chapter, we must remind ourselves of what makes a decision *strategic* in nature as opposed to one that is *operational*. We encountered these terms in Chapter 1 in the context of the nature of strategic objectives.

Strategic decisions are taken at the highest level of an organization. They concern decisions on how the whole organization broken down into its constituent SBUs will be positioned in respect to its product and resource markets, its competitors and its macro influences. Accordingly, the options at the strategic level are those that offer solutions to the 'big questions' in this regard.

Operational level decisions are those that are concerned with how the internal parts of the organization should be configured and managed so that they best achieve the strategic objectives.

The 'big questions' that are considered in strategic selection usually concern three major areas, all of which are discussed in detail elsewhere in this text.

- Decisions on competitive strategy (see Chapter 10).
- Decisions on products and markets relating to the direction of development (see Chapter 10).
- Decisions on methods of development (see Chapter 11).

In most cases, an organization will need to make continual decisions on all of these matters. We should not lose sight of the fact that the strategic process is just that – a process. Strategic selection is no more of a 'once for all' activity than either strategic analysis or strategic implementation. For organizations that exist in rapidly changing environments, decisions on strategic options will be required on a continual basis, hence the importance of ensuring we have a good grasp of the issues that are discussed in this chapter.

Competitive strategy decisions

Decisions over the organization's competitive or generic strategy (as discussed in Chapter 10) are important not only because they define the organization's competitive position, but also because they will determine the way that the internal value chain activities are configured (see Chapter 3 and Chapter 10).

If the company elects to pursue a differentiation strategy, for example, the implications of this will be felt in all parts of the organization. The culture and structure will need to be configured in such a way that they support the generic strategy and the product features and quality will also reflect it. Similarly, the way that the organization sources and configures its resource base will need to support the strategy.

The same issues will be considered if a cost-driven strategy is chosen, although the way in which the internal activities are configured will be somewhat different.

Product and market decisions

The questions over *which products* and *which markets* are extremely important, because they can determine not only the levels of profitability but also the survival of the organization itself. It is likely that strategy will involve a change in the SBU or company's size. If 'stability' is the chosen option this does not mean that nothing should be done, since to do so would invite competitors to enlarge their market shares. In such circumstances market share may be fiercely defended through such measures as pricing, promotional offers or increased levels of efficiency. Furthermore even if the market share remains stable if the market as a whole is growing then the size of the overall business will increase, i.e. to use the analogy of a cake, one's slice of the cake may remain constant but the overall size of the cake is growing. If retrenchment is the chosen option decisions have to be made concerning which product or market areas should be reduced, sold off or withdrawn.

In cases where growth is the chosen strategic option that the organization will pursue (see Chapter 10), decisions have to be taken about the direction of growth. These strategic choices arise from Igor Ansoff's (Ansoff, 1987) framework and should not be confused with Porter's generic strategies (Porter, 1985). Ansoff's generic growth strategies concern whether growth will involve new or existing markets and products.

There are a number of further product and market decisions that are normally required.

Market categories ◦ ◦ ◦

First, decisions must be made about the categories of markets that the business will be involved with. The organization will have to reach decisions on geographic coverage, international exposure and the benefits and risks that attend such options (see Chapter 14).

Product features ◦ ◦ ◦

Second, decisions must be made on the features that the product will possess. The mix of product benefits that a product will possess will not only strongly affect costs, but also the position that the product will assume in the market. We encountered Kotler's (1997) five 'levels' of product features (or 'benefits') in Chapter 6 and the inclusion or 'leaving out' of any of these will have a strong bearing upon any proposed strategy.

Product and market portfolios ◦ ◦ ◦

Third, product and market decisions must include a consideration of portfolio. The extent to which the products and markets are focused or spread can be very important. A broad portfolio (presence in many product market sectors) offers the advantages of the ability to withstand a downturn in one sector and to exploit opportunities that arise in any of the areas in which the business operates. Conversely, a narrow portfolio enables the organization's management to be more focused and to develop expertise in its narrower field of operation.

Life cycle considerations • • •

The final consideration to be made for products and markets concerns their life cycle positions. It is perhaps intuitively obvious to say that products or markets that are approaching late maturity or are in decline should be of particular concern, but there is also a need to produce new products or develop new markets on an ongoing basis.

Strategic method decisions

The third area for which strategic business level decisions are required relates to the methods or mechanisms that are to be used. A basic choice exists between internal (organic) development, mergers and takeovers, and some form of joint development such as alliances and franchising. The choice has important implications for:

- the resources that are required;
- the degree of control over future strategic decisions;
- the speed with which a change in the position of the SBU could be achieved;
- the need to re-configure the internal value chain of the organization.

For example, organic growth is normally viewed as a slower means of growth (since resources are provided by one organization only), than either some form of joint development or a merger or takeover, which involve a *step change* in size. However, internal growth retains full control within the existing organization with no control being ceded to other organizations.

Applying evaluation criteria

Identifying the criteria

When considering which course of action to pursue, it is normally the case that a number of options present themselves to an organization's top management. In order to ensure that each option is fairly and equally assessed, a number of criteria are applied.

For each option, four criteria are applied – questions to ask of each option. In order to 'pass', the option must usually receive an affirmative answer to each one. In some texts various acronyms are introduced to describe the criteria such as RACES (as described by Haberberg and Rieple, 2001), SCARE and CARES, which usually stand for Resources, Acceptable, Consistent, Effective and Sustainability, which are considered in the order required by the acronym. Here another widely used scheme is used: the SFA framework of Suitability, Feasibility and Acceptability, to which is added a fourth criterion, that of achieving competitive advantage. Thus each strategic option should be considered in relation to the four criteria by considering whether:

1 the strategic option is *suitable*;
2 the strategic option is *feasible*;
3 the strategic option is *acceptable*;
4 the strategic option will enable the organization to *achieve competitive advantage*.

The process of evaluation is an integral part of the overall strategy process as indicated in Figure 12.1

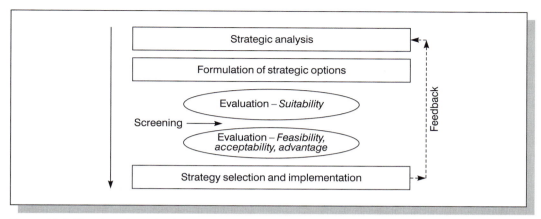

Figure 12.1 The strategic evaluation process

Suitability criteria

A strategic option is suitable if it will enable the organization actually to achieve its strategic objectives. If it will in any way fall short of achieving these objectives, then there is no point in pursuing it and the option should be discarded.

If, for example, an organization's objective is to spread its market portfolio by gaining a presence in foreign markets, then the option of increasing the company's investment in its domestic home would clearly be unsuitable.

The suitability of options must be assessed not only in relation to the objectives that have been set but also in relation to the SWOT. Options might be regarded as suitable when they:

- exploit *opportunities* in the environment and avoid the *threats*;
- capitalize on an organization's *strengths* and avoid or address the *weaknesses*;
- address the expectations of key stakeholder groups.

It is also important to recognize cases where strategic options may be unsuitable. For example:

- there may be options that are more suitable so that suitability might be seen in relative terms and the various options ranked according to their suitability;
- there is a need for internal consistency in the choice of options, in that the choice of competitive strategy (such as cost leadership or differentiation) the development direction (such as market development or diversification) and the development method (internal, acquisition or joint development) need to work together as a 'package' (Johnson and Scholes, 2002).

For example, a non-American airline seeking to grow through market penetration of a quality differentiated product in the large US aviation market (which accounts for over 40% of world demand) would be restricted in its choice of strategic method. Foreign ownership restrictions prevent the purchase of American airlines or the development of airlines by foreign based companies, leading to the need to develop joint development opportunities through alliance relationships (such as the longstanding strategic alliance between KLM and Northwest Airlines) to enter this important market.

Table 12.1 Some examples of suitability

Strategic option	Environment	Resources/competences	Expectations	Examples
Directions			**Why this option might be suitable in terms of:**	
Consolidation	Withdraw from declining markets Sell valuable assets Maintain market share	Build on strengths through continued investment and innovation	Better returns at low risk by exploiting current strategies	Declining American seaside resort of Atlantic City redeveloped as a gambling destination
Market penetration	Gain market share for advantage	Exploit superior resources and competences	Better returns at low risk by exploiting current strategies	Growth of multiple branch travel agencies in UK during the 1980s and 1990s
Product development	Exploit knowledge of customer needs	Exploit expertise in developing new or improved product offerings	Better returns at medium risk by exploiting current strengths or market knowledge	Development of all-weather tourism products such as Center Parcs for Northern Europe
Market development	Current markets saturated New opportunities for: geographical spread, entering new segments or new uses for existing products	Exploit current product portfolio	Better returns at medium risk by exploiting current strengths or market knowledge	Growth of hitherto UK outbound tour operators such as Airtours and Thomson into international markets during 1990s, particularly Scandinavia, Germany and North America
Diversification	Current markets saturated or declining	Exploit core competences in new arenas	Better returns at higher risk	Diversification of Disney Corporation during the 1990s into cruising
Methods				
Internal development	First in field providing *first mover* advantage Cautious controlled development	Learning and competence development Spread out the cost	Cultural and political ease Less disruptive	Development of low cost 'no frills' airline concept by Southwest Airlines from late 1970s
Merger/acquisition	Speed of development Alter supply/demand balance Improved ratios	Acquire competences Scale and scope economies	Returns in terms of growth or enhanced share value Problems of culture clash	The acquisition of Holland-America and Seabourn cruise lines by Carnival Cruise Lines during the 1990s
Joint development	Speed Access to markets Industry norm	Complementary competences Learning from partners	Required for market entry Dilutes risk Fashionable	The development of franchising by Holiday Inn from the 1950s onwards first in the USA followed by elsewhere in the world.

Source: adapted from Johnson and Scholes (2002)

Table 12.1 presents some examples of why some options might be regarded as suitable in terms of specific directions or methods of development (considered in Chapters 10 and 11).

Screening

Having applied the suitability criterion a further stage might be included in some cases – that of *screening*. If certain options are clearly unsuitable it makes little sense going through the time, effort and expense involved in applying the further criteria. Consequently, at the screening stage a decision is made as to whether it is worth continuing with the further stages of evaluation or that certain options should be disregarded at this stage of evaluation owing to their unsuitability.

Feasibility

A strategic option might be considered to be suitable only to be later found not to be possible. In other words, the option is not feasible. When evaluating options using this criterion, it is likely that the options will be feasible to varying degrees. Some will be completely unfeasible, others 'might be' feasible, whilst others still are definitely so.

Feasibility studies are often carried out prior to tourism projects being approved in order to secure financing. Such studies were discussed in Chapter 6 (page 143 and Figure 6.3).

The extent to which an option is feasible will depend in practice upon the following two areas.

1   Internal considerations – culture, skills and resources • • •

Culture, skills and resources are internally controlled by the organization. An organization might not have the culture, skills or resources which are necessary to carry out the options. A deficit in any of the key resource areas (physical resources, financial, operational, human and intellectual) will present a problem at this stage of evaluation. If an option requires capital that is unavailable, human skills that are difficult to buy in, land or equipment that is equally difficult to obtain or a scarce intellectual resource, then it is likely to fail the feasibility criteria.

For example, London's Heathrow Airport has been working at or close to capacity for a number of years. Take off and landing slots are a scarce resource and are controlled through the rights of airlines which have operated at the airport for a protracted length of time (so called *grandfather rights*). Many airlines would like to establish a presence at Heathrow as a key international transit hub but are prevented from doing so by the lack of slots. Consequently whilst establishing a presence at Heathrow might be a *suitable* aspect of a growth strategy it would not be *feasible* owing to the deficit in a key resource area, i.e. the failure to gain access to the physical resource of Heathrow.

The checklist shown as Figure 12.2 indicates some of the key internal feasibility issues to consider.

2   External considerations – competitive reaction • • •

The second area that needs to be considered with regard to feasibility relates to the consideration of competitive reactions and other considerations which are external to the organization. Specifically, the acceptance of customers and suppliers, competitive reactions and necessary approvals from government or regulatory bodies needs to be considered (Lynch, 2000).

- Capital investment required: do we have the funds?
- Projection of cumulative profits: is it sufficiently profitable?
- Working capital requirements: do we have enough working capital?
- Tax liabilities and dividend payments: what are the implications, especially on timing?
- Number of employees and, in the case of redundancy, any costs associated with this?
- New technical skills required, new operational equipment required: do we have the skills? Do we need to recruit or temporarily hire some specialists?
- New products and how are they to be developed: are we confident that we have a portfolio of fully tested new products? Are they breakthrough products or merely catch-up on our competition?
- Amount and timing of marketing investment and expertise required: do we have the funds? When will they be required? Do we have the specialist expertise such as advertising and promotions agency teams to deliver our strategic options?
- The possibility of acquisition, merger or joint venture with other organisations and the implications: have we fully explored other strategic options that would bring their own benefits and problems?
- Communication of ideas to all those involved: how will this be done? Will we gain the commitment of the managers and employees affected who are required to implement the required changes?

Figure 12.2 Checklist on internal feasibility (adapted from Lynch, 2000)

For example, a UK air-inclusive tour operator might wish to double its capacity within one year as part of its growth strategy. Given its past growth record, its financial position and its potential customer base this might appear a suitable strategic option. However, such capacity is licensed in the UK through the Air Tour Organizer's Licence (ATOL) system administered by the Civil Aviation Authority (CAA, a government body). The CAA might take the view that such growth in one year was excessive and financially unsustainable. Consequently allowable growth might be limited. Hence what might appear to be suitable strategy is not feasible due to the lack of regulatory approval.

The checklist shown as Figure 12.3 indicates some of the key internal feasibility issues to consider.

- How will our customers respond to the strategies we are proposing?
- How will our competitors react? Do we have the necessary resources to respond?
- Do we have the necessary support from our suppliers?
- Do we need government or regulatory approval? How likely is this?

Figure 12.3 Checklist on external feasibility (adapted from Lynch, 2000)

Acceptability

Acceptability is concerned with the expected performance outcomes of a strategy. Consequently the acceptability of a chosen strategy is often determined by using a range of analytical financial and non-financial tools such as those described later in the chapter. A strategic option is acceptable if those who must agree to the strategy accept the option. This raises an obvious question – who are those who agree that the option is acceptable?

We encountered the concept of stakeholders in Chapter 1. The extent that stakeholders can exert influence upon an organization's strategic decision-making rests upon the two variables, power and interest (see Chapter 1). Stakeholders that have the highest combination of both the ability to influence (power) and the willingness to influence (interest) will have the most *effective* influence. Where two or more stakeholder groups have comparable influence, the possibility of conflict over acceptability will be heightened. In most cases, the board of directors will be the most influential stakeholder. It is also important to consider the commitment from managers and employees. If important members of the organization are not committed to the strategy it is unlikely to be successfully implemented.

For example in the mid-1990s when the previously state owned British Airways was endeavouring to place its strategic emphasis on controlling its hitherto high cost base, it tried to change the working conditions of its cabin staff. Management tried to push through the changes in a way that showed little respect for the views of employees (Haberberg and Rieple, 2001). The dispute resulted in strike action during 1997 and the airline, having underestimated the power of this group of stakeholders, lost many millions of pounds and its reputation for customer service which had been assiduously built up over the preceding few years was seriously eroded.

Competitive advantage

We learned in Chapter 1 that one of the key objectives in strategy is to create competitive advantage. This criterion asks a simple question of any strategic option – what is the point of pursuing an option if it isn't going to result in superior performance (compared to competitors) or higher than industry-average profitability? In other words, a strategic option would fail this test if it were likely to only result in the business being 'ordinary' or average in relation to the industry or sector norm.

This is particularly important when considering product options. For example, if a new product option is forecast to receive an uncertain reception from the market, we might well ask what is the point of the launch at all. It would be unlikely to result in competitive advantage for the business.

Financial tools for evaluation

In the evaluation and selection stage, a number of 'tools' are available to managers which may assist in deciding upon the most appropriate option. Not all of them will be appropriate in every circumstance and some are more widely used than others. They are used to explore the implications of the options so that the decisions that are made are based upon the best possible information.

Accountants or financial analysts are usually very involved in strategic evaluation and selection because of their expertise in understanding the financial implications of the possible courses of action, and the reader is referred to more specialized texts such as Ellis and Williams (1993), Atkinson *et al.* (1995), Kotas and Conlan (1997) and Ambrosini *et al.* (1998), for further coverage. There are two major areas of financial analysis.

Cash flow forecasting

One of the most straightforward financial tools is cash flow analysis – sometimes called funds-flow analysis. Many businesses fail not because they fail to be profitable but because have run out of cash, i.e. they become insolvent in that they are unable to pay their bills as they become due. A business may have substantial assets such as cruise ships, aircraft and buildings, but creditors such as suppliers and staff need to be paid in cash.

Essentially, cash flow forecasting involves a forecast of the expected income from an option, of the costs that will be incurred and, from this, the forecast net cash inflows or outflows. For most options, the forecast will be broken down into monthly 'chunks' and a statement will be constructed for each month in which cash outflows and inflows are shown together with opening and closing bank balances. The closing bank balance in one month becomes the opening balance in the following month. The forecast allows for potential problems and solutions to be identified. If the same procedure is carried out for each option, the most favourable can be identified or suggestions can be made in order to improve the forecast cash position. The example from Eurojet below shows a cash flow forecast for a tour operator which experiences seasonal cash flow difficulties.

Cash flow forecasting for Eurojet

Eurojet is a fictitious tour operator with ambitious growth plans based upon a clear strategy involving market penetration based upon organic growth and differentiation. The company plans to increase its sales turnover by around 25% each year. However, like many tour operators and travel agents, the company experiences seasonal cash flow difficulties.

A cash flow forecast has been prepared for the following financial year and this is shown below. Figures in the table are in £000s.

	1	2	3	4	5	6	7	8	9	10	11	12	Total
INFLOWS													
Receipts from debtors	230	250	120	50	60	75	80	90	110	150	220	320	1755
Dividend on investment							45						45
TOTAL INFLOWS	230	250	120	50	60	75	125	90	110	150	220	320	1800
OUTFLOWS													
Payments to creditors		80		80		88		88		88		92	516
Wages and other expenses	102	77	58	103	79	59	105	80	62	108	83	63	979
Payments for fixed assets				70	10	15					5		100
Dividend payable			80										80
Corporation Tax									120				120
TOTAL OUTFLOWS	102	157	138	253	89	162	105	168	182	196	88	155	1795
NET IN/OUT	128	93	−18	−203	−29	−87	20	−78	−72	−46	132	165	5
Bank balance													
opening	30	158	251	233	30	1	−86	−66	−144	−216	262	−130	
closing	158	251	233	30	1	−86	−66	−144	−216	−262	−130	35	

a. As a tour operator most funds are received by customers as a deposit and subsequent payment of balance. On average this results in 3 months credit being granted to customers.

b. On average 6 weeks credit is taken from customers.

c. Capital expenditure budget:

New computer facilities	Month 4	£40 000
Routine replacement of motor vehicles	Month 4	£30 000
Computer software and programming costs	Month 5	£10 000
Progress payment on building extensions	Month 7	£15 000
Office furniture and equipment	Month 11	£5000

d. Negotiated overdraft facilities currently stand at £60 000.

Investment appraisal

An investment, at its simplest, is some money put up for a project in the expectation that it will enable more money to be made in the future. The questions surrounding investment appraisal concern *how much* will the organization make against each investment option (called the *return* on investment)?

There is a strong time element to investment appraisal techniques because the returns on the investment may remain for several years or even decades. It is for this reason that a factor is often built into the calculation to account for inflation.

Key measures of acceptability are the returns that are likely to accrue from specific options and the risks of potential losses. Returns are based upon forecasts. What risks arise if the forecast returns turn out to be inaccurate? One approach is 'what if?' or sensitivity analysis. Uncertainty is concerned with the risk, that some potential factors affecting returns cannot be forecast but arise unexpectedly.

A common method of assessing the financial acceptability of strategic options is through the application of investment appraisal techniques. Various methods of investment appraisal can be used which are briefly considered below.

Payback method

The first and most obvious thing that accountants want to know about any investment is the *payback period*. This is the time taken to repay the investment – the shorter the better. If, for example, an investment of £1000 is expected to increase profits by £100 a month, then the payback period will be 10 months.

In practice, payback periods are rarely this short and it is this fact that makes investment appraisal calculations a bit more complicated. When the effects of inflation are taken into account, the returns on an investment can be eroded over time. Consequently, accountants include a factor to account for the effects of inflation, usually on a 'best-guess' basis. The payback method can be justified on the grounds that it represents a simple, quick screening process. However it can be criticized in that it ignores the so-called 'time value of money' and also ignores inflows after the payback period.

Accounting rate of return (ARR)

The ARR is, as its title implies, an accounting measure. It is calculated in three steps:

1 Take average annual inflows over project life.
2 Deduct depreciation on the initial outlay.
3 Divide result by the average investment over the period.

The ARR can be justified (like the payback method) on the grounds that it represents a simple, quick screening process but can be criticized in that it ignores the so-called 'time value of money'.

Discounted cash flow (DCF) methods ● ● ●

DCF methods (Net present value and internal rate of return) are considered superior (but more complicated) than payback and ARR because such methods consider the timing of cash flows – *the time value of money*. The time value of money is based on the notion that companies or individuals need to be compensated for foregoing the use of money for a period of time if it has been invested in a project. Such methods are based on the concept of compound interest in reverse. If, for example, interest rates are 10% and a certain investment promises to pay $100 000 in 1 year's time, the amount we would need to invest now is:

$$\frac{\$100\,000 \times 100}{110} = \$90\,909$$

i.e. $90 909 now is equivalent to $100 000 received in 1 year. It is the *present value* of $100 000.

Net present value (NPV) ● ● ●

NPV is the value obtained by discounting the forecast cash inflows and outflows of a project at a chosen *acceptable* rate of return and taking the net total. If NPV is positive then the investment is worthwhile; if it is negative, the project or option should be rejected.

Internal rate of return (IRR) ● ● ●

The goal with this method is to find the interest rate at which inflow exactly equal outflows, i.e. where NPV = 0. Where IRR is higher than the rate deemed to be an acceptable level of return then the option should be considered as financially viable. For example, if 10% is viewed as an acceptable rate of return and IRR is calculated to be 15% then the project would be deemed to be viable.

NPV and IRR compared ● ● ●

IRR is easier to understand (because it is expressed as a percentage) but NPV is normally considered superior because:

1 NPV is easier to calculate.
2 IRR ignores relative size of the investment.
3 IRR rates are non-additive, i.e. the rates from two or more projects cannot be added together.
4 In some circumstances there may be more than one IRR.

A full consideration of investment appraisal techniques is beyond the scope of this chapter. A number of books, such as Dyson (2001), consider the topic in greater depth.

Limitations of the financial tools

The limitations of the financial tools rest in the problem of the unpredictability of the future. We learned in Chapters 7 and 8 that the macro- and microenvironments can change – sometimes rapidly. Accordingly, the actual returns that an organization makes on an investment may not always be what were expected.

A similar limitation applies to forecasting the level of inflation for net present value calculations. In the major First World economies such as those in Western Europe, North America, Japan and Australia, the level of inflation has historically been relatively stable at between 2 and 10%, with an occasional 'shock' such as in the mid-1970s when, in the UK, it reached 24% because of a quadrupling of oil prices caused by a Middle-Eastern conflict. In other parts of the world, however, problems with the supply of goods and the value of currency can lead to much higher inflation levels – sometimes exceeding 1000% a year. A presumption of low and stable inflation will therefore tend to encourage investment rather than high and unpredictable inflation.

Other tools for evaluation

Financial evaluation of strategic options is very important, but for most organizations, other tools can also provide useful information. These may require financial information as an input and so they should be seen not as 'instead of' financial analyses, but 'as well as'. They enrich the information enabling management to select the best strategic option.

Cost–benefit analysis

Cost–benefit analysis applies to almost every area of life, not just strategic evaluation and selection. The cost–benefit concept suggests that a money value can be put on all costs and benefits of a strategy, including tangible and intangible returns to people and organizations proposing the project. Each option will have a cost associated with it and will be expected to return certain benefits. If both of these can be quantified in financial terms, then the cost–benefit calculation will be relatively straightforward. The problem is that this is rarely the case.

The costs of pursuing one particular option will have a number of elements. Any financial investment costs will be easily quantifiable. Against this, the cost of not pursuing the next best option needs to be taken into account – the *opportunity cost*. There may also be a number of social and environmental costs which are much harder to attach a value to.

The same problems apply to the benefits. In addition to financial benefits, an organization may also take into account social benefits and others such as improved reputation or improved service. Intangible benefits are very difficult to attach a value to for a cost–benefit analysis as they can take a long time to work through to increased financial performance.

Whilst it is difficult to quantify non-financial benefits it is usually possible after some calculations have been made and often negotiations and research amongst the interested parties. Certainly the technique is commonly used to assess the acceptability of strategic options, particularly in the public sector (Williams and Giardina, 1993) and in cases where development involves public–private partnerships. The problem in many cases is to know just where the analysis should stop.

For example, in considering a major new airport development for a city it would seem appropriate that the increased costs of noise and emission pollution and congestion for the city should be costed. However, aircraft emissions are thought to be partly responsible for the global warming phenomena. Consequently, should the costs associated with global warming arising from increased air transport movements also be factored into the calculations or is this aspect too remote from the project under consideration?

Key concept: Social costs and benefits

All organizations have an impact upon the societies that are in their locality or that are affected by their products or activities. Although the term *social* is a bit nebulous, it is generally taken to mean the effect on the condition of employment, social well-being, health, chemical emissions, pollution, aesthetic appearance (e.g. 'eyesores'), charitable societies, etc.

A strategic option will have an element of social cost and social benefit. We would describe a social cost as a deterioration in any of the above – an increase in unemployment, higher levels of emissions, pollution, declining salaries, etc. Conversely, a social benefit will result in an improvement in the condition of society – increasing employment, cleaner industry, better working conditions, etc.

Impact analysis

When a strategic option may be reasonably expected to have far reaching consequences in either social or financial terms, an impact study may be appropriate. Essentially, this involves asking the question, 'If this option goes ahead, what will its impact be upon the local (regional) environment, community and economy?'

The aspects that might be impacted upon will depend upon the particular circumstances of the option. The impacts have been widely discussed in a travel and tourism context by authors such as Mathieson and Wall (1982), Archer (1996), Wager (1997), Mules (2000) and the World Tourism Organization (1994).

For a proposed development of a new theme park, for example, the impact study might typically take into account the development's implications for:

- Local employment.
- Primary and secondary levels of spending to be generated and *leakages* from the local economy.
- The effect of the development on other businesses.
- The capacity of the local infrastructure such as road and rail services but also utilities such as water and sewerage, waste disposal, gas and electricity.
- The environmental impact on the local flora and fauna and the effects of noise pollution.
- The aesthetic impact of the development on the local community.

In many cases, an impact study will be an intrinsic part of the cost–benefit calculation, and it suffers from the same limitations – that of evaluating the true value of each aspect that may be impacted.

'What if?' and sensitivity analysis

The uncertainties of the future, as we have seen, make any prediction inexact. Whilst an organization can never be certain of any sequence of future events, 'what if?' analysis (or scenario planning as it is sometimes called), and its variant, sensitivity analysis, can give an idea of how the outcome would be affected by a number of possible disruptions.

The development of computerized applications such as spreadsheets has made this activity easier than it used to be. A financial model on a spreadsheet that makes a number of assumptions such as revenue projections, cost forecasts, inflation rate, etc., can be modified to instantly show the effect of, say, a 10% increase in costs or a higher-than-expected rate of inflation. This is designed to show how sensitive the cash flow is to its assumptions – hence the name.

For example, an airline might produce a projection of future earnings based on the assumption that the average price it would have to pay for its jet-fuel requirements (a major constituent of airline costs) is US$0.60 per gallon. The airline obviously is unable to control the price of this key input and indeed has no accurate means of forecasting it. Consequently, when forecasting its future earnings the airline might regard it as a prudent step to produce alternative scenarios which ask the 'what if' question. The scenarios might suppose that:

- A major war breaks out or the Organization of Petroleum Exporting countries (OPEC) restricts supplies, thereby increasing jet fuel prices by 25%.
- Surplus supplies of jet fuel become available as a result of lower demand for air services leading to jet fuel prices falling by 10%.

Having produced the scenarios and calculated the impact of the events on the cost of jet fuel the airline would factor the costs into its overall calculations. As a result the airline might be able to produce a central or base earnings forecast based on the US$0.60 per gallon price, but would also have knowledge of the effect an increase or decrease in fuel costs would have on overall profitability. In other words, the *sensitivity* of earnings to fuel price changes would have been assessed. In some cases the analysis might go a stage further by applying weightings to the scenarios. Thus the airline might be fairly confident about its central assumption and assign a 50% weighting, i.e. its assessment of the situation is that there is a 50% chance of the central assumption of US$0.60 per gallon being realized. Similarly, the company might assess the situation and feel that if the central case is not borne out then a rise is more likely than a fall and consequently 30% and 20% weightings are assigned to the rising and falling fuel price scenarios respectively.

Qualitative variables can also be analysed. If an option has a high dependency upon the availability of a key raw material or the oversight of a key manager, a 'what if?' study will show the effect that the loss or reduction in the key input would have.

Strategic evaluation in emergent strategies

In Chapter 1, we encountered the idea that business strategies can be either deliberate (or prescriptive) or emergent. This is to say that some strategies are planned in advance, often following a rational sequence of events – deliberate strategies. Others are not planned in this way and are said to be emergent – they result from an organization's management following a consistent pattern of behaviour.

This distinction is important when it comes to strategic evaluation. Companies that employ the deliberate model are likely to use the criteria and the tools above whilst those that prefer the emergent model are less likely to do so explicitly. This is not to say, however, that the analytical process cannot form a part of an intelligent manager's intuitive thinking.

It is here that one of the potential limitations of emergent strategy becomes apparent. If an organization follows a deliberate process with its systematic and sequential events, then it can be more certain that all possible options have been identified and evaluated before the most appropriate one is selected. An intuitive emergent approach that relies upon patterns of behaviour cannot be certain that the best option is taken in all times of decision. It might get it right – but it might not.

References and further reading

Ambrosini, V., Johnson, G. and Scholes, K. (eds) (1998) *Exploring Techniques of Analysis and Evaluation in Strategic Management.* Harlow: Prentice Hall.

Ansoff, I. (1987) *Corporate Strategy.* London: Penguin.

Archer, B.H. (1996) Economic Impact Analysis. *Annals of Tourism Research,* 23(3), 704–7.

Atkinson, H., Berry, A. and Jarvis, R. (1995) *Business Accounting for Hospitality and Tourism.* London: International Thomson Business Press.

Brown, D.O. and Kwansol, F.A. (1999) Using IRR and NPV Models to Evaluate Societal Costs of Tourism Projects in Developing Countries. *International Journal of Hospitality Management,* 18(1), 31–43.

Bull, A. (1995) *The Economics of Travel and Tourism,* 2nd edn. Melbourne: Longman.

Dyson, J.R. (2001) *Accounting for Non-Accounting Students,* 5th edn. Harlow: Pearson Education.

Ellis, J. and Williams, D. (1993) *Corporate Strategy and Financial Analysis.* London: Pitman.

Haberberg, A. and Rieple, A. (2001) *The Strategic Management of Organizations.* Harlow: Pearson Education.

Holloway, S. (1998) *Changing Planes: A Strategic Management Perspective on an Industry in Transition.* Aldershot: Ashgate.

Johnson, G and Scholes, K. (2002) *Exploring Corporate Strategy.* Harlow: Pearson Education.

Kotas, R. and Conlan, M. (1997) *Hospitality Accounting,* 5th edn. London: International Thomson Business Press.

Kotler, P. (1997) *Marketing Management Analysis, Planning, Implementation, and Control,* 9th edn. Englewood Cliffs, NJ: Prentice Hall International.

Lynch, R. (2000) *Corporate Strategy,* 2nd edn. Harlow: Pearson Education.

Mathieson, A. and Wall, G. (1982) *Tourism: Economic, Physical and Social Impacts.* London and New York: Longman.

Mules, T. (2000) Globalisation and the Economic Impacts of Tourism, in B. Faulkner, G. Moscardo and E. Laws (eds), *Tourism in the 21st Century: Lessons from Experience.* London: Continuum.

Owen, G. (1998) *Accounting for Hospitality, Tourism and Leisure,* 2nd edn. Harlow: Longman.

Porter, M.E. (1985) *Competitive Advantage.* New York: Free Press.

Rumelt, R. (1980) The Evaluation of Business Strategy, in W.F. Glueck, *Business Policy and Strategic Management.* New York: McGraw-Hill.

Vogel, H.L. (2001) *Travel Industry Economics.* Cambridge: Cambridge University Press.

Wager, J.E. (1997) Estimating the Economic Impacts of Tourism. *Annals of Tourism Research,* 24(3), 592–608.

Williams, A. and Giardina, E. (1993) *Efficiency in the Public Sector: The Theory and Practice of Cost–Benefit Analysis.* London: Edward Elgar.

World Tourism Organization (1994) *Aviation and Tourism Policies: Balancing the Benefits.* London: Routledge.

Part Five

Strategic implementation

Introduction

Once a travel and tourism organization has selected the most appropriate strategic options, the organization must consider a number of key issues related to actually putting what is proposed into practice. As ever, the danger can lie in this more detailed level of strategic management. However well thought out the strategy may be, if sufficient thought is not given to the ways in which it should be implemented it is unlikely to prove to be successful. In this section of the book a number of the most important issues connected with strategic implementation are considered.

First, implementation requires a reconfiguration of the travel and tourism organization's resource base. Does the organization have the inputs it needs in terms of finance, people, physical inputs and intellectual assets to carry out the strategy? If not these will have to be obtained (Chapter 13).

Second, the travel and tourism organization will need to bring its structure and culture into such a position that they facilitate a successful outcome. It may be that the structure and culture are not initially supportive for the strategic changes the organization is trying to implement. In such a situation the organization will need to instigate the requisite changes (Chapter 13).

Third, implementation of strategy invariably involves change. This will affect employees' roles and responsibilities, may mean redundancies or additional appointments and external stakeholders such as shareholders will also be implicated. Change can be a difficult managerial challenge. While some may welcome proposed changes others may resist, thus risking the efficient implementation of the strategy. Managers may adopt different approaches according to the circumstances (Chapter 13).

Fourth, in an inherently international industry such as travel and tourism an important consideration is the approach of organizations to internationalization. International strategy is considered in Chapter 14.

It is likely that, following on from the four issues considered above, each functional area of the organization (finance, marketing, human resources, operations etc.) will need to consider implementing detailed strategies, which focus on each area of activity. This level of detail, however, is beyond the scope of this book.

The word 'implementation' perhaps implies that it is a 'one-off' process with the strategy being is implemented then left alone. This is not the case. Strategic management should be viewed as an on-going process, for lessons learned (both successes and failures) from the implementation stage can be fed back into the analysis phase. The external and internal environments of travel and tourism organizations are constantly changing so that such an organization needs continually to re-evaluate its environments. Changes in these may require modifications to the chosen strategies and consequently revisions to the ways in which they are implemented.

At the end of a book on strategic management for travel and tourism it is apposite to stand back and consider the changing nature of the subject matter. Thus the book concludes in Chapter 15 with a brief overview of present and future trends in the study of strategic management.

CHAPTER 13

Strategic implementation for travel and tourism organizations

Strategic implementation is concerned with the issues which are considered to be necessary for the successful execution of strategy. In a deliberate strategic process, strategic implementation would be carried out only after an organization has gathered sufficient information on its internal and external environments (this being the purpose of strategic analysis) and after it has undertaken the process of choosing strategic options. The evaluation of these options is followed by the selection of the most appropriate option (see Chapter 12).

In order to carry out a strategy successfully, an organization must consider several key areas. First, it must establish how the strategy will be resourced. Second, it should ask itself how well its current culture, structure and internal systems are able to meet the challenges of the strategy. Changes in any or all of these may become necessary. Finally, most strategies necessitate some degree of internal change and this process of change will need to be managed. This chapter discusses each of these matters in turn.

After studying this chapter, students should be able to:

- describe where implementation fits into the strategic process;
- describe the role of resource planning in strategic implementation;
- explain how and why corporate culture plays an important part in implementation;
- understand the link between structure and strategy;
- describe the essentials of change management.

Implementation and the strategic process

Most people intuitively understand that a lot of information is required before any big decision is made. We wouldn't normally buy a holiday (a relatively expensive purchase) without investigating the attractions of the destination or finding out something about the company we would be travelling with and the accommodation available. In the same way, an organization or business would be risking a great deal if it were to pursue a strategic option without first carrying out a detailed analysis of its internal and external environments.

Put simply, successful strategy selection and implementation relies upon the presupposition that the organization has carried out a meaningful strategic analysis and is consequently aware of its internal strengths and weaknesses and its external opportunities and threats. Without being 'armed' with this information, the company cannot be certain that the chosen strategy would be the correct choice. The process leading to implementation is shown in Figure 13.1.

In order to carry out (implement) a strategy successfully, an organization will need to work out how to resource it. This means how it will obtain the requisite finance, human resources (usually in the form of appropriately skilled employees) and the physical resources such as equipment and buildings. As part of this process a detailed strategy may be developed for each part of the organization, such as the marketing, finance operations and personnel functional areas. It should also reconfigure its culture and structure to 'fit' the proposed strategy. Finally, strategic implementation often means change inside the organization in order to achieve the agreed objectives. Change management is thus the third area to be considered in strategic implementation. This chapter will briefly consider each of these issues.

Resources and implementation

Resources – the key inputs

In the same way that people and animals need the inputs of air, food, warmth, etc., so also organizations need inputs in order to function normally. Economics textbooks would refer to these inputs as the *factors of production*. They fall into four broad categories:

1 Physical and operational resources (land, buildings, plant, equipment, etc.).
2 Financial resources (share and loan capital required for development and expansion).
3 Human resources (obtaining the requisite number of appropriately skilled employees).

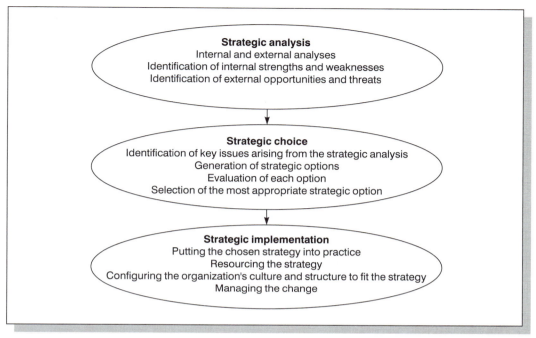

Figure 13.1 The linear–rational (prescriptive) strategic process

4 Intellectual or 'intangible' resources (non-physical inputs that may be necessary in some industries such as databases, legal permissions, brand or design registration, contacts, etc.

In most instances travel and tourism organizations must obtain resource inputs in competitive markets. This means that they must compete with other organizations for the best people, financial investment capital, the best locations for development, etc. For example, a travel agent setting up a new branch in a town will want to ensure that it occupies a site that has a large number of people passing the shop window (or *footfall* as retailers often refer to it). Other retailers may also want to gain access to such a site so the travel agent may have to compete for this scarce resource thus bidding up the price. At some point the price (in the form of rent) may become too great in relation to the expected revenues, so decisions have to made as to how much can be afforded.

Thus all of these inputs have a cost attached to them and so careful planning for resource requirement is usually a key calculation in strategic implementation.

Matching strategy with resources

Once a strategic option has been settled upon (following the strategic choice stage), management attention turns to evaluating the resource implications of the strategy. The extent to which the resource base needs to be adjusted will, of course, depend upon the degree of change that the proposed strategy entails.

Broadly speaking, resource planning falls into three categories (Johnson and Scholes, 1998).

Few changes strategies • • •

Some strategies, particularly those that are not particularly ambitious, require few changes in the resource base. They may require, for example, a slight increase in financing to fund modest expansion or the recruitment or retraining of some human resources to meet a skill shortage in one or two areas. Conversely, of course, a few changes strategy may require the disposal of some assets or a slight reduction in the human resource base.

Resource increase strategies • • •

Second, some strategies require an increase in the resource base in order to facilitate a more substantial programme of growth. This usually entails two things: an internal reallocation of resources and the purchasing of fresh resource inputs from external resource suppliers. Internal reallocation entails reducing resource employment in one area of the organization and moving it across to where it is needed, say by redeploying human resources or by selling some non-core activities to reinvest the money in the area of growth. New resources (from outside the organization) are obtained through the usual channels – from the job-market, the real estate market, the financial markets and so on.

Resource decrease strategies • • •

Third, some strategies involve a reduction in the resource base in order to manage decline successfully. If an organization finds, after a resource audit, that it has too many resources (say too many employees, too many aircraft, too many hotel properties in the wrong locations, etc.) then measures are put in place to carry out some reduction. Excess capital or physical resources can often be successfully reinvested in business areas that are in more buoyant markets whilst excess human resources must usually be released.

Key concept: Resource audit

An audit process can be used to make assessments of any or all of the resource inputs. In Chapter 3 we discussed in some depth the human resource audit, but the same procedures can be employed to audit financial, physical or intellectual resources.

The nature or audit of any kind (including resource audits) is of purposeful checking or testing. Resources are audited (or purposefully checked) for:

- *sufficiency* (is there enough for the purpose?);
- *adequacy* (is the condition, location, state, or quality of the resource adequate for the purpose?)
- *availability* (are the required resources available at the time and in the quantities required?)

An audit of a hotel group's chain of hotels (an example of physical resources) might take the form of assessing whether the number of rooms is *sufficient* for current needs and any planned expansion. This might be followed by an evaluation of *adequacy* – the location of the hotels relative to customers and those of competitors; the state of repair and decoration of the hotels; and, the ability of the hotels to support the prevailing business (leisure, business, conferences etc.). Finally, if more resources are required or if development of the land or buildings is needed, *availability* is examined, either of additional property or of permissions for development.

Developing and controlling resources

In order to meet the resource requirements of a proposed strategy, resources are developed and then controlled to ensure they meet the needs of the strategy.

Financial resource planning ● ● ●

Financial resource planning takes the form of financing the proposed strategy (see Chapter 5 for a more detailed discussion of these issues). *Capital budgeting* concerns projecting the capital needs of a strategy. This is usually a relatively straightforward operation as costs can normally be forecast with some accuracy. Once the capital requirements are known, a plan is put in place to finance any shortfall. Whilst some strategies can be financed from retained profits (depending upon how much retained profit the company has), others are financed from external sources such as share (rights) issues, debt capital or the issuing of corporate bonds or debentures. The pros and cons of these approaches to financing are discussed in Chapter 5.

Human resource planning ● ● ●

Human resource planning (see Chapter 4) involves projecting the human capital required for the successful implementation of the proposed strategy. It would typically take the form of forecasts of both the numbers of people required and the types of skills and abilities that will be in demand. If a shortfall in either of these is identified, the 'gap' will be filled by one or more of the following.

- Training, retraining or staff development – to close the skills gap by developing existing employees.
- Appointing new employees – entering the labour market and competing with other employers for the requisite number of appropriately skilled employees.

Physical and operational resource planning ● ● ●

Physical resource planning is slightly more complex than financial and human resource planning. The reason for this is that so many inputs fall into this category. We include in this category land, buildings, location, plant and equipment.

Some physical resources are more easily obtained than others. Most equipment is relatively easily obtained, unless the requirement is very specialized. However, careful planning may be necessary for some equipment needs require long lead times for their construction. For example, a cruise line or an airline seeking to update its fleet with new ships or aircraft would need to plan one or two years in advance in order to secure delivery on a particular date. Businesses that have requirements for key locations and buildings of particular specificity expose themselves to the possibility of having to settle for second best if they are unable effectively to compete in these particular resource markets.

Some sectors of the travel and tourism industry exemplify this competition for physical resources. The location of a travel retail outlet, a hotel or a visitor attraction will often be a key determinant in the success of the business. Successfully competing with competitors for prime locations and the best buildings will consequently be of paramount importance, especially when these locations are in short supply. Hong Kong has developed on Hong

Kong island (where the central business district CBD is located) and across the harbour in Kowloon on the Chinese mainland. On the island, especially in 'Central' (the CBD), the lack of suitable sites and the costs of development have forced hotels to seek other locations. Banks and other financial institutions have been willing to pay very high prices for prime sites, and consequently many of the new hotel developments have taken place elsewhere on the island or in Kowloon, where development sites are more plentiful and where land costs are lower. The Hilton Hotel in Central, for example, was demolished to make way for an office development.

Intellectual resource planning • • •

Intellectual resources – inputs that cannot be seen and touched – can be the most important resource inputs of all (see Chapter 1). Some proposed strategies have a requirement for a legal or regulatory permission, a database (say of key customers in a certain market segment), or experience of dealing with certain markets.

Organizational culture and implementation

Culture suitability

We encountered the concept of culture in Chapter 4. Strategic implementation usually involves making an assessment of the suitability of a culture to undertake the strategy. In the same way that human personalities differ in their readiness to undertake certain courses of action, so also some organizational 'personalities' differ.

In the context of implementation, culture is usually analysed for its suitability. If we consider human personalities, we can readily appreciate that not all personalities are equally suitable for all jobs or tasks.

Some people, for example, have a personality that is ready to embrace a new challenge and who take to change with vigour and excitement. They enjoy bungee jumping and parachute jumps. Other people prefer things not to change. They are conservative in nature and they would be likely to turn down the opportunity to engage in risky sports. These two personality types highlight the suitability contrasts that can exist.

In Chapter 4 we encountered two typologies of corporate culture. Handy (1993) identified four types of culture – power, role, task and person. Miles and Snow (1978) also identified four culture types by their reaction tendency, and this is probably the more useful typology in this context.

Miles and Snow's typology and cultural postures

Miles and Snow's (1978) typology divided culture types according to how they approach strategy. These distinctions are important as they tell us how each culture type will react to different strategic options.

A review of the Miles and Snow categories • • •

Defender cultures are suitable for organizations that exist in relatively well-defined market areas and where improving the position in existing markets is the most appropriate strategic option (e.g. market penetration). The culture would feel uncomfortable with having to develop new markets or diversification. The values resident within defender cultures work well if markets are stable and relatively mature.

Prospector cultures, in contrast to defenders, are continually seeking out new product and market opportunities. Accordingly, they often create change and uncertainty. The cultural norms within the culture are consequently more able to develop new markets and products.

Analyser cultures exhibit features of both defenders and prospectors. They have developed a culture that is able to accommodate both stability (which defenders like) and instability (which prospectors have learned to adjust to). The culture can be formal in some circumstances and flexible and 'organic' in others.

Reactor cultures can sometimes lack strategic focus and are consequently sometimes accused of being 'blown around' by changes in their environments. They do not innovate and tend to emulate the successes of competitors.

The purpose of examining Miles and Snow's typology ● ● ●

It is evident that the ability of cultures to undertake different strategic courses of action varies. It is likely, for example, that defender cultures and those like them would be less able to undertake a programme of radical change than, say, those that exhibit prospector characteristics.

Cultural differences between *what is* and *what is required* for a strategy is one of the most important aspect of strategic implementation. Incongruities between the two present a challenge to management in respect of either changing the culture or compromising on strategic objectives such that cultural change is required to a lesser extent. We will return to the nature of change – including cultural change – later in this chapter.

Cultural change at British Airways

During the 1970s and 1980s the publicly owned British airline British Airways or 'BA' as it was commonly referred to, had become synonymous with poor service. The common joke of the time was that BA stood for 'bloody awful'. Despite recent indifferent performance British Airways is often put forward as a successful example of cultural change. After the airline went public by floating on the stock exchange in 1987 a major cultural change programme was introduced which emphasized the service-led orientation of the business. Virtually the entire 37 000 workforce was put through a two-day culture-change training course entitled 'Putting People First'. Almost all of the airline's 1400 managers went through a five-day version entitled 'Managing People First'. What separated this programme from most normal management training programmes was its size, the consistency with which it was applied throughout the organization to all grades of employees, and the determination of senior management to drive the programme through.

The programme's emphasis was on instilling a new culture, but this ran alongside other changes. An appraisal scheme was introduced which measured not only what managers did but how they went about it and bonuses were introduced. An emphasis was also placed on informing staff of the competitive pressures facing the airline and on empowering staff to make decisions on their own initiative rather than being bound by inflexible rules.

Source: adapted from Tushman and O'Reilly (1996)

Structure and implementation

What is structure?

Organizational structure refers to the 'shape' of the business. The importance of structure to strategic success is intuitively easy to grasp by using the structure of a human body as a metaphor. Some people are naturally large and may be slightly overweight whilst others are smaller, lithe and fit. The skeletal and muscle structure of people is a major determinant of their suitability for certain activities. People who are large and overweight are less suitable for ballet dancing but are more suitable as sumo wrestlers or as members of tug-of-war teams. Conversely, smaller and fitter people are better at running, rowing and competitive horseracing.

There is no such thing as 'the perfect structure' since usually compromises have to be made in their design and often they are the result of ad hoc growth where parts are added over time rather than planned from the outset. However, in relation to strategy it is necessary to consider whether the proposed structure is capable of helping the organization achieve the objectives that have been set as part of its strategy. Organizational structures tend to be described in terms of their 'height,' their 'width' and their complexity. A fourth, related way of describing organizational structures is according to their method of division.

The 'height' of structures

Height refers to the number of layers that exist within the structure. It is perhaps intuitively obvious that larger organizations are higher than smaller ones. The guide to how high an organizational structure should be depends upon the complexity of the tasks that a proposed strategy entails. A small, single site travel agent is involved in competing in one location with an easily identified number of competitors and a single set of product types. This scenario is much less complex than a multinational, vertically and horizontally integrated travel company that competes in many national markets, in several product types and with a high dependence on innovation.

Essentially, height facilitates the engagement of specialist managers in the middle of an organization who can oversee and direct the many activities that some large organizations are involved in. Not all organizations have this requirement and it would be more appropriate for such organizations to have a flatter structure (see Figure 13.2). The trend in recent years has been for organizations to become flatter as increasingly technology can provide information directly from the point of sale to the highest levels. This process is often known as *delayering* and facilitates quicker decision-making and the faster communications between managers and operational employees who have to implement the decisions.

Key concept: Tall and short structures

Tall structures, involving more layers of specialist managers, enable the organization to coordinate a wider range of activities across different product and market sectors. It is more difficult for senior management to control and is obviously more expensive in terms of management overhead.

Shorter structures involve few management layers and are suitable for smaller organizations that are engaged in few products or market structures. They are cheaper to operate and facilitate a greater degree of senior management control.

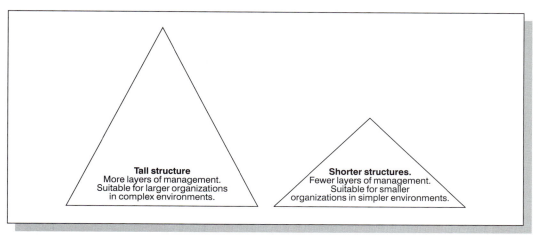

Figure 13.2 The height of organizations

The 'width' of structures

The 'width' of organizational structures refers to the extent to the organization is centralized or decentralized. A decentralized organizational structure is one in which the centre elects to devolve some degree of decision-making power to other parts of the organization. A centralized organization is one in which little or no power is devolved from the centre. In practice, a continuum exists between the two extremes along which the varying extents of decentralization can be visualized (see Figure 13.3).

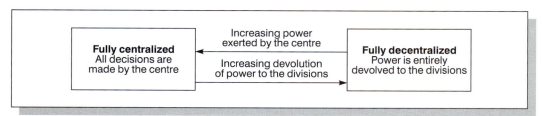

Figure 13.3 The centralization–decentralization continuum

As with the height of structures, there is a trade-off between the costs and benefits of width. The advantages of centralization are mainly concerned with the ability of the centre to maintain tighter direct control over the activities of the organization. This is usually more appropriate when the organization is smaller and engages in few product or market segments. Some degree of decentralization is advantageous when the organization operates in a number of markets and localized specialized knowledge is an important determinant of overall success. The main advantages of centralization and decentralization are summarized in Table 13.1.

Complexity of structure

The complexity of structure is usually taken to mean the extent to which the organization observes formal hierarchy in its reporting relationships. Strict hierarchy is not always an

Advantages of centralization	Advantages of decentralization
Managers at centre maintain tight control	Can engage in a wider range of activities
Avoids problems of complex structures	Enables increased specialization
Communications quicker and cheaper	Can reduce time taken to make key decisions
Delegation risks avoided	Can develop and improve the skills of managers

Table 13.1 The advantages of centralization and decentralization (which have both horizontal and vertical lines of reporting)

appropriate form of organization, especially when it cannot be automatically assumed that seniority guarantees superior management skill.

In some contexts, formal hierarchy is entirely appropriate in implementing strategy. In others, however, allowing employees to act with some degree of independence can in fact enable the organization to be more efficient. The use of so-called matrix structures (which have both horizontal and vertical lines of reporting) for example, can result in the organization being able to carry out many more tasks than a formal hierarchical structure. Many companies go 'half way' in this regard by seconding employees into special task forces or cross-functional teams that are not part of the hierarchical structure, and which act semi-independently in pursuit of its brief.

Culture and structure at easyJet

EasyJet favours an informal company culture with a very flat management structure, which, the company argues, eliminates unnecessary and wasteful layers of management. All office-based employees are encouraged to dress casually. Ties are banned, except for pilots! Remote working (away from the office) and 'hot desking' (sharing desks) have been characteristics of easyJet since the beginning.

Methods of divisionalization

The fourth and final way of understanding how structure fits into strategic implementation is by considering how the parts of the organization are to be divided. As with all of the other matters to be considered in structure, the method of division is entirely dependent upon the context of the company and its strategic position. It is a case of establishing the most appropriate divisional structure to meet the objectives of the proposed strategy.

Divisions are based upon the grouping together of people with a shared specialism. By acting together within their specialism, it is argued that synergies can be obtained both with and between divisions. There are four common methods of divisionalization:

1 by functional specialism (typically operations, HRM, marketing, finance, and operations);
2 by geographic concentration (where divisions are regionally located and have specialized knowledge of local market conditions);

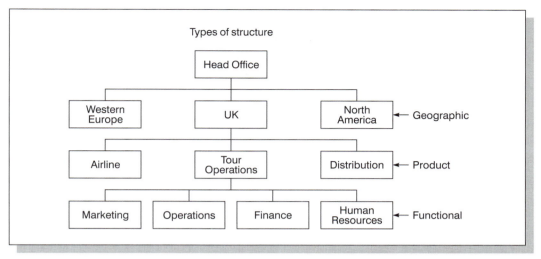

Figure 13.4 An example of a 'hybrid' divisional structure for a vertically integrated travel company

3 by product specialism (where divisions, usually within multi-product companies, have detailed knowledge of their particular products area);
4 by customer focus (where the company orientates itself by divisions dedicated to serving particular customer types, for example retail customers, industrial customers, etc.).

In many cases, a 'hybrid' approach to divisionalization might be appropriate. For example a vertically integrated tour operator, airline and travel retailer with sales in the UK, Western Europe and North America might have a hybrid divisional structure with geographical, product, and functional elements as shown in Figure 13.4. Each geographical region might have three product areas (the UK is used in Figure 13.4 for illustration), each having its own functional divisions.

Managing the changes in implementation

The need for change

At its simplest, strategy is all about change. In this chapter, we have encountered the importance of an organization's resource base, its culture and its structure. In order to bring about strategic repositioning (say in respect to products and markets), all of these may need to be changed.

Different organizations exhibit differing attitudes to change. We can draw a parallel here with different types of people. Some people are very conservative and configure their lives so as to minimize change. Such people will generally fear change and will resist it. Other people seem to get bored easily and are always looking for new challenges, new jobs, and so on. Organizations reflect this spectrum of attitudes. It is here that we encounter the concept of *inertia*.

Inertia – identifying barriers to change

Inertia is a term borrowed from physics. It refers to the force that needs to be exerted on a body to overcome its state in relation to its motion. If a body is stationary (i.e. at rest)

then we would need to exert a force upon it to make it move. The size and shape of the body will have a large bearing upon its inertia – compare the inertia of a football to that of a train.

In the same way, different organizations present management with varying degrees of inertia. Some are easy to change and others are much more reluctant. The willingness to change may depend upon the culture of the organization – its size, its existing structure, its product and/or market positioning and even its age (i.e. how long it has existed in its present form).

For most purposes, we can say that resistance to change on the part of employees can be caused by one or more of the following attitudes:

- It may be that those affected by the change *lack an understanding* of the details. They may not have had the reasons for the change explained to them or they may not be aware of how they will personally be affected. This particular barrier can normally be overcome relatively easily by management taking the requisite measures to close the information gap.
- There may be a *lack of trust* on the part of employees in respect to management.
- Employee inertia may be based upon fear – particularly in respect to their personal position or their social relationships. Those affected by the change may fear that the proposed changes will adversely affect their place in the structure or the relationships they enjoy in the organization.
- Some inertia is driven by *uncertainty* about the future. Attitudes to uncertainty vary significantly between people, with some showing a much more adverse reaction to it than others.

Kurt Lewin's three-step model of understanding change

Lewin (1947) suggested that organizational change could be understood in terms of three consecutive processes: unfreezing, moving and then refreezing.

Unfreezing

Unfreezing involves introducing measures that will enable employees to abandon their current practices or cultural norms in preparation for the change. In many organizations nothing has changed for many years and unfreezing is necessary as a 'shaking-up' phase. The impetus for unfreezing can come from either inside or outside the organization itself. Changing market conditions, for example, sometimes give employees warning that change will be imminent. A particular market crisis may precipitate the expectation amongst employees that change must happen as a result. Internally, a management shake-up, a profit warning or talk of restructuring may bring about similar expectations.

Moving to the new level

Moving to the new level involves bringing about the requisite change itself. The time period given over to this phase varies widely. Structural change can usually be brought about relatively quickly. Changes in internal systems sometimes take longer (such as the introduction of new quality or information systems), whilst changing culture can take years.

Refreezing • • •

Refreezing is necessary to 'lock in' the changes and to prevent the organization from going back to its old ways. Again, we would usually take cultural changes to require more 'cementing in' than some other changes and some resolve might be required on the part of senior management.

Step and incremental change

The pace at which change happens can usually be divided into one of two categories – step and incremental (see Figure 13.5). There are two factors that determine which is the most appropriate (Quinn and Voyer, 1998).

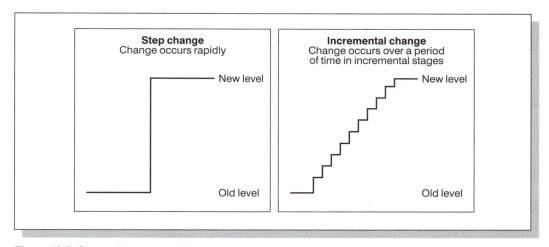

Figure 13.5 Step and incremental change

1 How urgent the need for change is. A market crisis will typically bring about an urgent need for rapid change whereas preparing for the introduction of a new legal regulation in five years' time will usually allow change to be brought about more slowly and perhaps more painlessly.
2 How much inertia is resident within the organization's culture. The time taken to unfreeze the inertia in some organizations will necessarily take longer than in others.

Step change offers the advantage of 'getting it over with'. It enables the organization to respond quickly to changes in its environment and hence enable it to conform to new conditions without lagging behind. Its disadvantages include the 'pain' factor – it may require some coercion or force on the part of management, which in turn may damage employee–management relationships.

Incremental changes offer the advantage of a step-by-step approach to change. For organizations with high inertia, it enables management to gain acceptance before and during the change process, and consequently, it tends to be more inclusive. The process is divided into a number of distinct phases and there may be periods of 'rest' between the phases. It would be an inappropriate technique to use in situations of rapid environmental change.

Models for managing change

The process of actually managing strategic change brings us to consider a number of managerial approaches and their appropriateness in various contexts. Writers in this area have tended towards two complementary approaches.

The management approaches

Some writers have suggested that change can be successfully managed by employing a range of managerial practices. We can conceive of this approach as an 'if this doesn't work, try this' mechanism.

Most academics and managers have agreed that the process should begin with *education* and *communication*. The purpose if this is to inform those (usually internal) stakeholders who will be affected by the change. The message communicated will usually contain an explanation of the reasons for the change and an overview of its timescale and extent. In some organizational contexts, this procedure alone will be sufficient to overcome inertia and get the change process under way. In others, this will not be enough.

The next step will thus be to progress to *negotiation* and *participation*. Affected stakeholders will be invited to contribute to the process and to participate in its execution. It is thus hoped, by this process, that employees will be 'on board' – that they will feel some sense of ownership of the change. Some managers may introduce some degree of manipulation (of employees) in this stage, possibly by appealing to the emotional responses of employees or by over- or under-stating the reality of the changes in the environment.

Finally, if all else has failed to bring about the willing participation of the employees, management may be able to introduce some degree of *coercion*. This tactic is far from being appropriate in all contexts, but where it is possible, it can be used to significant effect. Coercion is the practice of forcing through change by exploiting the power asymmetry between executive management and 'rank and file' employees. It is usually only used as a last resort – it can have a very negative effect on management–employee relationships after the change.

The change agent approach

Some texts refer to this approach as the 'champion of change' model. It is a change process that is managed from start to finish by a single individual (or a small team). The individual (or change agent) may be key manager within the organization or he or she may be brought in as a consultant for the duration of the process.

The change agent approach offers a number of advantages.

First, it provides a focus for the change in the form of a tangible person who becomes the personification of the process. A 'walking symbol' of change can act as a stimulus to change and can ensure that complacency is avoided.

Second, in many cases, the change agent will be engaged because he or she is an expert in the field. They may have overseen the same change process in many other organizations and so be well acquainted with the usual problems and how to solve them.

Third, the appointment of a change agent sometimes means that senior management time need not be fully occupied with the change process. The responsibility for the change is delegated to the change agent and management thus gain the normal advantages of delegation. Accordingly, senior management are freed up to concentrate on developing future strategy.

References and further reading

Hall, R. (1992) The Strategic Analysis of Intangible Resources. *Strategic Management Journal*, 13, 135–144.

Handy, C.B. (1993) *Understanding Organizations*, 4th edn. London: Penguin.

Heskett, J.L., Sasser, W.E. and Schlesinger, L.A. (1997) *The Service Profit Chain*. New York: Simon and Schuster.

Johnson, G. (1987) *Strategic Change and the Management Process*. Oxford: Blackwell.

Johnson, G. and Scholes, K. (1998) *Exploring Corporate Strategy*, 5th edn. Hemel Hempstead: Prentice Hall.

Lewin, K. (1947) Feedback Problems of Social Diagnosis and Action: Part II-B of Frontiers in Group Dynamics. *Human Relations, 1*, 147–153.

Lewin, K. (1951) *Field Theory in Social Science*. New York: Harper & Brothers.

Miles, R.E. and Snow, C.C. (1978) *Organizational Strategy, Structure and Process*. New York: McGraw-Hill.

Moss Kanter, R. (1989) *The Change Masters: Innovation and Entrepreneurship in the American Corporation*. Englewood Cliffs, NJ: Simon & Schuster.

Pettigrew, A.M. (1988) *The Management of Strategic Change*. Oxford: Blackwell.

Quinn, J.B. and Voyer, J. (1998) Logical Incrementalism: Managing Strategy Formation, in H. Mintzberg, J.B. Quinn and S. Ghoshal (eds), *The Strategy Process*. Englewood Cliffs, NJ: Prentice Hall.

Quinn, J.B. (1980) Managing Strategic Change. *Sloan Management Review*, Summer 1980, 3–20.

Quinn, J.B. (1980) *Strategies for Change*. Homewood, IL: Irwin.

Schein, E.H. (1985) Organizational Culture and Leadership. San Francisco: Jossey–Bass.

Stacey, R.D. (1993) *Strategic Management and Organizational Dynamics*. London: Pitman.

Tushman, M.L. and O'Reilly, C.A. (1996) *Winning Through Innovation: A Practical Guide to Leading Organizational Change and Renewal*. Boston, MA: Harvard Business School Press.

Williamson, O. (1975) *Markets and Hierarchies*. New York: Free Press.

International and global strategies for travel and tourism organizations

Introduction and Chapter Overview

One of the most important considerations in the implementation of strategy is the extent to which the organization's activities are spread across geographical regions. Some organizations are entirely domestically based, others operate in many countries, and others still operate in almost all regions of the world. This chapter is concerned with a discussion of the key issues surrounding the *why* and *how* questions: why do organizations expand in this way and how do they go about it? The *why* questions are covered in a discussion of the factors that drive increased internationalization. The *how* questions are answered in a discussion of the market entry options.

Learning Objectives

After studying this chapter, students should be able to:

■ define and distinguish between internationalization and globalization;

■ explain the factors that drive globalization;

- describe and demonstrate the application of Yip's framework for analysing the extent of globalization in an industry and market;
- explain the major global strategy alternatives;
- describe the international market entry strategies.

Internationalization and globalization

What is the difference?

Business has been international since the days of the ancient Egyptians, Phoenicians and Greeks. Merchants travelled the known world to sell products manufactured in their home country and to return with products from other countries. Initially, international business simply took the form of exporting and importing. The term *international* describes any business, which carries out some of its activities across national boundaries.

Globalization, on the other hand, is more than simply internationalization. A large multinational company is not necessarily a global business. In order for a business to become global in its operations, we would usually expect a number of important characteristics to be in place.

1 First, global organizations take advantage of the increasing trend towards a convergence of customer needs and wants across international borders (e.g. for fast foods, soft drinks, consumer electronics, hotel accommodation etc. – see Levitt, 1983).
2 Second, global organizations compete in industries that are globalized. In some sectors, successful competition necessitates a presence in almost every part of the world in order to compete effectively in its global market.
3 Third, global organizations can – and do – locate their value adding activities to those places in the world where the greatest competitive advantages can be made. This might mean, for example, shifting certain operations to a low cost region.
4 Finally, global organizations are able to integrate and coordinate their international activities between countries. The mentality of 'home base, foreign interests' that has been so prevalent amongst traditional multinational companies is eroded in the culture of global businesses. They have learned effectively to manage and control the various parts of the business across national borders and despite local cultural differences.

The development of an organization's global strategy, therefore, will be concerned with global competences, global marketing and global configuration and coordination of its value adding activities (see the discussion of value adding in Chapter 3).

Key concepts: Multinational and transnational companies

Both multinationals and transnational companies share the feature that they are usually large and they have direct investments in one or more foreign countries. The foreign investments may be part-shareholdings, but are more usually wholly owned subsidiaries.

The difference is in the degree to which the foreign investments are coordinated. We tend to think of a *transnational* company as one that has a high degree of coordination in its international interests. It will usually have a strategic centre, which manages the global operation such that all parts act in accordance with a centrally managed strategic purpose.

The term *multinational* company is usually taken to mean an international company whose foreign interests are not coordinated from a strategic centre.

Globalization of markets and industries

Levitt and market homogenization

It was Levitt (1983) who first argued that changes in technology, societies, economies and politics are producing a 'global village'. By this he meant that consumer needs in many previously separate national markets were becoming increasingly similar throughout the world. Developments in transport have not only made it easier to move products and materials between countries but they have also resulted in a huge increase in the amount that people travel around the world. Such travel educates people to the products and services available in other countries and, on their return home, they often wish to have access to products and services from overseas. This trend has been reinforced by changes in information technology, particularly those related to cinema and television, which have been important in some aspects of cultural convergence. The development of the World Trade Organization WTO (not to be confused with the other 'WTO' – the World Tourism Organization) and its predecessor, GATT (the General Agreement on Tariffs and Trade), has resulted in huge reductions in the barriers to trade between countries since the Second World War. Rising income levels throughout many parts of the world have also given economic impetus to the development of global markets.

It is not only markets which are in many cases becoming more global. Industries are also becoming more global. The value chains of businesses in many industries span the globe. In the case of a diversified tour operator for example, inputs in the form of destinations may be sourced from many parts of the world with the supply from one country varying from year to year based on the costs of the destination relative to other competing destinations. Organizations concentrate certain of their activities in locations where they hope to obtain cost, quality or other advantages. Other activities, like distribution, are also often dispersed around the world. The way that a business configures its activities across national borders can be an important source of competitive advantage. The spread of an organization's value adding activities around the world also means that there are important advantages to be gained from effective integration and coordination of activities.

Porter and multi-domesticity

Porter (1990) argued that industries can be either global or *multi-domestic*. Multi-domestic industries are those where competition in each nation is essentially independent. He gives the example of consumer banking where a bank's domestic reputation and resources in one nation have tended to have little effect on its success in other countries. The international banking industry is, Porter agued, essentially a collection of domestic industries.

Global industries are those in which competition is global. The consumer electronics industry is a good example where companies like Philips, Sony and Panasonic compete in almost all countries of the world. The implication would appear to be that businesses should adopt a global strategy in global industries and a multi-local strategy in multi-domestic markets. Yet the situation is not so simple as this. Even markets like consumer banking are becoming more global. The trend is for most industries to become more global, but even within industries major differences may occur.

One way of viewing globalization is as a continuum from globalization through international to local or multi-domestic (as shown in Figure 14.1). In travel and tourism the large computer reservations systems have a global reach, whereas towards the other end of the continuum most retail travel agents and rail and bus operators might be viewed as multi-domestic in their orientation. Large airlines often like to portray themselves as 'global' carriers, but close inspection of their route networks reveals that no carrier serves all parts of the world and even in those countries which are served, it is usually only the largest city that is served. Similarly, the large international hotel chains have expanded to include many countries but rarely penetrate local markets beyond the capital city. By way of contrast, the major soft drinks brands such as Coca-Cola are widely available throughout the world, and are widely dispersed within individual countries.

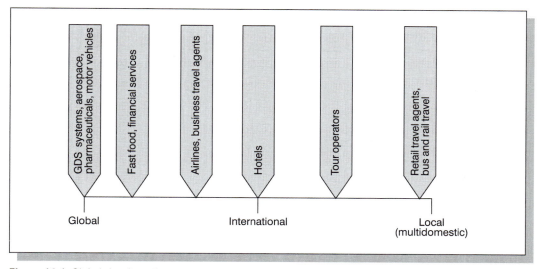

Figure 14.1 Global–local continuum

It is also the case that the degree of globalization of an industry or market may not be uniform. In other words, some aspects of an industry or market may be indicative of globalization while others may be indicative of localization. The degree of globalization of an industry can be assessed using Yip's globalization driver framework (1992). This is a more useful framework than Porter's because it makes it possible to evaluate both the overall degree of globalization of an industry and which features of the industry are more or less global in nature.

Globalization drivers

Yip's framework

Yip (1992) argues that it is not simply the case that industries are 'global' or 'not global', rather that they can be global in some respects and not in others. Yip's globalization driver

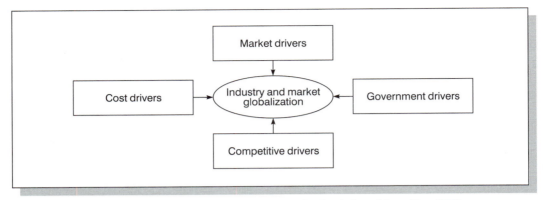

Figure 14.2 A framework describing drivers for internationalization (adapted from Yip, 1992)

framework makes it possible to identify which aspects of an industry are global and which aspects differ locally. Analysis using this framework can play an important role in shaping the global strategy of a business. A global strategy, according to Yip, will be global in many respects but may also include features that are locally oriented.

Yip argued that, 'to achieve the benefits of globalization, the managers of a worldwide business need to recognize when industry conditions provide the opportunity to use global strategy levers'. Yip identified four drivers (Figure 14.2) which determine the nature and extent of globalization in an industry. These are:

- market drivers
- cost drivers
- government drivers
- competitive drivers.

We will consider each of these drivers in turn.

Breakdown of globalization drivers

Market globalization drivers
- common customer needs
- global customers
- global distribution channels
- transferable marketing techniques
- presence in lead countries

Cost globalization drivers
- global scale economies
- steep experience curve effect
- sourcing efficiencies
- differences in country costs (including exchange rates)
- high product development costs fast changing technology

Government globalization drivers
- favourable trade policies
- common marketing regulations
- government owned competitors and customers
- compatible technical standards and common marketing regulations
- host government concerns

Competitive globalization drivers
- high exports and imports
- competitors from different continents
- interdependence of countries
- competitors globalized

Market globalization drivers

The degree of globalization of a market will depend upon the extent to which there are common customer needs, global customers, global distribution channels, transferable marketing and lead countries. It is not simply a case of a market being global or not global. Managers must seek to establish which, if any, aspects of their market are global.

Common customer needs

Probably the single most important market globalization driver is the extent to which customers in different countries share the same need or want for a product. The extent of shared need will depend upon cultural, economic, climatic, legal and other similarities and differences. There are numerous examples of markets where customer needs are becoming more similar. Examples include motor vehicles, soft drinks, fast food, but also beach and ski resorts, cruise ships and business travel The importance of American Express and Carlson Wagonlit in international business travel and the various international hospitality brands operated by Marriott Corporation as well as McDonald's, Burger King and Pizza Hut in fast food, or Coca-Cola and Pepsi Cola in soft drinks, are all illustrative of converging customer needs in certain markets. Levitt (1983) referred to this similarity of tastes and preference as increasing *market homogenization* – all markets demanding the same products, regardless of their domestic culture and traditional preferences.

Global customers and channels

Global customers purchase products or services in a coordinated way from the best global sources. Yip identifies two types of global customers:

1 *National global customers* – customers who seek the best suppliers in the world and then use the product or service in one country, e.g. a theme park operator might seek the best rides from many countries which are known for providing such engineering skills such as Germany, Switzerland, USA and Japan.
2 *Multinational global customers* – they similarly seek the best suppliers in the world but then use the product or service obtained in many countries, e.g. cruise lines source their ships from many countries such as Finland, France, Germany, Italy and Japan to ensure optimal quality standards delivered at a competitive price.

Alongside global customers there are sometimes global, or more often regional, distribution channels, which serve the global customers. Global customers and channels will contribute towards the development of a global market.

Transferable marketing

Transferable marketing describes the extent to which elements of the marketing mix like brand names and promotions can be used globally without local adaptations. Clearly, when adaptation is not required, it is indicative of a global market. In this way brands like McDonald's, Coca-Cola and Nike are used globally, and increasingly travel brands such as Hilton, Thomas Cook and Lufthansa also have global recognition. Yet advertising for such brands can be both global and locally adapted according the prevailing attitudes in local markets. If marketing is transferable it will favour a global market.

Lead countries • • •

When, as Porter (1990) found, there are certain countries that lead in particular industries, then, 'it becomes critical for global competitors to participate in these lead countries in order to be exposed to the sources of innovation'. Lead countries are those that are ahead in product and/or process innovation in their industry. These lead countries help to produce global standards and hence global industries and markets. The USA would clearly been seen as the lead country in terms of Internet travel distribution systems and different hotel formats for example, whilst Germany has taken a lead in developing vertically and horizontally diversified leisure travel companies.

Cost globalization drivers

The potential to reduce costs by global configuration of value adding activities is an important spur towards the globalization of certain industries. If there are substantial cost advantages to be obtained then an industry will tend to be global.

Global scale economies • • •

When an organization serves a global market then it is able to gain much greater economies of scale than if it serves only domestic or regional markets. Similarly, serving global markets also gives considerable potential for economies of scope. Thus internationally diversified travel companies such as Air France or Disney who market their activities in many countries gain large economies of scope in product development, marketing, procurement and financing.

Key concepts: Economies of scale and scope

Economies of scale describe the benefits that are gained when increasing volume results in lower unit costs. Although economies of scale can arise in all parts of the value chain, it is probably best understood by illustrating it using purchasing as an example. An individual purchasing one hotel room will pay more *per item* than a large company contracting to purchase hundreds of hotel rooms to provide for their customers for the season. It is said that the purchaser who is able to purchase in bulk (because of the size and structure of the buyer) enjoys scale economies over smaller organizations that buy in at lower volumes.

An economy of scope is a concept that describes the benefits that can arise in one product or market area as a result of activity in another. Another way of putting it is that the cost of providing two distinct offers from the same organization is less than providing both separately. Thus if a tour operator expands to market its activities in another country, the costs of the marketing activity can be shared with the activity in the countries in which it already operates through joint advertising, promotion and so on.

Steep experience curve effect • • •

When there is a steep learning curve in operations and marketing, businesses serving global markets will tend to obtain the greatest benefits. In many service industries there are steep learning curves yielding the greatest benefits to global businesses. Experience and good practices from one country can be shared with other countries and regions thereby increasing organizational learning and experience. Those organizations that are able to communicate the lessons from their experience, i.e. learning, around the organization quickly and effectively, are likely to be the most successful in global markets. For a hotel group expanding internationally, it is crucial that they get their market entry strategy right. However, experience of entering other country markets will help them make the correct decisions when they choose to enter subsequent markets.

Sourcing efficiencies

If there are efficiency gains to be made by centralized sourcing carried out globally then this will drive an industry towards globalization. Businesses like those in sports apparel and fashion clothing benefit from global sourcing to obtain lowest prices and highest quality standards, but this may also apply to cruise lines and airlines seeking crew.

Favourable logistics

If transportation costs comprise a relatively high proportion of sales value, there will be every incentive to concentrate production in few, large facilities. If transport costs are relatively small, such as with consumer electronic goods, production can be located in several (or many) locations, which are chosen on the basis of other cost criteria such as land or labour costs.

Differences in country costs

Operational costs (building, labour etc.) vary from country to country which can stimulate globalization. Thus, countries with lower operational costs will tend to attract businesses to locate activities in the country. Many Asian countries have attracted international hotel chains because of their favourable cost conditions. Although countries like Thailand have suffered in some respects because of the devaluation of their currency in 1997–98, from the point of view of being chosen as tourist centres, they have benefited.

Fast changing technology and high product development costs

Product life cycles are shortening as the pace of technological change increases. At the same time research and development costs are increasing in many industries. Such product development costs can only be recouped by high sales in global markets. Domestic markets simply do not yield the volumes of sales required to cover high R&D costs. Thus industries like pharmaceuticals and automobiles as well as cruising and airlines face very rapidly changing technology and hyper competition, together with high development and equipment purchase costs. As a consequence they must operate in global markets so as to ensure the volumes of sales necessary to recoup these costs.

Government globalization drivers

Since the Second World War many governments have taken individual and collective action to reduce barriers to global trade.

Favourable trade policies • • •

The World Trade Organization and its predecessor, the General Agreement on Tariffs and Trade, have done much to reduce barriers to trade, which have, in the past, hindered globalization of many industries. Although there are still significant barriers to trade in certain areas, the movement towards freedom of trade has been substantial, thus favouring globalization. The growth of customs unions and 'single markets' such as the European Union and the North American Free Trade Area (NAFTA) have also made an important contribution in this regard. In the airline industry deregulation occurred in the USA in 1978 and was followed by Europe in the 1990s.

Compatible technical standards and common marketing regulations • • •

Many of the differences in technical standards between countries, which hindered globalization in the past, have been reduced. For example, telecommunications standards, which have traditionally differed between countries, are increasingly being superseded by international standards. Similarly standards are converging in the pharmaceutical, airline and computing industries, which make it easier to produce globally accepted products.

There remain important differences in advertising regulations between countries, with the UK regulations among the strictest. Generally, however, these differences are being eroded and this is expected to favour greater globalization.

Government owned competitors and customers • • •

Government owned competitors, who often enjoy state subsidies, can act as a stimulus to globalization as they frequently compete with other global competitors, thus being forced to become more efficient and global market oriented. On the other hand, government-owned customers tend to favour domestic suppliers, which can act as a barrier to globalization The privatization of many state-owned businesses in many European countries (and elsewhere in the world) has reduced this barrier to globalization.

Host government concerns • • •

The attitudes and policies of host government concerns can either hinder or favour globalization. In certain circumstances, host governments may favour the entry of global businesses into domestic industries and markets, which will assist globalization. For example, the Malaysian government has, in recent years, done much to attract inward investment by Japanese, American and European-based hotel companies. The more governments that espouse such policies, the greater will be globalization of an industry. In other cases, host governments will seek to protect industries which they see as strategically important and will attempt to prevent foreign businesses from entry. Thus many countries such as the USA limit the ownership of American airlines by foreign companies and restrict access to foreign airlines for domestic airline routes.

Competitive globalization drivers

The greater the strength of the competitive drivers the greater will be the tendency for an industry to globalize. Global competition in an industry will become more intense when:

- there is a high level of trade between countries;
- the competitors in the industry are widely spread (they will often be on different continents);
- the economies of the countries involved are interdependent;
- competitors in the industry are already globalized.

High exports and imports

The higher the level of trade in products and services between countries the greater will be the pressure for globalization of an industry.

Competitors from different continents

The more countries that are represented in an industry and the more widely spread they are, the greater the likelihood of globalization.

Interdependence of countries

If national economies are already relatively interdependent, then this will act as a stimulus for increased globalization. Such interdependence may arise through, for example, multiple trading links in other industries, through being a part of a single market or through being in a shared political alliance.

Competitors globalized

If a competitor is already globalized and employing a global strategy then there will be pressure on other businesses in the industry to globalize as well. Globalization in the business travel sector is high because of the pressure on organizations to compete globally. Business travel agents are often required to serve the needs of their customers who themselves are global companies. Such companies often wish to deal with one organization, which is able to service its travel needs on a global basis.

Using the globalization driver framework

Yip's globalization driver framework provides an extremely useful tool for analysing the degree of globalization of an industry or market. Equally, it makes possible an understanding of which particular aspects of an industry or market are global and which aspects are localized. Each of the drivers must be analysed for the industry and market under consideration and the results of the analysis will play an important role in assisting managers to form the global strategy of their organization. The results will help to determine which features of the strategy are globally standardized and which features are locally adapted.

There are several models that explain the basis of global strategy. This chapter explains the frameworks developed by Porter (1986a, 1990) and Yip (1992). Porter focuses on adapting the generic strategy framework to global conditions and the role of configuration and coordination of value adding activities in securing global competitive advantage. Yip develops the concept of 'Total Global Strategy' based upon his globalization driver framework.

Although these are the models considered in this chapter, interested readers should consider reading the work of Bartlett and Ghoshal (1987, 1989), Prahalad and Doz (1987), Ellis and Williams (1995) and Stonehouse et al. (1999). There is also a large developing literature on globalization and its impacts on the travel and tourism industry. See, for example, Go and Pine (1995), Hanlon (1996), Keller (1996), Knowles (2001), Wahab and Cooper (2001).

Porter's global generic strategies

We learned in Chapter 10 that Porter (1980) argued that competitive advantage rests upon an organization selecting and adopting one of the three generic strategies (differentiation, cost leadership or focus) to modify the five competitive forces in its favour so as to earn higher profits than the industry average. In 1986 Porter extended the generic strategy framework to global business. The model suggests that a business operating in international markets has five strategy alternatives (Figure 14.3). The five strategic postures are defined according to their position in respect to two intersecting continua: the extent to which the industry is globalized (or country-centred horizontal axis) and the breadth of the segments served by the competitors in an industry (which, put simply, means the number of different customer groups served by an industry).

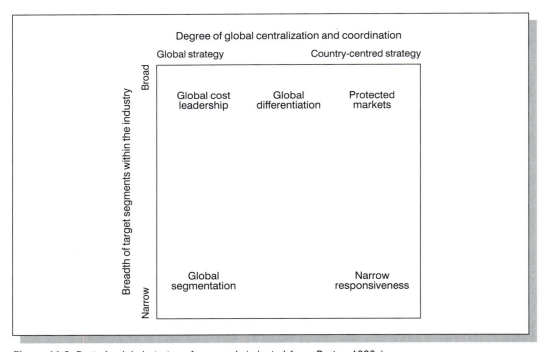

Figure 14.3 Porter's global strategy framework (adapted from Porter, 1986a)

The five strategic postures are described below.

1 *Global cost leadership* – the business seeks to be the lowest cost producer of a product globally. Globalization provides the opportunity for high volume sales and greater economies of scale and scope than domestic competitors.
2 *Global differentiation* – the business seeks to differentiate products and services globally, often on the basis of a global brand name.

3 *Global segmentation* – this is the global variant of a focus strategy when a single market segment is targeted on a worldwide basis employing either cost leadership or differentiation.

4 *Protected markets* – a business identifies national markets where its particular business is favoured or protected by the host government.

5 *National responsiveness* – the business adapts its strategy to meet the distinctive needs of local markets (i.e. not a global strategy). Suitable for purely domestic businesses.

The model suffers from similar flaws to those discussed in Chapter 10 relating to the generic strategy framework. As in the case of the conventional understanding of generic strategy, it is possible for a business to pursue a hybrid international strategy. Expedia.com, the online travel product distributor, for example, concentrates on both cost control (with regard to its supplier) and also on ensuring that it differentiates its products on the basis of reliability of delivery and the scope of its operations.

Porter's global strategy – configuration and coordination of internal activities

One of Porter's most important contributions to understanding global strategy was his work on the global value chain (1986a, 1990). Porter made the case that global competitive advantage depends upon configuring and coordinating the activities of a business in a unique way on a worldwide basis. To put it another way, competitive advantage results from the global scope of an organization's activities and the effectiveness with which it

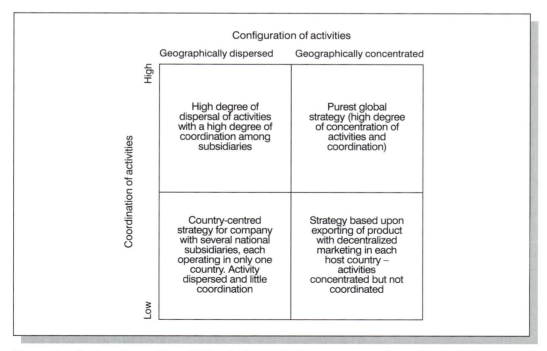

Figure 14.4 Configuration and coordination for international strategy (adapted from Porter, 1986a)

coordinates them. Porter (1986a, 1990) argued that global competitive advantage depends upon two sets of decisions:

1 *Configuration of value adding activities* – managers must decide in which nations they will carry out each of the activities in the value chain of their business. Configuration can be broad (involving many countries) of narrow (few or one countries).
2 *Coordination of value adding activities* – managers must decide the most effective way of coordinating value adding activities, which are carried out in different parts of the world.

Configuration and coordination present four broad alternatives, illustrated in Figure 14.4. In the case of configuration, an organization can choose to disperse its activities to a range of locations around the world or it may choose to concentrate key activities in locations that present certain advantages. Many businesses concentrate the manufacture of their products in countries where costs are low but skill levels are good. Many call centres are located in India where labour costs are low but the workforce is skilled, motivated and flexible. An organization can decide to coordinate its worldwide activities or to mange them locally in each part of the world. The latter approach misses the opportunity for global management economies of scale. For Porter, the 'purest global strategy' is when an organization concentrates key activities in locations giving competitive advantages and coordinates activities on a global basis. In the long term, according to Porter, organizations should move towards 'purest global strategy' as far as is practicable.

'Total' global strategy

Yip's stages in total global strategy

Yip (1992) argued that successful global strategy must be based upon a comprehensive globalization analysis of the drivers we encountered above. Managers of a global business must, he contends, evaluate the globalization drivers for their industry and market and must formulate their global strategy on the basis of this analysis. If, for example, they find that customer demand is largely homogeneous for their product then they can produce a largely standardized product for sale throughout the world. If, on the other hand, they find that there are few cost advantages of global concentration of operations because of adverse economies of scale or scope, they may choose to disperse their operational activities around the world to be close to their customers in different parts of the world. Thus the 'total global strategy' of an organization can be a mix of standardization and local adaptation as market and industry conditions dictate.

Yip went on to identify three stages in developing a 'total global strategy'.

1 *Developing a core strategy* – this will, in effect, involve building core competences and generic or hybrid strategy which can potentially give global competitive advantage.
2 *Internationalizing the core strategy* – this will be the stage at which the core competences and generic strategy are introduced to international markets and when the organization begins to locate its value adding activities in locations where competitive advantages like low cost access to resources are available. This will include choice of which markets the business will enter and the means by which it will enter them.
3 *Globalizing the international strategy* – this stage is based upon coordinating and integrating the core competences and strategy on a global basis. It will also include deciding which elements of the strategy are to be standardized and which are to be

locally adapted on the basis of the strength of the globalization drivers in the industry and market.

Key strategic decisions

Once a business has developed core competences and strategies which can potentially be exploited globally, the decisions must be made as to where and how to employ them. Initial moves into overseas markets will involve market development as such markets and segments can be regarded as new to the business. The initial market development may then be followed by product development and, perhaps, diversification (see Chapter 10).

When a business enters international and global markets it will be necessary to build new competences, alongside those that have brought about domestic competitive advantage. These new competences could well be in the areas of global sourcing and logistics, and global management.

The globalization of a business does not happen overnight. It may well involve entry to key countries with the largest markets first, followed by entry to less important countries later. In the initial stages of globalization the key decisions are usually as follows:

- Which countries are to be entered first?
- In which countries are value adding activities to be located?
- Which market development strategies are to be employed to gain entry to chosen overseas markets?

Market entry decisions

Decision criteria

The decision as to which countries and markets are to be entered first will be based upon a number of important factors.

- *The potential size of the market* – is the market for the product in the country likely to be significant? This will, in turn, be determined by the factors following.
- *Economic factors* – are income levels adequate to ensure that significant numbers of people are likely to be able to afford the product?
- *Cultural and linguistic factors* – is the culture of the country likely to favour acceptance of the product to be offered?
- *Political factors* – what are the factors that may limit entry to markets in the host country?
- *Technological factors* – are levels of technology adequate to support provision of the product in the host market and are technological standards compatible?

To begin with a business will choose to enter markets in those countries where the above conditions are most favourable.

Location of value adding activities

Managers must determine within which countries they will locate key value adding activities of their business. They will seek to gain cost, skill and resource advantages. In other words, they will attempt to locate activities in countries where there are production advantages to be gained.

Such advantages depend upon:

- *wage levels* – low wage levels will assist in low production costs;
- *skill levels* – there must be suitably skilled labour available;
- *availability of materials* – suitable materials must be accessible;
- *infrastructure* – transport and communications must be favourable to the logistics of the business.

The existence of these conditions within a country will, in turn, depend upon:

- *economic factors* – level of economic development, wage levels, exchange rate conditions;
- *social factors* – attitudes to work, levels of education and training;
- *political factors* – legislation favouring investment etc.;
- *technological factors* – levels of technology, and transport and communications infrastructure of the country.

Market development methods

Once decisions have been made as to which countries' markets are to be entered and where value adding activities are to be located, the task for management becomes the determination of which method of development to employ to enter another country. Broadly speaking, a business can choose either *internal or external methods for development* of overseas markets (see Chapter 11). Internal methods are usually slower, but tend to entail lower risk. External methods involve the business developing relationships with other businesses. Internal methods of development include direct exporting, overseas sourcing of suppliers, local processing and establishing overseas subsidiaries. External methods include joint ventures and alliances, mergers and acquisitions, franchising and licensing. The choice of method will depend upon a number of factors:

- the size of the investment required or the amount of investment capital available;
- knowledge of the country to be entered and potential risk involved (e.g. of political instability);
- revenue and cash flow forecasts and expectations;
- operating cost considerations;
- control considerations (some investment options will have implications for the parent to control activity in the host country).

Internal development methods

Internal methods are based upon the organization exploiting its own resources and competences and involve the organization carrying out some of its activities overseas. This may be exporting its products or setting up some form of production facilities abroad. The advantages of internal methods of development are that they maximize future revenue from sales abroad and they make possible a high degree of control over overseas activities. On the other hand, they can involve significant risk if knowledge of the host country and its markets are limited, and they may require considerable direct investment from the business.

The major internal methods of development overseas are direct exporting and development of overseas facilities.

Direct exporting • • •

Direct exporting is the transfer of services across national borders from the home operation. The service may simply be provided from the home country. For example, a cruise line might advertise its products in a particular country but the line might not have any staff in that country. Instead customers are directed to a sales office in the cruise line's home country. As sales increase, a sales office may be set up in the overseas country.

To avoid some of the pitfalls of direct exporting (like lack of local knowledge and access to distribution channels), many exporting businesses make use of local sales agents or distribute their products (often known as a *piggyback* distribution arrangement).

Overseas operations • • •

Organizations may choose to offer their products themselves directly in foreign countries. There are a number of reasons for such direct investment. The investment allows the company to gain local knowledge, to maintain control over the operations and to tailor the products and marketing to local demands. Relationships can also be forged with local suppliers and government, which might be helpful in developing the business.

Internal development may involve establishing a foreign subsidiary of the business. This is the case when it is favourable for the parent company to have total control of its overseas operations, decision-making and profits. Such a subsidiary may carry out the full range of activities of the parent business or it may be only an operational or marketing subsidiary.

External development methods

External methods of development involve the organization entering into relationships with businesses in a host country. External development methods can take the form of alliances or joint ventures, mergers or acquisitions, or franchises (see Chapter 11 for a discussion of these topics). Such methods have the advantages of providing local knowledge, potentially reducing risks, and reducing investment costs (except in the case of mergers or acquisitions). The major disadvantages (again except in the case of mergers and acquisitions) are reduced revenues and reduced control of activities as optimal income is traded off against the advantage of lower financial exposure.

International alliances and joint ventures • • •

Alliances and joint ventures allow a business to draw upon the skills, local knowledge, resources and competences of a locally based company. They reduce the risks of entry to overseas markets by providing local knowledge and help reduce investment costs.

International mergers and acquisitions • • •

A business may use mergers or acquisitions to enter overseas markets. Such mergers and acquisitions give a business access to the knowledge, resources and competences of a business based in the host country thus reducing some of the risks of market entry.

International franchising and licensing • • •

A franchise is an arrangement under which a franchiser supplies a franchisee with a tried-and-tested brand name, products and expertise in return for the payment of a proportion of profits or sales. The major advantage to the franchiser is that the risk, investment and operating costs of entering overseas markets are reduced considerably. At the same time the franchisee can contribute their local knowledge whilst also benefiting from the lower risks associated with an established business idea. Much of Burger King and Holiday Inn, or the Choice hotel expansion in overseas markets for example have come through franchise development.

References and further reading

Bartlett, C. and Ghoshal, S. (1987) Managing Across Borders: New Organizational Responses. *Sloan Management Review*, Fall, 45–53.

Bartlett, C. and Ghoshal, S. (1989) *Managing Across Borders: The Transnational Solution*. Cambridge, MA: Harvard Business School Press.

Campbell, A.J. and Verbeke, A. (1994) The Globalization of Service Sector Multinationals. *Long Range Planning*, 27(2), 95–102.

Douglas, S.P. and Wind Y. (1987) The Myth of Globalization. *Columbia Journal of World Business*, Winter, 19–29.

Doz, Y. (1986) *Strategic Management in Multinational Companies*. Oxford: Pergamon Press.

Ellis, J. and Williams, D. (1995) *International Business Strategy*. London: Pitman.

French, T. (1998) The Future of Global Distribution Systems. *Travel and Tourism Analyst*, 3.

Glaister, K.W. and Buckley, P.J. (1996) Strategic Motives for International Alliance Formation. *Journal of Management Studies*, 33(3), 301–332.

Go, F. and Pine, R. (1995) *Globalization Strategy in the Hotel Industry*. London: Routledge.

Hamel, G. and Prahalad, C.K. (1985) Do You Really Have a Global Strategy? *Harvard Business Review*, July/August.

Go, F. (1996) A Conceptual Framework for Managing Global Tourism and Hospitality Marketing. *Tourism Recreation Research*, 21(2), 37–43.

Hamel, G. (1991) Competition for Competence and Inter-Partner Learning within International Strategic Alliances. *Strategic Management Journal*, 12 (Special Summer Issue), 83–104.

Hamel, G., Doz, Y.L. and Prahalad, C.K. (1989) Collaborate with Your Competitors – and Win. *Harvard Business Review*, Jan/Feb, 133–139.

Hanlon, P. (1996) *Global Airlines: Competition in a Transnational Industry*. Oxford: Butterworth-Heinemann.

Heene, A. and Sanchez, R. (eds) (1997) *Competence-Based Strategic Management*. New York: John Wiley.

Henzler, H. and Rall, W. (1986) 'Facing Up to the Globalization Challenge', *McKinsey Quarterly*, Winter.

Keller, P. (1996) Globalization and Tourism. *Globalization and Tourism*, 38 (Editions AIEST). Switzerland: St Gallen.

Knowles, T., Diamantis, D. and El-Mourhabi, J.B. (2001) *The Globalization of Tourism and Hospitality: A Strategic Perspective*. London: Continuum.

Levitt, T. (1983) The Globalization of Markets. *Harvard Business Review*, May/June.

Litteljohn, D. (1997) Hotel Chains and Their Strategic Appraisal, in M. Foley, J. Lennon and G. Maxwell (eds), *Hospitality, Tourism and Leisure Management*. London: Cassell.

Mintzberg, H., Quinn, J.B. and Ghoshal, S. (1995) *The Strategy Process: Concepts, Contexts and Cases, European Edition*. Englewood Cliffs, NJ: Prentice Hall.

Nickson, D. (1997) Continuity or Change in the International Hotel Industry, in M.

Foley, J. Lennon and G. Maxwell (eds), *Hospitality, Tourism and Leisure Management*. London: Cassell.

Mules, T. (2001) Globalization and the Economic Impacts of Tourism, in B. Faulkner, G. Moscardo and E. Laws (eds), *Tourism in the 21st Century: Lessons from Experience*. London: Continuum.

Ohmae, K. (1989) The Global Logic of Strategic Alliances. *Harvard Business Review*, March/April, 143–154.

Ohmae, K. (1989) Managing in a Borderless World. *Harvard Business Review*, May/June, 152–161.

Porter, M.E. (1980) *Competitive Strategy: Techniques for Analysing Industries and Competitors*. New York: Free Press.

Porter, M.E. (1985) *Competitive Advantage*. New York: Free Press.

Porter, M.E. (1986a) *Competition in Global Business*. Cambridge, MA: Harvard University Press.

Porter, M.E. (1986b) Changing Patterns of International Competition. *California Management Review*, 28(2), 9–40.

Porter, M.E. (1990) *The Competitive Advantage of Nations*. New York: Free Press.

Prahalad, C.K. and Doz, Y.L. (1987) *The Multinational Mission: Balancing Local Demands and Global Vision*. New York: Free Press.

Prahalad, C.K. and Hamel, G. (1990) The Core Competence of the Corporation. *Harvard Business Review*, pp 79–91

Sessa, R. (1996) Tourism Production, Tourism Products. *Globalization and Tourism*, 38 (Editions AIEST). Switzerland: St Gallen.

Smeral, E. (1996) Globalization and Changes in the Competitiveness of Tourism Destinations, in *Globalization and Tourism*, 38 (Editions AIEST). Switzerland: St Gallen.

Smeral, E. (1998) The Impact of Globalization on Small and Medium Enterprises: New Challenges for Tourism Policies in European Countries. *Tourism Management*, 19(4), 371–380.

Stonehouse, G.H, Hamill, J., Campbell, D. and Purdie, A. (1999) *Global and Transnational Business – Strategy and Management*. London: John Wiley.

Wahab, S. and Cooper, C. (2001) *Tourism in the Age of Globalization*. London: Routledge.

Yip, G.S. (1992) *Total Global Strategy – Managing for Worldwide Competitive Advantage*. Englewood Cliffs, NJ: Prentice Hall.

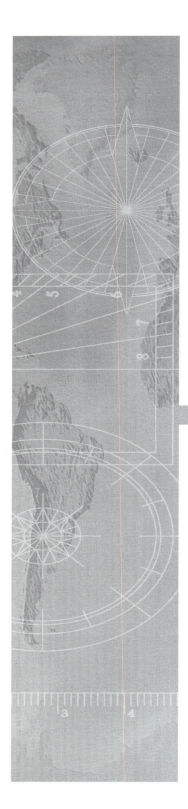

CHAPTER 15

Strategic management – present and future trends

Introduction and Chapter Overview

In travel and tourism, as in other industrial sectors, managers are learning that adopting a strategic and holistic approach to management can benefit organizational competitiveness. However, strategic management is not a mature discipline, if indeed it can be called a discipline when it is in fact a multi- and inter-disciplinary field of study. Strategists draw heavily upon disciplines as diverse as organization theory and behaviour, human resource management, economics, accounting and finance, and marketing as well as attempting to formulate their own theories and analytical frameworks. The future of strategic management will undoubtedly be longer than its past. For this reason, the theories, tools and techniques employed in strategic management in many cases are far from fully formulated. The subject will continue to evolve and the sophistication of its methods and methodology will develop and improve over time.

At the heart of strategic management is the desire to explain why certain organizations achieve competitive advantage through superior performance. The view in the 1980s was that competitive advantage was based upon the competitive positioning of the organization in its environment based upon highly systematic planning (Argenti, 1965; Porter, 1980, 1985). This view has since been challenged by strategists who believe that in a turbulent business environment, strategy can be developed incrementally and that competitive advantage depends upon the ability of the business to build core competences that cannot be easily replicated by competitors (Prahalad and Hamel, 1990; Kay, 1993; Hamel and Prahalad, 1994; Heene and Sanchez, 1997). This chapter, intended to be a summary of the book, serves the dual purpose of identifying the origins of strategic management before considering recent developments which will shape its future.

Learning Objectives

After studying this chapter, students should be able to:

- outline the development of strategic management as an academic discipline;
- explain and explore the planned/prescriptive approach to strategic management;
- explain and explore the emergent/incremental approach to strategic management;
- explain and explore the competitive positioning approach to strategic management;
- explain and explore the resource/core competence approach to strategic management;
- identify likely developments in strategic management, namely collaborative advantage and knowledge management.

Themes in strategic management

The 'big' controversies

The developing nature of strategy as a coherent academic discipline is reflected in two related debates revolving around what constitutes the most appropriate approach to strategic management (Figure 15.1). There is some disagreement among strategists on the

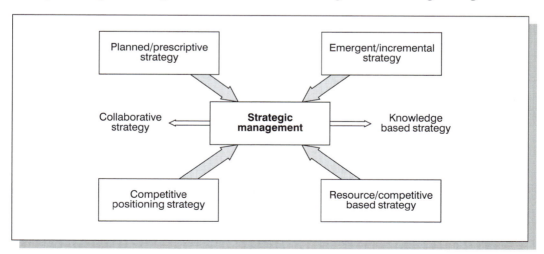

Figure 15.1 The development of strategic management

best way of understanding the determinants of competitive advantage. Some writers advocate an approach to strategic management which is *planned* or *prescriptive* (sometimes called *deliberate*) while others argue that it is better to evolve strategy incrementally (the *emergent* approach to strategy – see the key concept in Chapter 1). A parallel debate centres upon whether competitive advantage stems primarily from the competitive position of the business in its industry or from business-specific core competences. These themes are explored in the following sections of this chapter.

The debate surrounding the development of strategic management can be summarized under two broad headings:

1 The planned/prescriptive versus emergent/incremental controversy.
2 The competitive positioning versus resource/core competence based strategy controversy.

We discussed the first of these debates in Chapter 1 and the second in Chapter 10. Here, we summarize the main features of these approaches and briefly explore their advantages and disadvantages (see Table 15.1). The arguments are discussed below.

The prescriptive versus emergent strategy debate

Planned or prescriptive strategy

The planned or prescriptive approach views the formulation and implementation of strategic management as a logical, rational and systematic process. After analysis of the business and its environment, strategists must set well-defined corporate and business objectives and formulate, select and implement strategies which will allow objectives to be achieved. Such an approach has been criticized on the grounds that there is often a major discrepancy between planned and realized strategies (Mintzberg, 1987). It is also argued that the increasing turbulence and chaos of the business environment makes highly prescriptive planning a nonsense. Rigid plans prevent the flexibility which is required in an environment of volatile change. Being over-prescriptive, it is argued, also stifles the creativity that often underpins successful strategy.

On the other hand, it is argued that systematic planning makes it possible to organize complex activities and information, unite business objectives, set targets against which performance can be evaluated and generally increases the degree of control which can be exercised over the operation of the business. The planned or prescriptive approach is often linked to the *competitive positioning* approach (see later in this chapter).

Emergent or incremental strategy

The emergent or incremental view of strategy adopts the position that strategy must be evolved incrementally over time. This view is based upon the premise that businesses are complex social organizations operating in rapidly changing environments. Under such circumstances, strategy will tend to evolve as a result of the interaction between stakeholder groups and between the business and its environment. It is argued that an emergent approach has the advantages of increased organizational flexibility. It can form a basis in organizational learning and can provide an internal culture for managers to think and act creatively rather than have to act within the rigid framework of deliberate strategy . The danger is that an emergent approach may result in a lack of purpose in

Approach	Theory	Advantages	Criticisms
Prescriptive or planning strategy	Strategic management is a highly formalized planning process Business objectives are set and strategies are formulated and implemented to achieve them	Clear objectives provide focus for the business Objectives can be translated into targets against which performance can be measured and monitored Resources can be allocated to specific objectives and efficiency can be judged The approach is logical and rational	There are often major discrepancies between planned and realized strategy Rigid planning in a dynamic and turbulent business environment can be unproductive Prescriptions can stifle creativity Rigid adherence to plans may mean missed business opportunities
Emergent or incremental strategy	Strategy emerges and develops incrementally over time in the absence of rigid planning	Emergent strategy increases flexibility in a turbulent environment allowing the business to respond to threats and exploit opportunities Changing stakeholder interactions can mean that strategy is often, of necessity, emergent	There is a danger of 'strategic drift' as objectives lack clarity It is more difficult to evaluate performance as targets are less well defined
Competitive positioning approach to strategy	Competitive advantage results from an organization's position in respect to its industry The business analyses the strength of the competitive forces in its industry and selects an appropriate generic strategy. The business configures its value adding activities to support this generic strategy The approach to strategy is 'outside-in'	Well-developed analytical frameworks like Porter's five forces, value chain and generic strategies Structured approach helps to simplify the complexity of business and the business environment Good for identifying opportunities and threats in the environment	Neglects the importance of business-specific competences as opposed to industry wide factors Some of the analytical frameworks (e.g. generic strategies) have been widely criticized
Resource or competence based approach to strategy	Organizations must identify and build core competences or distinctive capabilities which can be leveraged in a number of markets The approach to strategy is 'inside-out'	The approach emphasizes the importance of the individual business in acquiring competitive advantage Strategic intent, vision and creativity are emphasized	Analytical frameworks are in their infancy and are currently poorly developed The importance of the environment in determining competitive advantage is underestimated

Table 15.1 Approaches to strategic management

strategy and it can make it difficult to evaluate performance (because if an organization has no explicit objective, performance against it cannot be measured).

To counter the criticisms of emergent strategy, Quinn (1978) and Quinn and Voyer (1994) see a role for some planning in the context of emergent strategy, advocating 'purposeful incrementalism'. This approach places a strong emphasis on *organizational learning* (see later in this chapter).

The competitive positioning versus resource/core competence debate

Competitive positioning

This school of thought dominated strategic management in the 1980s and still had considerable significance in the 1990s. Although the approach has now been widely criticized, the analytical frameworks devised by Porter in the 1980s (1980, 1985) are still widely used by both managers and academics. The major strength of the approach lies in the ready applicability of these frameworks to analysis of the business and its environment. The approach to strategy is essentially 'outside-in' to establish a competitive position for the business in its environment which results in its outperforming its rivals.

In terms of procedure, the process of analysing competitive position begins with the *five forces framework*. This is used to analyse the nature of competition in the organization's industry. This is followed by selection of the appropriate *generic strategy* together with *value chain analysis* to ensure that the business configures its value adding activities in such a way as to support a strategy based on either differentiation or cost leadership.

In the 1990s, this approach was criticized for its overemphasis of the role of the *industry* in determining profitability and its underestimation of the importance of the individual business (Rumelt, 1991). Porter's frameworks have also been criticized as being too static, although Porter argues that they must be applied repeatedly to take account of the dynamism of the environment. The reality is that without Porter's work, strategic management would be devoid of many of its most practical and applicable analytical tools.

Resource or core competence based strategy

The 1990s witnessed the rise of what is known as *resource* or *core competence based* strategic management (Prahalad and Hamel, 1990; Kay, 1993; Heene and Sanchez, 1997). The major difference to the competitive positioning approach is that the importance of the individual business in achieving competitive advantage is emphasized rather than the industry. The approach is therefore 'inside-out'. Although this approach came to prominence in the 1990s, its origins lie in the work of Penrose (1959), who emphasized the importance of the business and its resources in determining its performance. Interest in the approach was revived by Prahalad and Hamel's 1990 work 'The core competence of the corporation'. A core competence is some combination of resources, skills, knowledge and technology which distinguishes an organization from its competitors in the eyes of customers. This distinctiveness results in competitive advantage.

The approach also emphasizes organizational learning, knowledge management and collaborative business networks as sources of competitive advantage (Demarest, 1997; Sanchez and Heene, 1997).

The resource/core competence approach has focused the search for competitive advantage on the individual business but its critics argue that it lacks the well developed analytical frameworks of the competitive positioning school and, perhaps, understates the potential importance of the business environment in determining success or failure.

Towards an integrated approach to strategy

Similarities and differences between the approaches

The prescriptive and competitive positioning approaches are often seen as related to each other because they both adopt a highly structured view of strategic management. Similarly, the emergent and competence based approaches are often linked because of their shared focus on organizational knowledge and learning.

On the other hand, the prescriptive and emergent approaches are often presented as being diametrically opposed, as are the competitive positioning and competence based approaches. The reality is that the approaches are in many ways complementary as they present different perspectives of the same situation.

Mintzberg, Quinn and Ghoshal (1995) argue that the competence based and competitive positioning approaches ought be seen as 'complementary, representing two different forms of analysis both of which must be brought to bear for improving the quality of strategic thinking and analysis'. Similarly, Quinn and Voyer (1994) recognize that within logical incrementalism 'formal planning techniques do serve some essential functions'.

Acknowledging the contribution of each approach

The point is that each approach has its merits. By acknowledging the contribution of each approach, managers can arrive at an enriched method of understanding the complex area of strategic management. The contribution of each approach to an integrated understanding is summarized below.

- *Planned/prescriptive* – a degree of planning is necessary to provide focus for the strategy of the organization and to assist in the evaluation of performance.
- *Emergent/incremental* – plans must always be flexible to allow organizations to learn and adapt to changes in the environment.
- *Competitive positioning* – emphasizes the importance of the environment and provides useful tools for analysing the business in the context of its industry.
- *Resource/competence based* – focuses on the importance of the business and assists in identifying company-specific sources of competitive advantage.

Accordingly, we suggest that strategy must be both inward and outward looking, planned and emergent. By adopting this synthesis, a broader understanding of competitive advantage can be gained.

The future of strategic management thinking

This book has discussed the 'state of the art' in strategic thinking at the beginning of the twenty-first century. In attempting to predict the areas that will focus the minds of academics in the near future, two central areas of interest are prominent – *collaborative advantage* and *knowledge management*.

Collaboration and competitive behaviour in industries

In recent years, considerable research and theorization has focused on the extent to which collaboration between businesses (as opposed to competition) may contribute towards the attainment of competitive advantage (Contractor and Lorange, 1988; Hamel *et al.*, 1989; Quinn *et al.*, 1990; Reeve, 1990; Davidow and Malone, 1992; Heene and Sanchez, 1997).

Collaboration in non-core activities • • •

The competence based approach suggests that businesses should concentrate upon developing core competences so as to achieve competitive advantage. Any activities that are not seen as core can be outsourced to other organizations for whom those activities are core. Most networks centre on a focal business whose strategy drives the operation of the network. Quinn, Doorley and Paquette (1990) suggest that such are the changes in service technologies that they now 'provide sufficient scale economies, flexibility, efficiency and specialization potentials that outside vendors [sellers] can supply many important corporate functions at greatly enhanced value and lower cost. Thus many of those functions should be outsourced.'

Rather than abandoning control to outside vendors it is sometimes best to form some sort of alliance or network with them. Collaborative networks potentially provide several advantages by:

- allowing businesses to concentrate on their core competences and core activities;
- allowing businesses to pool core competences, thus creating synergy between them;
- reducing bureaucracy and allowing flatter organizational structures;
- increasing efficiency and reducing costs;
- improving flexibility and responsiveness;
- making it difficult for competitors to imitate.

The formation of a collaborative network will involve:

- identification of the core competences of the organization;
- identification and focus upon activities which are critical to the core competence of the organization and outsourcing those which are not;
- achieving the internal and external linkages in the value/supply chain which are necessary for effective coordination of activities and which enhance responsiveness.

Collaboration can be:

- *horizontal* – partners are at the same stage of the value system and are often competitors;
- *vertical* – partners are at different stages of the value system (this includes collaboration with suppliers, distributors, and customers).

Collaboration can provide benefits including the linking of core competences (of the two parties in the relationship), access to resources and technology, risk reduction, greater control over supplies, betters access to customers and reduced competition. Collaboration, however, can create problems which include conflicting objectives between the participating businesses, cultural differences, changing requirements among the partners and coordination and integration problems.

Virtual organizations • • •

Developments in information and communications technology (ICT) have greatly increased the potential for collaboration between businesses by making it much easier to integrate and coordinate network activities. These changes in technology have made possible the development of 'virtual' organizations. A virtual organization is a network of linked businesses who coordinate and integrate their activities so effectively that they give the appearance of a single business organization.

There is considerable potential for such virtual organizations to enhance competitive advantage. ICT linkages greatly increase flexibility and efficiency, and make it difficult for competitors to replicate the activities of the network. Linkages to suppliers and customers are greatly improved as are flows of the information required for strategic decision-taking. The net result is that the virtual corporation is more flexible, more responsive and better able than its non-virtual rivals to compete on the bases of time and customer satisfaction.

Organizational learning and knowledge management

Closely related to the rational/logical approaches to strategy (such as the prescriptive and competitive positioning schools of thought) is the notion that organizations must continually learn both about themselves and their environment. At the same time – and here this point is in agreement with the core competence approach – it is widely acknowledged that organizational knowledge underpins many core competences. Accordingly, organizational learning and knowledge management have been the subject of considerable recent research and theorization (see for example Argyris, 1992; Demarest, 1997; Grant, 1997). Grant (1997) argues that 'the knowledge-based view represents a confluence of a number of streams of research, the most prominent being "resource-based theory" and "epistemology"'.

Explicit and implicit knowledge • • •

Organizational learning and knowledge management are concerned with the creation, development and dissemination of knowledge within an organization. This 'knowledge' can be either explicit or implicit.

- *Explicit knowledge* is knowledge whose meaning is clearly stated, details of which can be recorded and stored (such as important formulations, procedures, ways of acting, etc.).
- *Implicit or tacit knowledge* (Demarest, 1997) is often unstated, based upon individual experience and difficult to record and store. Implicit knowledge is often a vital source of core competence and competitive advantage as it is most difficult for competitors to emulate (such as experience in a given sector, an understanding of a particular technology or the multiple contact networks that have been built up over many years by managers and sales people).

Both forms of knowledge begin as individual knowledge but, to substantially improve performance, they must be transformed into organizational knowledge. This is a particularly difficult transformation for implicit knowledge. It is the role of knowledge management to ensure that individual learning becomes organizational learning.

Types of organizational learning • • •

Argyris (Argyris and Schon, 1978; Argyris, 1992) argues that organizations must develop 'double loop learning'. In other words, learning is not just a case of learning how to solve an immediate problem but must also aim at developing principles that will inform and determine future behaviour. It must also result in the ability to generalize from specific learning. Such learning takes place when individual solutions are reached and then generalized to apply in other circumstances.

Senge (1990) identifies two types of learning found in leading organizations: 'adaptive learning' and 'generative learning'. Adaptive learning centres on changing in response to developments in the business environment. Such adaptation is often necessary for business survival. Generative learning is, on the other hand, about building new competences or identifying or creating opportunities for leveraging existing competences in new competitive arenas. For example, the entry of MyTravel plc into the low-cost airline sector in 2002 was based upon leveraging existing competences. The competences related to charter airline operations were complemented by new competences based upon learning about the nature of scheduled air services.

The keys to successful knowledge management • • •

Knowledge management incorporates organizational learning but it is also concerned with the management of existing stocks of knowledge. Effective knowledge management must overcome:

- barriers to learning and knowledge creation;
- difficulties in storing and sharing knowledge (particularly tacit knowledge);
- difficulties in valuing and measuring knowledge (based on Demarest, 1997).

Knowledge management is, therefore, primarily concerned with the creation of new knowledge, storage and sharing of knowledge and the control of knowledge. Knowledge management is an important element in building core competences, which must be distinctive and difficult to imitate.

The often intangible nature of knowledge tends to make it distinctive and difficult to copy. In the case of a company like Microsoft, it is evident that its core competences are largely knowledge based. Quinn (1992) argues that 'most successful enterprises today can be considered intelligent enterprises' as they focus on building knowledge based core competences. Similarly, Grant (1997) points out that many companies are now developing corporate-wide systems to track, access, exploit and create organizational knowledge. Within such organizations, questioning and creativity are encouraged, as are trust, teamwork and sharing. At the same time, they have created infrastructures which support learning, which assist in the storage and controlled diffusion of knowledge, and which coordinate its application in creating and supporting core competences.

There is some way to go in understanding the role of knowledge and its management in strategy. It is likely that significant developments will take place in this area as the new millennium proceeds.

Conclusion

Strategic management is fundamentally concerned with understanding the nature of competitive advantage and the means by which it is acquired and sustained. This chapter has explored the major approaches adopted by strategists seeking to better understand the factors that underpin competitive advantage, allowing certain organizations to outperform their competitors. The different approaches should not be regarded as mutually exclusive, but rather they provide alternative methods for better understanding the means by which strategy is formulated and implemented. A degree of planning of strategy is required but equally, strategy might also emerge incrementally. Heracleous (1998) argues that 'strategic thinking' (which is distinctive and creative) is required in the formulation of new strategies while 'strategic planning' (which is analytical and conventional) is needed successfully to implement new strategy.

Future developments in strategic management are likely to centre on the role of collaborative networks and knowledge management in producing competitive advantage. The discipline is in its adolescence and, as with all adolescents, it is difficult to predict what will happen next!

References and further reading

Ansoff, I. (1987) *Corporate Strategy*. London: Penguin.

Argenti, J. (1965) *Corporate Planning*. London: Allen and Unwin.

Argyris, C. (1977) Double Loop Learning in Organizations. *Harvard Business Review*, September–October, pp. 115–125.

Argyris, C. (1992) *On Organizational Learning*. London: Blackwell.

Argyris, C. and Schon, D. (1978) *Organization Learning: A Theory of Action Perspective*. Reading, MA: Addison Wesley.

Contractor, F. and Lorange, P. (1988) Why Should Firms Cooperate? The Strategy and Economic Basis for Cooperative Ventures. In F. Contractor and P. Lorange (eds), *Cooperative Strategies in International Business*, Lexington, MA: Lexington Books, 3–30.

Cravens, D.W., Greenley, G., Piercy, N.F. and Slater S. (1997) Integrating Contemporary Strategic Management Perspectives. *Long Range Planning*, 30(4), 493–506.

Davidow, W.H. and Malone, M.S. (1992) *Structuring and Revitalizing the Corporation for the 21st Century – The Virtual Corporation*. London: Harper Business.

Demarest, M. (1997) Understanding Knowledge Management. *Long Range Planning*, 30(3), 374–384.

Grant, R.M. (1991) The Resource Based Theory of Competitive Advantage: Implications for Strategy Formulation. *California Management Review*, 33 (Spring), 114–135.

Grant, R.M. (1997) The Knowledge-based View of the Firm: Implications for Management Practice. *Long Range Planning*, 30(3), 450–454.

Hamel, G. and Prahalad, C.K. (1989) Strategic Intent. *Harvard Business Review*, 67(3), 63–76.

Hamel, G. and Prahalad, C.K. (1994) *Competing for the Future*. Cambridge, MA: Harvard Business School Press.

Hamel, G., Doz, Y. and Prahalad, C.K. (1989) Collaborate with Your Competitors and Win. *Harvard Business Review*, January–February.

Heene, A. and Sanchez, R. (eds) (1997) *Competence-Based Strategic Management*. London: John Wiley.

Heracleous, L. (1998) Strategic Thinking or Strategic Planning. *Long Range Planning*, 30(3), 481–487.

Kay, J. (1993) *Foundations of Corporate Success*. Oxford: Oxford University Press.

Kay, J. (1995) Learning to Define the Core Business. *Financial Times*, 1 December.

Lenosky, T.J., Kress, J.D., Collins, L.A., Kwon, I. and McKiernan, P. (1997) Strategy Past; Strategy Futures. *Long Range Planning*, 30(5), 790–798.

Mintzberg, H. (1987) Crafting Strategy. *Harvard Business Review*, July–August.

Mintzberg, H. (1991) *The Strategy Process – Concepts, Contexts, Cases*. Englewood Cliffs, NJ: Prentice Hall.

Mintzberg, H., Quinn, J.B. and Ghoshal, S. (1995) *The Strategy Process: Concepts, Contexts and Cases*, European edn. Englewood Cliffs, NJ: Prentice Hall.

Penrose, E. (1959) *The Theory of the Growth of the Firm*. Oxford: Oxford University Press.

Porter, M.E. (1980) *Competitive Strategy: Techniques for Analysing Industries and Competitors*. New York: The Free Press.

Porter, M.E. (1985) *Competitive Advantage*. New York: The Free Press.

Prahalad, C.K. and Hamel, G. (1990) The Core Competence of the Organization. *Harvard Business Review*, 90, 79–93.

Quinn, J.B. (1978) Strategic Change; Logical Incrementalism. *Sloan Management Review*, Fall.

Quinn, J.B. (1992) *The Intelligent Enterprise*. New York: The Free Press.

Quinn, J.B. and Voyer, J. (1994) *The Strategy Process*. Englewood Cliffs, NJ: Prentice Hall.

Quinn, J.B., Doorley, T. and Paquette, P. (1990) Technology in Services: Rethinking Strategic Focus. *Sloan Management Review*, 31(2), 79–87.

Reeve, T. (1990) The Firm as a Nexus of Internal and External Contracts, in M. Aoki, M. Gustafsson and O.E. Williamson (eds), *The Firm as a Nexus of Treaties*. London: Sage.

Rumelt, R. (1991) How Much Does Industry Matter? *Strategic Management Journal*, 12, 167–185.

Sanchez, R. and Heene, A. (eds) (1997) *Strategic Learning and Knowledge Management*. New York: Wiley.

Senge, P. (1990) The Leader's New Work: Building Learning Organizations. *Sloan Management Review*, 32(1), 7–22.

Part Six

Case analysis in strategic management

Introduction

Case study analysis invariably forms a part of most courses in strategic management. Originally developed as a teaching tool in the major American Business Schools, particularly Harvard, case studies are now widely used by most business schools. Case studies are used so as to enable students to understand the complex nature of strategic decision-making and the inter-related nature of such decisions, i.e. a decision taken in one part of a business will have a knock-on effect upon other parts of the business. Although there is perhaps no substitute for management experience in the real world, case studies represent the next best thing.

The case studies you are asked to analyse indicate the broad range of strategic decisions managers need to take in the real world. The cases may vary in a number of ways which may affect the type of analysis that is carried out and the way in which the results of the analysis are presented. Cases may relate to:

- large or small scale organizations;
- organizations that are complex in their structure and management or which are relatively simple to understand;
- organizations with exposure to particular types of risk;
- organizations that are successful or organizations that are in difficulties;
- organizations and their circumstances that are known to you or organizations in which their true circumstances will be changed in order to illustrate particular points;
- organizations that are totally fictitious and created just for illustrative purposes or companies in which the name of the company and the names of managers and so on will be altered so as to disguise the real company being considered;
- organization activities in the present day or at a date in the past.

In all cases considered, however, it is important to realize that what you are normally being asked to do is to place yourself in the position of a manager of an organization or within an industry sector at a particular moment in time. The important point is not what actually happened to the company in reality, but given the available information, how would you have made sense of the information available to you at the time and what actions you would have recommended in the circumstances.

Reading and studying the case

In considering cases you are expected to go beyond merely describing the circumstances of the case. The case method requires you to analyse the cases in detail and to develop sound, reasoned judgements that will lead to recommendations being made. In so doing it is important to recognize the key or strategic points of the case and to distinguish these points from less substantial or trivial points.

Many cases contain 'red herrings', which are designed to mislead and confuse, and in so doing replicate the real world in which information comes from several directions and reaches managers by different means. A manager has to make sense of the information and discern the important or urgent from the less important or less urgent. So in analysing a case ask yourself, 'What are the central issues in the case?'

There will be instances when you feel that you do not have all the information you need to make the best decision. The information presented in the case, however, is often incomplete by design and again reflects the situation pertaining in the real world. Managers often have to make decisions based on the information available to them at the time, and although they might wish they had further information, it is either unavailable or not available within the necessary time-scale with the resources available. Thus you are required to make the best possible use of the information that you actually have at your disposal.

You are also asked to make your analysis at the time of the case. Managers do not have the benefit of hindsight when managing their companies (much as they might want it), they have to manage with the information available to them at that time and so it is with case studies. A tour operation set in 2000 would not have known, for instance, of the terrorist attacks on America in September 2001 and its subsequent effects upon the travel industry.

One of the difficulties in analysing cases is the lack of a *'right'* answer. Whilst there may be some answers that are clearly *'wrong'*, it is less easy to prove that an answer is right. If for instance you propose that a one-branch travel agency that has demonstrated growth of 10% per annum over the past five years should grow to become the largest travel agency group in the country over the next three years, it would almost certainly be unrealistic and therefore wrong. However, there may be several strategic options available and the strength of the answer depends upon the strength of the arguments presented, which in turn depend upon the analysis carried out. The analysis should be based upon the facts of the case, sound reasoning and importantly the application of strategic principles, theories and concepts from the academic literature.

Doing the analysis

A few tips on the analysis of cases are presented below:

- *Read the case thoroughly.* Read the case twice initially. First read the case quickly as if you were reading a newspaper, getting a feel for the structure and layout of the case. On the second reading, make notes, underline important passages, mark sections for later analysis and identify the central issues. Once you have an adequate grasp of the case and the issues presented you can begin an in-depth analysis.

- *Organize the case facts.* The facts of a case may be presented in a bewildering or misleading way. It may be necessary for you to reorganize the information or label the data so that it makes more sense. For instance, sometimes it might be necessary to reorder the material chronologically or to separate the organization into its constituent parts.

- *Avoid vacuous terms.* Terms that are hollow and lacking in content make the analysis unsound. For example 'good', 'bad', 'many', 'few' are vacuous, as each individual could interpret them in a different manner. Instead use precise language.

- *Do not contact the company.* The case provides the information you need to analyse and the information may have been changed for teaching purposes. The case is designed to put you in the position of a company manger at a particular point in time. What actually happened is not relevant and companies should not be burdened by numerous student enquiries.

- *Appeals to authority.* Use of references, concepts and empirical evidence to support your case are valid ways of justifying your arguments. However, care must be taken. Just because an expert supports a view does not necessarily make it correct and different experts can present different views.

- *Apply concepts.* If you use a concept to organize the information or to support your views make sure that it is applied appropriately. For example, Porter's five forces model may be an appropriate way of analysing the competitive environment but make sure that it is applied to the facts of the case and not merely presented in its abstract form. A common mistake is to use every conceivable strategic concept or framework available. Be selective, usually some concepts are more appropriate in the circumstances than others. The concepts are only useful inasmuch that they aid understanding. Which concepts are appropriate will depend upon the facts of the case and the material presented to you.

- *Look for linkages.* The case may be presented in a confusing manner but look for opportunities to make links between different parts of the case and thereby demonstrate that you have understood the case and its complexities. For instance, the case may state within the text that a new sales and marketing director was appointed. In another part of the case a table may indicate a falling sales trend and the financial statements may indicate a vastly increased advertising budget. By bringing together the three disparate pieces of information, appropriate conclusions might be drawn. Similarly, bringing together information from differing parts of the case and presenting it in a different form may be useful to aid understanding. For example putting figures into a graph or table.

- *Look for ways of adding value to the information.* Look for opportunities when analysing a case to add value through your analysis. In other words, it is of far more value to interpret the information rather than merely to repeat the information contained in the case in your answer. For example, a case on an airline might state that the aircraft fleet contains 10 Boeing 737–400 and 6 Boeing 757 aircraft purchased at various stated dates between 1986 and 1997. Rather than repeat this information in your answer it is much more useful to calculate the average age of the fleet. Is the fleet relatively young or relatively old? Similarly a tour operator may present sales figures for the last ten years. A calculation showing the percentage growth (or decline) of sales from year to year would add value. Such a calculation would clearly show whether the rate of growth has risen or declined.

Case 1

Strategic alliances in the airline industry

Nigel Evans

Introduction

The airline sector has a long history of working in partnerships. In 1999, 513 international alliances existed between airline companies, an increase of about 80% from the 1994 level. Under the auspices of the International Air Transport Association (IATA), a tradition of cooperation between airlines was built up and on individual routes cooperation has commonly included revenue-pooling agreements between the carriers operating a route.

During the 1990s, airlines have rushed to form alliances in the fear of being left behind and the stage has now been reached where the international airline sector is coalescing into a small number of large alliance groupings such as the *Star Alliance* which includes Lufthansa, United Airlines and Scandinavian Airlines System (SAS), the *Oneworld Alliance* which includes British Airways, American Airlines and Qantas, and the longstanding alliance between KLM and Northwest Airlines. It is not only the number of airline alliance agreements being made that is significant, but the deepening relations between partners in these alliances. 'No longer are alliances mere loose arrangements between a couple of carriers to share flight codes and cross-sell tickets', the alliances are now so wide ranging that 'they are aiming at virtual mergers, despite national rules forbidding foreign ownership' (*The Economist*, 1998).

Motivations for alliance formation in the airline sector

British Airways attempted to introduce a degree of empiricism to the analysis of the external forces driving alliance formation. It used scenario-planning techniques to develop strategies for the future given the uncertainties in the macroenvironment. Scenarios representing possible futures were developed which sought to identify the key driving forces shaping the world economy and in turn the airline industry. Enormous changes have

occurred in technology, education, world trade and finance over the past 50 years with a quickening pace of change. The combination of these forces has helped to bring about the information 'revolution', global economic restructuring and global competition.

External drivers

The information 'revolution'

In the 1960s and 1970s information technologies mainly played a facilitating role in international tourism. The US Airline Deregulation Act of 1978 introduced airlines operating in the USA to a new world of competitive threats and opportunities. The key change, whereby price regulating power was removed from the Civil Aeronautics Board (CAB), enabled airlines to increase the variety of fares offered and the increased frequency by which fares were changed necessitated the extensive development of advanced computer reservations systems (CRS). The CRS systems allowed airlines to monitor, manage and control their capacity through yield management and their clients through 'frequent flyer' programmes. The growth in CRS systems, first in the USA and then in Europe and elsewhere, created a marketing tool of considerable power, given travel agents' preferences for booking flights on their screens as the customer is waiting. In the past the airlines that owned the CRSs undoubtedly favoured their own flights (or those of their code sharing partners), but to a significant extent such bias has now been eliminated, at least in Europe and North America, through codes of conduct. The power given to airlines by the CRS system has now been replicated by the power given directly to consumers by the Internet. A vast amount of information is available to consumers to compare prices and the Internet's growth has allowed airlines to communicate directly with consumers thus cutting out the need for intermediaries to be involved. Some airlines such as easyJet are making extensive use of the technology, reporting that over 80% of bookings are being made through the Internet.

Economic restructuring

Economic restructuring through the philosophy of 'economic disengagement' by governments in many parts of the world, has, since the 1970s, had a major impact on airline industry structure. This philosophy influenced by the widespread adoption of the theory of 'contestable markets' (which advocated the removal of restrictive industry entry barriers) from the early 1980s, manifested itself in the forms of deregulation and privatization. The Chicago Convention of 1944 established the bilateral system of air service agreements (between pairs of national governments), which have since governed international air transport. The international industry that developed was characterized by national airlines from each country serving routes, airlines charging the same fares, and often sharing markets and revenues. Some bilateral agreements also involved agreement on such matters as ground handling. The terms of the bilateral agreements reflected the negotiating power and current aviation policies of the countries involved and resulting productivity was often low and costs were high.

Deregulation of domestic services occurred in the United States in 1978 followed by Canada, the United Kingdom, Australia and New Zealand in the 1980s, and the completion of deregulation within the European Union in April 1997. However, parallel liberalization in international air services has taken place much more slowly. Notwithstanding the change that has occurred in some markets, even the liberalized structures are restrictive on industry entry. Requirements for designated airlines to be owned by nationals of the states involved are common and airport congestion and slot allocation practices often further impede effective industry entry. There was some evidence, however, that the removal of bilateral agreements and similar intervention barriers can reduce fares.

Another, and linked, aspect of economic disengagement is the worldwide movement towards the privatization of state owned airlines. Despite this gradual process, however, many international airlines remain publicly owned or have major government shareholdings. Controls on foreign ownership remain in most national industries but some foreign ownership now exists, and with planned privatizations, this will increase.

The European Union's third air transport package (implemented from April 1997), for instance, sets no limit on the stake an EU national or EU airline can hold in an airline registered in another European Union state. With limited exceptions, however, non-European Union investors cannot hold a majority stake in any EU airline. In the USA, foreign shareholdings of up to 49% of equity under certain circumstances and 25% of voting stock is possible, although the US government also imposes an *ad hoc* control test to determine whether the foreign shareholder would substantially influence decision-making irrespective of equity held.

Liberalization, privatization, foreign ownership and transnational mergers will have a major impact upon the future structure of the airline industry but many regulatory and ownership barriers remain in force worldwide. As a result alternative methods of strategic development, namely internally generated growth, and mergers and acquisitions are often precluded as viable growth strategies for international airlines, and consequently the formation of strategic alliances is, in many cases, the only available form of new market entry.

Global competition

Organizational 'type' has been dramatically influenced by the rise of globalization and it has been argued that success or failure of larger businesses in the future will depend upon their ability to compete globally. Certainly many industries in the post-war era have seen a rapid concentration of activity with the emergence of a few dominant companies. Global competition is clearly well advanced in industries such as motor vehicles, pharmaceuticals, soft drinks and, more recently, financial services, but globalization is a more recent phenomenon in the airline business, having been restricted for so long by regulation, government ownership and consumer preferences.

Airlines are seeking to maximize their 'global reach', in the belief that those that offer a global service (with a competitively credible presence in each of the major air travel markets) will be in the strongest competitive position. The importance of the 'triad' markets of Japan, North America and Europe is shown in Appendix 6. In a global airline context, the triad is modified so as to broaden the

Japanese leg of the triad to include the wider Asia–Pacific region and for the crucial markets to include not only the constituent markets of the triad but also the flows between them. Thus, globalization, and particularly developments in the key markets, is an important external driver for alliance formation.

Internal drivers

Risk sharing

Strategic alliances are seen as an attractive mechanism for hedging risk because neither partner bears the full risk and cost of the alliance activity. The need to spread the costs and risks of innovation has increased as capital requirements for development projects have risen. Developing new or existing routes, for instance, becomes far less risky if the partners operating the routes have firmly entrenched marketing strengths in the two markets at either end of the routes.

Economies of scale, scope and learning

A prime driver for alliance formation is for airlines to achieve cost economies, which can be categorized as economies of scale, scope and experience. Economies of scale exist where the average cost per unit of output declines as the level of output increases. Empirical evidence reveals little evidence of economies of scale, however, except for the smallest operators and in specific areas such as marketing. Indeed one study of US domestic aviation suggests possible diseconomies at the largest airlines. Furthermore, the evidence also suggests that airlines' unit costs do not fall greatly as they expand their networks. Cost savings stem from attracting more traffic to a given network rather than expanding it to cover more destinations.

The airline industry may lack substantial scale economies, but other economies related to the size and nature of operations exist which help to explain the growing industry concentration and the move towards alliances. Economies of scope occur when the cost of producing two (or more) products jointly is less than the cost of producing each one alone. Such economies can be achieved if alliance partners link up their existing networks so that they can provide connecting services for new markets, and where marketing costs can be shared between alliance partners.

For example, the alliance between KLM and Northwest formed in 1989 has had a substantial impact on passenger numbers, market share and both airlines' financial performance. Through the alliance, KLM has gained access to Northwest's extensive North American route network based on its Minneapolis, Detroit and Boston hubs, whilst Northwest can advertise that it serves KLM's sizeable international network.

A number of observers have suggested that an important motivator in forming alliances is the benefit to be derived from economies of learning (or experience). Incumbent suppliers have more information on the market being served and can tailor their services to specific customer needs. Whereas new entrants would have to sink resources to acquire such information in order to win market share, alliances allow the information to be gained from existing suppliers.

Access to assets, resources and competences

Specific resource, skill or competence inadequacy can be addressed by collaborating with partners which have a different set of such attributes and can therefore compensate for internal deficiencies. The regulatory framework of 'bilaterals' and landing rights means that slots at congested airports are important and marketable assets that are attractive to alliance partners. Alliances can thus offer relatively easy access to a route through allowing access to a partner's assets which may have been established over prolonged periods and which may have been previously protected by government intervention.

Shape competition

Strategic alliances can influence the companies that a firm competes with and the basis of competition. They can also reduce the likelihood of retaliatory behaviour by binding two firms together as allies. Furthermore, current strategic positions may be successfully defended against forces that are too strong for one firm to withstand alone. Strategic alliances may, therefore, be used as a defensive ploy to reduce competition since an obvious benefit of strategic alliances is converting a competitor into a partner. Smaller and weaker airlines may view alliances as the only viable way in which to compete with larger, more sophisticated rivals. The announcement in March 1998 by

Air Lanka that it was to sell a 40% stake to Emirates Airlines, for instance, was viewed as part of a defensive alliance strategy aimed at retaining international competitiveness through allying with a commercially stronger rival.

Alternatively, alliance formation may form part of an offensive strategy. By linking with a rival pressure can be put on the profits and market share of a common competitor. The proposed alliance between British Airways and American Airlines announced in June 1996 was seen as such a case since it represented the combining of (arguably) the two strongest airlines on the trans-atlantic routes. It therefore attracted widespread criticism from competing airlines and later failed to win regulatory approval from either the US or EU authorities.

Alliance structure and scope

Considerable time and effort may be expended in developing the structure and scope of an alliance. The unique nature and operating environment of the airline sector means that alliances must be structured around diverse requirements. Determining the structure and scope of an alliance requires detailed consideration of issues across a broad spectrum. Issues that must be taken into account include marketing, products, computer system technologies, equipment, and equipment servicing and logistics.

Evaluation of alliance performance

Evaluating the performance of alliances is complex given the multifaceted objectives of many alliances and the difficulties involved in ascribing financial measures. The situation is often further complicated by the asymmetric performance: one firm achieves its objectives while others fail to do so. For instance several alliances have resulted in a situation where one partner raced to learn the other's skills while the other partner had no such intentions.

Despite these evident measurement obstacles, several observers have attempted empirical studies of alliance performance, primarily through examining the factors leading to the termination of alliance arrangements. These contributory factors include partner asymmetry, competitive overlap between partners, the presence of other concurrent ties, and the characteristics of the alliance itself, such as autonomy of operations and flexibility. It

should be borne in mind, however, that not all alliance terminations can be viewed as failures since in some cases they may have been intended as time-limited arrangements. Furthermore, it should not be assumed that all continuing alliances are successful since inertia or high exit costs may provide an explanation for their continuation.

Examples of airline alliance success and failure

The 'Alcazar' alliance involving Scandinavian Airline System (SAS), Swissair, Austrian Airlines and KLM failed in the early 1990s partly because the individual airlines were technologically incompatible (they used different CRS systems). In another example, British Airways held discussions at various times with KLM, Sabena and United Airlines regarding strategic alliances before forming such an alliance with US Airways in July 1992 as part of its strategy of building up several key global collaborative agreements.

The agreement between British Airways and US Airways (which involved the acquisition of approximately 44% of US Airways' equity share capital by British Airways), has now been broken, with British Airways writing off 50% of its initial investment. The British Airways/US Airways alliance provides an example of poor long-term positioning in that the alliance stood in the way of more recent strategies by both partners. In June 1996, British Airways announced its intention to form a wider alliance with American Airlines (which still awaits regulatory approval as at year 2002), and US Airways responded with a lawsuit seeking damages. US Airways is said to have been anxious to extricate itself from its alliance with British Airways because it failed to deliver the projected earnings enhancement. British Airways on the other hand viewed American Airlines as a larger strategically, more important alliance partner. The long list of failed airline alliances, supposedly bolstered by equity stakes, includes Air Canada/Continental Airlines, Scandinavian Airlines System/Continental Airlines and Sabena/Air France.

Political sensitivities lay behind the failure of another proposed airline alliance between the Dutch airline KLM and Belgian airline Sabena in the early 1990s. Both airlines had held talks with British Airways before talking to each other about a possible alliance or merger. Both were loss-making and feared absorption by larger competitors, but the failure to cement an alliance highlighted the uniquely political nature of the airline sector. Political considerations are transparent when both companies involved are 'national flag carriers' carrying the prestige of the home country around the world. For Sabena to ally with KLM would have created a predominantly Dutch-speaking company which would have proved politically unacceptable in bilingual Belgium. Sabena had to bow to political pressure from Belgium's French-speaking community and pull out of negotiations.

The airline alliance between KLM and the American airline Northwest dating from 1989 can claim to be a success, at least in part, since it has shown uncharacteristic sustainability, and appears to have been revenue-enhancing for the two partners. The alliance, which encompasses collaboration on a broad front including code-sharing, flight scheduling, joint marketing, and integration of frequent flyer programmes, had generated additional revenues of between $125 million and $175 million for Northwest and $100 million for KLM by 1994. Through the alliance KLM gained access to Northwest's extensive North American route network based on its Minneapolis, Detroit and Boston hubs, whilst Northwest can advertise that it serves KLM's sizeable international network through its Amsterdam hub.

The alliance was borne out of necessity when KLM, (in return for a 20% equity stake), contributed $400 million to the $700 million that was required when senior Northwest executives put together a leveraged buyout of the airline. Notwithstanding the financial success of this strategic alliance, cultural differences and personal incompatibilities between the two parties have repeatedly threatened to force them apart and have at times soured the relationship. One writer noted that, 'the alliance has been a saga of personal spats, fights over "creeping control" and threats of separation that until recently were hidden behind a marriage that works well on a daily basis'. KLM, it is said, is inclined to be quiet, stay out of the limelight and focus on strong operational expertise whereas the US partner (Northwest) is more inclined to Hollywood lifestyles and a financial engineering approach to management.

Conclusion

Clearly the growth of airline strategic alliances is one of the most fundamental developments in the airline industry over recent years. Airlines have rushed to form alliances in the fear of being left behind, and many have later changed their partners as they have become more sophisticated at identifying the potential 'strategic fit' between partners. To some degree alliance formation can be viewed as an inevitable result of the regulatory framework within which the international airline industry operates. Regulatory and legal restrictions often prevent the full ownership of airlines by foreign companies and consequently alliances have been perceived as the only viable market entry mechanism at least in the short to medium term. However, some observers view strategic alliances as inherently unstable and transitory forms of organization, a 'second-best' solution that is disturbingly likely to break up under commercial pressure.

The airline industry is littered with examples of alliances that have been broken up (the alliance between British Airways and US Airways for instance) and planned alliances that failed to materialize. However, the role and characteristics of the strategic alliances have continued to evolve. In the late 1980s strategic alliances were seen as a rather crude way in which to grow quickly through the avoidance of bilateral restrictions and some airlines rushed to form alliances in the fear of being left behind. The cyclical slump and heavy losses of the early 1990s turned attention to the efficiency improvements made possible by alliances, and consequently airlines focused more clearly on the strategic logic of the particular partners that had been chosen. The importance of 'strategic fit' thus came to be stressed, i.e. that the proposed partner should have a culture, management style and geographical coverage that were compatible.

Consumers receive several benefits from those alliances that are successful in producing integrated products. Consumers are provided with an enhanced choice of destinations through the marketing of alliance partners' route networks. Schedule coordination between partners often produces shorter transfer times between connections, and coordination of flight timings can avoid bunching of flight schedules. Additionally consumers benefit from one-stop check-in for passengers, the pooling of frequent flyer programmes, shared airport lounge facilities, ground handling arrangements and the improvement in technical standards brought about through the sharing of expertise.

A number of trends relating to strategic airline alliances are discernible.

- The number of airlines involved in alliances has continued to grow. Four key alliances have emerged, each headed by one of the major American airlines. The focus in the coming years will be on these alliances adding further airlines so as to fill gaps in their global coverage. Equally, second level feeder airlines will be added to the existing alliances.

- Substantial new alliances may be difficult to form since the major international players from the 'triad' countries are all now involved in alliances and new alliances would therefore lack the substantial marketing presence that appears to be necessary to ensure success.

- Airlines from outside the 'triad' countries will increasingly become involved with the established alliances. To date, airlines from Africa, South America and parts of Asia have largely been excluded from the major alliances. Although many such airlines are currently operating in highly protected domestic markets, the degree of protection will progressively decrease and these airlines will increasingly

want to secure their commercial future through involvement with the major alliance groupings.

- Increasing consumer pressure is likely to be evident. Whilst the case for alliances has robustly been made by the airlines, less attention has been focused on consumers. This has started to change with the intense investigation into the effects of the British Airways–American Airlines alliance and possible retrospective investigation of the Star Alliance by competition authorities. Increasingly, international regulators will be attempting to ensure that the supposed cost savings (that the airlines argue result from alliance activity) are passed on to consumers and that the dominant positions at hub airports are scaled down so as to allow more 'contestability' of markets.

- Competition between the alliance groupings as entities (as opposed to the individual airlines comprising them) is likely to increase. The alliances will start to look more like 'umbrella' brands with the individual airlines being sub-brands, offering similar service standards and an increasing level of integration between the constituent airlines will be evident.

Appendix 1.1

Airline alliances in the global airline industry, 1994–1999

	1994	1995	1996	1997	1998	1999	% Change 99/94
Number of alliances	280	324	389	363	502	513	+183%
with equity stakes	58	58	62	54	56	53	−8.6%
non-equity alliances	222	266	327	309	446	460	+207.2%
New alliances	–	50	71	72	121	26	
Number of airlines	136	153	159	177	196	204	+150.0%

Source: adapted from Airline Business, 1999

Appendix 1.2

Major international airline alliances as at July 1999

Alliance members	Date joined	Passenger traffic 1998 (RPK bn)	Passenger traffic 1998 world share	Passenger numbers millions	Revenue $ billions
Atlantic Excellence/Qualifier					
Atlantic Excellence					
Austrian Airlines	Jun 96	7.3	0.3%	3.4	1.3
Delta Air Lines	Jun 96	166.3	6.3%	105.4	14.4
Sabena	Jun 96	15.3	0.6%	8.7	2.4
Swissair	Jun 96	28.0	1.1%	11.9	7.8
Sub totals		*216.9*	*8.2%*	*129.5*	*25.9*
Qualifier					
Air Europe	May 99	5.8	0.2%	0.8	0.2
AOM	Mar 98	8.5	0.3%	2.9	0.6
Austrian Airlines	Mar 98	7.3	0.3%	3.4	1.3
Crossair	Mar 98	2.7	0.1%	4.4	N/a
Lauda Air	Mar 98	2.9	0.1%	0.8	N/a
Sabena	Mar 98	15.3	0.6%	8.7	2.4
Swissair	Mar 98	28.0	1.1%	11.9	7.8
TAP Air Portugal	Mar 98	9.4	0.4%	4.5	0.9
THY Turkish Airlines	Mar 98	13.0	0.5%	9.9	1.4
Sub totals		*93.0*	*3.5%*	*47.4*	*14.6*
Total		*259.3*	*9.9%*	*152.8*	*29.0*
Oneworld					
American Airlines	Sep 98	175.2	6.7%	81.4	19.2
British Airways	Sep 98	116.0	4.4%	36.6	14.6
Canadian	Sep 98	26.9	1.0%	8.3	2.1
Cathay Pacific	Sep 98	40.7	1.5%	10.3	3.4
Qantas	Sep 98	56.9	2.2%	16.4	5.2
Sub totals		*415.7*	*15.8%*	*153.0*	*30.0*
Future members					
Finnair		10.2	0.4%	6.8	1.5
Iberia		32.5	1.2%	21.8	3.6
Lan Chile		8.7	0.3%	4.0	1.1
Total		*467.1*	*17.8%*	*185.5*	*36.2*
Star Alliance					
Air Canada	May 97	37.3	1.4%	15.0	4.0
Lufthansa	May 97	75.4	2.9%	38.5	12.8
SAS	May 97	20.8	0.8%	21.5	5.2
Thai International	May 97	34.4	1.3%	15.6	2.5
United Airlines	May 97	200.4	7.6%	88.6	17.6
Varig	Oct 97	27.1	1.0%	11.0	3.0
Ansett Australia	Mar 99	13.1	0.5%	11.7	2.0
Air New Zealand	Mar 99	19.4	0.7%	6.2	1.7
Sub totals		*428.0*	*16.3%*	*206.3*	*48.8*
Future members					
All Nippon Airways		54.4	2.1%	42.3	7.1
Singapore Airlines		58.2	2.2%	12.4	2.7
Total		*540.6*	*20.6%*	*261.0*	*58.6*
Northwest/KLM					
Alitalia	May 99	35.6	1.4%	24.2	5.0
Continental	Jan 99	86.7	3.3%	43.6	8.0
KLM	1989	57.3	2.2%	15.0	22.0
Northwest Airlines	1989	107.4	4.1%	50.5	9.0
Total		*287.0*	*10.9%*	*133.3*	*44.0*

RPK, Revenue passenger kilometres.
Source: adapted from Airline Business (1999)

Appendix 1.3

External driving forces underpinning strategic alliance formation in the airline industry

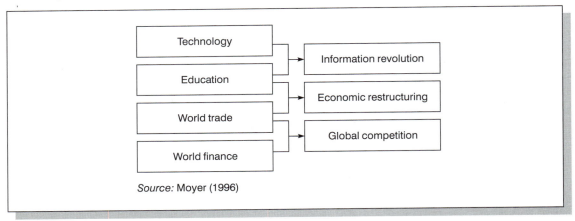

Source: Moyer (1996)

Appendix 1.4

CRS market share in European countries

Country	Amadeus (% of locations)	Galileo (% of locations)	Sabre (% of locations)	Worldspan (% of locations)
Austria	34.8	60.4	3.1	1.6
Belgium	21.1	30.1	16.0	32.8
Denmark	54.2	14.1	6.9	24.8
Finland	98.1	–	1.7	0.2
France	81.7	4.1	10.1	4.1
Germany	91.6	1.4	4.7	2.3
Greece	–	39.9	34.9	25.2
Hungary	–	97.6	2.4	–
Ireland	–	84.6	6.0	9.4
Italy	–	76.9	17.8	5.3
Luxembourg	57.1	–	42.9	–
Netherlands	–	61.6	10.3	26.8
Norway	74.5	11.2	7.7	6.6
Portugal	6.0	65.5	0.2	28.3
Spain	88.7	5.2	2.6	3.5
Sweden	77.0	–	13.0	10.0
Switzerland	–	87.7	9.9	2.4
UK	0.2	65.6	20.0	14.2

Notes:
Amadeus – developed by Air France, Lufthansa, Iberia, Sabena.
Galileo – developed by British Airways, KLM, Swissair, Austrian, Aer Lingus, Air Portugal, Olympic.
Sabre – developed by American Airlines.
Worldspan – developed by Delta, Northwest, TWA.
Source: Humphreys, (1994)

Appendix 1.5

Foreign ownership of selected airlines

Country	Airline	Stake held by	% stake	Date first acquired
Europe				
Austria	Austrian	Air France Group	1.5	1988
		All Nippon Airways	9.0	1989
		Swissair	10.0	1988
	Lauda Air	Austrian	35.9	1996
		Lufthansa	20.0	1993
Belgium	Sabena	Swissair	49.5	1995
France	Air Liberté	British Airways	70	1992
Germany	Deutsche BA	British Airways	100	1992
Luxembourg	Luxair	Lufthansa	13.0	1992
Spain	Spanair	SAS	49.0	1986
Switzerland	Swissair	Delta Air Lines	4.5	1989
		Singapore Airlines	2.7	1991
Ukraine	Ukraine Int'l Airlines	Austrian Airlines	14.3	1996
		Swissair	4.1	1996
United Kingdom	British Midland	SAS	40.0	1988
North America				
USA	Delta Airlines	Singapore Airlines	3	1991
		Swissair	3	1989
Canada	Canadian Airlines	American Airlines	33.0	1994
Asia/Pacific				
Australia	Ansett Australia	Air New Zealand	50.0	1996
	Qantas	British Airways	25.0	1993
China	Dragonair	Cathay Pacific	25.5	1990
Malaysia	Malaysia Airlines	Royal Brunei	10.0	Not reported
Singapore	Singapore Airlines	Delta Air Lines	2.7	1991
		Swissair	0.6	1991
Other				
Argentina	Aerolinas Argentinas	Iberia Airlines	10.0	1990
		American Airlines	10.0	1997
Mauritius	Air Mauritius	Air France	12.8	1975
		Air India	8.8	1975
		British Airways	12.8	1975
Kenya	Kenya Airways	KLM	26.0	1995

Source: adapted from *Airline Business* (1999)

Appendix 1.6

Share of world RPKs* and world RPK growth

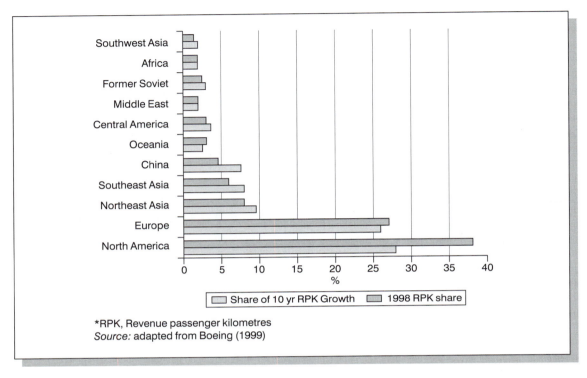

*RPK, Revenue passenger kilometres
Source: adapted from Boeing (1999)

References and sources

Airline Business (1999) Circling the Globe – Annual Alliances Survey, *Airline Business*, July, 33–65

Boeing Aircraft Company (1999) *Current Market Outlook – Economic Basis of Traffic Growth*, http://www.boeing.com/commercial/cmo/3eb06.html regional

The Economist (1998) Airline Alliances: Mergers in Mind, *The Economist*, 26 September, p. 96

Humphreys, B.K. (1994) The Implications of International Code Sharing, *Journal of Air Transport Management*, 1(4), 195–207

Case 2

Holidaybreak plc: adapting for success

Nigel Evans

Origins and development

Holidaybreak plc is, together with MyTravel plc and First Choice plc, one of only three quoted tour operators currently trading on the London Stock Exchange. Although considerably smaller than the other two, Holidaybreak plc evolved from the Eurocamp camping business and is a specialized travel business of significant scale. It operates on a pan-European basis.

The camping holiday market has seen many developments over the past 30 years or so. Camping was viewed as an activity merely for scouts and the adventurous, and was associated in the public mind with leaking canvas tents lacking adequate ground sheets. There was clearly a gap in the market – to provide camping holidays that would appeal to the wider public. The first company to exploit this gap with self drive camping holidays was Canvas Holidays, which was established in 1965 by Jack Cuthbert. The company's first site was in Brittany, France, utilizing traditional tents, but gradually the product evolved to provide the luxury tents which later became associated with camping at destinations in numerous European countries.

The year 1973 marked the founding of Eurocamp with the provision of self-drive camping holidays to a single French camp site, offered to British customers through direct sales. The company enjoyed a decade of growth under its founder Alan Goulding, culminating in the sale of the company to Combined English Stores plc (CES) in 1983. At this time the company's capacity had grown to over 50 camp sites, mainly in France but also in Switzerland, Germany and Italy. Mobile home holidays were also added in that year.

By the mid-1980s, Eurocamp had established itself as the market leader in the provision of self-drive camping holidays to continental Europe from the UK. In 1984 the offering of Eurocamp holidays to the Dutch market through a sales agent was initiated and some holidays were sold in the UK through agents. Two smaller direct sell camping operators were acquired by CES in 1986: Carefree Camping Ltd and Sunsites Ltd. Eurocamp Independent was launched in 1987 providing holidays for customers using their own tents.

Next Plc, a leading fashion retailer (which had been expanding rapidly in the early 1980s), bought CES in 1987 and it later became apparent that it was seeking potential purchasers for some of its non-core activities in order to reduce its high levels of debt. Richard Atkinson, Holidaybreak's chief executive, explained that, 'Next was unloading its peripherals, the classic scenario for a management buyout. We wanted independence and there was a significant financial incentive.'

Management and organization

Richard Atkinson had spotted his chance. He had begun his career in classic travel industry fashion as a courier, being Eurocamp's first full-time employee in 1976 after graduating from Manchester University. Good career moves often occur by accident, and his move stemmed from nothing more than, 'a vague desire to work in France'. Atkinson turned down a job offer from Canvas Holidays, the market leaders from the early 1970s.

Eurocamp was lucky with the timing of its entry to the market because in a niche market that was in its infancy, the company was able to learn from established competitors. As one of the first companies to compete with Canvas, Eurocamp had the opportunity to learn from Canvas and avoid the mistakes that had previously been made in the fledgling sector. Atkinson grew with the company, taking responsibility for operations and marketing before becoming general manager in 1979, when he took over day-to-day running of the company. Following the resignation of the founder in 1983, he became managing director.

Atkinson recalled, 'by 1981 we were number two in the market. There were a lot of companies trying to do the same thing, but we had looked at what Canvas Holidays did and tried to do it better, rather than just accepting we were second fiddle, and we overtook them a few years later.' Recession hit the travel trade in the early 1980s and the number of companies involved in the camping holiday market contracted sharply with Eurocamp strengthening its position as a result in a market that continued to exhibit growth.

Two of Eurocamp's original executive board members, Martin Leppard (operations) and Julian Rawel (sales and marketing), both followed similar routes into the company. The fourth member of the management team, Gordon Harman, a chartered accountant (who became finance director in 1984 after joining the company in 1982), brought with him much needed financial expertise. The management team was strengthened by the appointment of Jim Crew (group systems) in 1989 after five years' involvement with the company on a consultancy basis. The group also had non-executive involvement at board level. Tom Neville was appointed non-executive chairman in July 1990 having previously retired as the finance director of Vickers plc, a major defence company. Gil Thompson, the chief executive of Manchester Airport was appointed to the board in March 1991.

In the early days the group was very much dominated by the forcefulness of its founder. The chairman based decisions very much on instinct and rarely were these decisions challenged. As the company grew, and when the founder left the company, the company's management began to evolve in different ways. A group of senior managers developed, taking decisions together after consideration of the issues, while management expertise of a more technical nature was bought in as required. Although senior managers took increasingly specialized roles within the group and a well-defined reporting structure existed, members of the management team took an active interest informally in other areas of the business in order to maintain an overall perspective.

In November 1988 a management buy-out was led by the management team and Eurocamp plc was formed. 'We had a great deal of experience of the way the business was growing,' said Atkinson, who believed this to be an important prerequisite for any management buy-out. 'When everyone knows each other and the team is experienced, there can be continuity of business, despite changes in company ownership.' A number of institutional investors, led by Barclays Development Capital Ltd, backed the buy-out in the form of loans and equity totalling £32 million.

After the management buy-out the group continued to expand and develop and was floated as Eurocamp plc on the London Stock Exchange in 1991. Several directors later left the company and other directors joined the main board as businesses were added. The group, which became more diverse and complex, was organized into three divisions (Camping, Hotel Breaks and Adventure), each of which was represented at main board of director level. In recent years Holidaybreak has sought to operate quality, market-leading businesses in sectors of the holiday business which appear to offer good growth potential. The low-margin, short-haul air-inclusive tour package holiday market has been avoided, thereby choosing not to compete head-to-head with the large vertically integrated tour operators.

The board of directors has overall responsibility for ensuring that the company maintains a system of internal financial control to provide them with reasonable assurance regarding the reliability of financial information used within the business and that assets are safeguarded. Subsidiary businesses produce monthly management accounts information, which is used to compare actual performance with budget and medium term plans. These accounts include updated forecasts and other information to enable the board to assess the prospects of all group businesses. The group has an established internal organizational structure with clear well defined reporting lines, which determine responsibilities and areas of accountability.

The group maintains offices in various locations to manage the individual businesses. However, certain of the group's key functions, including the company secretariat, legal, taxation, cash and currency management (treasury) and business risk insurance, are carried out centrally under the direct control of the group chief executive and the group finance director. The board has applied Principle D2 of the 'combined code' on corporate governance, which was published by the London Stock Exchange in 1998. The principle establishes a continuous process for identifying, evaluating and managing the significant risks that the group faces. Furthermore the process itself is regularly reviewed. Such a system is designed to manage rather than to eliminate the risk of failure to achieve business objectives, and can only provide reasonable not absolute assurance against losses or misstatements in the accounts.

Activities and operations – camping

The principal activity of the group remains the provision of self-drive camping holidays in Europe, which are provided by the Camping division. This includes the hiring out of 'luxury' fully equipped tents and mobile homes at an extensive range of high standard European camp sites. The choice of holiday destinations amounts to over 250 in France and many other countries. The standard of accommodation provided is far removed from the traditional camping image. This is reflected in the standard of quality of the tents, mobile homes and camp sites provided. The majority of sites are included in their country's top official category (four star in France).

It is an important feature of the holidays that the character and ambience of the camp sites is preserved. In order to facilitate this aim, it is unusual for the group to rent more than 30% of the pitches on any one site. Furthermore, contracted pitches are usually spread throughout a site. Holidays offered by the group differ from the standardized 'typical package' in a number of important respects. Holidays are not for standardized periods or at just one destination. Customers are offered freedom, flexibility and independence through a 'tailor made' combination, normally including cross-channel ferries of the customer's choice, insurance and accommodation. Motorail, fly/drive and en-route stops can also be added. On site the group have trained couriers.

The price of holidays offered cover a broad spectrum from but an important thrust of Eurocamp marketing at all price points is to be perceived as offering value for money. Well-established relationships have been developed with a large number of individual camp site owners. The highest number of pitches for tents and mobile homes rented from any one owner represents less than 5% of total group capacity. Ferry bookings are made with a number of different operators, principally Stena-Sealink, P&O, and Brittany Ferries. On-site operations are overseen by a team of experienced area managers. These managers supervise, train and support seasonal courier staff and monitor the quality of the product. They are also responsible for setting up and clearing the camp sites at the end of the season. On-site seasonal staff are employed mainly as couriers usually on full or half season contracts. In the past seasonal employees have been important sources of recruitment for permanent posts. Typically the group's products, in both the UK and overseas, are aimed at the family holiday market, with parents in the 30–45 age range from the ABC1 social categories. The holidays are also popular with couples, particularly at inland destinations outside the school holiday period. The majority of customers book direct although the Keycamp brand also receives a significant number of UK bookings through travel agents. A high level of customer satisfaction is achieved and a considerable amount of customers represent repeat bookings.

The group is the largest provider of self-drive camping holidays in Europe. The UK market is served by a small number of fairly long-established specialist operators but during recent years there has also been increased competition from other tour operators diversifying into this sector. The number of competitors in this sector of the market has increased markedly over recent years with about 100 companies currently competing in it. Traditionally, the sector has been dominated by specialists that have grown with the growth of the sector. These companies include Canvas Holidays, which is a well-established family owned concern, and French Life, a relatively small family-controlled business. Increasingly though, larger tour operators and companies with parent companies outside the travel industry have been attracted to the sector. These competitors included:

- Keycamp, which was owned by a diversified plc before its purchase by Holidaybreak.
- Haven, owned by Bourne Leisure (a privately owned company which also runs UK caravan parks and owns Butlins Holiday Centres).
- Eurosites, owned by MyTravel plc, which entered the market in the early 1990s.

Like its parent company, Eurosites is strongly price conscious, and sells its products both through the trade and 'direct sell'. The company has rapidly built up market share in this sector. Eurosites has a very fresh image. The identity is strong, easily remembered and used consistently throughout the company. The company's colours (blue and red), logo and brochure layout with widespread use of a white background all serve to establish its strong public image.

Holidaybreak has a number of brands. The *Eurocamp* brand (which together with the *Sunsites* and *Eurocamp Independent* brands is run from the company's Cheshire Head Office) is a direct sell business, aimed very much at the ABC1 markets. It is the clear market leader. The company has established a strong market identity using the company logo and the company colours (red and green) extensively. The Eurocamp brand competes directly with the well-established Canvas Holiday's product, which enjoys a loyal clientele. Canvas promotes its independence, its record and its informality.

Sunsites is a more simplified product based around the sun, sea, sand formula of Mediterranean holidays and is aimed particularly at families with small children. It is relatively easy for the trade to sell on a commission basis and is positioned slightly down-market of the Eurocamp brand.

The *Eurocamp Independent* brand allows people to take their own tents with them instead of using the company's contracted equipment. The company's role is to take care of the troublesome details, such as reservations, ferry bookings and insurance.

The *Keycamp* brand, which is managed from the brand's offices in Sutton, south-west London, has a strong following among travel agents as well as receiving many bookings through direct selling. The brand also has a far higher proportion than the Eurocamp brand of customers opting for mobile homes rather than camping.

The group has to compete in the wider market for overseas summer holidays. This involves competing with mainstream package holiday operators as well as other companies offering self-drive and self-catering family holidays in continental Europe. The self-drive sector represents only a small part of the total market, but in spite of the general trend away from the traditional package, it is believed that this sector will continue to grow.

Whilst it offers a cheaper alternative to air inclusive holidays, the quality of the product, wider choice of destinations and the willingness of the British to increasingly make their own way abroad, has produced a strong sector of the industry in its own right. Competition comes not so much from the Spanish Costas, but the country cottage market. The group has actively developed its holiday products so as to make them appeal to a wider customer base. Improvements in the level of comfort and quality of facilities have been made and the diversity and choice of destinations offered has been increased. The same high quality accommodation is available at all locations, but the nature of the holiday varies according to the style and environment of the camp site, the range and type of facilities and the approach of the site management.

The majority of bookings received by the group are secured through direct marketing and sales techniques, which offer a number of significant advantages. Additionally in recent years a number of new markets have been successfully developed. The group endeavours to manage its costs and capacity in a flexible way so as to match effective demand with supply as completely as operationally possible. Group companies rent space on selected camp sites usually on a seasonal basis. Unlike many other holiday companies, the group does not have a high level of committed costs, because there is not the requirement to charter aircraft seats for instance. Typically a contract gives considerable ability for the group to adjust the number of pitches rented. A substantial proportion of bookings is received prior to the turn of the calendar year and expenditure on camping equipment can be managed flexibly in accordance with requirements.

In contrast to most other package operators, therefore the business is more predictable, and phenomena such as 'consolidations', which see customers sent to a different location than the one originally booked, rarely happen. Holidaybreak is, however, susceptible to various problems of transportation arrangements caused by factors usually beyond the company's control such as problems with ferry operators or the operations of the Channel Tunnel.

One of Holidaybreak's main capital expenditure items is mobile homes. A popular form of holiday, the company has kept to strict limits on the proportion of capacity which such holidays represent, because of the need to retain flexibility in matching demand and supply. Cancellation rates are relatively high at about 10–12% of early bookings and perhaps 6% overall. Increasingly, the group has been able to spread demand across a number of months rather than being limited to the UK school summer holiday, resulting in high capacity utilization throughout the season. Ferry crossings and insurance are not subject to fixed quotas, but are arranged as required. A large number of staff are employed on a seasonal basis only. The group thus has considerable flexibility in varying its major fixed and operating expenses in line with demand and thereby reducing the risk of late discounting of holiday prices. As a result the group is able to operate at far higher margins than have normally been associated with overseas tour operators.

Camping is the most mature of Holidaybreak's businesses, but several developments are taking place in this sector of the industry. Although the UK market is now fairly well served by well-established operators and is growing quite slowly, Holidaybreak has much lower levels of penetration in several European markets. Germany and mainland European markets are viewed as relatively under-exploited. There has also been a discernible move away from camping and towards mobile homes which offer greater degrees of comfort for customers. Mobile homes provide higher sales revenue at substantially higher margins.

Hotel breaks

The group's second business is represented by its Hotel Breaks division, with which it has been involved since 1995. The business has agreements with about 1400 UK hotels which provide allocations to enable Hotel Break's brands, which include the market leading Superbreaks, to sell UK hotel short breaks normally for leisure customers and particularly at weekends. The company takes a 30% margin on the selling price, and a guarantee is provided to customers that they would not be able to book more cheaply by going directly to the hotel.

Although travel agents have hitherto provided the main distribution channel, direct sales and the Internet are growing in importance. There is a clear trend in the market for people to be taking more frequent short holidays, and weekend breaks are very much the current fashion.

Adventure

The Adventure division is the group's third business area and is the field in which the company has been most active in terms of acquisitions over recent years. A growing number of people demand more adventurous and exotic holidays as alternatives to lying on the beach or by a swimming pool. These customers, which come from a wide spectrum of age ranges, whilst wanting something a bit different, nevertheless want to feel secure in the quality of arrangements that are made. Explore Worldwide, which is based in Aldershot in Hampshire, is the UK market leader and the largest European operator of worldwide adventure holidays, with an estimated 40% of the UK market. Explore offers some 200 winter and summer tours to nearly 100 countries. An experienced tour leader leads each tour group comprising up to 18 people and customers will usually stay in middle range hotel accommodation, although some tours necessitate the use of more basic accommodation or camping.

The second business in this division is the much smaller Regal Diving, which is based in Cambridge. Regal travels mainly to the Red Sea organizing scuba diving holidays and are the leading specialist operator in this particular market niche.

Financial information

The Holidaybreak group has had a successful record of growth over the past five years, with an increasing number of sales being made in continental Europe. In addition, it has been possible to apply consistent pricing policies, thereby avoiding significant recourse to discounting. The group's business is of a highly seasonal nature, resulting in unbalanced profitability through the year and cyclical cash flows. However, in a typical year the group is net cash generative, with capital expenditure incurred at the beginning of the calendar year and normally significant cash balances being held by year end. During the winter months the group faces a negative cash position financed by bank overdrafts, with the peak overdraft requirement falling in January or February. Net cash flows into the group from February onwards, so that positive cash balances are held by the group for the remainder of the year. These balances peak in June or July.

The management of the cash flow of the group ('cash management') is thus a significant part of running the business. It is important to be able to forecast the size and timing of the major inflows and outflows of cash and the resulting cash balances or deficits that may result. With this information overdraft requirements can be planned for, negotiated and agreed with the bank. Additionally, interest income on cash balances represents a highly significant source of revenue for the group.

As part of the cash management process, consideration is given to the nature of the booking terms, asking for payments from customers slightly earlier than the norm in order to improve cash flow. Inducements for early payment and rewards for returning customers in the form of discounts are given in some cases. The group's business is thus of a highly seasonal nature, with sales and profits being recognized in the second half of the year as holidays are taken. Intensive marketing of the following season's camping holidays commences in October each year, with the majority of bookings taken by April of the following year.

There remain accounting oddities inherent in Holidaybreak's business, not least because it has only limited fixed assets, with the value of the business resting largely in the goodwill associated with the brand names and the management expertise in place. Even so, the company has more fixed assets than many travel companies, with net book value camping equipment (mainly tents and mobile homes) representing substantial assets.

Currency exposure is always a topic of interest to companies offering overseas holidays. The company's net currency exposure is, however, very limited. Since there is also a substantial inflow of Euros from the foreign selling operations in Holland, Germany and to a lesser extent Ireland and other countries, a 'natural hedge' is provided against the principal expenses which are incurred in France (predominantly) and other countries. Any remaining net exposure to the risk of movements in currency rates is managed through the taking out of forward foreign exchange contacts with major banks.

Appendix 2.1
Holidaybreak plc organization chart – 2002

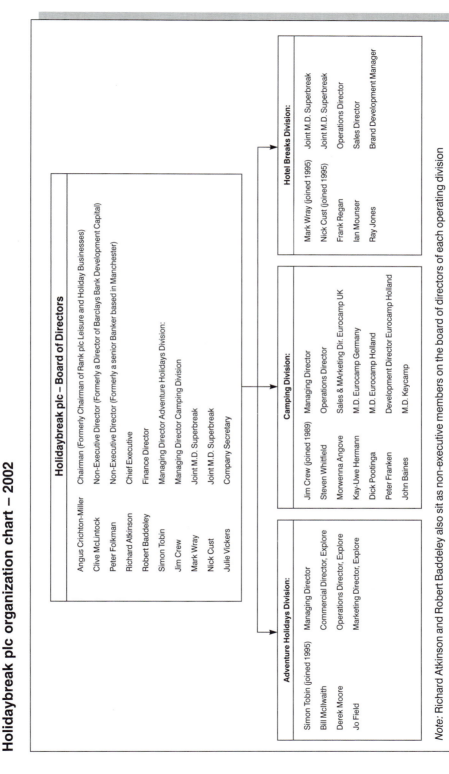

Holidaybreak plc – Board of Directors

Angus Crichton-Miller	Chairman (Formerly Chairman of Rank plc Leisure and Holiday Businesses)
Clive McLintock	Non-Executive Director (Formerly a Director of Barclays Bank Development Capital)
Peter Folkman	Non-Executive Director (Formerly a senior Banker based in Manchester)
Richard Atkinson	Chief Executive
Robert Baddeley	Finance Director
Simon Tobin	Managing Director Adventure Holidays Division:
Jim Crew	Managing Director Camping Division
Mark Wray	Joint M.D. Superbreak
Nick Cust	Joint M.D. Superbreak
Julie Vickers	Company Secretary

Adventure Holidays Division:

Simon Tobin (joined 1995)	Managing Director
Bill McIlwaith	Commercial Director, Explore
Derek Moore	Operations Director, Explore
Jo Field	Marketing Director, Explore

Camping Division:

Jim Crew (joined 1989)	Managing Director
Steven Whitfield	Operations Director
Morwenna Angove	Sales & MArketing Dir. Eurocamp UK
Kay-Uwe Hermann	M.D. Eurocamp Germany
Dick Pootinga	M.D. Eurocamp Holland
Peter Franken	Development Director Eurocamp Holland
John Baines	M.D. Keycamp

Hotel Breaks Division:

Mark Wray (joined 1995)	Joint M.D. Superbreak
Nick Cust (joined 1995)	Joint M.D. Superbreak
Frank Regan	Operations Director
Ian Mounser	Sales Director
Ray Jones	Brand Development Manager

Note: Richard Atkinson and Robert Baddeley also sit as non-executive members on the board of directors of each operating division

Appendix 2.2
A brief history of Holidaybreak plc

Holidaybreak plc was founded in 1973 as Euro-camp Travel Limited – a family-run business, based in Knutsford, Cheshire, offering camping holidays in Brittany. From modest beginnings the business grew steadily benefiting from the growing interest in France as a holiday business. In the early 1980s mobile-homes and destinations outside France were added to the product range. Ownership of the business changed in 1981, with the founder Alan Goulding selling to the London based retail group Combined English Stores plc. Alan Goulding finally left the company in 1983 when Richard Atkinson, currently chief executive, became managing director.

The 1980s were years of innovation and growth as the UK market to France expanded rapidly and Eurocamp took over leadership of the camping sector. Product developments included the introduction of a much wider range of destinations both inside and outside France, development of services for children and opening up camp sites for overnight stops. There were also a series of milestones in the development of the business and a number of small competitors were absorbed into the business as the market consolidated. Key events included:

1984 Launch of Eurocamp on the Dutch market
1986 Acquisition of Sunsites and Carefree Camping
1987 Launch of Eurocamp Independent
Take-over of Combined English Stores by Next plc
1988 Launch of Eurocamp on the German market
Management buy-out from Next
1991 Flotation on the London Stock Exchange

Since flotation the business has continued to develop. The marketing reach of the Eurocamp brand has been extended into several new territories, notably Switzerland, Belgium, Denmark and most recently Poland, whilst customers have increasingly opted for mobile home rather than tent accommodation. From the mid-1990s expansion came through several acquisitions within the holiday sector as well as through organic growth.

1995 Superbreak – leading provider of UK hotel short-breaks acquired.
1996 Acquired Camping in Comfort and Tesh Travels – Eurocamp's sales agents in Holland and Germany
1998 Keycamp Holidays – the UK's Number 2 camping and mobile home operator acquired
2000 Explore Worldwide – worldwide adventure holidays specialist acquired
Regal Holidays – scuba diving specialist tour operator acquired
Hotelnet – Internet hotel portal
Rainbow Holidays – UK short-break specialist acquired

2001 and 2002 have represented a period of greater stability as the company has integrated its purchases into the group and reorganized its management structures. Recent years have seen other important changes. In 1998, after 25 years in Knutsford, the Camping and Group head offices were relocated to a country house at Hartford, near Northwich, Cheshire. The holding company name was also changed from Eurocamp plc to Holidaybreak plc to better reflect the aspirations and range of activities of the group.

Appendix 2.3

Profit and loss account – divisional breakdown

	Camping (£ m)	Hotel breaks (£ m)	Adventure holidays (£ m)	Group (£ m)
Turnover				
2001	103.7	57.8	31.0	192.5
2000	102.3	46.1	16.1	164.5
Gross profit				
2001	35.8	11.0	9.2	56.0
2000	34.7	8.7	4.9	48.3
Operating profit				
2001	17.8	5.5	3.4	26.7
2000	17.0	4.4	2.4	23.7

Balance sheet

	Holidaybreak plc Group 2001 (£'000)	Holidaybreak plc Group 2000 (£'000)
Fixed Assets		
Intangible assets – goodwill	31,600	32,753
Tangible assets	57,728	53,779
Investments	1,896	1,079
	91,224	87,611
Current assets		
Assets held for disposal	2,626	3,463
Debtors	13,421	12,690
Cash at bank and in hand	49,169	47,803
	65,216	63,956
Creditors:		
Amounts falling due within 1 year	(61,925)	(52,553)
Net current assets (liabilities)	3,291	11,403
Total assets less current liabilities	94,515	99,014
Creditors:		
Amounts falling due after 1 year	(60,499)	(73,619)
Provisions for liabilities and charges	(6,022)	(5,482)
Net Assets	27,994	19,913
Capital and reserves		
Called up share capital	2,317	2,290
Reserves	25,677	17,623
Equity shareholders' funds	27,994	19,913

Appendix 2.4

Operating divisions of Holidaybreak plc – background information

Camping division

Some 450 000 UK customers (mainly family groups) took a European camping or mobile-home holiday in 1999 in pre-sited accommodation provided by Holidaybreak's various companies or another tour operator. The equivalent figures for the two other most sizeable markets, Holland and Germany, are approximately 250 000 and 150 000 respectively. Holidaybreak customers are generally families from the ABC1 social categories, or the equivalents in their own countries. The holidays are also popular with couples, particularly at inland destinations outside the school holiday period. Each brand offers a very similar core product. Differentiation is through presentation, distribution and peripheral aspects.

Hotel breaks division

Superbreak and its associated brands offer breaks in almost 1400 hotels in the three to five star category throughout the UK. These are featured in catalogue style brochures, which are distributed primarily through UK travel agents. A sustained growth in short-breaks and multiple holiday-taking has been a feature of the UK travel market in recent years. On-line bookings can be made at Superbreak's own site www.superbreak.com. Customers come mainly from the ABC1 social categories. Couples predominate but families are also an important target group. This is a high volume business with relatively low transaction values per booking. Agency commissions, in those cases where they are payable, represent entirely variable costs and no upfront commitments for rooms, transport, theatre tickets etc. are incurred. Fixed costs are very low.

With minimal capital expenditure requirements and year round sales, the business is profitable and cash flows are strong throughout the year. In July 2000 the Internet hotel booking business Hotelnet was acquired. This is one of the leading UK Internet portals for hotel bookings.

Adventure holidays division

Explore

Explore offer some 200 winter and summer tours in nearly 100 countries in six continents. Types of tours include:

- *Culture/adventure* – Trips that explore exciting places but do not necessarily involve any particular physical activity, usually focusing on local cultures, historic sites or dramatic locations.

Market share estimates (2000)					
UK	**Ireland**	**Holland**	**Germany**	**Denmark**	
Holidaybreak	61%	70%	64%	71%	49%
Eurosites (MyTravel)	20%	1%	16%	29%	51%
Haven (Bourne Leisure)	10%	12%	8%	–	–
Canvas Holidays	9%	–	13%	–	–
Campotel	–	17%	–	–	–

Sales by brand		Sales by market	
Eurocamp	53%	UK/Ireland	68%
Keycamp	38%	Holland	15%
Sunsites	4%	Germany	11%
Independent/other	5%	Others	6%

- *Ethnic or tribal encounters* – Offering the opportunity to meet, and sometimes stay with, traditional local people or tribal groups.
- *Easy to moderate hikes* – A few days easy or moderate walking, usually in open countryside, based in hotel or tented accommodation.
- *Major treks* – This type of trip is recommended to strong mountain walkers who enjoy a challenge. Participants need to be physically fit.
- *Wildlife and natural history* – A particular emphasis on wildlife or natural wonders. Sometimes visiting some of the world's greatest game reserves.
- *Wilderness experience*– Trips that venture into areas where man's influence is limited.
- *Sailtrek/seatrek* – Involving the use of sailboats, ships, ferries or even tallships.
- *Raft or river journeys* – Lasting anything from a few hours to several days. This category includes a wide range of activity type, from whitewater rafting to easy-going cruising and river exploration.

Nearly 80% of Explore's customers come from the UK, booking direct with the company's headquarters in Aldershot. Overseas customers come mainly from English speaking countries – Australia, New Zealand, Canada, USA etc. They book through appointed sales agents in those countries. The customers are typically professional people who are reasonably active and want a change from more traditional holiday types. They will often be interested in local cultures and history or wildlife and landscapes. The age profile varies, depending on the tour, but 90% of customers are aged between 25 and 65, with an average age of 44.

Tour costs are largely variable. There are no commitments to airline seats and accommodation costs will depend on the number of travellers in a party. Vehicles and equipment are normally rented locally. Management systems ensure healthy load factors and efficient control of overseas costs. The diversity of the product range and destinations provides considerable resilience and the year-round nature of business (with about 45% of revenues coming in the UK winter period) means that the business is profitable throughout the year. Capital expenditure requirements are limited ensuring strong, year-round cash flows and dollar denominated revenues from overseas customers provide a partial currency hedge.

Regal

Regal Holidays has been arranging diving holidays worldwide since 1987 and is considered to be the UK's leading dive tour operator. Regal offer year-round holidays for both novices and qualified divers. In the 2000/01 brochure there are holidays in 24 destinations, offering over 11 diving activities, plus snorkelling for all ages too. The learn-to-dive market continues to grow and is one in which Regal has been active in developing. There are an increasing number of divers who will take at least two dive holidays per year, one of which would be to a value for money destination such as the Red Sea or a short break in Gozo, and the second one would be to a longer-haul destination such as the Maldives, Grenada etc. The age profile of clients varies but the main sector is aged between 25 and 45 years old. They all tend to be fairly active and want more from their holiday than just a sun tan. Some are dedicated divers who have been diving for years whilst a growing sector are young and single and want to go and learn to dive. Capital expenditure requirements are limited and cash flows are strong year round, allowing for a profitable product throughout the year.

Sources

Company reports – various years; newspaper articles – various

Case 3

Leicester Promotions: destination management for maximizing tourist potential

Amanda Miller
Manchester Metropolitan University

An introduction to Leicester

Leicester is the largest city in England's East Midlands and the tenth largest in the country, with a history dating back to Roman times when it was a strategic stronghold in the control of the Midlands region. It is a major commercial and manufacturing centre, with a thriving ethnic minority drawn from a range of cultural traditions (particularly from the Indian sub-continent), which accounts for over a quarter of Leicester's population. This cultural mix provides opportunities for a wide range of cuisines in the city's many restaurants. Within the city centre there are newly pedestrianized shopping streets, a marketplace which has its origins back through some seven centuries and a modern purpose-built shopping centre. It was also the first British city to be awarded the title of 'Environment City' by the Royal Society for Nature Conservation and the Civic Trust in recognition of the city's pioneering environmental programmes. Tourist attractions include the Leicestershire Museum and Art Gallery, the Haymarket Theatre, (which sometimes hosts shows prior to their West End debut) and the newly completed National Space Centre.

Company background

Tourism as an area of interest is problematic for many local authorities charged with delivering local government services in the UK. Local areas and communities have often recognized the potential income that can be derived from tourism (both leisure and business related) and in the UK they have traditionally been responsible for providing local tourist information facilities through a network of tourist information centres (TICs). The TICs provide tourism information for visitors and are able to book accommodation but usually have a restricted commercial focus, often limited to selling a narrow range of souvenirs from their offices.

Many local authorities have also recognized that tourist related activities can form an important constituent part of urban renewal. Thus Liverpool, Cardiff and Edinburgh's waterfront redevelopments, and Birmingham's investment in conference facilities as 'Europe's Meeting Place' for example have important tourism components.

However, in terms of direct public spending at the local level, tourism spending has often been small when compared to education and social services and it has sometimes appeared to be low down the pecking order of political issues. Furthermore, decision-making in local authorities, although democratic and accountable, is often slow and lacking entrepreneurial flair. Against this background many cities such as Sheffield, Coventry and Manchester (and some counties) have sought to move the management of tourism outside direct public control through public–private partnerships of various types and configurations.

Leicester Promotions Ltd, the marketing and tourism agency for the City of Leicester, was established in 1993 as a non-profit-making organization to undertake the marketing and promotion of Leicester with a £1.1 million grant from Leicester City Council. Prior to 1993, tourism promotion services were delivered directly by the city council. With increasing financial pressures and the refocusing of the city council on other services, the delivery of tourism services was transferred out of the public sector. The move from the public sector to the private sector led to dramatic changes in the culture of the organization and the need to concentrate on activities that were commercially viable. Since 1993 it has become increasingly independent, with less than 50% of its funding coming from Leicester City Council for the year 2001/2.

Business activities

The principal activity of the company is the marketing and promotion of the City of Leicester and surrounding area and the delivery of tourism services. The company is actively involved in helping the city and county of Leicestershire fulfil their objectives relating to economic growth and social welfare. An objective is to raise the profile of the city, locally, regionally and nationally, and to do so the company specializes in tourism development, marketing and promotion. It aims to balance the delivering of services for local residents with developing the number of visitors to the area.

As partners on the city's key profiling events – Leicester Comedy Festival, Leicester's Diwali celebrations and annual festivals – the company is directly involved in marketing and promotional activities. The marketing and promotional support provided for a major festival 'Festival 2000' was carried out in partnership with the City Council. Direct public relations support was provided to the Comedy Festival and a range of activities was undertaken for the National Space Centre (direct mail, advertising, familiarization visits and telesales campaigns). Partnerships are undertaken with a wide range of organizations. Other partners include: Leicestershire County Council Tourism Department and many of the city's festivals, local hotels and attractions. Leicester Promotions also continues to be involved in the organization of the annual Leicester and Leicestershire Tourism Awards. This is done through partnerships with sponsors and it represents a way of recognizing and rewarding achievements by venues and attractions around the city and county.

Leicester's Christmas campaigns have proved very successful and have involved partnerships with a number of organizations. The aim has been to promote the city as one of the region's major destinations raising its profile in the region and promoting the Christmas experience of the city to local people. The campaigns have included: producing a TV campaign with The Shires shopping centre and City Centre Management team, producing a 36 page Christmas Guide in partnership with local retailers and the *Leicester Mercury* newspaper, and Leicester on Ice (an outdoor ice rink) as a result of collaboration between an international ice company and sponsorship by GAP.

A further step taken has been the establishment of 'Mosaic' as its in-house marketing communications and design function. Mosaic financially supports the projects Leicester Promotions continues to undertake as part of its commitment to the city. Clients to date have included both of Leicester's Universities, the National Institute for Adults

Continuing Education, Leicester Festival 2000 and a variety of regeneration projects across the city. As part of regeneration proposals Mosaic has also produced strategic and marketing plans for the run-down Leicester North West area.

Tourist information centre (TIC) and UK Holiday Shop

The city councils tourism services are contracted out to Leicester Promotions. As part of their activities they are responsible for the running of Leicester's tourist information centre and they see themselves as offering a leading edge TIC service. The TIC has been awarded the title of Heart of England's Best TIC. The TIC distributes a wide variety of information on attractions, events and hotels and takes bookings for all Leicester's major venues. It is located by the Town Hall and is thus not in a prominent high street position. It has very limited passing trade and they have succeeded in maximizing the number of customers despite its disadvantageous position in the city centre. Additionally, it offers a unique UK Holiday Shop and Box Office for local and London events, and also offers ancillary travel services. The other travel agents in the city are clustered together in the main shopping district and the UK Holiday Shop is isolated.

The income received from Leicester City Council is provided directly for information provision activities rather than for retailing or UK Holiday Shop operations. The city council is very clear in its contract with Leicester Promotions that they are divorced from the commercial enterprises of the company. As part of the services delivered to the city council Leicester Promotions represent the council at the Heart of England Tourist Board. They are seen as local authority members in terms of paid subscriptions but their own needs as a commercial marketing and tourism agency may at times be seen as providing points of conflict with their local authority status within the tourist board.

The UK Holiday Shop is the only Association of British Tour Operators (ABTA) bonded travel agency that is part of a tourist information centre and it specializes in UK domestic holiday products racking brochures from a range of tourism suppliers, including the following:

- Blakes
- Box Office (event tickets)
- Country Cottages

- Flightlink
- Haven
- Highlife
- Hoseasons
- Leisure Breaks
- Luxury Hotel Collection
- National Rail
- National Express
- Oasis
- Pontins
- Shearings
- Superbreaks
- Wallace Arnold
- Warner
- Wightlink

The UK Holiday Shop operated in its first year without an ABTA bond and in doing so there were obstacles to its efficient and effective operation as the range of products that could be offered was limited. Difficulties were encountered in setting up agency agreements with tour operators. In explaining to tour operators that they were a TIC there was confusion and suspicion with what that actually meant. For more traditional travel agents there is a good system of support and regular contact but tour operators have not established such links with the UK Holiday Shop. Tour operators are not used to dealing with a travel agent that deals solely with UK domestic holiday products. Administrative working capital problems have arisen from the need to provide cash up front to tour operators without which tour operators would cancel reservations. This has involved a fundamental change in policy, as the inherited local authorities approach (where payments were processed within 30 days) was not an acceptable practice to tour operators. Not only do they have an ABTA bond as a travel agent but they are also required to maintain a bond as a tour operator because Leicester Promotions Ltd are involved in the packaging of the Leicester tourism product.

Their customers typically take a brochure away and do not necessarily return to them to make a booking. There is no way of recognizing that the customer has obtained their holiday brochure from the UK Holiday Shop and that they have actually helped the supplier obtain that booking. Even when customers do book at the UK Holiday Shop return custom is not very common, and they tend to attract customers from the older generations who pay for their holidays with cash. Travel agents located in the high street in Leicester frequently send customers to the UK Holiday Shop as they consider the commission from selling domestic holidays too low to bother with so they would rather pass their custom on. They assure customers that they would get better choice from this alternative shop.

Within the industry a key issue is the low level of commission (usually less than 10%) and how this discourages the selling of the domestic tourism products by travel agents. Domestic tour operators and hoteliers appear to be attempting to decrease commission levels and a number of significant domestic operators (such as Center Parcs, which operates rural activity based holidays) sell directly rather than through agents. The UK Holiday Shop has recently won attention as one of the leading sellers of 'Superbreaks' (a major operator for hotel based UK short breaks).

Appendix 3.1

Leicester Promotions Ltd: management

Martin Peters, the Managing Director of Leicester Promotions Ltd, has 19 years' experience in tourism and place marketing within both the public and private sectors. On a national level, he is a former Chairman of the 'British Association of Conference Destinations' and remains a director of that Company. He is also a member of the steering group of the British Cities Marketing Board which represents the shared interests of many of the larger British cities. Locally, he has represented Leicester at home and overseas to both the business and leisure tourism markets. In Leicester, he was responsible for introducing the strategies into Leicester's tourist information centre that culminated in the TIC being the first in the country to be awarded ABTA bonding. Formerly Director of Operations, Martin has been with Leicester Promotions since its inception in 1993 and was part of the original team transferred out of the City Council to form the Company.

Martin is supported by a small but enthusiastic team and Leicester Promotions' controlling Board of Directors reflects the city's strengths and diversity. Board members include:

- The Leader of Leicester City Council
- The Chief Executive of Leicester Rugby Club
- The Bishop of Leicester
- The manager of the Belmont House Hotel

Appendix 3.2

Income and expenditure account

	2001 £	2000 £
Turnover	1,613,807	1,496,785
Operating costs	(1,561,397)	(1,602,435)
Operating surplus/(deficit)	52,410	(105,650)
Surplus/(deficit) on ordinary activities before taxation	56,892	(99,310)
Surplus/(deficit) for the financial year transferred to/(from) reserves	56,041	(95,110)

Operating costs

	2001 £	2000 £
Promotional costs	147,974	320,665
Tourist information centre costs	361,964	341,206
Conference/tourism costs	73,817	163,955
Rent, rates, heat and light	77,498	44,611
Salaries and national insurance	531,206	498,365
Other operating costs	368,938	233,633

Notes:
Transactions with related parties. The company's turnover in 2001 included sales of £839,523 to Leicester City Council. Of this amount £798,000 related to core funding.

Appendix 3.3

Tourism facts and figures: UK domestic tourism

	All tourism trips (millions)	All tourism nights (millions)	Holiday tourism trips (millions)	Holiday tourism nights (millions)	Holiday tourism spending (£millions)
1995	121.0	449.8	66.2	302.1	8915
1996	127.0	454.6	64.8	295.8	9365
1997	133.6	473.6	70.8	313.3	10 355
1998	122.3	437.6	65.1	284.2	9800
1999	146.1	495.3	75.3	319.6	11 095

Sources

Personal interviews

Case 4

MyTravel plc (formerly Airtours): competing in the travel industry big league

Nigel Evans

An entrepreneurial beginning

David Crossland's introduction to the business world was not very promising. On leaving Burnley Grammar School in 1963 he took a job as a glorified coffee boy in a local travel agent and it was difficult to imagine that he would in time become the Chairman of what itself became one of the world's leading travel companies and rank 86th in *The Sunday Times* 'Rich List' of Britain's wealthiest 1000 people. From acorns oak trees grow, and so it was with this Lancastrian entrepreneur.

During the 1970s Crossland developed his own travel agency business, Pendle Travel, together with his brother-in-law Tom Trickett. Entry costs were at the time relatively low and the powerful multiple chains were far less the threat to the independent travel agency business that they were later to become. Trickett backed Crossland in 1972 with an £8000 investment in the first travel agency, and he remained a large shareholder in the Airtours business until the mid-1990s. What later evolved into the MyTravel group emerged with the Airtours name in 1978 when Pendle Travel launched a tour operations division within the successful travel agency business. When the first tours took to the air the company operated from a tiny office above a travel agency in the small Lancashire village of Haslingden. The initial specialization of the company was low cost package holidays to Malta which found a ready market in north-west England. The speed of development of the tour operating business outstripped that of the travel agency chain and the competitive pressures on independent travel agents were becoming ever greater with 'the march of the multiples', as it was later termed.

From 1985, Crossland, recognizing that the development of the business required professional inputs from others, started to draw around him a strong management team to help him build the business. The sale of the 22-branch chain to Hogg Robinson (which operated a nationwide branch network) was concluded in 1986 and in that year Airtours carried 300 000 holidaymakers. This period culminated the following year with a major step in the company's strategic development. The company was floated on the London Stock Exchange to become a public limited company (plc), making it one of a very small number of tour operators to have a full stock market listing at that time.

After flotation

As Airtours plc, the management could raise capital for investment, and although this allowed opportunities for expansion, it also imposed financial disciplines on the management team. As a plc, every move was carefully scrutinized by the City and by the media. The company had to deliver satisfaction to customers, shareholders and bankers, and balancing these competing demands was not always easy. Still based in its north-west England heartland (the company today has its corporate headquarters in the Manchester suburbs), Airtours had established a reputation throughout the travel industry for its relatively low staffing costs and the loyalty it was able to engender in its staff: 'They stay a long time because they are determined that one day they will get to the office before me,' Crossland once joked. Although he became less 'hands-on' as he approached retirement in the late 1990s, he remained as chairman and the days in which he regularly arrived at the office by 5.30 a.m. are still fondly remembered by staff.

Despite many developments in the company, tour operations remained at the core of the group's activities with airline, distribution networks and accommodation developing largely to service the needs of the tour operations activity. The Aspro brand was positioned at the value for money or price-led end of the market while Airtours was positioned as the main market brand with particular appeal to families. A large number of different brochures were produced in the UK using the Airtours name and representing a variety of holiday types. The brochures included: Summer Sun, Far and Away, Turkey, Greece, Florida, Fly-Drive USA, Cruises, Florida and Caribbean Cruise and Stay Holidays (featuring Carnival Cruises), All-Inclusive Suncenters, City and Short Breaks, and Lakes and Mountains. The Tradewinds brand offered more exclusive and exotic holidays, mainly utilizing scheduled flights to destinations all over the world.

In 1990 Airtours introduced EuroSites by establishing a subsidiary operating self-drive holidays with pre-arranged camping locations. By the late 1990s EuroSites had become the second largest company (after Eurocamp) in this area of the market. EuroSites offered tent and mobile home holidays across Europe, selling since its launch in the UK and more recently in the Dutch and German markets. Further capacity was added progressively from one season to the next through the adding of capacity at sites and by adding additional camp sites to its portfolio. Demand for the product proved to be strong with good levels of profitability, high levels of customer satisfaction and high levels of repeat business. During 1990 'The Cottage Directory' product selling UK country cottages was also developed. However, sales levels achieved were lower than forecast and the product proved operationally difficult, involving as it did close liaison with a large number of individual property owners and a comparatively low value of sales per brochure page. After the end of its first season an offer for the business was received and accepted, thereby incurring a relatively limited loss overall.

Throughout the 1990s, the UK outbound tour-operating sector was characterized by intense competition and was highly seasonal and cyclical in its booking patterns. A number of factors combined to create a substantial imbalance between supply and demand for the summer of 1995. Tour operators had anticipated the arrival of the much talked about 'feel good factor' in the UK economy and sales in the pre-Christmas selling period were encouraging. However, this did not continue into the peak booking months of January–March and all operators maintained capacity in the expectation of an upturn in demand. Several companies also declared their aim of gaining market share in 1995. Onto this market position was added the effect of the excellent, record-breaking UK weather during the summer months. With supply greater than demand in the increasingly important 'late sales' market, many prices fell to unprofitable levels across the industry and discounting was substantially higher than in most years.

The alternatives indicated by the 1995 market were straightforward. The industry could either downsize by offering fewer holidays at realistic margins or continue on the same basis as pre-1995 with higher and higher late sales discounts giving customers little incentive to book early.

Launched ahead of schedule on 18 March 1991, Airtours International was set up. Unlike some other charter carriers, Airtours International's airline capacity was intended solely to serve the group's tour operations. Its capacity was fully utilized on Airtours business and was not dependent upon third party customers. The growing needs of the Airtours' tour operations required assurance that sufficient seat capacity could be acquired at the right price and of a consistent quality. The airline's growth, however, was limited by Airtours' winter tour operations since it was during the winter that any excess charter capacity was likely to become apparent. With this factor in mind, the airline provided over 90% of the winter tour operations flying programme, dropping to between 60 and 70% for the summer programme.

Airtours' northern roots were emphasized by the position of Manchester airport. In 1986 76% of Airtours bookings were for Manchester departures and although growth from the airport continued in terms of absolute numbers, its relative position declined since it represented only 46% of UK departures in 1991 and this proportion subsequently fell further. The company's in-house airline, Airtours International, was, from its inception in 1991, based at the airport.

In September 1992 Airtours re-entered the UK retail travel agency business with the purchase of 335 branches of the third largest retail chain, Pickfords. This was followed by the purchase in June 1993 of 210 branches acquired from Hogg Robinson, moving the group to second position behind Lunn Poly in UK retail distribution. The branches served as outlets for the distribution of Airtours products and importantly provided market intelligence on customer preferences and market trends. A major re-branding exercise took place during December 1993 in which the division was re-launched under the Going Places name. Within seven days every one of the company's 545 retail shops had been fitted out with new fascias, signage and stationery. Later in the year, the 40 strong Winston Rees chain was added to the Airtours network.

The merging of the large retail networks inevitably resulted in a degree of duplication with some shops being closer to others than would be considered ideal. Little merit was seen in closing branches despite the close proximity of a second Going Places outlet as long as each shop continued to make a satisfactory contribution to central overheads. Nevertheless, the profitability of each shop was continually reviewed and while many new sites were subsequently developed by Going Places, several poorly performing shops were closed and sold off. In 1995 Going Places had over 650 branches operating in the UK compared to 795 operated by Lunn Poly the market leader. Late Escapes, a telephone sales business specializing in the sales of holidays within eight weeks of departure, was purchased in 1994. Late Escapes, based in north-east England, made extensive use of the teletext information services for the marketing of its services directly to customers in their homes.

In January 1993 Airtours launched a hostile take-over bid for Owners Abroad (later known as First Choice Holidays), another large tour operator, which served many of the same destinations. The acrimonious battle fought over several months and widely reported by the media led to a narrow defeat for Airtours and incurred costs of some £9 million.

International expansion

After 1994 the group expanded internationally, most significantly in Scandinavia and subsequently in North America. The acquisition from Scandinavian Airways in June 1994 of the Scandinavian Leisure Group (SLG) gave Airtours ownership of the largest leisure travel company in Scandinavia, albeit one that served many of the same destinations as Airtours in the UK market. SLG operates the Ving, Always and Saga brands, with particular strengths in Norway and Sweden. Seventy per cent of its sales were made directly to the public either by 'direct sell' methods or through dedicated retail outlets with the remaining 30% of bookings being made through third party travel agents.

During the winter of 1994/95 SLG undertook a major restructuring exercise of its operations

which together with an improvement in the Scandinavian economies resulted in a greatly enhanced performance by this division. SLG carried 915 000 customers in 1995 increasing to 1 028 000 in 1996. The acquisition of the Spies group, Scandinavia's third largest tour operator during 1996, added a further 397 000 customers under the Spies and Tjaerborg brands. The Spies group was extensively reorganized and re-focused on acquisition with most administrative functions being integrated into SLG's Stockholm headquarters and respective overseas resort offices being rationalized. Following its major expansion SLG had approximately 50% of the Scandinavian market with the leading position in each of the Scandinavian countries. The acquisition of Spies gave Airtours full control of Scandinavia's largest charter airline Premiair.

The Scandinavian acquisitions brought with them hotel and holiday complex portfolios of 16 properties in the case of SLG and 25 properties in the case of Spies, located in many of the principal resorts served by the group's tour operations. Accommodation ownership allowed retention within the group of a higher proportion of resort expenditure and allowed the company to more accurately monitor customer tastes and preferences. By limiting hotel ownership to less than 20% of total accommodation requirements within any one area, the group was able to ensure high occupancy levels. Distinct accommodation brands were developed in order to satisfy the differing demands of the group's tour operations. The successful Sunwing brand was primarily designed for Scandinavian customers, whilst the Suncenter product was marketed through Airtours Holidays and catered largely for the needs of the UK market. Suncenters offered families an action packed home-from-home with many activities, lots of entertainment and children's clubs.

The acquisition of Sunquest Vacations in August 1995 established Airtours' presence in the North American market through its tour operating businesses in Ontario and western Canada and this was followed by the acquisition in August of Alba, another significant Canadian tour operator, in August of the following year. Airtours also made its first foray into the vast US market during 1996, deciding that the most cost effective entry vehicle would be through a 'greenfield' start-up operation capitalizing on the Sunquest brand name. Accordingly, Sunquest Holidays was formed under the leadership of John Trickett, who had previously held management positions within the Airtours Group in the UK prior to moving to California in 1989 where he had subsequently worked for other tour operators. The company operated its first programme of holidays in 1997, flying largely from California and focusing on Mexico, the Caribbean and Hawaii, all of which were also served by existing tour operations within the Airtours group. In 1996 Airtours' North American Leisure Group had built a business carrying almost 500 000 customers a year.

Cruising as a holiday choice grew in popularity during the 1990s in most Western economies. The UK market was still relatively small (representing about 500 000 customers in 1994) due to its image of high cost, exclusivity and older age group appeal, but this market doubled in size between 1994 and 2000. It also grew elsewhere in Europe but accounted for only 2% of European package holidays as at the year 2000. The North American cruise market developed in a different way with rapid growth in the later 1990s, a much younger customer base, specialist targeted cruise programmes and a product that offered high standards at competitive prices.

In 1994 Airtours created a cruise product, Sun Cruises, at a price level that would appeal to its existing customer base, and two ships containing a total of 1900 berths were purchased. Passengers flew from local airports in the UK, Scandinavia and North America to their point of embarkation (mainly in traditional Mediterranean resort areas and the Caribbean). The operational management of the ships was sub-contracted to an experienced cruise operator. Utilizing many of the services of the group's tour operating businesses and taking advantage of its distribution network substantially reduced costs and enabled a high quality product to be offered at prices significantly below those offered by traditional cruise operators. In only its second year of operation Sun Cruises achieved load factors approaching 100% and a UK market share of 18%.

The principal risks usually perceived by external observers of the travel industry for a group such as Airtours are those of under-utilized aircraft and excess hotel accommodation for which payment has already been made. The reality was that Airtours, in common with other major tour operators, had considerable flexibility in its contracting of both of these services. Aviation contracts with third party suppliers usually had a variety of cancellation options, which could be exercised once booking patterns have been established. This provided a margin of comfort when coupled with the way in which Airtours' in-house flying capacity was tailored to provide 60–70% of expected summer requirements. With regard to accommodation, only 10% of Airtours' requirements were booked on an irrevocable basis.

Perhaps more critical to the business, and common to other businesses dealing with international conditions, were changes in exchange and interest rates and aviation fuel. Airtours developed a policy of 'hedging' against all major risks on the financial and commodity markets prior to each brochure launch. Specifically, the group developed the practice of negotiating a range of forward contracts and options. In this way the costs of hedging these risks were built into the brochure selling prices.

The holiday business is well-known for generating substantial cash flows as customers traditionally pay in advance and the holiday companies pay their suppliers in arrears. There is a degree of seasonality to this cash flow but even at its lowest point, substantial cash balances are usually held by the tour operating companies. Effective 'cash management' of these balances therefore became a very important part of managing the business and interest receivable, as, with other tour operators, this represented a significant source of income. Surplus funds were placed on deposit with established international banks, but other investment opportunities were examined at times of falling interest rates.

Airtours – competing in the big league

For many years Airtours was seen as the darling of the City – a travel company that was professionally run and which reported steadily increasing turnover and profits. Its shares peaked at 540 pence in mid 1999 but then languished at prices of between 200 and 300 pence as a series of problems beset the company over 2000 and 2001. Europewide consolidation of the sector led to the emergence of powerful new competitive groupings while its own deals largely failed to impress. The years 1998 and 1999 saw a flurry of take-over activity in the UK tour operating sector with Airtours and other large groups consolidating their leading positions following a Monopolies and Merger Commission (now the UK Competition Commission) investigation. Thus Airtours added to its portfolio of activities by acquiring medium sized British operators (such as Cresta, Bridge, Panorama and Direct Holidays and the Bridge Travel Group) whilst Thomson added Crystal Holidays, and First Choice added Unijet.

Problems began for the group in 1999 when Airtours bought Travelworld, a 120 strong Yorkshire based travel agency for £12 million. Airtours had to beat off competition from rival companies to buy Travelworld, and post acquisition it rebranded the shops and bolted them on to its existing Going Places chain. Travelworld's financial position was less robust than it had been hoped at the time of the purchase and this raised questions about Airtours' management's astuteness in making the deal. Of greater strategic significance to the group however was the impact of the consolidation that swept through the sector.

'Scale matters in a business where the better performers only make a 4% profit margin,' said John Donaldson, Thomas Cook chief executive. 'If you can get cost efficiencies of 1 to 2 per cent through better buying, such as hotel rooms and aircraft fuel, that has a very material impact on profitability. That's what's driving consolidation.' Tour operating has always been viewed as a risky business where most profits are made during a short summer period. The tour operators responded to this in several ways. In the 1990s the sector increasingly became vertically integrated and horizontal expansion followed, first at the national level and then internationally when domestic opportunities became more limited. The new century, however has been characterized not by the largest players purchasing smaller, weaker rivals, but by consolidation among the largest players themselves, which has seen the emergence of four key groups: Preussag and Thomas Cook based in Germany and Airtours and First choice based in the UK.

The shape of the European industry was largely determined at corporate headquarters in Toronto, Canada and Hanover in Germany by the changing strategies of two large industrial companies. Thomson, the Canadian media group, withdrew from the sector by floating its Thomson Holiday group in the UK during 1998. Preussag AG, a German industrial and logistics group, decided to withdraw from these sectors in order to concentrate its activities on the travel industry. In 1999 Preussag purchased Germany's largest travel group (TUI) and followed up this purchase

a year later with the acquisition of Thomson Travel. The TUI purchase left Preussag with a stake in Thomas Cook, a first class brand name in the travel industry. European Community rules meant that the Thomas Cook holding had to be sold by Preussag when Thomson was subsequently purchased. C&N Touristic, Germany's second largest tour operating group (which was owned jointly by Lufthansa and Karstadt, a department store group) subsequently purchased Thomas Cook and later changed its name to Thomas Cook AG.

Airtours purchased its means of entry into the German market in 1998 when it purchased a minority stake in Frosch Touristik International (FTI), Germany's fourth ranked tour operating group. That sun-starved Germany and Britain emerged to dominate the industry in Europe is not surprising. They are the two largest European markets, with the Germans, who typically have six weeks annual holiday, spending £40 billion on international tourism – 20% more than the British figure. Airtours, however, in common with other British companies expanding in Germany, found the going difficult. Airtours discovered it had bought trouble in that the 2000 season produced losses of some £100 million for FTI, which resulted in Airtours taking full control of the company in late 2000. The difficulties were attributed to the overestimation of capacity requirements for the summer season and being left with unfilled allocations.

Although (as at 2002) further consolidation remained likely, there were legal constraints upon further consolidation. In 1999 Airtours' £950 million bid for First Choice plc was blocked by the European Commission on the grounds that it would have left three vertically integrated tour operators (Thomson, Airtours and Thomas Cook) controlling over 80% of some short-haul tour operating destinations. Although Airtours did not rule out a further bid in the future, and lodged an appeal against the decision, First Choice emerged reinvigorated having modified its strategic positioning. First Choice's emphasis began to shift away from high volume; low margin businesses towards a portfolio of individually branded more specialist products offering potentially higher returns. Nevertheless, cost efficiency was maintained through the utilization of centralised systems and corporate buying power.

The vertically integrated model whereby a single group became the full owner (or had equity in) airline operations, tour operations and travel retailing was, however the subject of further development. Until the mid to late 1990s most groups avoided investment in accommodation, believing that the high capital costs and inherent interest rate and property risks involved were at variance with the types of businesses they had traditionally run. Competition from operators around Europe, the growth of new markets in Eastern and Central Europe, and a slow-down in the rate of new building led to a shortage of good quality accommodation at key resorts (particularly in the Balearic and Canary Islands). The shortage increasingly led to a re-assessment of the position with regard to property and hotel ownership on the part of the big travel groups.

Airtours became hoteliers with the purchase of Scandinavian Leisure Group and then further embraced accommodation ownership with the purchase of several hotels and apartment complexes. In January 2000, for example, the company purchased for £63.4 million the Bellevue apartments, Europe's largest complex situated in Majorca. This not only gave the company access to high quality accommodation in an important location, but it also denied others such access at a time when increasingly stringent planning procedures prevented large scale new developments.

In 1997 Airtours and Carnival Cruise Line (the world's largest) agreed to jointly purchase the Costa cruise line based in Florida at a cost (to Airtours) of £59 million. Sales through Airtours' distribution network were significant but far from spectacular and the sale of the assets to the partner Carnival in summer 2000 for £350 million represented an opportunity to realize the value of a non-core asset at a time when a large amount of additional cruising capacity was about to enter the market. The transaction left Airtours better positioned to exploit its business model in Europe and North America and to seek investments, which would further support and enhance the group's core activities.

Management, staff and systems

The transition from its single business core of tour operating into an integrated international travel business was rapid, and this placed considerable demands on management, staff and systems. Considerable resources were devoted to staff recruitment, management training and the pro-

curement of the necessary computer hardware and software in order to enhance the group's competitive position. As at the year 2002, Airtours, now renamed the MyTravel group, was managed on a decentralized basis with a small head office team and a separate Board of Directors for each of the main divisions: UK Tour Operations, UK Retail, Scandinavian Leisure Group, North American Leisure Group, Aviation division, and Cruise and Hotels division.

Such rapid development did not always run smoothly. Airtours was a long-time favourite target for attacks by sections of the media, attracting poor ratings by reports from The Consumers' Association, and attracting more than its share of press criticism over quality standards. During the late 1990s, Airtours made strenuous efforts to ensure that customers knew what they were buying and that they got what they were promised. Each of the group's divisions operated its own quality control initiatives relying heavily on customer feed-back, and although it remained an area for some concern relative to competitors, there was a marked reduction in the proportion of complaints relative to holidays sold.

Management clashes led to a series of high profile departures from Airtours. A new director was brought from a cinema chain to shake up the UK Retail division during 2000, and subsequently sacked five directors of Going Places. The sacked directors launched actions in the High Court to recover money they claimed they were owed with two of them later being re-employed by First Choice plc. Meanwhile at the group level, Harry Coe and Hugh Collinson, longstanding board members and Airtours' founder David Crossland's 'right hand men', both retired. Perhaps the most damaging, however, was the defection of two senior executives during 2001 to arch-rival, Thomson.

The imponderable factor for all firms was the future of direct dealings with customers as opposed to dealings through intermediaries such as travel agents. Airtours invested heavily in call centres, and channels such as TV text services and TV channels dedicated to travel grew in importance, but capturing e-commerce business remained the elusive prize. Airtours chief executive Tim Byrne hoped to make huge savings by persuading people to book direct rather than on the High Street. Just two years after a big UK retail expansion (of Going Places) he closed 120 of 867 shops in 2001, and more were expected to follow.

Airtours struck a £20 million deal with TV text service Teletext to distribute holidays on digital channels, but it was the £240 million purchase of US Travel Services International (which included mytravel.com) in 2000, which was viewed as the key deal in distribution.

The acquisition brought expenditure by Airtours on its net strategy to more than £340 million, with few discernible signs of success. The MyTravel brand was launched in Autumn 2001 and was rolled out across the shops and brochures to raise visibility. The Airtours name had served the group well and continued to be the largest tour-operating brand, Airtours Holidays, but it was thought that benefits could be gained from aligning the plc name with the new branded distribution. The new name was placed on each of the 115 million brochures produced each year, the 1000 retail outlets and on each piece of stationery.

Although it cost 15% of turnover to book through travel agents and just 5% online everything hung on persuading people to book their holidays in this way. Consumer purchasing behaviour was deeply embedded and slow to change. Travel agents, like shoe shops, were often found clustered on a high street allowing comparisons to be made and bargains to be struck by customers. Going to buy the holiday was associated with the excitement of the holiday itself and so the change to online booking was not expected to be fast growing. Internet bookings struggled to get off the ground in the UK as elsewhere, with, as at 2002, package holidays bought in this way only accounting for 1% of business.

Appendix 4.1

MyTravel Plc group structure (2002)

		Markets			
		United Kingdom	Scandinavia	Germany	North America
Products	Distribution	Going Places Late Escapes MyTravel	Spies Tjaerborg Ving Shops MyTravel	Fti Touristik	World Choice Travel MyTravel Cruises Only
	Tour operations	Airtours Aspro Tradewinds EuroSites Direct Holidays Manos Panorama Cresta	Ving Always Saga Spies Tjaerborg	Fti Touristik	Sunquest Vacations AlbaTours Vacation Express
	Aviation	Airtours International	Premiair		Skyservice*
	Cruise and Hotels	Resort Hotels: Sunwing, Tenerife Sol†, Hotetur† Cruise: Sun Cruises			

* Long term contract
† Joint ventures

Note: The Board of Directors comprises the chairman (David Crossland), chief executive (Tim Byrne) the group finance director, chairmen of the operating divisions (UK Leisure Group, Scandinavian Leisure Group, German Leisure Group, MyTravel North America and the Aviation division) and three non-executive directors. Each operating division had its own directors chaired by a main board member

Appendix 4.2

Some comments on David Crossland – MyTravel Chairman

Speaking in 1992 chairman David Crossland said, 'I certainly can't claim that I sat down 20 years ago and created a master plan for a travel business, but I did always believe that if you really wanted to achieve something you could.' From the earliest days, Crossland wanted to give holidaymakers a good value-for-money product and believed that if they received such a product that they would come back for more. That desire is something that has not changed and it proved to be correct. He recently said that '[the only people] I really worry about are those who buy our products, the end users. I care passionately about them.'

Initially, Airtours was very much a family business. It had very little capital and Crossland knew the only way the company would grow was through reinvestment and hard work. Today it is a big organization, but Crossland argues that the management and staff all share that original commitment towards passengers and they work extremely hard and show great loyalty. 'My enthusiasm seems to be infectious and rubs off on them,' he said. 'It is still a family business, but now it has become the Airtours family rather than the Crossland family.'

Crossland has said that he only really has one talent and that is the ability to appoint managers who are far cleverer than he is – people who are extremely professional and absolute experts in their fields. The success of the company has a great deal to do with them. Another key to the success, he said was that 'we believe in our product. We believe we have a really good product, that our brochures are clear, clean and easily understood, and that our advertising is effective. We have grown and changed, but our roots are in travel retailing and we understand, from inside knowledge, just how retailers work.'

In 2002 David Crossland appointed Tim Byrne, Airtours' managing director, as chief executive to oversee the day-to-day running of the company. Crossland's plan was then to concentrate on exploring new opportunities. This came in the wake of news that Airtours' underlying profits had fallen 30% against the previous year. Pre-tax profits were up to £211.4m from £125.9m, but the problem with FTI, its German business (which lost £100m during these two years) is still being addressed. MyTravel's mistake was entering the German market with a minority stake. It acquired control only during 2001, but not in time to reverse the damage caused by excess capacity in the local holiday market. Yet Crossland saw the problems as a blip: 'You've got to get it into perspective,' he said. 'When we floated in 1987 we were making £2m and when we started we employed two people.'

A key mistake was made in 1999 when the company thought it was taking a low-risk route by only buying 30% of FTI but it actually turned out to be worse because, in Crossland's words, 'We did not have control and if we had had control this year, which has been a difficult year in the German market, the losses would not have been as bad.' Airtours finally took full control of FTI in September 2001 and big changes were made in the German subsidiary. Overseas bed rates were renegotiated using the MyTravel bargaining strength, the cost of sales were brought down and the company was restructured. Crossland added that 'it grew very fast. It had an entrepreneur who would not take advice about putting a structure in and was trying to manage all the divisions himself.'

Having been the driving force behind MyTravel's growth and then the architect of its move into Germany, Crossland's challenge became to restore investor confidence. It has been suggested that MyTravel is a one-man band, but Crossland responds by saying that 'we have some strong managers and directors who run big businesses all over the world . . . but I'm the front person and take responsibility when we have a difficult year.' The appointment of Tim Byrne was clearly important for the group; as Crossland explained, 'We need one guy sitting on the top of each division and driving out the costs and sweeping the synergies across the matrix rather than just down it. It will leave me able to spot opportunities, which is what I'm good at.'

Appendix 4.3

Statement from Airtours 1996 report and accounts

Three years ago we concluded that in order to maintain our rate of growth we would need to develop our business overseas. At that time we stated our objectives of achieving, in the medium term, an even split of profits between UK and overseas businesses.

In a short period of time, Airtours has transformed itself from a purely UK based company into an internationally diversified leisure group which is now the largest air inclusive tour operator in the world. The growth of the group continues to produce economies of scale and by managing capacity across our different markets we obtain the maximum utilization of our aircraft, cruise ships and hotels.

For future growth we shall seek to develop or acquire businesses operating in markets which we understand, where we can add value and where the acquired business has high quality management or alternatively can be readily integrated into our existing management infrastructures.

Appendix 4.4

Statement from Airtours 2001 report and accounts

Reorganization and consolidation

The consolidation of the major UK tour operator into a single site in Rochdale has been successfully implemented and the reorganization of Scandinavian businesses from a brand based to a country based organization was completed in early 2001. The most dramatic changes were seen within the German business. A new management team was put in place and the complete reorganization led to significant reductions in the German workforce as efficiencies were identified. The closure of the dedicated charter carrier FlyFTi will result in significant savings going forward. The consolidation of the North American charter operations under the Airtours North America name was also completed.

Operational flexibility

The business model favoured by MyTravel ensures inherent flexibility to deal with capacity reductions. The under-sizing of the aircraft fleet and to an even greater extent hotels and cruising ensures capacity can be reduced to meet market conditions without significant exposure to the costs associated with under-utilized assets. Over-capacity in distribution however enables the group to widen its product offerings through featuring favoured products provided by third parties.

Appendix 4.5

Tui AG

According to Dr Michael Frenzel, the boss of German holiday giant Preussag, the package tour must become more European. Although there will still be room for diversity and differences in national tastes will still be important, Preussag believes that further integration at a European level will take place. Preussag's £1.8 billion take-over of Thomson Travel in August 2000 made it the largest package holiday firm in the world. Frenzel's opinion is one that cannot be ignored.

Frenzel, 53, manages Preussag from an austere headquarters in Hanover, where for the past six years he has plotted the company's transformation from an industrial conglomerate into a more focused package holiday giant. After joining the company in 1994, Frenzel has embarked on a high-risk strategy. While rapidly withdrawing from the group's poorly performing industrial interests, he has set about acquiring prized assets amongst European holiday companies. As an industrial group there were about 50 separate businesses but importantly Preussag were not number one at anything.

Leisure and tourism presented major opportunities for growth. Rivals cannot help but admire the single-mindedness demonstrated in his plans for the tour group. In 1998, the German travel giant Tui and airline Hapag-Lloyd were acquired, followed by British holiday and financial services group Thomas Cook. Then, after acquiring a couple of travel agency chains, Frenzel went for his holiday dream in the form of Thomson Travel. He snatched it at the eleventh hour from C&N Touristic, Germany's second-biggest travel company. He had promised to turn Thomas Cook into the British market leader ahead of Thomson and Airtours (MyTravel), but sold Thomas Cook to another German tour operator as soon as Thomson came on the market. Thomson represented the bigger opportunity.

Control of two of the UK's biggest tour companies make the two German operators the two most powerful holiday firms in Europe. This is all a far cry from just a few years ago, when British firms such as MyTravel were homing in on German companies. After a period of aggressive selling and buying Tui as it is now called is concentrating on digesting and integrating the companies. Twelve teams of executives have been established to ease the integration of the various new companies in what has been dubbed Operation Titan.

'It's not a question of cost savings,' Frenzel maintains 'it's about being more flexible in our destinations, in buying fuel for our airlines and negotiating on hotel beds. Shifting over-capacity of tourists from one subsidiary's resort to another to take advantage of synergies also offers opportunities.'

Appendix 4.6

MyTravel in the wake of the 11 September 2001 terrorist attacks

The large tour operators faced a difficult situation in the wake of the 11 September terrorist strikes The events caused early bookings for summer 2002 to crash by between 30 and 40 per cent. However, instead of the lean pickings which many experts predicted for tour operators, swift and firm action restored 2002's profit prospects. In an industry often criticized for targeting market share over profitability, the events of 11 September provide an illustration of the vulnerability of the industry to external shocks, whilst the events following the attacks show a new willingness amongst managers to target profitability by cutting capacity.

After 11 September, the large tour operators cut (by about 15%) the number of holidays and aircraft seats they were willing to supply to the UK market for the 2002 season. At the same time research predicted a strong recovery in customer booking. By cutting supply while demand remained strong, holiday prices remained firm, boosting yields and profits. For investors used to seeing the holiday companies swamp the market with cheap deals to drive market share rather than earnings, this was good news. A study by the Centre for Economic Business Research into the impact of 11 September and subsequent conflicts suggested that a 5 per cent reduction in demand for overseas holidays was likely, which means the industry's capacity cuts more than compensate.

Appendix 4.7

MyTravel – financial statements

MyTravel – financial summary (1986–2001)

	2001	2000	1999	1998	1997	1996	1995	1994	1993	1992	1991	1990	1989	1988	1987	1986
Turnover (£m)	5061.4	3949.0	3309.3	2753.4	2235.6	1717.9	1317.8	971.7	615.6	405.6	289.5	183.0	155.6	102.5	68.3	55.0
Profit before tax (£m)	81.3	211.4	125.9	125.7	117.2	86.8	59.1	75.8	45.6	36.5	27.5	6.3	5.2	4.1	2.0	2.0
Earnings per ordinary share	6.28p	35.98p	19.74p	21.14p	20.62p	45.63p	32.76p	41.79p	29.22p	24.47p	24.68p	6.69p	5.12p	17.43p	8.55p	8.53p
Dividends per ordinary share	9.50p	9.00p	8.25p	7.50p	6.67p	16.00p	14.00p	12.00p	9.00p	7.25p	5.75p	2.03p	1.72p	6.25p	n/a	n/a
No. of employees	27 868	24 316	20 226	17 354	14 565	12 198	9896	6337	3819	1349	946	571	389	310	212	283

MyTravel – Business Segment Analysis

	Turnover (£m)		Profits before tax (£m)		Net assets (£m)	
	2001	2000	2001	2000	2001	2000
UK						
Continuing	2672.2	2323.8	110.6	279.9	106.9	282.6
Other Europe						
Continuing					286.5	273.3
Scandinavia and Netherlands	1018.3	926.8	31.2	20.7		
FTi	684.4	92.8	–52.6	–13.3		
Acquisitions	14.0	–	0.8	–		
Discontinued	22.3	143.3	–2.0	–36.1		
North America						
Continuing	641.8	462.8	–10.8	–19.3	128.5	–12.3
Acquisitions	8.4	–	–	–		
Joint Ventures						
Continuing						
FTi	–	293.9	–	–49.6		
Other	28.1	8.5	4.1	2.2		
Discontinued						
Costa Cruises	–	183.4	–	26.9		
TOTAL	5089.5	4435.3	81.3	211.4	521.9	543.6

Appendix 4.7
MyTravel – financial statements – continued

MyTravel Balance Sheet

		2001	2000	1999	1998	1997
Fixed assets	Tangible	431.1	513.5	417.8	310.7	261.4
	Intangible	540.2	534.8	36.9	–	–
	Investments	83.7	55.3	116.9	82.7	63.0
	TOTAL	1055.0	1103.6	571.6	393.4	324.4
Current assets	Stock	13.3	17.2	11.4	17.0	6.4
	Debtors	838.5	712.2	550.5	403.5	331.7
	Investments	0	0	0	0	0
	Bank and Deposits	378.6	793.3	554.2	364.2	406.6
	TOTAL	1230.4	1522.7	1116.1	784.7	744.7
Current liabilities	Creditors	–359.0	–462.6			
	Loans/overdraft	–16.9	–33.8			
	Other	–827.4ᵃ	–777.5ᵃ			
	TOTAL	–1203.3	–1273.9	–948.8	–802.0	–747.2
Non current liabilities		–560.2	–695.4	–490.8	–210.1	–562.6
Total assets less liabilities		521.9	543.6	248.1	166.0	240.7
Shareholders funds	Share capital	49.3	49.1	47.8	47.5	47.2
	Reserves	263.0	285.7	200.3	118.5	193.5
Non equity preference shares		209.6	208.8	–	–	–
	TOTAL	521.9	543.6	248.1	166.0	240.7

Notes: ᵃOf which Revenue received in advance = 310.8 (2001), 333.4 (2002) and Accruals and deferred income = 330.2 (2001), 250.5 (2000).

Appendix 4.8

Major competitors – financial statements

Major competitors – turnover and profits

		2000	1999
Turnover	Tui (Euro m)	21,854.0	16,501.0
	of which tourism (Euro m)	10,562.1	7,164.8
	F Choice (£ m)	1,880.7	1,465.8
	Thomas Cook (DM m)	9,740.8	9,073.9
Profit Before Tax	Tui (Euro m)	402.5	345.4
	of which Tourism (Euro m)	423.3	307.5
	F Choice (£ m)	68.9	38.0
	Thomas Cook (DM m)	220.4	209.5

Note: Euro/£ = 1.65, DM/$ = 3.20, $/£ = 1.40

Balance sheet First Choice Holidays plc (£M)

		2000	1999	1998	1997	1996
Fixed assets	Tangible					
	Intangible					
	Investments					
	TOTAL	462.1	134.3	58.3	51.3	58.9
Current assets	Stock					
	Debtors					
	Investments					
	Bank and Deposits					
	Prepayments					
	TOTAL	704.9	417.6	380.9	264.4	238.5
Current liabilities	Creditors					
	Loans/overdraft					
	Other					
	TOTAL	−660.1	−375.2	−325.4	−227.2	−206.2
Non current liabilities		−89.6	−57.5	−45.7	−28.1	−30.8
Total assets less liabilities		417.3	119.2	68.1	60.4	60.4
Shareholders funds	Share capital	213.2	13.1	13.1	13.1	7.1
	Reserves	204.1	106.1	55.0	47.3	53.3
	TOTAL	417.3	119.2	68.1	60.4	60.4

Note: Royal Caribbean Cruise Lines invested £200 million in a strategic alliance with First Choice during 2000. The alliance provides the cruise line with a 20% stake and enhanced distribution whilst providing First Choice with access to high quality cruising products.

Sources

Company reports – various years; newspaper articles – various

Case 5

Competitive strategy at Ryanair

Nigel Evans and David Campbell

The launch and early development

Ryanair, now firmly established as Europe's largest low fares airline, began operations back in 1985 with the launch of a daily flight on a 15 seater turbo prop aircraft between Waterford Airport in the south east of Ireland and London Gatwick. The company had a commitment to low fare air travel and making air travel affordable for people in Ireland and the UK, but in the early years problems were encountered in delivering this commitment. In the company's first year, its 57 employees carried just over 5000 passengers on its one route. In 1986, Ryanair broke the high fare cartel, which was then operated by the two state airlines Aer Lingus and British Airways, on the Dublin–London route. The Dublin–London route had stagnated at about 1 million passengers per annum between 1975 and 1985, and was then characterized by some of the highest air fares in Europe. Prior to Ryanair, the normal air fare between Dublin and London in 1985 was £209 return. Ryanair began services on the 23 May 1986 with two turbo prop BA 748 aircraft and an introductory launch fare of £94.99 return. Ryanair was the first European airline specifically set up to offer low fares on short-haul intra-European routes.

Over the next three years (1987–9) Ryanair expanded rapidly, opening many new routes between Ireland and the UK, increasing the fleet by adding BAC 1–11 jets, and ATR 42 turbo prop aircraft. Whilst customers continued to flock to Ryanair for the low airfares, costs were not controlled, and the company continued to rack up losses. By 1989, the company employed 350 people, operated 14 aircraft (four different types), was carrying 600 000 passengers a year, but had managed to lose £20m in just four years.

New management team

Under a new management team, a major overhaul of the airline was undertaken in 1990/91, with Ryanair relaunched as the first of a new breed of 'low fares/no frills' airline. In relaunching the airline in this way, the management was adapting the formula so successfully pioneered by Southwest Airlines in the USA in the period since deregulation of the American aviation market in 1978. Non-profitable routes were eliminated, the network was cut back from nineteen to only five routes, the turbo prop aircraft were disposed of and air fares across the remaining network were substantially reduced with 70% of all seats offered at the two lowest fares. On Dublin–London, for example, a new promotional fare of just £69 return was launched which stimulated a whole new era of growth for Ryanair. By 1991, Ryanair was operating an all-jet fleet of 6 BAC 1–11 aircraft, employing 350 people, carrying 700 000 passengers on just five routes, and it had recorded its first ever profit (despite the damage done to the airline industry by the Gulf War in 1991).

Over the next couple of years, schedules on the key Dublin–London route were increased, average air fares were lowered, new routes were launched from Dublin to Birmingham, Glasgow, Manchester and Gatwick, while traffic continued to grow strongly. By 1994, Ryanair was employing over 500 people, carrying over 1.5 million passengers per annum, offering lower than ever air fares of just £49 return on the Dublin–London route, and it recorded its fourth continuous year of profitability. In 1994 also came the acquisition of Ryanair's first Boeing 737 aircraft, with an order for six 737–200 series aircraft (130 seats) being purchased direct from Boeing. Over the following three years a further 15 737–200 aircraft were purchased, bringing the fleet to 21 737–200s. To coincide with this expansion of the fleet, many more new routes were opened by Ryanair between Ireland and the UK. Increased frequencies were offered on all routes and air fares were lowered yet further. As a result, in 1995, by the time of the airline's tenth anniversary, Ryanair had become the biggest passenger carrier on the Dublin–London route, with total passengers of 2.25 million per annum and a work force of over 600 people.

1997 – a milestone year

The year 1997 marked a milestone for Ryanair. Thanks to the full EU air transport deregulation, the airline was free for the first time to open up new routes to continental Europe. Services were launched from London Stansted to Stockholm and Oslo, as well as from Dublin to Paris and Brussels. Again, Ryanair entering these markets offered air fares which were more than 50% lower than the cheapest fares then provided by the flag carrier airlines. Passengers responded enthusiastically and in great numbers to the arrival of low fares for the first time in these European markets. Ryanair was the first low fare airline to offer scheduled services from the UK to Continental Europe and vice versa. The same year, 1997, also saw Ryanair Holdings plc float on the Dublin and New York stock exchanges enabling all of its then 700 people to become shareholders in the airline. At the time the airline was capitalized at a market value of IR£300m, and was carrying over 3 million passengers per annum on its network of 18 routes. Ryanair was competing head to head with many of Europe's biggest airlines including British Airways, SAS, Alitalia, Lufthansa, Air France and Aer Lingus.

Continuing growth

In 1999, Ryanair announced its next major investment programme with a US$2 billion order for up to 45 new Boeing 737–800 series aircraft. These are the latest and most modern aircraft manufactured by Boeing. The first five aircraft were delivered to Ryanair in 1999, and five more were scheduled for delivery each year thereafter. In 1999 Ryanair announced another set of record results, operating 35 routes to 11 countries, and carrying almost 6 million passengers. The company was then employing over 1200 people, and also had its shares listed on the London Stock Exchange as well as in Dublin and New York (Nasdaq). In 1999, Ryanair was awarded 'Airline of the Year' by the Irish Air Transport Users Committee, and was voted one of the 'best managed' airlines in the world by the International Aviation Week magazine. In 2000, the airline launched its website at www.Ryanair.com, which within three months of its launch was taking over 50 000 bookings per week by offering low air fares which started from as little as £1 return plus taxes on the Glasgow–London and £9 return plus taxes on the Dublin–London routes.

The airline continues to grow through the addition of extra routes and hubs carrying about 7 million passengers a year with hubs at Dublin and London (Stansted), and further hubs under development at Brussels (Charleoi) and Frankfurt (Hahn). The total network has grown to over 45 routes across 11 countries served with a fleet of 31 aircraft and 1400 people.

An interview with Ryanair chief executive

[The interview with Micheal O'Leary reproduced below was conducted by Tom Chesshyre and appeared in the *Travel* section of *The Times* newspaper in January 2002.]

Michael O'Leary is late, just like so many of his aeroplanes. 'I'm terribly sorry,' gasps Ryanair's chief executive, as he rushes in 15 minutes after our scheduled appointment. 'You haven't been waiting long have you? Let me get you a tea. Or would you prefer coffee? Would you like a muffin, or something? No, are you sure? OK back in a couple of seconds.' And off he dashes to the counter of the Metro cafe at Stansted airport, hub for the airline's operation in the UK – looking apologetic and glancing over anxiously at me as he makes his order. All of which is making me feel just a little bit confused. You see, the *Times Travel* desk receives more complaints about Ryanair than any other airline – regarding everything from delays, to poor in-flight service, to damaged luggage, to lengthy check-in queues.

The Irish-based carrier, which has spearheaded the low-cost airline phenomenon in the past decade and which carried ten million passengers in the past year, crops up time and again in letters. A new complaint arrives virtually every week. Yet, as O'Leary is only too quick to point out, Ryanair rarely apologises or tries to make up for these problems. 'Are we going to say sorry for our lack of customer service?' he asks rhetorically, putting down his cheese and ham croissant (after offering part of it, most un-Ryanairishly, to me). 'Absolutely not. If a plane is cancelled will we put you up in a hotel overnight? Absolutely not. If a plane is delayed, will we give you a voucher for a restaurant? Absolutely not.'

But isn't this a bit harsh, I ask. Surely Ryanair and O'Leary – who has agreed to meet *Times Travel* to counter some of the complaints we have received about his airline – must care about customer service, to some extent? It can't just be a matter of saying 'tough luck' if a flight is delayed – can it? Whatever happened to that old business maxim: the customer is always right? 'Listen,' he says bullishly. 'Our customer service is about the most well-defined in the world. We guarantee to give you the lowest airfare. You get a safe flight. You get a normally on-time flight. That's the package. We don't and won't give you anything more on top of that.' He pauses to take a sip of his tea – something passengers would have to pay for on board Ryanair flights. You even have to shell out for a packet of peanuts or a glass of mineral water. 'Listen, we care for our customers in the most fundamental way possible: we don't screw them every time we fly them.' (O'Leary, I soon realise, doesn't mince his words.) 'We care for our customers by giving them the cheapest airfares. I have no time for certain large airlines which say they care and then screw you for six or seven hundred quid almost every time you fly.'

I'm getting the picture. But the fact is, *Times Travel* still receives more complaints about Ryanair than any other airline. And many people are sick of the 'we've-got-the-cheapest-flights-so-grin-and-bear-it' approach – as the Air Transport Users' Council (AUC), which monitors airline complaints in the UK, testifies. The AUC says that Ryanair is one of the worst offending airlines; that it seems to 'stick two fingers up' at its disgruntled passengers; and that its delays record is poor for many European destinations. Recent findings from the Consumers' Association also show that fewer people would recommend Ryanair to a friend than any of the other main low-cost carriers: easyJet, buzz and Go. Isn't it time Ryanair moved on a bit and stopped thinking about customers as cattle to be transported from A to B? This sets off an O'Leary tirade, about the 'British Airways of this world', so I ask him about some of the specific complaints received from readers in recent weeks. For example, several have complained about how difficult it is to talk to anyone at the airline when they have a problem. Frustrated customers say they have to make endless phone calls before finally getting through to an operator. Doesn't this seem as though Ryanair is treating them with disdain?

'Our position is simple,' O'Leary says. 'Generally speaking, we won't take any phone calls because they keep you on the bloody phone all day. We employ four people in our customer care department,' he continues. 'Every complaint must be put in writing and we undertake to respond to that complaint within 24 hours. Anyway, do you know what 70 per cent of our complaints are about?' he says, sounding a bit aggrieved. 'They're about people who want to make changes to what are clearly stated as being "non-changeable, non-transferable and non-refundable" tickets.' He adopts a 'complaining' voice, mimicking a customer: 'I've changed my mind. My granny wasn't feeling well. I couldn't travel because I couldn't take time off work.' Aren't you being slightly cruel? 'No because even if you can't change your ticket and you've got to buy a second one, you're still going to save money compared with buying a single ticket from the major airlines. Anyway, with our new system you can make some changes. If you pay 20 euros (£12.30) you can change the time of your flight, but not the name on the ticket.' Which is a start.

Moving on to other reader gripes, I ask why Ryanair isn't more explicit about its use of secondary airports that are often miles from the destination that the airline headlines in its adverts. For example, Ryanair says it flies to Frankfurt, when it actually flies to Frankfurt's secondary airport, Hahn, 60 miles and a one-hour bus ride from Frankfurt City centre. Although it says so in the small print, surely the use of such airports should be made crystal clear to potential passengers? 'We'll be happy to do that some day, when other airlines describe Heathrow as being 35 miles outside London,' O'Leary says. 'This secondary airport matter is a typical one run up by the big airlines. They constantly say low-cost airlines take you to the middle of nowhere. It's what they said about Stansted ten years ago when we first flew here. They said: 'Oh, but Stansted's in Essex'. What? Like Heathrow's in Pall Mall or something?' But Hahn is still twice as far from the centre as Heathrow. And it doesn't have a 15-minute rail link. 'Look,' O'Leary says. 'The more experienced traveller fundamentally wants to know: "Is that airport close to my destination?" If it's the main airport or not, that makes no difference to them.'

Regardless, many *Times* readers say they are frustrated at lead-in fares that are often unavailable. They say advertisements for £1 tickets encourage them to contact Ryanair, only to find that available tickets are much more expensive. The Advertising Standards Authority has upheld several complaints regarding fares headlined in Ryanair promotions. This really gets O'Leary going: 'When British Airways did its low-fares promotion it was only on a tiny percentage of sales,' he says. 'This compares with 75 per cent of our airfares that are sold in the two lowest categories. No other airline even comes close. And look what we did after September 11: instead of sitting aircraft on the ground, we carried more passengers. We gave out 300,000 seats for free. We sold a million seats for £9.99. That's caring, for you.'

Which brings us back to the whole question of customer service – and O'Leary's argument that low-cost airlines can get away with a no-frills service precisely because the fares themselves are low-cost. We don't seem to be getting anywhere. O'Leary says the proof of the pudding is that Ryanair attracts ten million passengers a year, a number he claims will treble by 2010 – more than BA. 'You can look at us in the most caustic light possible, that we're cheap Bush Paddies – but you can't get around the fact that people want to fly with us. In 16 months flying to Hahn airport, we've gone from nowhere to an 18 per cent market share.'

So how come we receive more complaints about Ryanair than easyJet, buzz and Go, its low-cost competitors? 'Just look at Frankfurt,' O'Leary says. 'That growth suggests to me that people really don't have much of a problem with us, do they?'

Sources

Tom Chesshyre, 'It's cheap but why not more cheerful?', *The Times, Travel Section*, Saturday 5 January 2002. Reproduced with permission, ©Times Newspapers Limited 2002
www.Ryanair.com
UK Outbound Tour Operations

Case 6

The UK outbound tour operations industry

Nigel Evans

The 'package' concept

Tourists travelling abroad can purchase each separate component of a holiday – accommodation, transportation, activities, ground handling, etc. – as individual items. During the 1960s, however, the foreign inclusive tour or 'package' holiday became established in Western Europe and brought with it a substantial expansion in the numbers of tourists venturing abroad.

A 'package' was defined by the European Commission in 1990 as a pre-arranged combination, sold or offered for sale at an inclusive price, of not less than two of the following three elements: transport; accommodation; and other tourist services not ancillary to transport or accommodation and accounting for a significant part of the package.

The role of the tour operators was the key element in the expansion of the package concept, which has continued to grow since it began in the 1950s. This role goes beyond that of the whole-saler, in that tour operators not only purchase or reserve the separate components in bulk but, in combining these components into an 'inclusive tour', they also become producers, since a new product, the inclusive tour or package holiday, is created. The traditional appeal of the tour operators' product has been to offer a complete holiday package at the lowest price to a population often lacking the linguistic knowledge or the knowledge and confidence to organize independent travel. As a result tour operation has become the dominant feature of the holiday market not only in the United Kingdom but also in most tourist-generating countries.

Benefits of the package concept

Despite some industry commentators' comments over the years suggesting that the package holiday's days may be numbered (because many tourists have become more 'worldly-wise' and are prepared to travel independently), growth in the industry has been fuelled by three key selling points:

- the convenience of purchasing all the elements of the product in one purpose designed 'bundle';
- delivery of product quality assurance, reliability and protection;
- perceived good value prices.

But although the future of the 'package' seems assured, changes in consumer preferences and in the business environment are changing the characteristics of these packages, which will, in turn, have an effect on the future structure of this industrial sector. The tour operating sector as a whole (and the independent sector in particular), is facing a number of pressures which have led to a marked differences in recent performance.

The growth of UK outbound tour operations

Vladimar Raitz, a Russian émigré, is widely credited with operating the first air inclusive tour (AIT) charter to Corsica in 1950, at an all-inclusive price of £32.10. Part of his original company, Horizon, continued until recent years as a trading name of Thomson. Others who pioneered AITs during the 1950s in the UK were Captain Ted Langton, who set up Universal Skytours (which was also later to become part of Thomson); Joe and Syril Shuman, founders of Global Holidays; Christopher and Stephen Lord whose Lord brothers firm was later absorbed by Laker Airways; George Jackman and Wilf Jones, who built up Cosmos; and Harry Chandler, whose family continues to control The Travel Club of Upminster, founded in 1936.

Other companies missed out on the early market opportunities. Thomas Cook never achieved the market leadership in air holidays that it had in rail holidays, while British European Airways (BEA), a forerunner of British Airways, was slow to react to the threat posed by the charter airlines. In the 1950s foreign travel remained a luxury commodity within the reach of only a privileged few who had both plenty of free time and considerable purchasing power. The market changed during the 1960s, from that of a privileged 'niche' market to a 'mass' tourism market as a result of innovations in aircraft technology, changes in labour legislation (which provided for paid holidays in most European countries), and

changes to the structure of the tour operating industry itself. Large companies had begun buying into tour operating as early as 1956 when Great Universal Stores acquired Global, but the industry remained highly fragmented during the 1950s and early 1960s.

The industry of the early 1960s was also beset by a number of company failures, including the failure in 1964 of Fiesta Tours, a major tour operator of the period. The Association of British Travel Agents (ABTA) had to step in to rescue customers stranded abroad and in the aftermath calls were made for statutory controls of the burgeoning tour operating sector. ABTA responded from November 1966 with the introduction of the so-called 'Stabilizer Resolution'. Stabilizer was an attempt by ABTA to regulate the UK travel industry whereby ABTA member agents could sell only the foreign inclusive tours of ABTA tour operators, while ABTA tour operators could only sell through ABTA agents (or direct). It thus became impossible to build up a major market presence without belonging to ABTA. The Stabilizer Resolution did indeed help to stabilise the industry as the rate of failures fell after its introduction. Stabilizer remained in force until 1993 when ABTA relinquished the requirement upon the introduction of the EC directive on Package Travel, one effect of which was to require tour operators to provide financial protection to customers under law.

New entrants and consolidation

The strategic entry into the marketplace of the International Thomson Organization (ITO) in 1965 proved to be a major turning point for the industry. It represented the initiation of a period of consolidation within the industry which continued until the late 1980s. The introduction of ITO meant the entry to the UK tour operations industry of a large, sophisticated and diversified international group of companies. During the summer of 1965 Thomson had around 100,000 holidays on offer. The air inclusive tour (AIT) market (which is regulated in the UK by the Civil Aviation Authority (CAA) through the Air Travel Organizers' Licences (ATOLS) it issues each year) grew enormously during the period, but detailed figures are only available from 1976. Although many operators do not use their full ATOL allocation, the licences issued give an indication of the size of the total market and relative market shares.

The reasons for the rapid growth of the UK outbound AIT market and that of the operators are inextricably linked but perhaps two major factors stand out. First, many UK residents travel abroad for their holidays in order to obtain reliable sunshine and warmth. The UK's island location has necessitated the development of well-organized, packaged transportation to service this need. Second, UK residents accord holidays and travel a high priority in terms of their discretionary expenditure even in times of relative economic hardship.

Relatively low barriers to entry and continual striving among operators for increased market share led to price wars (particularly in the early 1970s and the mid 1980s), which resulted in a highly volatile record of profitability over the period. The price wars, low margins and the vulnerability of the travel industry to external economic and political factors inevitably took their toll on operators. For example, Clarksons, which had expanded rapidly in the late 1960s, was losing money by 1971 and was taken over by the Court Line Group. The group had invested heavily in jet aircraft, but the 1973 oil crisis and economic recession led to the collapse of the company at the height of the summer season in August 1974. Parallels can be drawn between the International Leisure Group (ILG), which, when it failed in March 1991 was Britain's second largest tour operator, and Clarksons. The downturn in business at the time of the Gulf War exposed ILG's strategy of using strong tour operating cash flows to diversify into scheduled air services through its airline Air Europe.

During the 1970s and the 1980s the large tour operators came to increasingly dominate the AIT market, as mass market operators were determined to increase their market share and to reap the anticipated rewards of market dominance. Thomson, the market leader, had since its inception faced major challenges to its market leadership position, but had hitherto always successfully defended its position. Major competitors had disappeared from the scene: Clarksons collapsed in 1974; ILG collapsed in March 1991. Thomson's major challengers in the current marketplace are of more recent prominence. Owners Abroad (now renamed First Choice) was founded in 1972 and, as its name suggests, was a 'seat-only' specialist serving the needs of expatriate overseas property owners. Airtours started in 1978 as Pendle Airtours, a small operating division of David Cross-

land's travel agency Pendle Travel. The demise of ILG removed from the industry a privately held company that had targeted Thomson through aggressive pricing in a bid for an ever-greater share of the market. Both Airtours (since 1989) and First Choice are public limited companies (PLCs). Their status as PLCs necessitated the targeting of profitability rather than market share as the primary objective of the two companies and as a result, competition since 1991 has focused on matching supply much more closely to demand, and thereby avoiding damaging price wars.

By 1990 a marked polarization had occurred in the industry, dividing competitors into a relatively small number of 'mass' tour operators and a much larger number of 'independent' operators largely serving specialized niche markets. The term 'independent' tour operator has become widely used in the UK but it has no precise meaning. The term is often used loosely to describe any operator that is not one of the largest mass tour operators. One of the key features of independent tour operators is that they are not vertically integrated and they therefore rely on the supply in the marketplace for individual components of the package. With regard to the distribution of the products, the choice depends very much on the size of the organization in terms of the number of passengers carried. Many of the smaller tour operators choose to apply direct sell methods. As one of the components of an air inclusive package is transport by air, the independents also need to secure capacity with either charter or scheduled airlines in order to assemble their products. In the UK the term 'independent' tour operator also has a more precise meaning, in that it can refer to those companies that are members of the Association of Independent Tour Operators (AITO). AITO was formed in 1976 in the wake of the Clarksons crash primarily to represent the views of smaller tour operators during the setting up of the CAA's bonding scheme. The association has grown to represent about 150 members that collectively carry some 1 500 000 customers per annum.

AITO members range from those carrying less than 500 customers per year to those carrying in excess of 100 000. The membership includes well-known companies that are part of the second tier of operators such as Balkan Holidays and Simply Travel, and less well-known names such as Sunvil Holidays. The membership also includes many tour operators that predominantly use car and ferries as means of transport. These companies, particularly a large number of French specialists, include well known names such as Eurocamp (which is a subsidiary of Holiday Break which has the status of a public limited company and carries over 250 000 customers a year), but do not appear in the ATOL listings, which solely cover AITs.

Competition, therefore, took place in two competitive arenas – the larger AITs competed with each other for the major 'volume' business whilst the independents, usually smaller companies, offered specialist products to niche markets. The temptation among the AITs to acquire within the independent sector was, however, limited by two factors: the constant threat of anti-monopoly legislation and a fear that the larger tour operators may be unable to 'think small' and flexible in a way that maintains quality for clients.

Clearly, given the scale and complexity of their operations, and the vertically and horizontally integrated structure of their businesses, the four largest operators in the UK can now be viewed as constituting a category of their own. Increasingly, however, given the size and international complexity of the companies concerned, it is apparent that a pan-European view of competition issues in the tour-operating sector will need to be taken in future. Expansion through integration does not only apply to the UK but the travel industry is also experiencing rapid internationalization of ownership. If a company wants to be regarded as a major player in this sector it now needs to be part of a pan-European partnership, alliance or ownership structure of some sort. The aim of such international integration is to increase buying power abroad together with improvement of margins through airline fleet integration and combined ground handling.

The take-over of Thomson by its German rival Preussag during 2000, which required European Commission approval (that was granted during August 2000) is indicative of this trend. This purchase signalled a further round of merger and acquisition activity. C&N Touristic (Germany's second largest tour operator) gained control of Thomas Cook in December 2000 after Preussag had been forced to sell its controlling stake as a consequence of its purchase of Thomson.

Industry features
Economies of scale

One of the reasons often cited for ever-greater concentration by a few large suppliers of activities for an industry is that larger companies enjoy the advantages to be derived from economies of scale. These economies clearly exist in tour operating, in terms of marketing and purchasing economies for instance, but perhaps the influence of such economies is on the wane. The trend away from standard 'summer sun' packages towards a more diverse range of package options in the UK means that such economies of scale are harder to achieve. Tour operators are increasingly being forced to respond to a much more complex holiday market than has hitherto existed, through diversification, narrower market segmentation, catering for independently minded travellers and increasingly experienced customers. All of these trends reduce, to some extent, the advantages to be derived from economies of scale.

Furthermore, it is by no means clear that economies of scale are great beyond a certain size threshold in the industry. The increasing bureaucracy, expense of systems and the inflexibility of a larger scale of operations, can lead to diseconomies of scale resulting in higher not lower unit costs. The tour operating industry may well have many of the same characteristics as the airline industry. In the USA, the lowest cost 'producer' that other airlines seek to emulate is not one of the major carriers, but a medium sized airline called Southwest.

The four largest tour operating companies operating in the UK have become vertically (as well as horizontally integrated) in recent years, that is to say, that they own both inputs to the operating process and control a part of the distribution channels for their products. To this end, the largest four tour operating brands of Thomson, Airtours, First Choice and JMC are part of groups which own airlines: Britannia, Airtours, Air 2000 and JMC respectively. The four companies also have extensive interests in travel agencies. Thomson, Airtours and JMC are part of groups which control the country's first, second and third largest travel agency chains: Lunn Poly, MyTravel (a re-branding of the former Going Places chain) and Thomas Cook respectively. First Choice, as well as owning the Travel Choice and Bakers Dolphin chains, has also developed a successful 'out of town' format with its Holiday Hypermarket concept which is spreading across the country.

The larger travel agency chains (which have themselves expanded their aggregate share of the total travel agency market), have increasingly favoured the larger operators that are able to offer bulk capacity and sufficient brochures to 'rack'. This trend has intensified as vertical integration has led to travel agencies favouring the operating brands of their owners, and operators seek preferential terms with agents. The tour operators have also developed direct forms of distribution through the development of dedicated call centres where staff are able to earn higher salaries than most travel agents if sales targets are met.

Regulatory investigations

The increased concentration in the industry resulted in referral to the UK Mergers and Monopolies Commission (MMC – now known as the Competition Commission) on two occasions in 1989 and 1997. The MMC sought to investigate the issues arising out of possible anti-competitive behaviour by the largest tour operators in the UK. Later, in 2000, the European Commission investigated the UK industry in relation to the proposed take-over of First Choice plc by Airtours plc.

In 1989 the Thomson Travel Group was investigated for its takeover of Horizon plc as the industry worried that the long-term effects of the merger would cause the withdrawal of a number of operators from the industry, thereby increasing concentration and leading to adverse effects on price, choice, availability and standards of service. The takeover (of the UK's third largest tour operator of the time by its first) was allowed to proceed. The sector was investigated again in 1997 owing to the increase in the level of vertical integration by the larger tour operators. Smaller tour operators and travel agents again argued that this increase would bring about anti-competitive practices which would eventually squeeze them out of the market, leading to higher prices and less choice for consumers. However, in both investigations, the Commission found that the industry was broadly competitive and saw no significant reason to intervene, although in relation to vertical integration, recommendations were made in the 1997 report to:

- prevent tying discounts to the purchase of travel insurance;
- make travel agency ownership links more explicit;
- outlaw the practice of specifying discount levels to travel agencies by major operators.

The smaller tour operators were not only worried about the distribution of their products but also the supply of charter seats. In this regard the MMC concluded that, 'while there may be a shortage of capacity at weekends, there appears to be no shortage during the week'. One industry observer noted that the 1997 MMC investigation effectively gave a go-ahead for further consolidation in the industry.

Many of the smaller companies have successfully developed a niche in the market, usually by targeting particular customer types or by focusing on specific destinations. Furthermore, a number of niche operators have been acquired by the 'big four'. Innovative companies, which have created new products and discovered new destinations, have fallen to their more predatory competitors searching for greater economies of scale and scope. In doing so they have tried to combine the benefits of scale with the higher margins to be derived from the exploitation of successful niche markets. Nevertheless many middle-ranking operators remain vulnerable since, on the one hand, they fail to derive the benefits of scale, and on the other, they have failed to develop a niche market they can effectively defend. This vulnerability is likely to be greatest in the short-haul markets due to the structural characteristics of the industry. Concentration specifically in key short-haul markets is even higher than the figures indicated for overall concentration, a point that was to be emphasized by the European Commission investigation

In November 1999 the European Commission prohibited a merger of two of the largest tour operators within the UK AIT market (Airtours and First Choice), on the grounds that the three largest operators effectively would control a large share of the short-haul market. The report stated that, 'the four large integrated suppliers already sell between them over 90% of all packages to mainland Spain, the Balearic Islands, the Canary Islands and Tunisia and 80% to [most] other significant short-haul summer destinations.' Concern was given in the report to the position of the remaining smaller tour operators since they would become further marginalized with regard to distribution, flight capacity and general competitiveness in the industry. The European Commission indicated that an excessively concentrated industry structure would emerge as a result of the proposed take-over. The potential removal of First Choice from the market would, the commission argued, remove the last remaining medium sized tour operator (and the only one with the potential to grow rapidly to the size of the three major suppliers). Finally, the take-over would have reduced competition at all three levels of the supply chain.

New technologies

Tour operators in the UK have played an important part in the development of computerized bookings for tour packages. The investment in on-line interactive view data systems (during the 1970s and 1980s) resulted in the majority of the larger tour operators relying on this technology for most of their bookings. Other smaller operators have chosen not to automate and to rely instead on using conventional telephone calls as the main vehicle for bookings. This has worked to the advantage of the larger tour operators as travel agents have endeavoured to reduce telephone call charges and improve efficiency.

Foremost amongst the newer technologies is the development of Computerised Reservation Systems (CRS). CRS systems were first developed in the USA in the 1960s and 1970s as databases and booking systems for US airlines. They continued to develop and now include vast amounts of information on other transport providers, hotels, car hire provision, attractions and so on. Additionally, the reach of systems such as Amadeus and Galileo has expanded throughout the developed world as non-US airlines have forged partnerships with the US instigators of the systems.

In the USA 96% of travel agents are linked to a CRS system. CRS systems give travel agencies the ability flexibly to package exactly what the consumers want, thereby undermining the role of the traditional mass market tour operator. They can combine hotels, flights, car hire and so on using the CRS database. However, the role of the CRS in a British 'leisure traveller' context should not be overstated. There is a marked polarization of business and leisure travel agencies with a low level of CRS penetration in the leisure travel agency sector. Many leisure travel agents are owned by tour operators which have invested heavily in their own view-data technology, and therefore have a vested interest in delaying the diffusion of CRS systems to the leisure travel agent sector.

Other technological developments are also important. Distribution options include home shopping, point of sale multi-media booths, mail order and booking, particularly booking through the Internet.

The emerging tools of the Internet enable consumers to search on-line for information, to access reliable, accurate and up to date information, and quickly to compare comparative product offerings. Furthermore, the availability of such information enables consumers to make reservations in a fraction of the time necessary for some other methods and with a minimum of inconvenience. The Internet is driven by both the increasing volume and diversity of tourism demand and by the power it gives consumers to buy personalized 'bundles' of tourism products. In some cases this leads to the avoidance of the traditional tourism 'packages' leading instead to consumers assembling their own packages from individual component parts on offer.

Booking habits, however, are slow to change, and use of the Internet for international travel requirements (other than flights) is comparatively small when compared to other forms of distribution – as at the year 2002 at least. Most Internet users, however, match the profile of the most desirable market segments in that they tend to be relatively well-educated professionals who travel frequently and have a higher disposable income. Furthermore, the Internet allows (at reasonable cost) suppliers an unprecedented opportunity to communicate globally with their target markets and to establish direct relationships with consumers.

Legal and regulatory developments

The EC Directive on Package Travel, Package Holidays and Package Tours was adopted on 13 June 1990 and EU member states were required to implement its measures prior to 31 December 1992. The main provisions of the directive are outlined below:

- Article 2, Definitions: The directive covers 'packages' which are defined as a pre-arranged combination of not less than two of three elements: transport; accommodation; and other tourist services.
- Article 3, Descriptions and advertising: The directive does not impose a legal obligation to provide a brochure, but where one is available it must contain in a legible, comprehensive and accurate manner both the price and adequate information concerning certain specified items such as the itinerary and the meal plan.
- Article 4, The package travel contract: Certain information is specified, such as information

relating to passport and visa requirements, that the tour operator and/or the travel agent must provide to the consumer prior to travelling.

- Article 5, Liability. The tour operator becomes responsible for ensuring that all services under the package are rendered effectively and efficiently (whether rendered directly or by a third party).
- Article 7, Financial security: The tour operator must provide evidence of security for the refund of money paid over and for repatriation of the consumer in the event of insolvency.

The goal of the directive was to codify and harmonize existing EC legislation relating to package travel. In so doing much of the detailed implementation of the directive was left to the discretion of member states. In the UK, the Department of Trade and Industry took the view that it wanted to place a minimum of additional burdens on the sector and consequently opted for a self-regulating system.

As a result, 'bonding' in the UK is undertaken by a number of 'approved' schemes including those operated by ABTA, AITO, the Federation of Tour Operators (FTO) and the CAA. Under these systems a tour operator has to pay for a bond representing the value of an agreed proportion of their licensed capacity. The bond is forfeited in the event of failure to help reimburse customers. One effect of the implementation of the directive in the UK has been to include surface transport, and domestic packages as 'packages' requiring financial protection for the first time. The Directive, in requiring financial protection and greater scrutiny of activities, has raised the entry barriers to the tour operating sector in Europe, and forced some of the smaller, specialized tour operators to carry heavy additional financial burdens.

Changing consumers

Mass tourism can be seen as a phenomenon of large-scale packaging of standardized leisure services at fixed prices for sale to a mass clientele. Clearly such tourism remains central to the outbound tourism product of the UK and several other north European countries, but underlying trends towards a new type of more independent and experienced traveller have been discerned.

These 'new tourists' have been described as consumers who are flexible, independent and experienced travellers, whose values and lifestyles

are different from those of mass tourists. Six key attributes are characteristic of these 'new tourists'.

- *New consumers are more experienced.* In the UK the proportion of adults who had ever been on holiday abroad rose sharply from the 1960s through to the mid-1980s, reaching 67% in 1985. The figure has stayed close to this level ever since. In other words, first time buyers with sufficient income to enter the market had been captured and future growth (or decline) would reflect the motivations of experienced travellers. More experienced travellers are more knowledgeable and consequently more quality and value conscious, they demand greater choice and flexibility and are more certain of what they want and what they find unacceptable
- *New consumers have changed values.* Values of conservation, health and nature are being reflected in the tour operators' products and there are growing signs that the fashion for the sun is beginning to fade.
- *New consumers have changed lifestyles.* One industry-watcher argued that society has moved through three key phases between the industrial era and today. First, from the industrial era in which people live to work to the post industrial era in which they worked to live, to the third phase where a new unity exists between work and leisure, and travel and leisure become integral aspects of daily life. These changes in the role of travel and leisure in society have implications for the travel industry. People who live to work have simple holiday and travel motivations while people who work to live view leisure as the counterpoint to everyday life. Those seeking unity of everyday life want to reduce the polarity between work and leisure and are looking for fulfilment throughout all sectors of life, during working time, through 'humanized' working conditions, and at home through more habitable cities and a more colourful everyday life. The varying motivations of these three groups are summarised on page 385:
- *New consumers are the products of changing population demographics.* Population demographics in the tourism generating countries are changing. In particular the population is ageing. These demographic changes will have profound effects upon buyer behaviour in tourist generating countries. It has been forecast that the early

Table 1 Motivations for travel

People who live to work	People who work to live	People seeking a unity between work and leisure
to recover	to experience something different	to broaden their horizon
to recuperate	to explore	to learn something new
to rest	to have fun	to encourage introspection and communication with other people
to be served	to play	to discover the simple things in life and nature
to switch off	to be active	to foster creativity
	to relax without stress	to experiment
	to enjoy proximity to nature	to take personal risks
	to do as one pleases	

years of the twenty-first century will witness demographic shifts in Europe including a slight growth in the proportion of elderly people aged over 65, a large growth in the middle age categories and a relative decline in the 18–35 category. A significant European demographic trend was the rise of the 'baby boomers', that is those born between the Second World War and the mid-1960s, currently aged between their mid-30s and mid-50s. This category is inheriting wealth on a large scale leading to the higher net worth of middle-age households. They take wealth for granted, have higher expectations of the products and services that they buy and are likely to buy such products and services for their intrinsic qualities rather than for their status.

- *New consumers are more flexible.* Consumers are becoming 'hybrid' in nature in that they may consume in an unpredictable way, making the traditional stereotypical categories of rich, poor or middle income people no longer sufficient to segment holiday markets. Some consumers may, for instance, take the cheapest charter flight available but stay in the most luxurious accommodation available at the destination. Other consumers may stay in relatively modest accommodation but partake in expensive sporting activities such as heli-skiing or hot air ballooning. Another aspect of the flexible consumer is the spread of impulse buying to the travel industry. There are shorter lead times before booking and paying for holidays – a changing consumer preference which partially explains the growing number of shorter and more frequent breaks.

- *New consumers are more independent.* Consumers are increasingly asserting their individuality and independence, and seeking more flexible and custom-made travel and leisure options. They tend to resist the standardized and sanitized product options. This trend towards independence, individuality and more experimentation in travel and leisure is clearly underpinned by the value, lifestyle and demographic changes. Such changes are likely to manifest themselves in the continuing demand by consumers for the core advantages provided by packaged travel products relating to pricing, convenience, reliability and easy access. However, consumers are likely to increasingly reject some of the traditional drawbacks of packaged travel products relating to the inflexibility of products, and resistance to travelling in organized groups.

Appendix 6.1

Total ATOL capacity

Year	Total ATOL capacity (000s)	Year	Total ATOL capacity (000s)
1976	8345	1989	13 982
1977	7424	1990	13 065
1978	8578	1991	10 061
1979	5303	1992	14 920
1980	6164	1993	15 468
1981	6661	1994	18 539
1982	7067	1995	22 723
1983	7938	1996	22 951
1984	8623	1997	24 980
1985	8647	1998	27 926
1986	9843	1999	27 942
1987	12 598	2000	30 652
1988	14 567	2001	32 470

Source: CAA, various

Appendix 6.2

Largest tour operators licensed capacity

Year	5 largest tour operators' market share (000s)	Tour operators in order of market share
1976	1553	Thomson, Cosmos, Silverwing, Laker Air, Horizon-Midlands
1977	1502	Thomson, Cosmos, Silverwing, Horizon-Midlands, Laker Air
1978	1521	Thomson, Cosmos, Silverwing, Horizon-Midlands, Laker Air
1979	1875	Thomson, Silverwing, Cosmos, Horizon, Laker Air
1980	2165	Thomson, Silverwing, Horizon, Cosmos, Owners Services
1981	2263	Thomson, Silverwing, Horizon, Cosmos, Owners Services
1982	2913	Thomson, Silverwing, Intasun, Horizon, Cosmos
1983	3142	Thomson, British Airways, Intasun, Horizon, Rank
1984	3076	Thomson, Horizon, Intasun, British Airways, Rank
1985	3456	Thomson, Horizon, Intasun, Rank, British Airways
1986	5041	Thomson, Horizon, Intasun, Rank, British Airways
1987	8493	Thomson, ILG, Horizon, British Airways, First Choice
1988	8985	Thomson, ILG, Horizon, Redwing, First Choice
1989	10 022	Thomson, ILG, First Choice, Redwing, Airtours
1990	8899	Thomson, ILG, First Choice, Airtours, Yugotours
1991	6088	Thomson, First Choice, Airtours, Yugotours, Sunworld
1992	8353	Thomson, First Choice, Airtours, Cosmos, Sunworld
1993	8600	Thomson, First Choice, Airtours, Cosmos, Sunworld
1994	10 719	Thomson, Airtours, First Choice, Cosmos, Sunworld
1995	11 799	Thomson, Airtours, First Choice, Cosmos, Sunworld
1996	10 253	Thomson, Airtours, First Choice, Cosmos, Unijet
1997	11 952	Thomson, Airtours, First Choice, Thomas Cook, Cosmos
1998	16 009	Thomson, Airtours, First Choice, Thomas Cook, Carlson
1999	15 921	Thomson, Airtours, Thomas Cook, First Choice, Cosmos
2000	18 218	Airtours, Thomson, Thomas Cook, First Choice, Cosmos
2001	18 518	Airtours, Thomson, Thomas Cook, First Choice, Cosmos

Note: Tour operator figures are for the group of companies, where an operator has more than one operating brand
Source: CAA, various

Appendix 6.3
Largest tour operators' capacity

Tour Operator	1990 ATOL capacity (000s)	1991* ATOL capacity (000s)	1992 ATOL capacity (000s)	1993 ATOL capacity (000s)	1994 ATOL capacity (000s)	1995 ATOL capacity (000s)	1996 ATOL capacity (000s)	1997 ATOL capacity (000s)	1998 ATOL capacity (000s)	1999 ATOL capacity (000s)	2000 ATOL capacity (000s)	2001 ATOL capacity (000s)
Thomson	4348	3015	3326	3488	3801	4281	4032	4440	5080	5080	4725	4568
ILG	1798	a										
First Choice	798	1621	2275	1939	2042	2373	2029	1917	3164	3068	3210	3557
Airtours	635	828	1488	1692	2438	2946	2671	3083	3841	3930	5330	5540
Cosmos	b	b	822	1081	1805	1453	831	1049	b	1132	1294	1269
Yugotours	320	340	b	f								
Sunworld[d]/T. Cook	b	284	442	400	633	746	b	1463	2711	2711	3659	3584
Unijet	b	b	b	b	b	b	690	b	e	e		
Carlson	b	b	b	b	b	b	b	b	1213	g		
Total Largest five	8899	6088	8353	8600	10719	11799	10253	11952	16009	15921	18218	18518
Total All tour operators	13065	10061	13575	14545	17136	18813	21995	19819	22231	23264	24039	25362

Notes:
a ILG was placed in receivership in March 1991.
b Not placed in the top five tour operators.
c Airtours' 1994 and 1995 figures include Aspro which was acquired in June 1993.
d Became Thomas Cook after 1997
e Part of First Choice after 1997
f Ceased trading
g Traded as part of Thomas Cook from 1999
* Gulf War.
Source: CAA, various

Appendix 6.4
Actual carryings

Tour operator	1991 carryings (000s)	1992 carryings (000s)	1993 carryings (000s)	1994 carryings (000s)	1995 carryings (000s)	1996 carryings (000s)	1997 carryings (000s)	1998 carryings (000s)	1999 carryings (000s)	2000 carryings (000s)	2001 carryings (000s)
Thomson	2850	3247	3481	3950	4208	3657	3917	4679	4869	4037	3917
First Choice	1658	2094	1878	1915	1928	1992	1875	2919	2973	2844	2949
Airtours	993	1437	2135	2427	2720	2488	2877	3618	3961	4338	5087
Cosmos	600	864	1135	1562	1091	931	965	957	991	1084	1134
Sunworld/TCook	239	461	429	661	705	a	1050	2352	2901	3232	3292
Unijet	a	a	a	a	a	649	b				
First tier Sub-total	6340	8103	9058	10515	10652	9717	10684	14525	15695	15535	16379
Others	4040	4807	5192	6085	7648	10983	11416	9975	10605	11965	12821
TOTAL	10380	12910	14250	16600	18300	20700	22100	24500	26300	27500	29200

Notes:
Figures relate to all licences for 12-month periods to the end of September.
[a] Not placed in the top five tour operators.
[b] Part of Thomas Cook.

Source: CAA, various

Since 1990 the Civil Aviation Authority (CAA) has published data on the actual carryings of the total AIT market and from 1991 this data has been broken down to itemize the actual carryings of individual ATOL holders. The CAA data on actual carryings can be categorised in order to distinguish between two groupings of tour operators:

- First tier operators – consisting of the largest five tour operators.
- Other operators – which include all remaining actual carryings by ATOL holders.

Following the introduction of new ATOL regulations in May 1995, three kinds of business are specified in licences. These are:

- 'Fully Bonded' – scheduled or charter based inclusive packages and seat-only travel on charter flights (1406 licences December 1996).
- 'Lower Bonded' – scheduled seat-only tickets covered by a bond. These are bonded at a lower level than packages and charters, usually 5% (186 licences December 1996).
- 'Agency' – scheduled seat-only tickets where an airline guarantees the business of a consolidator and provides a 'Deed of Undertaking' to the CAA (63 licences December 1996).

The introduction of Lower Bonded and Agency ATOLs from 1995 accounts for a large (although not precisely quantifiable) part of the increase in ATOL capacity between 1995 and 1996.

Appendix 6.5
Number of ATOL holders

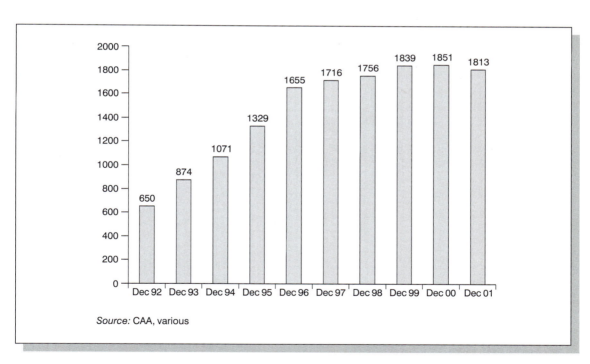

Source: CAA, various

Appendix 6.6

Average prices total revenue and retail price indices

	1992	1993	1994	1995	1996	1997	1998	1999	2000	2001
Average holiday price	£318	£346	£356	£361	£388	£415	£415	£421	£438	£447
Total revenue (£bn)	4.1	4.9	5.9	6.6	7.8	9.2	10.2	11.0	12.0	13.1
Retail price index (1987 = 100)	138.5	140.7	144.1	149.1	152.7	157.5	162.9	165.4	170.3	173.3

Note: Table shows actual average prices charged by tour operators for 12 months to September.
Source: CAA, various

Sources

D. Buhalis (2001) The tourism phenomenon: the new tourist and consumer, in S. Wahab and C. Cooper (eds), *Tourism in the Age of Globalisation*, Routledge, London

Civil Aviation Authority, *ATOL Business*, Civil Aviation Authority, London, 1992–2001

European Commission, *Council Directive of June 13 1990 on Package Travel*, Package Holidays and Package Tours (90/314/EEC)

J. Krippendorf (1986) Tourism in the system of industrial society, *Annals of Tourism Research*, 13(4)

J. Krippendorf (1987) *The Holidaymakers: Understanding the Impact of Leisure and Travel*, London, Heinemann

Victor T.C. Middleton (1991) Whither the package tour? *Tourism Management*, September

Auliana Poon (1993) *Tourism Technology and Competitive Strategies*, Wallingford, CABI

Chris Ryan (1991) UK package holiday industry, *Tourism Management*, March 1991

C. Smith and P. Jenner (1998) Travel agents in Europe, *Travel and Tourism Analyst*, 4, 5–15

TTG (1998) The year that shook the travel world, *Travel Trade Gazette*, 6 January

Glossary

Acquisition
The purchase of a controlling interest of one business's shares by another. The acquired business becomes a subsidiary of the acquirer but may be subsequently absorbed fully into the parent's structure.

Added value
The difference between the full cost of a product and its financial value to the market. High added value is one of the objectives of strategy. It tends to be measured in terms of profit.

Annual report and accounts
Audited annual communication between a limited company and its shareholders. In the UK, it has five compulsory statements by law (the chairman's statement, the auditors' statement, the profit and loss statement, the balance sheet and the cash flow statement). Also called *corporate reports*.

Augmented benefits
Benefits added to core (or basic) benefits that are intended to differentiate a product.

Backward vertical development
The acquisition of one or more parts of the backward direction in the supply chain. This is typically done by acquisition of or merger with a supplier.

BCG matrix (Boston Consulting Group matrix)
Framework used to rationalize and understand a business's product portfolio. It divides products according their market share and the rate of market growth. Four categories are identified, stars (high market share in high growth market), cash cows (high market share in low growth market), question marks (low market share in high growth market) and dogs (low market share in low growth market).

Benchmarking
A collection of techniques used to compare certain aspects of business practice and the transfer of good practice procedures from benchmark companies to 'followers'.

Business ethics
An area of research in which the nature of the relationship between business organizations and their role as moral agents is explored. It also describes research into the interface between business organizations and their social constituencies..

Capacity
In travel and tourism, capacity refers to the number of people that can be accommodated in a hotel, aircraft, bus, resort etc. The important figure is how much of the capacity is actually used at any time. This is the occupancy rate for accommodation or the load factor for transportation.

Capital
The finance used to invest in a business with a view of making a return from it in future years. It is used to purchase the other resource inputs that enable an organization to carry out business activity.

Change agent
One of the models of change management wherein the change process is overseen and managed by a single individual (the change agent). Offers the advantages of specialist management of a change process and the personification of the need for change.

Collaboration
Businesses are said to collaborate when, instead of (or perhaps as well as) competing, they choose to work together in pursuit of both parties' strategic objectives.

Competences

The abilities that an organization possesses that enable it to compete and survive in an industry. It includes an element that is tangible (its physical resource base) and another which is intangible (know-how, networks etc.).

Competitive advantage

The ability of an organization to out-perform its competitors. It can be measured in terms of superior profitability, increase in market share or other similar performance measures.

Competitive positioning (school of thought)

The approach to business strategy that argues that an organization's success in strategy rests upon how it positions itself in respect to its environment. This is in contrast to the resource based approach.

Consortia/consortium

Various types of collaborative arrangements in which more than two organizations join together to undertake a certain tasks (such as marketing and promotion) or for the duration of a certain project.

Core competences

Competences are core when they become the cause of the business's competitive advantage. Also called *distinctive capabilities*.

Corporate reports

Same as **annual report and accounts**.

Cost benefit analysis

One of the non-financial tools sometimes used in evaluating strategic options. It involves weighing up the benefits that will arise from a course of action against its costs.

Cost leadership (in generic strategy framework)

The approach to business that seeks to achieve higher than industry-average performance by keeping unit costs lower than those of competitors. It is characterized by an emphasis upon the high volume production of standard products.

Critical success factors (CSFs)

Those features owned by an organization that are the cause of its superior performance. Management approach to CSFs is to lock them in as far as possible.

Culture

The character or personality of an organization. A culture can be understood by examining its manifestations under the categories of the cultural web.

Deliberate strategy

Strategy that is planned in advance and which follows a rational process through each stage from analysis through to implementation.

Demerger

The disposal of a business (usually a subsidiary) by making it into a stand alone business and selling it off, usually via a flotation.

Differentiation (in generic strategy framework)

The approach to business that seeks to achieve higher than industry-average performance by being distinctive rather than cheap (more distinctive than competitors). It presupposes that markets will pay more for extra product features.

Distinctive capability

See **core competence**

Diversification

Business growth that involves developing new products for new markets.

Earnings

Profit after interest and tax. Attributable to the company's shareholders who may elect to not withdraw the total earnings as dividends in order to leave some retained profit for future investment.

Economies of scale

The benefits gained in unit costs (cost per item) from increases in size, and hence, the dilution of fixed costs.

Efficiency

A comparison of a system's output to its inputs with a view to testing how well the input has been turned into output.

Emergent strategy

Strategy that is not planned in advance and that arises from a consistent pattern of behaviour.

Empowerment

See **job enrichment**

Entry barriers
The obstacles that a new entrant to an industry needs to negotiate in order to gain market entry. Examples include the cost of capital, the legal and regulatory obstacles, access to supply and distribution channels, the costs of competing (especially lack of scale economies) etc.

Environmental analysis
Essentially the same as strategic analysis – an analysis of an organization's internal environment and its external macroenvironment and microenvironment.

External analysis
The analysis of the external environments in which an organization exists (micro and macro) with a view to identifying opportunities and threats.

External growth
Growth of a business by merger or acquisition (in contrast to organic or internal growth).

Factors of production
Inputs into an organizational process that make normal operation possible (otherwise called resources).

Fiscal policy
Regulation of a national economy by the use of government revenues and expenditure.

Five forces analysis
A conceptual framework for understanding an industry's or organization's position in respect to the forces in its microenvironment. Can be used to explain the structure of the industry and the performance of competitors within it.

Focus strategy (in generic strategy framework)
Competitive advantage gained through serving one (or few) market segments.

Foreign exchange risk
Arises out of uncertainty about the future exchange rate between two currencies. The risk can be categorized as transaction, translation or economic exposure to risk.

Forward vertical development
The acquisition of one or more parts of the forward direction in the supply chain. This is typically done by acquisition of or merger with a buyer.

Franchising
An arrangement for business growth where the idea or format is rented out (from a franchisor to a franchisee) rather than directly developed by the originator of the idea. Not to be confused with *licensing*.

Generic strategy
A distinctive posture that an organization adopts with regard to its strategy. It is suggested that superior performance arises from adopting a cost leadership or differentiation strategy with either a narrow or broad product and market scope.

Globalization
The most extensive stage of business development in which an organization's interests are spread throughout the world and are configured so as to compete and respond to differing customer requirements in many different national and local cultures.

Heterogeneity (of services)
Services, unlike mass produced manufactured goods, are never identical. The human element and other factors in delivering services, ensures that services will be heterogeneous, i.e. varied.

Horizontal development
Merger with or acquisition of a competitor or a business at the same stage of the supply chain. Increase in market share.

Hostile takeover
An acquisition attempt that is not supported by the board of the target company.

Human resource
One of four resource inputs that can be deployed to help create competitive advantage. Comprises skills of the employees and of any other people who are used by the organization (such as consultancy skills that it has access to).

Human resource audit
An investigation into the size, skills, structure and all other issues surrounding those currently employed by the organization.

Hybrid strategy
An approach to generic strategy that adopts elements of both cost leadership and differentiation.

Implementation
The part of the strategic process that involves carrying out the selected strategy. It involves making the requisite internal changes and reconfiguring the organization's resource base to make it possible.

Incremental change
Organizational change that is carried out in many small steps rather than fewer large steps.

Industry
A group of producers of close substitute products. The players in an industry compete against each other for resource inputs and in product markets.

Industry (competitive) analysis
Part of strategic analysis. The analysis of an industry, usually using the five forces framework, with a view to gaining a greater understanding of the microenvironment.

Inseparability (of services)
The production and consumption of service products are inseparable. The implication of this inseparability is that the consumers have direct experience of the production of the service in contrast to the production of a physical product.

Intangible resources
Sometimes called *intellectual resources* – resource inputs that are not physical but which can be amongst the most important at causing competitive advantage. Examples include patents, legal permissions, licences, registered logos, designs, brand names etc.

Intangibility of services
Services cannot normally be seen, touched, smelt, tasted, tried on for size or stored on a shelf prior to purchase. Their intangibility makes them harder to buy but easier to distribute.

Integration
The collective name given to mergers and acquisitions.

Intellectual resources
See **intangible resources**

Intermediaries
The individuals and companies that act as 'middlemen' by purchasing and packaging products and services from their owners (the principals) and selling them on to customers. Travel agents and tour operators are examples of intermediaries.

Internal analysis
Part of strategic analysis (along with external analysis) wherein the internal parts are examined for strengths and weaknesses. The value chain framework is often used to assist the process.

Internal growth
Growth in the size of a business without the use of mergers and acquisition; also referred to as *organic growth.* It involves the reinvestment of previous years' retained profits in the same business venture.

Internationalization
Business growth involving development across national borders. Can be achieved by using market entry strategies such as exporting, direct investment, international joint ventures, alliances or franchising.

Job enrichment
Employees are given a greater deal of discretion or *empowerment* to make decisions.

Job rotation
Employees rotate jobs between them so that teamwork is encouraged and knowledge and skills are gained.

Job sharing
Employees' jobs are shared between two or more employees, thereby sharing burdens and responsibilities.

Joint ventures
A collaborative arrangement between two or more companies. JVs tend to be for limited time periods, usually for a project or similar. Can also take the form of multi-partner consortia.

Just in time
An operational philosophy which aims to carry out (usually) production without any waste. Sometimes called *stockless production.*

Key issues
The issues that 'fall out' of the SWOT analysis which is, in turn, the summary of the strategic analysis. In practice, key issues are those issues

that are the most pressing, the most important and the most critical.

Licensing
The renting out of a piece of intellectual property so that the licensee enjoys the benefits of the licensor's innovation upon the agreement of a royalty payment. Most commonly applied to recipes, formulations, brands (such as lager brands) etc. Not to be confused with *franchising*.

Macroenvironment
The outer 'layer' of environmental influence – that which can influence the microenvironment. It comprises five categories of influence – socio-demographic, political, economic, natural and technological influences.

Management buy-out (MBO)
Occurs when a company is sold to its current management.

Management contracts
A popular form of joint development method whereby the ownership of the physical asset (such as a hotel or other accommodation) is separated from its management.

Market
The group of customers that a business or industry can sell its outputs to. Can also mean the specific part of a total market that an individual business sells to. In economics, market is taken to mean the 'place' or arena in which buyers and sellers come together.

Market segmentation
The practice of subdividing a total market into smaller units, each of which shares a commonality of preference with regard to a buying motivation. Markets are segmented by applying segmentation bases – ways of dividing customers in a market from each other.

Market share
The proportion (usually expressed as a percentage) of the market for a product type held by a supplier to the market. Can be defined in terms of value of volume.

Mergers
A form of external growth involving the 'marriage' of two partners of (usually) approximately equal size. The identities of both former companies are submerged into the new company.

Microenvironment
The near or immediate business environment which contains factors that affect the business often and over which individual businesses may have some influence. Usually comprises competitors, suppliers and customers.

Mission statements
A formalized statement of the overall strategic purpose of an organization.

Moment of truth
See **service encounter**

Near environment
See **microenvironment**

Objectives
The state of being to which an organization aims to reach. It is the end point to which the strategy is aimed.

Operational objectives
To be distinguished from strategic objectives. The level of objective which tends to be short- to medium-term in timescale and which has the sole purpose of helping to achieve the higher level strategic objective.

Organic growth
See **internal growth**

Package holiday
A package holiday is a pre-arranged combination, sold or offered for sale at an inclusive price, including at least two of transport, accommodation and other tourist services ancillary to transport or accommodation.

Paradigm
The worldview or way of looking at the world held by an individual or organization. It is a very powerful determinant of the culture and behaviour (and hence performance) of a business.

Perishability (of services)
Since production and consumption are simultaneous, services are instantly perishable if they have not been sold at the time of production.

PEST analysis
Same as **STEP analysis**.

Planned strategies
See **deliberate strategy**

Portfolio
Can refer to the spread of interests in respect to either products or markets. The principle behind any portfolio is to spread opportunity and risk with a view to making the organization less vulnerable to trauma in any one product or market segment and to enable it to be in the position to exploit any opportunities quickly.

Prescriptive strategy
See **deliberate strategy**

Price elasticity of demand
The relationship between the price of a product and the quantity of the product sold. Price elastic products are those whose quantity sold is relatively price responsive. Price inelastic products are those where a change in price would be expected to bring about a proportionately lower change in quantity sold.

Product
The output of an organization intended for consumption by its markets. The result of the adding value process.

Product life cycle
The concept is based on the analogy with living things, in that all products would be expected to have a finite life, whether it is long or short, and that products move from introduction through growth towards maturity and eventually decline.

Profit
The surplus of sales against total costs. Tends to be measured either before or after tax.

Profit Impact of Market Strategy (PIMS) study
Study that examined thousands of companies in many industries and found that one of the primary determinants of profitability was market share.

Profit and loss (P&L) account
One of the three compulsory financial statements in a company annual report. The P&L statement reports on the total sales, the costs incurred in creating those sales and hence (by subtraction) the profit made over a reporting period.

Public–private partnerships
Various forms of collaborative activity bringing public and private sector involvement together to develop assets and resources.

Quality
Usually defined as 'fitness for the purpose'. It is not to be defined in terms of luxury or premium.

Ratio analysis
A comparison (by quotient) of two items from the same set of accounts.

Related diversification
External growth by developing new products for new markets. Related diversification suggests that the new products or markets have something in common with existing products or markets such that the risk of the diversification is lessened. Related diversification is in contrast to *unrelated diversification*.

Resources
The key inputs into an organization that enable normal functioning to take place. There are four categories of resource – physical (e.g. stock, land, buildings etc.), financial, human and intangible (or intellectual).

Resource based approach
A way of understanding the source of competitive advantage as arising from the way in which an organization obtains and deploys its resources to build and develop core competences.

Resource immobility
Many resources that are used cannot be moved or are difficult to move either in terms of place or time.

Resource markets
The markets in which a business competes with other businesses for resource inputs. Examples include labour markets, real estate and property markets, finance markets (for capital) etc.

Resource substitution
The substitution of one resource category with those of another.

Retained profit
A balance sheet measure of the profit that is attributable to the shareholders once all other allocations are accounted for, i.e. profit after interest, tax and extraordinary items.

Selection of strategy
The second stage in the overall strategic process which takes the information gained in the strategic analysis and uses it to evaluate options and to decide upon the most appropriate option.

Service encounter
The time and place where the customer interacts with the organization. Sometimes referred to as *moment of truth*.

Service Profit Chain
Assesses the sources of profitability and growth in labour-dominated service firms.

SERVQUAL
A framework developed to consider service quality.

Stakeholders
'Any group or individual who can affect or [be] affected by the achievement of an organization's objectives' (Freeman, 1984:46 – see Chapter 1).

Stakeholder theory
The belief that the objectives of an organization are determined by the relative strengths of the various stakeholders.

STEP analysis
Same as *STEEP analysis* (see below), but omitting environmental influences.

STEEP analysis
The key stage in macroenvironmental analysis. It involves auditing the macroenvironment for socio-demographic, political, economic, environmental and technological influences.

Stockholder position
The belief that business objectives should be determined predominantly for the financial benefit of the owners (shareholders). In practice, this position is taken to mean that the objectives of a business should be to maximize its profits.

Stockless production
See **just in time**

Strategic alliances
A collaborative arrangement between two or more businesses where part or all of the companies' value chains are shared for a mutually beneficial strategic purpose.

Strategic analysis
The first part of the strategic purpose. Its purpose it to gather information about a business's internal and external environments so that sufficient information is available to make possible the informed evaluation of options.

Strategic groups
The subgroups within an industry that compete head on with each other for the same types of customers or for similar resource inputs. The members of a strategic group will normally consider an ongoing monitoring of each other's activities to be an essential part of their strategic analysis.

Strategic implementation
See **implementation**

Strategic objectives
In contrast to operational objectives, strategic objectives are those pursued at the highest level of an organization. They concern the whole organization or a significant part of it, are concerned with the overall product and market scope, and tend to concern longer time scales than operational objectives.

Strategic options
Generated as part of the second stage of the strategic process (evaluation and selection). The options that are considered as possible courses of action for the future.

Strategic process
One way of looking at strategy is to conceptualize it as an iterative process. According to this view, the process has three distinct stages – strategic analysis, strategic evaluation and selection and then finally, strategic implementation. In practice, all stages are carried out continually.

Strategic selection
See **selection of strategy**

Strategy
The many definitions of strategy are perhaps best understood in terms of Mintzberg's five Ps – plan, ploy, pattern, perspective and position. A strategy is usually taken to mean the process that is performed in order to close the gap between where an organization is now and where it aims to be in the future.

Strengths

Those internal features of an organization that can be considered to add to its ability to compete in its strategic group (or industry) and to increase its competitive advantage. Strengths are positive attributes that an organization owns.

Structure

The term used to describe the shape of an organization. In strategy, a consideration of structure usually refers to its height, width, complexity and the extent to which it is decentralized.

Stuck in the middle

A phrase used to describe the position of an organization that, in respect to the generic strategy framework, is neither purely cost leadership nor differentiation. It has been argued that to be stuck in the middle is to expose an organization to the probability of returning below-average profits because the organization experiences competition from those pursuing all other competitive strategies (narrow and broad, cost and differentiation). This view has been challenged.

Substitute products

Products that provide identical or comparable benefits to those of the organization's products.

Supply chain

Not to be confused with the *value chain*. Usually refers to the entire path that a product and its component parts take from the primary industry stage to when it is sold to the final consumer on the chain.

SWOT analysis

Standing for Strengths, Weaknesses, Opportunities and Threats, it is the key technique for presenting the results of strategic analysis, and provides a platform for going on to formulate the strategy for the future. Strengths and Weaknesses should be based upon the internal analysis of the organization whilst the Opportunities and Threats should be based upon an analysis of the organization's external environment.

Synergy

The effect that is observed after two or more parties (e.g. businesses in a merger) come together and the whole becomes greater than the sum of the parts. Sometimes expressed as 2 + 2 = 5.

Targeting

When the possible range of segments has been identified and the characteristics of each of the segments has been analysed, an organization then has to decide which market segments to target.

Tour operator

Tour operators purchase or reserve the separate components of a package holiday in bulk and combine these components into an 'inclusive tour' or package.

Tourism

Defined by the World Tourism Organization as comprising 'the activities of persons travelling to and staying in places outside their usual environment ... for leisure, business and other purposes'.

Tourist Area Life Cycle (TALC)

Destinations go through a similar evolution to that of products, but visitor numbers are substituted for product sales. Destinations move from evolution through involvement, development, consolidation before reaching stagnation Decline will follow unless actions are taken which result in rejuvenation.

TOWS analysis
Same as **SWOT analysis**

Travel

A journey of any length from one place to another. A variety of modes of transport may be used, i.e. air, land or sea, and the travel may be undertaken for a range of purposes, including both business and leisure. All tourism includes some travel.

Unrelated diversification

External growth by developing new products for new markets. Unrelated diversification suggests that the new products or markets have little or nothing in common with existing products or markets such that the risk of the diversification is increased, but that portfolio benefits are maximized. Unrelated diversification is in contrast to *related diversification*.

Value adding
See added value

Value chain analysis

A conceptualization of the internal activities of an organization. The framework divides the internal

activities of an organization into two categories –
those that directly add value (primary activities)
and those that support the primary activities
(support or secondary activities). The analysis of
an organization's value chain is intended to show
up the strategic importance of any key linkages or
any blockages – points where value is added less
efficiently than it might be.

Vertical development
The acquisition of forward or backward competences, such as through merger with, or acquisition of a supplier (backward vertical development)
or a customer (forward vertical development).

Waste
Anything that does not add value in an organizational process (such as machine inefficiencies,
tooling up and tooling down, bad quality, stock
etc.).

Weaknesses
Those internal features of an organization that can
be considered to detract from its ability to compete
in its strategic group (or industry) and to reduce its
competitive advantage. Weaknesses are negative
attributes that an organization owns.

Index

Page numbers in italics refer to definitions in the Glossary. Abbreviations: Fig = Figure; Tab = Table